Democracy Distorted

High-profile controversies surrounding the funding of political parties have shown how inequalities in wealth can enter the political process. The growth of the professional lobbying of MPs and the executive raises similar questions about money in politics. More broadly, inequalities emerge in terms of the opportunities the public have to participate in political debate. This analysis of the ways wealth can be used to influence politics in the UK explores the threat posed to the principle of political equality. As well as examining lobbying and party funding, the discussion also focuses on the ownership and control of the media, the chance to be heard on the Internet and the impact of the privatisation of public spaces on rights to assemble and protest. Looking at this range of political activities, the author proposes various strategies designed to protect the integrity of UK democracy and stop inequalities in wealth becoming inequalities in politics.

Jacob Rowbottom is a lecturer in Law at the University of Cambridge, and a Fellow of King's College, Cambridge.

The Law in Context Series

Editors William Twining (University College London),
Christopher McCrudden (Lincoln College, Oxford) and
Bronwen Morgan (University of Bristol).

Since 1970 the Law in Context series has been in the forefront of the movement to
broaden the study of law. It has been a vehicle for the publication of innovative scholarly
books that treat law and legal phenomena critically in their social, political and
economic contexts from a variety of perspectives. The series particularly aims to publish
scholarly legal writing that brings fresh perspectives to bear on new and existing areas of
law taught in universities. A contextual approach involves treating legal subjects broadly,
using materials from other social sciences, and from any other discipline that helps to
explain the operation in practice of the subject under discussion. It is hoped that this
orientation is at once more stimulating and more realistic than the bare exposition of
legal rules. The series includes original books that have a different emphasis from traditional legal textbooks, while maintaining the same high standards of scholarship. They
are written primarily for undergraduate and graduate students of law and of other dis-
ciplines, but most also appeal to a wider readership. In the past, most books in the series
have focused on English law, but recent publications include books on European law,
globalisation, transnational legal processes, and comparative law.

Books in the Series
Anderson, Schum & Twining: *Analysis of Evidence*
Ashworth: *Sentencing and Criminal Justice*
Barton & Douglas: *Law and Parenthood*
Beecher-Monas: *Evaluating Scientific Evidence: An Interdisciplinary Framework for
Intellectual Due Process*
Bell: *French Legal Cultures*
Bercusson: *European Labour Law*
Birkinshaw: *European Public Law*
Birkinshaw: *Freedom of Information: The Law, the Practice and the Ideal*
Cane: *Atiyah's Accidents, Compensation and the Law*
Clarke & Kohler: *Property Law: Commentary and Materials*
Collins: *The Law of Contract*
Cranston: *Legal Foundations of the Welfare State*
Davies: *Perspectives on Labour Law*
Dembour: *Who Believes in Human Rights?: The European Convention in Question*
de Sousa Santos: *Toward a New Legal Common Sense*
Diduck: *Law's Families*
Elworthy & Holder: *Environmental Protection: Text and Materials*
Fortin: *Children's Rights and the Developing Law*
Glover-Thomas: *Reconstructing Mental Health Law and Policy*
Gobert & Punch: *Rethinking Corporate Crime*

Goldman: *Globalisation and the Western Legal Tradition: Recurring Patterns of Law and Authority*

Harlow & Rawlings: *Law and Administration*

Harris: *An Introduction to Law*

Harris, Campbell & Halson: *Remedies in Contract and Tort*

Harvey: *Seeking Asylum in the UK: Problems and Prospects*

Hervey & McHale: *Health Law and the European Union*

Holder & Lee: *Environmental Protection, Law and Policy*

Kostakopoulou: *The Future Governance of Citizenship*

Lacey, Wells & Quick: *Reconstructing Criminal Law*

Lewis: *Choice and the Legal Order: Rising above Politics*

Likosky: *Transnational Legal Processes*

Likosky: *Law, Infrastructure and Human Rights*

Maughan & Webb: *Lawyering Skills and the Legal Process*

McGlynn: *Families and the European Union: Law, Politics and Pluralism*

Moffat: *Trusts Law: Text and Materials*

Monti: *EC Competition Law*

Morgan & Yeung: *An Introduction to Law and Regulation, Text and Materials*

Norrie: *Crime, Reason and History*

O 'Dair: *Legal Ethics*

Oliver: *Common Values and the Public–Private Divide*

Oliver & Drewry: *The Law and Parliament*

Picciotto: *International Business Taxation*

Reed: *Internet Law: Text and Materials*

Richardson: *Law, Process and Custody*

Roberts & Palmer: *Dispute Processes: ADR and the Primary Forms of Decision-Making*

Rowbottom: *Democracy Distorted: Wealth, Influence and Democratic Politics*

Scott & Black: *Cranston's Consumers and the Law*

Seneviratne: *Ombudsmen: Public Services and Administrative Justice*

Stapleton: *Product Liability*

Tamanaha: *Law as a Means to an End: Threat to the Rule of Law*

Turpin & Tomkins: *British Government and the Constitution: Text and Materials*

Twining: *Globalisation and Legal Theory*

Twining: *Rethinking Evidence*

Twining: *General Jurisprudence: Understanding Law from a Global Perspective*

Twining: *Human Rights, Southern Voices: Francis Deng, Abdullahi An-Na'im, Yash Ghai and Upendra Baxi*

Twining & Miers: *How to Do Things with Rules*

Ward: *A Critical Introduction to European Law*

Ward: *Law, Text, Terror*

Ward: *Shakespeare and Legal Imagination*

Zander: *Cases and Materials on the English Legal System*

Zander: *The Law-Making Process*

Democracy Distorted

Wealth, Influence and Democratic Politics

JACOB ROWBOTTOM

CAMBRIDGE
UNIVERSITY PRESS

CAMBRIDGE
UNIVERSITY PRESS

Shaftesbury Road, Cambridge CB2 8EA, United Kingdom

One Liberty Plaza, 20th Floor, New York, NY 10006, USA

477 Williamstown Road, Port Melbourne, VIC 3207, Australia

314–321, 3rd Floor, Plot 3, Splendor Forum, Jasola District Centre, New Delhi – 110025, India

103 Penang Road, #05–06/07, Visioncrest Commercial, Singapore 238467

Cambridge University Press is part of Cambridge University Press & Assessment,
a department of the University of Cambridge.

We share the University's mission to contribute to society through the pursuit of
education, learning and research at the highest international levels of excellence.

www.cambridge.org
Information on this title: www.cambridge.org/9780521876650

First published 2010

A catalogue record for this publication is available from the British Library

Library of Congress Cataloging-in-Publication data
Rowbottom, Jacob.
    Democracy distorted : wealth, influence and democratic politics / Jacob Rowbottom.
        p.   cm. – (Law in context)
    ISBN 978-0-521-87665-0 (hardback)
    1. Campaign funds–Great Britain.   2. Political parties–Great Britain.   3. Mass
    media–Ownership–Geat Britain.   4. Political participation–Great Britain.   5. Great
    Britain–Politics and government–2007–   I. Title.   II. Series.
    JN1039.R69 2010
    324.241–dc22
    +2010007558

ISBN   978-0-521-87665-0   Hardback
ISBN   978-0-521-70017-7   Paperback

Contents

Preface and acknowledgements

I first started thinking about money, politics and political equality a decade ago while working as a researcher in a senatorial campaign in the United States. It was a fascinating experience and I found much to admire about the US democratic system. Yet the vast amount of money spent in the election campaigns was striking. It is not much of an insight to say that money is important in US politics, but seeing the system in action brought the matter home to me. When I returned from the United States, there was similar talk about money and wealth being used to secure political influence in the UK, particularly in relation to some very large donations being made to political parties. Yet compared to the United States, UK politics is relatively inexpensive, and this is partly the product of the political system and its regulatory environment. The arguments advanced in this book seek to defend those features that have kept the costs of politics down, as well as propose some new strategies.

The way wealth can be used to secure political influence will depend on the particular features of the system in question. In the United States, many of the electoral battles are fought out through television advertisements. By contrast, in the UK the election campaigns and political debate tend to be conducted through the political coverage of the national media. As a result, particular attention will be given to the role of the mass media in later chapters. There are other broader trends that impact on people's opportunities to engage in politics. One example discussed here is the privatisation of certain public spaces. The aim is to examine these different activities and areas to see how various separate trends can be connected when looking at the impact on political equality. The argument is not based on a conspiracy theory and does not suggest that any problems are the result of deliberate design. Instead it examines the ways certain features of the political system leave open the potential for inequalities in wealth to become political inequalities, and the possible solutions to those problems.

For the comments and feedback on draft chapters and the ideas in this book, I am very much indebted to Trevor Allan, Jocelyn Alexander, Nick Barber, Eric Barendt, Michael Birnhack, Alan Bogg, John Dunn, Mark Elliott, Keith Ewing,

Thomas Gibbons, David Good, David Feldman, Dori Kimel, Anne Rowbottom, David Rowbottom, Tony Smith, Marc Stears and James Weinstein. Thanks are also due to Finola O'Sullivan, Sinead Moloney and Richard Woodham at Cambridge University Press. Finally, and not least, thanks to Lucia Perez for her patience and support.

1

Political equality, wealth and democracy

Wealth, power and influence are often mentioned together as symbols of status and prestige. Yet in a democracy, they can make an unhappy combination. If a democratic society is one that treats people as equals, then can it be consistent with an economic system in which the differences in wealth are so great? This tension between the distribution of wealth and democracy can emerge in different ways. Economic inequalities are thought to heighten divisions in society, where the lives and concerns of rich and poor barely seem to have any connection. Such a division based on extreme inequalities in wealth may thereby undermine the prospect for democratic decision-making to be a truly collective enterprise and for citizens in one economic group to understand the position of others. The tension between wealth and politics can also arise more directly, where the former is thought to secure political influence. Concerns about the influence of wealth in politics make the news headlines on a fairly regular basis, relating to a range of topics such as the funding of political parties, lobbying and the power of the media. For example, if MPs and ministers grant privileged access to political donors, or if media moguls command the attention of the public and politicians, it raises a problem for a democracy. Sometimes such influence is thought to have a corrupting effect on politics, suggesting that political influence has been 'bought'. However, a broader objection can be made against such influence, that it is contrary to the principle of political equality. It is the concern with political equality that will be the focus here, in particular looking at the democratic system in the UK.

The basic problem lies in the tension between inequalities in wealth and the egalitarian ideals underlying democracy. Inequalities in wealth are, to some extent at least, accepted as a part of the economic system, while equality is a defining feature in a democracy. That latter principle is compromised whenever people can convert wealth into political influence. Arguments based on political equality therefore provide a powerful intuitive argument that explains why it is wrong for a political party to become indebted to large donors or for a lobbyist to secure privileged access in return for a fee. It will also be argued that this same principle is compromised when people lack certain resources to participate in the political process. For example, political equality is affected when the private owner of a town centre space forbids people handing out leaflets. Yet despite its simple appeal, political equality, under closer examination, is a complex principle. This chapter will explore some of these complexities to give a basic account of political equality, how that principle fits with certain democratic theories, and why inequalities in wealth stand in tension with principle. While it advances a particular, and contested, account of political equality, it is one that is compatible with a number of approaches to democracy. It will also be advanced to provide a rationale for a number of measures, discussed in later chapters of this book, that aim to create a separation between the political and economic spheres and stop inequalities in wealth becoming political inequalities.

Wealth and democratic politics

The relationship between economic wealth and democratic politics is complex, and the two come into contact in various contexts. Politics often focuses on policies relating to the distribution of economic resources and the opportunities to acquire such resources, such as the appropriate level of taxation. Yet at the same time, economic resources can shape that political debate and impact on which speakers and arguments are heard. The complexities and various dimensions in this relationship were recently examined in Larry Bartels' study of US politics, which found some US politicians to be more responsive to those on middle and high incomes, while the opinions of those on low incomes were found to be 'utterly irrelevant'.[1] While much of Bartels' study is concerned with the reasons why US democracy often produces inegalitarian policies, the concern here is not with the policies produced by the political process. Instead, the focus is on the various mechanisms by which inequalities in wealth can impact on politics.

In most cases, any influence secured through wealth arises not through buying votes or making backroom deals for cash. Instead, there are a number of different ways that inequalities in wealth can affect political decisions, five of which will be identified in the following discussion. While the categorisation given is not exhaustive and the presence of any of these factors will vary in different political systems, the discussion will show the different directions from which inequalities in wealth can shape political decisions. A first may flow from various biases among the decision-makers. For example, while politicians are accountable to their constituents, the channels of accountability have limits and the politicians may have considerable autonomy to pursue their own ideological views.[2] The system may therefore benefit wealthier people if the politician's ideological commitments are closer to those held by people in middle or higher socio-economic groups, or reflect their interests. This connection between wealth and politics depends on showing that politicians in the system in question do in practice have itments. However, even if this can be shown, it

---

[1] L. Bartels, *Unequal Democracy* (Princeton University Press, 2008) ch. 9. See also M. Gilens, 'Inequality and Democratic Responsiveness' (2005) 69 *Public Opinion Quarterly* 778.
[2] See Bartels, *Unequal Democracy*, ch. 6–8.

does not explain why politicians' views may serve the interests of higher income groups more than any other.[3] One possible explanation arises if politicians share similar characteristics to those on high incomes, for example being drawn from high-income groups and receiving a relatively high income while in office. Under this view, the socio-economic background of the decision-maker may shape their political priorities and subsequent decisions.

A second way that wealth can impact on politics is through structural biases, in which those with greater economic power naturally command the attention of politicians and decision-makers. Under this view, given the importance of economic growth to government policies, politicians and other officials will give considerable weight to the views and interests of those businesses or actors that are seen as essential to that goal. This is what Charles Lindblom referred to in his classic study of the US political system, *Politics and Markets*, as the 'privileged position' of business.[4] Along these lines, if the government wishes to increase employment in the private sector, it will need to listen and cater to the needs of businesses to encourage further investment in the UK. Such priority may be afforded not just to business, but to any persons with substantial economic resources or a high income. For example, criticisms have been made about the influence of the so-called 'super-rich' individuals. The desire to ensure that the very wealthy continue living in the UK is sometimes thought to influence tax policy, and the prospect of such people leaving the UK advanced as an argument against redistributive policies.[5] The privileged position also arises as a result of the range of public functions carried out by the private sector. In the UK, this can be seen in policies such as privatisation, contracting out, and public–private partnerships. The role of the private sector in these policies means that the government will give priority to the interests of those businesses performing public functions and the businesses will also influence the way those policies are implemented. While none of this means that businesses are always successful in influencing policy, and there is debate about the extent to which other interests have a countervailing influence, this argument suggests that big businesses and wealthy interests will tend to have a constant and influential presence in policy-making.[6] In these examples, wealth generates influence not through direct political activity or campaigning, but

---

[3] See B. Page, 'Perspectives on *Unequal Democracy*' (2009) 7 *Perspectives on Politics* 148 at 149.

[4] C. Lindblom, *Politics and Market. The World's Political-Economic Systems* (New York: Basic Books, 1977). For discussion in the context of British politics see W. Grant, *Business and Politics in Britain*, second edition (Basingstoke: Macmillan, 1993) pp. 32–45; D. Marsh, 'Pluralism and the Study of British Politics', in C. Hay, *British Politics Today* (Cambridge: Polity, 2002) p. 26; A. Gamble, 'Policy Agendas in a Multi-Level Polity', in P. Dunleavy, A. Gamble, I. Holliday and G. Peele (eds.), *Developments in British Politics 6* (Basingstoke: Macmillan, 2000) pp. 303–5.

[5] This pressure does not always block such policies. However, redistributive policies (such as the 50 per cent tax band on people earning £150,000 introduced in the 2009 budget) are often met with concerns that a 'brain drain' will follow, see *Guardian*, 23 April 2009. While the merits of such criticisms are open to debate, the presence of such arguments highlight the importance attached to such concerns and may act as a brake on further redistributive policies.

[6] See Grant, *Business and Politics in Britain*, pp. 39–41.

flows from the importance of the economy to the success of government policies.

While the arguments given above look at the ways decision-makers may give priority to wealthier people or groups, the third way that wealth can impact on politics is through advantages secured in the opportunities for political participation. Studies have shown that those in higher socio-economic groups tend to participate in politics more,[7] and as a result the formal political process may amplify the voices of those with greater wealth. There are a number of possible reasons for this, for example that those in higher socio-economic groups have greater motivation to become involved in politics. However, one factor may be that those on higher incomes have more resources available to participate in politics.[8] Wealth is itself a political resource, which can be spent on lobbying, publicity campaigns, to pay for research or to donate to political parties.[9] The availability of such resources does not determine whether a person will be active in politics, and many rich people do not get involved in politics. However, people need to have the necessary resources before they can exercise the choice whether to participate in politics.[10] The relevance of wealth will also vary according to particular type of participation. In a study of US politics, Verba et al. found, unsurprisingly, that income is the key factor as to whether people engage in those forms of political participation that entail giving money, such as donating to a political campaign.[11] Consequently, if political activities become more capital intensive (for example through reliance on advertising, direct marketing and hiring lobbying firms) and the political groups demand contributions as the main form of support, the inequalities in participation may be heightened.[12]

A fourth way that economic power can impact on politics is by shaping public opinion and the agenda for political debate. Through this channel, economic resources can be used to gain access to or control the main forums for communication, providing greater opportunities to persuade the public on certain political issues. For example, the corporate control of the mass media may impose a pressure on it to disseminate content that is more favourable to the economic interests of its owners or advertisers. Such a channel for influence was central to what Lindblom described as the principle of circularity in which the views of citizens can be shaped to fit with the interests of business.[13] While Lindblom did not suggest that all businesses agree on every political issue, he

[7] C. Pattie, P. Seyd and P. Whiteley, *Citizenship in Britain* (Cambridge University Press, 2004) p. 85.
[8] See S. Verba, K. Schlozman and H. Brady, *Voice and Equality* (Cambridge, MA: Harvard University Press, 1995) ch. 9, and for discussion of their model see Pattie et al., *Citizenship in Britain*, ch. 5.
[9] Bartels found some evidence to be consistent with the view that patterns of political donations explain the differing responsiveness of senators on some issues, Bartels, *Unequal Democracy*, p. 280.
[10] Verba et al., *Voice and Equality*, p. 354. [11] *Ibid.*, p. 516.
[12] See Pattie et al., *Citizenship in Britain*, p. 268, on the growth of chequebook participation.
[13] Lindblom, *Politics and Market*, pp. 202 and 207.

argued that many arguments that threaten the privileged position of business are taken off the table and political discussion tends to focus on a relatively narrow set of issues. While accepting that it is impossible to completely exclude certain viewpoints,[14] he suggested that the constraints on public opinion meant that democracy is 'crippled though not paralyzed by circularity'.[15] This line of argument is open to a number of criticisms, for example it may be thought that the media in the UK are willing to criticise businesses and their underlying interests.[16] Furthermore, the argument also rests on certain assumptions about the effects of the mass media on the formation of people's political opinions. However, Lindblom's argument is just one among many that emphasises the importance of control of the main forums for communication in the political system.[17] While favourable coverage on the mass media does not guarantee political success, it is at least an important part of a political strategy and provides an opportunity to persuade a large audience. Consequently, a more basic point is that ownership or control of the media, or the influence of advertisers over content for example, can be used to promote or disadvantage political viewpoints, and provides another channel in which wealth and property ownership can impact on the political process.

Finally, economic inequalities form the background conditions which impact on peoples' chances to participate and influence decisions. While wealth has been considered as a political resource in itself, it also plays a role in securing other political resources. For example, if those with greater wealth can secure access to better education, then they are likely to be provided with the skills necessary to participate in politics effectively and given greater opportunities to gain those positions which offer influence over political decisions. Those in better paying jobs may also acquire more skills that can be deployed in political participation. Furthermore, if someone lives in poverty or does not know where their next meal is coming from, they are unlikely to become fully active citizens. Again, here the complaint is not that wealth has bought political power or that it has been used directly to influence political decisions. Instead, it is that the economic background conditions will impact on who can go on to become influential. Consequently, this concern supports arguments that certain material needs have to be met before people can participate or have any influence in politics. According to such a view, democracy requires some redistribution of wealth to ensure 'freedom from desperate conditions' (requiring 'police protection, shelter, or medical care'), 'opposition to caste systems' and 'rough equality of opportunity' (such as the provision of a good education).[18]

The discussion so far has not sought to specify the extent to which these channels allow inequalities in wealth to impact on collective decisions in

---

[14] *Ibid.*, p. 213.   [15] *Ibid.*, p. 230.   [16] Grant, *Business and Politics in Britain*, p. 35.
[17] The issues relating to the mass media will be considered in Chapters 2 and 7.
[18] C. Sunstein, *The Partial Constitution* (Cambridge, MA: Harvard University Press, 1993) pp. 137–8.

practice, but has identified some of the various ways that such an impact can arise. The practices that will be considered here will be largely limited to direct attempts to use wealth for political influence and the use of the forums for communication and debate, those methods primarily falling in the third and fourth categories. The argument advanced here will focus on attempts to insulate the political process from inequalities in wealth. The discussion will leave out some of the broader issues, for example that certain human needs have to be met as a condition of democracy, or that contracting out government functions gives too much power to unaccountable bodies. These issues are important, but raise broader questions beyond the scope of this book. The discussion of wealth and influence here is also limited to attempts to influence government decisions, and will not look at arguments to democratise the workplace, for example.

It is, however, important to think about the ways wealth can generate political influence as a whole rather than simply look at each channel of influence in isolation. If one use of wealth in politics is restricted, it may work to enhance the relative influence of other uses of wealth. For example, if all the ways that wealth can be used to directly secure influence in the formal political process were taken out of the equation, then advantages in education and other resources will become more important. The same point applies when looking at the various ways that wealth can directly influence politics. Strict limits on political donations may encourage those seeking to influence politicians to turn to lobbying or to influence the media. This argument reflects the 'hydraulicist' critique of party funding laws, that no matter what limits are imposed, money, like water, will always find somewhere to go.[19] In this view, those who have the resources and seek to influence collective decisions look for loopholes in the law, and find new ways to spend money that will generate influence. Yet this does not defeat the rationale for such measures, and in any event the law has a symbolic role that shows a commitment to equality and can define the ethical standards in politics. Beyond the problem of loopholes, a further concern is that some controls on wealth in politics will have an adverse impact on those individuals or groups that are already under-represented in the political process. For such groups, media campaigns or small donations to a politician may be the most accessible channels of influence. Those groups may also lack the skills, background and contacts that make possible the less visible forms of influence, such as insider lobbying.[20] Strict controls on one particular use of wealth could potentially impact some groups more than others. The criticisms do not mean that attempts to limit wealth in politics should be abandoned, but that it is important to look at the overall effects of reforms on the system as a whole.

---

[19] P. Karlan and S. Issacharoff, 'The Hydraulics of Campaign Finance Reform' (1999) 77 Tex. L. Rev. 1705.

[20] S. Verba and G. Orren, *Equality in America: the View from the Top* (Cambridge, MA: Harvard University Press, 1985) p. 216.

Political equality

The focus here is with the tension between economic inequalities and political equality. To explain this tension, more needs to be said about the role of equality in the democratic process. While the various theories of democracy are generally committed to some form of political equality, the place of equality and what it requires in a democracy is often explained in different ways. For example, Gutmann and Thompson draw a distinction between 'procedural democrats' and 'constitutional democrats', both of which are committed to political equality. The former approach is associated with majority rule as a central feature in a democracy, in which disagreements are resolved by giving each person an equal say.[21] The judgement of each citizen is given equal value in deciding what the outcome of a collective decision should be. The commitment to equality therefore translates into equality in the decision-making process. Equality in the procedure lies at the heart of this account of democracy, and the results it produces 'are legitimate because the procedure is fair, not because the results are right'.[22]

The constitutional democrat will also emphasise equality in the decision-making procedures, but may also require that the substance of collective decisions treat people as equals. As a result, the constitutional democrat may demand that the possible outcomes of the process be constrained in order to protect certain fundamental rights and 'the vital interests of individuals'.[23] An example of such an account can be seen in Ronald Dworkin's view that 'the best form of democracy is whatever form is most likely to produce the substantive decisions and results that treat all members of the community with equal concern'.[24] Under this view, giving people an equal say in some collective decisions is an important way of treating members with equal concern and recognises the equal status of the citizen.[25] However, equality in the procedural sense forms one aspect of a broader commitment to equality. That broader commitment to treating people with equal concern may require limits on the outcomes of the process, restricting what decisions can be made, to safeguard the rights or interests of the individual from majoritarian laws.

These two contrasting approaches illustrate how the commitment to equality can produce very different approaches to democracy. It is also important to note that despite the differences, both versions provide citizens with a right to participate in collective decisions as equals. There are a range of other democratic theories that take different routes leading to equality in decision-making. Some emphasise the value of the process in reaching the best outcome, whereas

---

[21] A. Gutmann and D. Thompson, *Democracy and Disagreement* (Cambridge, MA: Harvard University Press, 1996) p. 26.

[22] *Ibid.*, p. 27.   [23] *Ibid.*, p. 27.

[24] R. Dworkin, *Sovereign Virtue: the Theory and Practice of Equality* (Cambridge, MA: Harvard University Press, 2000).

[25] *Ibid.*, pp. 187–8.

others assign an intrinsic value to equality and make no reference to the outcome.[26] While relying on different justifications, a common feature among the
theories of democracy is the presence of some procedural rights in relation to
collective decisions. It is equality in the procedure for making decisions that is
of concern here, namely the equal rights of citizens to participate in collective
decisions. However, with this meaning, political equality remains a complex
and contested concept.

A basic requirement of political equality is that each citizen has an equal
vote in an election. One-person one-vote provides a classic statement of political equality in collective decision-making. People should also be free to stand
for elected office. Yet these rights do not exhaust the requirements of political
equality. A right to vote would not be worth much if people had no information
or the chance to debate the merits of the various options. The role of the citizen
goes beyond voting and includes the ability to influence decisions and policies
made by officials in-between elections. Non-electoral political activities can
also convey more specific information to the official, such as strength of feeling
or an opinion on a specific issue, which cannot be communicated through voting. Those activities also provide a chance for people to form their own views
and persuade others in relation to political issues. Consequently, the commitment to political equality means that people have the right to speak, associate
and form political groups. Denial of those rights would undermine the value of
the vote and would cut the person off from collective decisions in-between elections. However, a difficulty arises in deciding what political equality requires in
relation to such activities, and different approaches can be taken.

At one extreme is the view that people should have approximately the
same influence over political decisions, a standard of equality of influence.
However, while strict equality of input may be appropriate for voting, which
gives each citizen equal power over an outcome, it is difficult to extend to
other forms of participation. When making a political speech, taking part in
a protest or letter-writing campaign, a person has an impact on a decision by
influencing others.[27] An argument is influential because the person hearing it
chooses to be persuaded, for example where it is supported by more convincing reasons. Consequently, political equality cannot require that each person have the same level of influence, and no approach to democracy would
take such a standard in this extreme form. For example, it would not be desirable for someone expressing a weak argument to be as influential as someone
expressing one that is well thought out. Furthermore, even if it were desirable,
its enforcement would require a severe restriction on politics, such as a ban on
political expression to prevent citizens being able to influence one another.[28]
It would also be difficult to devise a standard to measure each citizen's level

---

[26] For discussion, see C. Beitz, *Political Equality: an Essay in Democratic Theory* (Princeton
University Press, 1989).

[27] See Dworkin, *Sovereign Virtue*, pp. 191–4.   [28] *Ibid.*, p. 197.

of influence, since that would require identifying what factors led a citizen to form a particular view.

If equality of influence is to be rejected, an alternative is to modify the standard so that citizens have an *equal opportunity* to influence collective decisions. A standard of equality of opportunity demands that people have an equal 'starting point', but not that people are equal in the final result.[29] The idea of an equal opportunity means that some people may be more influential than others. If everyone has an equal opportunity to persuade, some will end up persuading more people than others. However, if equality of opportunity means that people have an equal starting point, it raises the question of what needs to be equalised to ensure everyone has a fair chance. Consequently, a standard of equality of opportunity requires a distinction between those sources of unequal influence that are legitimate and those that are not.[30]

So far it has been assumed that persuasiveness is a legitimate basis for unequal influence. The persuasiveness of the argument is what makes the difference in determining whether the participant is influential or not. By contrast, non-legitimate sources of unequal influence are those that need to be distributed equally in order to provide each citizen with an equal opportunity. As Wojciech Sadurski notes, if we accept more sources as legitimate grounds of differentiation, then such sources do not need to be equally distributed and the demands of political equality become more limited.[31] By contrast, if more sources are seen as illegitimate grounds of differentiation, and require equal distribution, then this model becomes closer to equality of influence. The difficulty lies in determining which political resources need to be equally distributed.

An approach that distinguishes between the various potential sources of influence raises the question of whether political resources ranging from wealth, celebrity, expertise and experience are all legitimate grounds for unequal influence. As such questions cannot be answered solely by reference to equality of opportunity, that standard thereby has limited value as a guiding principle. As a result, any simplicity that procedural equality held as a standard for designing a fair democratic process seems to disappear and some other standard or values will be needed to help distinguish the different sources of influence. For this reason, some theorists reject simple accounts of political equality in which people have 'equal procedural opportunities to influence political decisions' as a central organising principle and instead think about the requirements of fair democratic process.[32] However, this does not render equality of opportunity

[29] S. Fredman, *Discrimination Law* (Oxford University Press, 2002) p. 14.
[30] A. Marmor, 'Authority, Equality and Democracy' (2005) 18 *Ratio Juris* 315, at 332. While Dworkin rejects equality of influence, he states that the crucial issue is whether the source of influence is legitimate; see Dworkin, *Sovereign Virtue*, p. 199.
[31] See W. Sadurski, 'Legitimacy, Political Equality, and Majority Rule' (2008) 21 *Ratio Juris* 39, at 58.
[32] For criticism of the 'simple' view see Beitz, *Political Equality*, ch. 1. Charles Beitz's account of political equality is based on a contractarian approach in which: 'Fair terms of participation are those upon which democratic citizens may reasonably expect each other to enter into the cooperative political activity required for self-government.' Equality is reflected in the process

redundant, as it can at least serve as a default rule, departures from which have to be justified.

Given these difficult questions about what needs to be equalised, there are different approaches as to what equality of opportunity requires. An important distinction can be made between formal political equality and substantive political equality. Under the formal approach, each citizen holds the same political rights, and equality is secured by preventing arbitrary distinctions being made by government that stop any person being influential. Under this approach an absence of state censorship will be a crucial factor in ensuring that each person has an equal opportunity to persuade regardless of her viewpoint. This approach to political equality is 'formal' in the sense that it prevents legal barriers to participation being imposed, but does not attempt to equalise the various other background conditions which might affect people's opportunities to participate in politics. Various differences, such as those in time, money, location and knowledge, can therefore impact on the extent to which people can influence political decisions under the formal version of political equality. The approach avoids the difficult questions in distinguishing the sources of influence and how to remedy any inequalities in those sources. However, this type of formal equality is open to criticism on the grounds that it assumes the background conditions in which people participate are fair, or at least unproblematic in a democracy. Yet in practice many people will be unable to influence, or face relative disadvantage in influencing, decisions because they have unequal access to certain political resources. Such inequalities may undermine the reasons why equality in the decision-making process was demanded in the first place.

These criticisms of formal political equality may lead to a more demanding account of substantive political equality. This account requires that people have the effective opportunity to influence political decisions and have the means to do so.[33] A version of this approach can be seen in John Rawls' account of the 'fair value' of political liberties, in which the worth of the political liberties 'must be approximately equal or at least sufficiently equal in the sense that everyone has a fair opportunity to hold public office and to influence the outcome of political decisions' regardless of their social or economic position.[34] This approach therefore takes the view that certain sources of influence, social or economic position, are not legitimate grounds for differentiation in democratic politics. While Rawls provides a liberal justification, substantive political equality may also be demanded as a requirement of democracy in republican political

---

for deciding the fair terms, rather than in the institutional arrangements themselves; see Beitz, *Political Equality*, pp. 217–18.

[33] See H. Brighouse, 'Democracy and Inequality', in A. Carter and G. Stokes (eds.), *Democratic Theory Today* (Cambridge: Polity Press, 2001).

[34] J. Rawls, *Political Liberalism* (New York: Columbia University Press, 1996) p. 327. Similarly, Harry Brighouse prefers the term 'equal availability of political influence', see H. Brighouse, 'Egalitarianism and Equal Availability of Political Influence' (1996) 4 *The Journal of Political Philosophy* 118, at 127.

theories. In some republican theories, a democratic process that is inclusive and gives each person an equal voice is important in ensuring non-domination (meaning mastery by others). In Philip Pettit's account, this requires that people or groups 'are enabled to speak out' and contest those political decisions that 'offend against someone's interests or ideas'.[35] Securing the equal political resources provides a way to facilitate such participation. However, if economic resources can be used to secure greater voice in the democratic process, the concern is that binding collective decisions can become a form of domination of the wealthy over others.[36] As a result Pettit states that 'One of the greatest challenges for republican research must be to identify measures for effectively separating the worlds of government and business'.[37]

The account of political equality advanced here will be a version of substantive equality of opportunity, but one that focuses on the economic position and does not look at broader concerns, such as a person's social position as a source of influence. This version of political equality also explains why the concern with wealth and politics is not based on an objection that money is used to directly buy influence. The concern does not depend on showing that, for example, political advertisements do actually change election results or that lobbying determines particular decisions. The concern is that wealth can be used to provide unequal *opportunities* for such influence.

If a substantive account of political equality is taken, further difficulties arise in elaborating the demands of that principle. For example, one problem is in determining the period over which equality is to be assessed. If political resources are equally distributed each year, one citizen may save up and, after twenty years, decide to use those stored resources to influence one decision. That citizen would have more resources to influence that particular decision, but it is not clear that this would violate political equality as any advantage flows from that citizen's choice. The difficulty, however, is that by saving all her political resources her relative voice may outweigh that of others in relation to that decision, and her potential to influence other decisions in the previous twenty years will have been limited. With voting, equality is defined with reference to a specific decision and citizens cannot save up votes and deploy more in one election than another. Away from elections, it becomes harder to identify when these differences represent an inequality or represent differences based on choice or level of interest. Yet while the standard is not clear-cut, political equality is still a useful standard in identifying the gross disparities. Some inequalities may be so great and violate the principle, whichever period is assessed.

---

[35] P. Pettit, *Republicanism* (Oxford University Press, 1997) p. 190.

[36] *Ibid.*, p. 194. See also R. Bellamy, *Political Constitutionalism* (Cambridge University Press, 2007) who makes a strong connection between non-domination and equality in the political process. In particular, at p. 162, explaining that wealth does not dominate when it merely allows a person to 'indulge a taste for classic cars', but does so 'when the wealthy man is able to influence public affairs more than the poor simply on account his wealth'.

[37] Pettit, *Republicanism*, p. 194.

This discussion does not exhaust the various meanings of political equality. The approach so far has focused on discussing political equality in relation to economic resources. One objection is that it is not the resources that are most important, but what people can do with those resources to achieve their goals. Arguments that people should have the same resources to spend on political activities, 'presupposes the equal capacity to make effective use of such resources'.[38] Consequently, an alternative account of political equality may seek to develop people's capacities to participate in politics rather than equalise resources. Yet this approach raises difficulties due to the complexities in identifying the relevant capacities and measuring the extent of any inequalities.[39] While the focus on inequalities in wealth has its limits, it at least provides an identifiable standard and helps to recognise some major disparities in influence.

Inequalities in wealth may also raise other issues for political inequality that have not been touched on so far. For example, Anne Phillips has argued that political equality requires not simply a particular distribution of political resources, but recognition of the equal status of citizens. Under this approach, disparities between rich and poor are problematic for democracy, not just for giving the rich more to spend on political activities, but because the disparity 'shapes [and damages] perceptions of fellow citizens' and 'discourages the capacity to view others as equals'.[40] This argument suggests that inequalities in wealth undermine the premise on which democracy rests and a more equal distribution of income is a condition for the working of a democratic process. Such concerns about the recognition of equal status do arise in relation to the distribution of political resources. For example, where one citizen can spend large sums on an independent political campaign that most citizens could not afford, a signal is sent out about the comparative status of citizens. The problems of recognition that are reflected in the general distribution of income and wealth, however, implicate a broader approach to political equality, which remains beyond the scope of this book.

The account of political equality given so far has focused on the relationship between different citizens and has omitted an account of the inequality between citizens and elected representatives.[41] Representatives have greater influence than other citizens, by voting or deciding issues in the legislature or executive on which individual citizens do not have any formal input. Much debate surrounds the role of representatives, and there is potential for greater direct citizen involvement in some government and legislative decisions to address this type of inequality.[42] However, for the

---

[38] J. Bohman, 'Deliberative and Effective Social Freedom: Capabilities, Resources and Opportunities', in J. Bohman and W. Rehg (eds.), *Deliberative Democracy: Essays on Reason and Politics* (Cambridge, MA: MIT Press, 1997) pp. 329–30.

[39] For discussion see J. Knight and J. Johnson, 'What Sort of Equality Does Deliberative Require?' in Bohman and Rehg, *Deliberative Democracy*, p. 298.

[40] A. Phillips, *Which Equalities Matter?* (Cambridge: Polity Press, 2000) pp. 79–83.

[41] Dworkin refers to this as the 'vertical dimension'; Dworkin, *Sovereign Virtue*, p. 190.

[42] For a recent contribution combining representative democracy with greater citizen participation, see P. Ginsborg, *Democracy: Crisis and Renewal* (London: Profile Books, 2008).

present purposes, it is assumed that such an unequal opportunity to influence is legitimate given that representatives owe their position to the choices made by equal citizens.[43] Furthermore, the channels of accountability ensure that such influence is constrained and the representatives are answerable to citizens. The role of political accountability in justifying the representative's opportunities to influence stresses the importance of citizens having an equal chance to communicate with, persuade, or question their representatives between elections.

Democratic models and political equality

Having identified the standard of substantive political equality and noted some of its complexities, this section will consider how that standard can fit with different models of democracy. There are a wide range of democratic theories, each characterising the process in different ways. Some give a fairly minimalist account of democracy as a process for authorising political leaders through periodic elections, while other theories have a more optimistic view and aim to give citizens much greater involvement and say in collective decisions. Across this spectrum, the various models of democracy take differing approaches to political equality and explain the principle in different ways. To illustrate these different approaches, the next section will contrast three models of democracy that reveal some of the key faultlines in democratic theory. These theories can be labelled: elite competitive, aggregative and deliberative democracy.

Elite competitive democracy

The elite competitive theory characterises democracy as a competition between rival groups of political leaders that are chosen through an election.[44] The central role for citizens is therefore casting the vote. Beyond elections, the public should be free to discuss the different electoral choices and organise political parties with an absence of state interference.[45] However, under this account the individual's ability to understand or participate in political decisions is thought to be limited, and the details of policy are left to the experts that form the political elite.[46] Under this view, the democratic process does not generate a clear will of the people or show the electorate's choice of policies, but merely signals the approval of one group of political leaders over another.

---

[43] See D. Copp, 'Capitalism versus Democracy', in J. D. Bishop, *Ethics and Capitalism* (University of Toronto Press, 2000) p. 86.

[44] See J. Schumpeter, *Capitalism, Socialism and Democracy*, fifth edition (London: Routledge, 1976) p. 269; 'the democratic method is that institutional arrangement for arriving at political decisions in which individuals acquire the power to decide by means of a competitive struggle for the people's vote'.

[45] *Ibid.*, p. 272.

[46] D. Held, *Models of Democracy*, second edition (Cambridge: Polity Press, 1996) p. 179.

Such an account justifies democracy as a mechanism to remove incompetent or bad leaders.

Given the limited role assigned to individual citizens, the elite competitive model points to a formal understanding of political equality that protects free discussion and the right to vote. However, the political system needs to be structured in a way that makes the removal of political leaders possible.[47] The opportunities to participate therefore have to be distributed sufficiently widely to ensure that no single elite is very secure in government. This may justify some limits on the greatest inequalities, in order to prevent leaders with access to more economic resources than any competitor staying in power without a serious challenger. Such an approach could call for some restrictions on media ownership, for example, in order to increase the chance that citizens know about bad or incompetent leaders.[48] While the elite approach demands little in the way of an equal distribution of political resources, there are arguments for limiting extreme inequalities to ensure democratic procedures provide a method to remove any bad rulers.[49]

Aggregating preferences

A second approach sees the democratic process as a way of adding up or collecting the existing preferences of citizens. An aggregative model establishes 'a scheme of collective choice – majority or plurality rule, or group bargaining – that gives equal weight to the interests of citizens in part by enabling them to present and advance their interests.'[50] Unlike the elite competitive theory, which views the democratic process primarily as a safeguard to remove bad leaders through election, the aggregative approaches aim to connect collective decisions with citizens' preferences. Under this approach, citizens do not have to justify their choices or provide reasons and the democratic process seeks to collect those preferences.[51]

The most obvious method of aggregating preferences is through voting, although the extent to which the election outcome really does reflect preferences has been subject to extensive criticism.[52] However, voting is not the only way that

[47] In William Riker's minimal account of democracy, the removal of 'offending' officials by citizens at an election must be at least a possibility; see W. Riker, *Liberalism against Populism: a Confrontation between the Theory of Democracy and the Theory of Social Choice* (San Francisco: W. H. Freeman, 1982) pp. 242–3.

[48] Given that so little weight is placed on the ability to acquire and assess political information, citizens may be more easily influenced by the mass media and groups with an 'ax to grind'; see Schumpeter, *Capitalism, Socialism and Democracy*, pp. 263–4.

[49] See I. Shapiro, *The State of Democratic Theory* (Princeton University Press, 2003) pp. 74–5.

[50] J. Cohen, 'Procedure and Substance in Deliberative Democracy', in T. Christiano (ed.), *Philosophy and Democracy* (Oxford University Press, 2003) p. 20. For discussion see also Sunstein, *The Partial Constitution*, ch. 6.

[51] A. Gutmann and D. Thompson, *Why Deliberative Democracy?* (Princeton University Press, 2004) p. 15.

[52] For discussion, see A. Weale, *Democracy*, second edition (Basingstoke: Palgrave, 2007) ch. 7.

citizens' preferences can be collected into decisions. The activities taking place outside an election, in particular campaigning, bargaining and negotiating with officials, can provide a way of influencing collective decisions. Under this view, political activities signal preferences to officials and provide a method of convincing others to support particular policy options.

This approach to aggregation can be seen in the example of interest-group pluralism.[53] Under this approach, citizens organise into groups that promote particular sets of interests. The primary political actor is not the individual, but the group, which will seek to exert pressure on decision-makers. Such group influence may arise where a state agency meets with various groups prior to making a decision and the final result is the product of a bargain struck between the various interests. Through these methods, the decision-makers are responsive to outside interests. Furthermore, through a fluid process in which different factions mobilise and become part of the governing coalition, no single faction forms a permanent majority.[54] This account sees politics as a competition between actors seeking to advance their own interests, and the goal of the democratic process is to seek some form of equilibrium between these interests. While the process of bargaining does not provide a mechanical method to collect and weigh preferences, the outcome is seen to be a balance between the various factions and is a very approximate way to aggregate preferences into collective decisions.[55]

This approach is most commonly associated with formal political equality: by allowing citizens to pool their resources, their voices will not be excluded and their activities can act as a check on other powerful groups. This version of pluralism places faith in a wide dispersal of political resources, thus preventing any group gaining a monopoly of power. While some groups may have more of one particular type of resource, whether it is money or expertise, any advantage in the political process will be challenged by other groups that have greater access to a different type of political resource.[56] Furthermore, decisions are taken by a range of agencies and actors dealing with separate areas of policy, so one group may be influential in one area, but less so in another. Defenders of this approach acknowledge its limits, recognising that 'control over decisions is unevenly distributed; neither individuals nor groups are political equals'.[57] There is still an element of elitism, given the role of group leaders that speak

---

[53] For an overview of pluralist theories, see P. Craig, *Public Law and Democracy in the United Kingdom and the United States of America* (Oxford University Press, 1991); Held, *Models of Democracy*; F. Cunningham, *Theories of Democracy: a Critical Introduction* (London: Routledge, 2002).

[54] Held, *Models of Democracy*, p. 206.

[55] See A. Ware, 'The Concept of Political Equality: A Post-Dahl Analysis' (1981) 29 *Political Studies* 392, at 394–6.

[56] For such an argument in relation to British politics, see S.E. Finer, *Anonymous Empire* (London: Pall Mall Press, 1966) pp. 118–21.

[57] R. Dahl, *Preface to Democratic Theory* (University of Chicago Press, 1956) p. 145.

for the interests of the group and engage in bargaining over policy.[58] Yet it is defended as a realistic account of the process, providing 'a high probability that an active and legitimate group in the population can make itself heard effectively at some crucial stage in the process of decision'.[59]

In so far as interest group pluralism provides a descriptive account of politics, it has been subject to a number of criticisms.[60] Most important for the present purpose is the criticism that political resources are not as widely dispersed as the theory suggests and some groups thereby hold a persistent advantage in the process. Far from securing equilibrium, critics argue that the theory merely serves to legitimise the perpetuation of existing power.[61] The privileged position of business provides one example of the structural constraints on the process which give an advantage to certain groups. Aside from such a structural advantage, some groups also have a financial advantage over others on account of their wealth. If a group has more money at its disposal, it may have a persistent advantage through its ability to spend more on campaigning, communications and research.

Interest group pluralism may have started out as a description of a political system, but it was developed into a normative account of politics. One variant of this normative account is 'egalitarian pluralism', in which 'an outcome is legitimate only if it emerges from a process of representation and bargaining in which all interests have substantively equal chances of being heard and influencing the outcome'.[62] A number of measures can be pursued to secure the conditions for an egalitarian pluralist system, such as 'strategies of affirmative action for underrepresented groups' and some redistribution of the resources 'that are relevant to organization'.[63] While this could include a broad range of measures, attempts to address the impact of economic inequalities in politics and to secure a fairer distribution of political resources provide one strategy. However, it is not clear how the equal opportunity to influence decisions fits within the pluralist model. In particular, it raises difficult questions about whether equality should be required between groups or individuals.[64] The former approach would attempt to ensure the equal representation of interests by giving equal political resources to each group. By contrast, the latter approach views the appropriate level of resources for the group as depending on its numerical support and would seek to make

[58] Cunningham, *Theories of Democracy*, p. 80.   [59] Dahl, *Preface to Democratic Theory*, p. 145.

[60] One line of argument was that its account of power failed to look at who determines which issues will be subject to a decision, and any possible resulting biases, see S. Lukes, *Power: a Radical View*, second edition (Basingstoke: Palgrave, 2005) p. 39.

[61] See Craig, *Public Law and Democracy*, p. 69; Held, *Models of Democracy*, p. 213.

[62] J. Cohen and J. Rogers, 'Secondary Associations and Democratic Governance' (1992) 20 *Politics & Society* 393, at 411. For the discussion of some of the difficulties in reconciling pluralism with political equality, see K. Schlozman, 'What Accent the Heavenly Chorus? Political Equality and the American Pressure System' (1984) 46 *The Journal of Politics* 1006.

[63] Cohen and Rogers, 'Secondary Associations', p. 413.

[64] See R. Dahl, *Dilemmas of Pluralist Democracy* (New Haven: Yale University Press, 1982) pp. 99–100.

the groups responsive to citizens' preferences, giving people equal resources to organise groups for themselves and build new coalitions. Both approaches reflect substantive political equality, but differ as to the unit that is to be equally weighed and aggregated. Even with this modification, limits on wealth would not address all the inequalities that critics identified, such as the privileged position of some interests. Nor would it address the broader criticisms about the way aggregative models characterise democracy as a contest between self-interested actors. However a substantive account of political equality can still be pursued within this model of democracy.

Interest group pluralism has been particularly influential in the United States, but has also been important in the study of pressure groups in the UK.[65] Yet there are other accounts of the role of the group in UK politics. For part of the twentieth century certain outside interests were organised more formally in a corporatist system of decision-making. Furthermore, greater weight has also been placed on political parties as the central institution in representative democracy. However, the point being made is that these various approaches to some extent use representative groups to connect citizens' preferences with collective decisions. There are also other theories that take a similar approach, but place greater emphasis on the individual rather than the group.[66] Pluralism, however, has been outlined to illustrate a way that egalitarian approaches can fit within a framework that aims to make collective decisions responsive to preferences and how the egalitarian standard can be distorted by inequalities in wealth.

Deliberative democracy

Deliberative democracy is used to describe a number of different theories, a common feature of which is the emphasis on democratic processes doing more than aggregating individual preferences.[67] The central idea underlying the model is that 'central to democracy should be a particular kind of communication, involving the giving of good reasons and reflection upon points advanced by others'.[68] Consequently, a deliberative process requires 'conditions of free public reasoning among equals' in which citizens offer 'justifications for the exercise of collective power framed in terms of considerations that can, roughly speaking, be acknowledged by all as reasons'.[69] While deliberating with others, the individual does not simply attempt to advance his preformed views. Instead, deliberation is a process in which citizens' preferences

[65] For discussion see W. Grant, *Pressure Groups and British Politics* (Basingstoke: Macmillan, 2000) ch. 3.

[66] Craig, *Public Law and Democracy*, p. 64.

[67] See Gutmann and Thompson, *Why Deliberative Democracy?*, and J. Dryzek, *Deliberative Democracy and Beyond* (Oxford University Press, 2000).

[68] J. Dryzek and P. Dunleavy, *Theories of the Democratic State* (Basingstoke: Palgrave, 2009) p. 215.

[69] J. Cohen, 'Democracy and Liberty', in J. Elster (ed.), *Deliberative Democracy* (Cambridge University Press, 1998) p. 186.

are formed and transformed. A citizen seeking to persuade another of the merits of a particular view may change his own view during the course of that discussion. Deliberation is valued not simply as a way for citizens to discover their true preferences, which could arguably be achieved through the provision of information. The benefits of deliberation include the provision of reasons to those whose views do not prevail in the democratic process, the promotion of 'mutual understanding and empathy' and possibly a greater level of agreement.[70]

The conditions for deliberative democracy are demanding. Substantive political equality fits within this model by ensuring that the process is inclusive and that people can participate regardless of their economic position. However, political equality in a deliberative democracy demands more than citizens having an equal opportunity to take part, and some versions require that in deliberation people present reasons that are accessible and appeal to all citizens,[71] do not rely on self-interest and show some degree of respect to the other participants.[72] It is argued by some that this emphasis on moral reasoning in deliberation itself can help to check any advantages secured by the use of wealth.[73] Furthermore, deliberative democracy requires that people be able to hear a range of different views and ideas, which ensures that citizens can revise and adapt their views. To meet this more demanding account of equality, deliberative democracy therefore requires that the agenda be both diverse and inclusive. As a result, the citizen's equal opportunity to influence may be complemented by a distribution of political resources that ensures that alternative views get a hearing (which can be described as 'equality of ideas', as opposed to the equal political resources among citizens).[74] In this context, each relevant political position or viewpoint should be granted an equal opportunity to be heard and considered.

Given that this model moves away from a characterisation of democracy as aggregation, some deliberative theorists argue for a shift away from voting as the central act in the democratic process. Dryzek, for example, states that deliberative democracy attempts to ensure that public policy is 'responsive to public opinion through non-electoral means',[75] which includes processes for 'reasoned agreement' such as mediation and citizen juries.[76] Furthermore, much research on deliberative democracy has focused on 'mini-publics',

[70] W. Kymlicka, *Contemporary Political Philosophy: an Introduction* (Oxford University Press, 2002) pp. 291–2.

[71] Gutmann and Thompson, *Why Deliberative Democracy?*, p. 4.

[72] See discussion of Rawls in Knight and Johnson, 'What Sort of Equality Does Deliberative Require?', pp. 283–4.

[73] For example, Gutmann and Thompson argue that moral arguments can be used to expose and critique the use of wealth in politics; see Gutmann and Thompson, *Why Deliberative Democracy?*, pp. 48–51.

[74] Along similar lines Christiano distinguishes between qualitative and numerical equality. See T. Christiano, *The Rule of the Many* (Oxford: Westview Press, 1996) p. 91.

[75] Dryzek, *Deliberative Democracy and Beyond*, p. 47.   [76] *Ibid.*, p. 50.

small-scale settings such as citizens' juries or consensus conferences, where the demanding conditions for deliberation can be more easily secured. For example, a small deliberative panel will have more opportunities for face-to-face interaction, briefing by and questioning of experts.[77] This model faces greater challenges if it is to be applied to mass democracy, such as politics on the national scale, where deliberation is 'asymmetrical, highly mediated and distorted by the structural inequalities in society'.[78] However, there are still ways that the deliberative model can be pursued in mass politics and the existing constitutional framework. For example, Robert Goodin argues that election campaigns are unlikely to serve some deliberative goals, as campaigns are less likely to be places for 'rational arguments involving careful deductions of conclusions from well-grounded premises' and participants are unlikely to show 'respect for opposing groups, their interests, and their arguments'.[79] However, in Goodin's view, election campaigns serve the deliberative goals of 'openness', in which any person can participate, and have a 'common good focus'.[80] While the different qualities of an election campaign can be debated, the point shows that there is scope for elections to meet some, even if not all, of the conditions for a deliberative democracy. Furthermore, steps can be taken to enhance those qualities. For example, substantive political equality can strengthen the openness of the process, making it more inclusive and preventing the debate being distorted by economic inequalities. Along these lines, Joshua Cohen has argued that deliberative democracy supports measures such as the public funding of political parties, to prevent inequalities in the deliberative arena and to ensure that the parties address issues that affect society as a whole, as opposed to those sectional interests that give money to the party.[81]

Aside from elections, the various forums for communication, discussion and dissemination of information can help to serve some deliberative goals in mass politics. Jurgen Habermas has emphasised the importance in a democracy for citizens to freely engage in 'rational-critical debate' with one another. Such activities can take place in the 'informal political public sphere' that is independent of the state and market, in which opinions are formed and communicated, and can then be taken up by the formal political institutions, such as the legislature.[82] In his earlier work, Habermas described how the coffee houses of the eighteenth century and the early press in Europe led to the development of such a public sphere in which people could engage in debate and participate as

---

[77] For discussion of the various types of 'mini-public' see R. Goodin, *Innovating Democracy* (Oxford University Press, 2008) ch. 2.

[78] S. Chambers, 'Rhetoric and the Public Sphere: Has Deliberative Democracy Abandoned Mass Democracy?' (2009) 37 *Political Theory* 323, at 339.

[79] Goodin, *Innovating Democracy*, pp. 199–200.

[80] *Ibid.*, p. 199.

[81] J. Cohen, 'Deliberation and Democratic Legitimacy', in J. Bohman and W. Rehg (eds.), *Deliberative Democracy: Essays on Reason and Politics* (Cambridge, MA: MIT Press, 1997) pp. 85–6.

[82] See J. Habermas, *Between Facts and Norms* (Cambridge: Polity, 1996) ch. 8.

equals.[83] However, much of Habermas' work has been critical of the commercial mass media. For example, criticisms include its potential to turn people into spectators of politics rather than participants, and that the reliance on advertising (alongside the growth of public relations) has made the media a space for the pursuit of private interests. In later work, Habermas has outlined how the mass media can, under certain conditions, still play an important role in a deliberative democracy.[84] Along these lines, while the mass media may not provide many opportunities for face-to-face contact or conversation, it can play an important role in ensuring that people have access to information and provide a space where a range of diverse views can be openly debated. This role, however, also highlights the danger that inequalities in wealth will distort the process if it means that some speakers cannot acquire the means to communicate in the media, or that a wealthy minority is able to use its resources to shape the political agenda and dominate the deliberative forums.[85] Measures related to substantive political equality can therefore help to serve deliberative goals, for example through regulations that prevent concentrated media ownership, secure access to the forums for communication or which ensure that diverse viewpoints reach audiences.[86] The discussion shows that while the practices of mass democracy may not meet all the conditions of a deliberative democracy, some steps can be taken to make it more deliberative, including insulating the process from inequalities in wealth.

This section has gone down a well-trodden path in contrasting three democratic models. Each gives an indication of the broad spectrum of democratic theories, with the minimalism of the elite theory at one end, and the more demanding (and optimistic) deliberative version at the other. The discussion is not exhaustive, and has missed out a number of other leading theories, notably participatory democracy.[87] The point, however, has been to show that inequalities in political resources can potentially distort the workings of these different types of democracy. It has also shown that the ideal distribution of resources may vary according to the goals of each theory. For example an egalitarian version of an aggregative model suggests resources should

---

[83] J. Habermas, *The Structural Transformation of the Public Sphere* (Cambridge: Polity, 1989).

[84] J. Habermas, 'Does Democracy Still Enjoy an Epistemic Dimension?' (2006) 16 *Communication Theory* 411. For discussion of the importance of the mass media and the forums for communication in a deliberative democracy, see also Sunstein, *The Partial Constitution*, ch. 8.

[85] Shapiro, *The State of Democratic Theory*, p. 24 and pp. 30–2.

[86] See C. Calhoun, 'Introduction', in C. Calhoun (ed.), *Habermas and the Public Sphere* (Cambridge, MA: MIT Press, 1992) p. 28. Under the Habermasian model, the use of certain legal regulations could be met with the objection that it undermines the independence of the informal public sphere from the state, in which the process of opinion formation is supposed to be 'wild' and 'anarchic'. See Habermas, *Between Facts and Norms*, pp. 307–8. However, in later chapters it will be argued that such regulations attempt to secure an equal opportunity to participate without political debate being subject to government direction.

[87] The participatory model can be placed close to deliberative democracy in the spectrum, as its requirements are more demanding and it emphasises that democracy is about more than just aggregating preferences, see Goodin, *Innovating Democracy*, p. 2.

ideally be distributed equally among the relevant unit that is to be aggregated, such as the individual or the group. The deliberative approach will also seek to ensure each individual has the opportunity to influence the outcomes, but also emphasises the need to ensure that the agenda for deliberation is diverse and inclusive of the relevant viewpoints. Below it will be argued that these different approaches can, to some extent, be accommodated at different stages of the democratic process. To make this point, a distinction will be drawn between three stages of the process: the voting stage; the pre-voting stage; and the agenda-setting stage.

Stages of the democratic process

Equality at the voting stage

The voting stage of the democratic process takes place after the arguments have been heard and discussed.[88] At this stage, each citizen is given roughly the same direct and unmediated input into a decision, a standard of 'one person, one vote'. Such a standard is reflected in the European Court of Human Rights' (ECtHR) statement that free and fair elections require 'equality of treatment of all citizens in the exercise of their right to vote'.[89] In the UK, this standard applies not only to elections and referenda, but also to the process for decision-making within elected bodies, such as the legislature or council chamber (where members of those bodies have equal votes). Despite the apparent simplicity of the standard, it leaves a number of questions unanswered and equality in voting needs to be defined with greater precision when designing an electoral system.[90] Various features of the electoral system will be subject to disagreement, such as who should be eligible to vote, whether first-past-the-post or proportional representation is to be used, and how electoral constituencies should be drawn up. Consequently, while requiring equality in the treatment of votes, the ECtHR gives considerable discretion to the state when answering these questions.[91] At the voting stage, the ideal of political equality provides a point of reference that can be used to rule out certain features that are clearly incompatible with any version of the principle. For present purposes, it is sufficient to say that allocating votes or the weight of

---

[88] It is important not to overstate the finality of voting, given that the outcome of a decision may impact on the agenda for future political decisions and citizens' preferences. Instead of seeing voting as a final matter that disposes of an issue, it is a part of a continuous feedback loop that can shape the future decision-making, and potentially questions a rigid distinction between voting and other stages.

[89] *Mathieu-Mohin* v. *Belgium* (1988) 10 *EHRR* 1 at [54].

[90] See J. Still 'Political Equality and Election Systems' (1981) 91 *Ethics* 375.

[91] For example in *Mathieu-Mohin* v. *Belgium* (1988) 10 *EHRR* 1, the Court stated at [54] that the 'equal treatment' of votes does not mean that 'all votes must necessarily have equal weight as regards the outcome of the election'. Similarly, in *Aziz* v. *Cyprus* (2004) 19 BHRC 510, the Court stated at [28] that while the rules regulating elections may 'vary according to the historical and political factors peculiar to each State, these rules should not be such as to exclude some persons or group of persons from participating in the political life of the country'.

each vote according to a citizen's wealth would fall foul of any version of political equality in a democracy.[92]

Equality at the pre-voting stage

Prior to the voting stage, political equality is more complex, and does not mean that every person has the same direct input into a decision. In this context an equal opportunity to influence is the standard for political equality. This stage includes a range of different activities,[93] including debate and deliberation, in which people participate by providing reasons and listening to those of others. Other activities apply pressure and advance a particular view which the participants have formed. For example, a letter-writing campaign to an MP may not try to convince the legislator through reasons or new arguments, but persuades through sheer numbers that support the position. Activities at the pre-voting stage can therefore have aggregative and deliberative elements, and the two may be difficult to distinguish. However, the two approaches can also complement one another.[94] Deliberation precedes the aggregative parts of the democratic process, and can lead to the formation and changing of preferences. Once deliberation has taken place, there will come a point where preferences have to be counted or collected in some way, which can be done through bargaining or pressure activities, as well as voting. Consequently, the approach to political equality at this stage should attempt to accommodate both those democratic goals by distributing resources in a way that ensures collective decisions are responsive to citizens and representative groups, but also supports deliberative goals. Under this approach, certain resources should be ideally distributed equally to each person, but other or additional resources may be distributed to promote a diverse and inclusive deliberative agenda.

Agenda-setting

Prior to deliberation and pressure activities comes the agenda-setting stage. This stage determines what the deliberation or pressure will be about, and which options will be subject to a vote. Agenda-setting occurs at a range of different levels.[95] For example, it can refer to the policy options that will be subject to a decision in the formal political institutions, such as the issues for

---

[92] Equality provides one, but by no means the only reason for restricting vote buying. See discussion in P. Karlan, 'Not by Money but by Virtue Won? Vote Trafficking' (1994) 80 Va. L. Rev. 1455 and R. Hasen, 'Vote Buying' (2000) 88 Calif. L. Rev. 1323.

[93] It may be misleading to describe all these activities as pre-voting, given that some decisions will be made by a minister or civil servant without a vote. These activities may seek to influence such decisions, so may be better described as pre-decision, rather than pre-voting.

[94] S. Besson, *The Morality of Conflict* (Oxford: Hart, 2005) ch. 7; Christiano, *The Rule of the Many*, pp. 83–93; Weale, *Democracy*, p. 80.

[95] See R.W. Cobb and C.D. Elder, *Participation in American Politics: the Dynamics of Agenda-building* (Boston: Allyn and Bacon, 1972) p. 14.

inclusion in a legislative programme. Agenda-setting is also used to describe the activities which give certain issues salience and provide a focus for public discussion. Much political activity attempts to get issues to move from this broader, more informal agenda to become a possible policy option in the formal political institutions. When taken in such a broad sense, agenda-setting is not really a distinct stage, but an ongoing process that overlaps with the pre-voting stage activities.[96] Furthermore, in practice, the agenda is not simply the product of people's choices and is formed through a range of different factors. For example, it may be shaped by unpredictable events such as a natural disaster. However, the agenda can be set by a number of political actors, such as the government when deciding the agenda in Parliament, the media when determining which issues to publicise, and political parties when writing an election manifesto. Given the importance of the agenda in shaping the final outcome, an equal opportunity to influence the political agenda is an important part of the political process. In so far as the agenda shapes deliberation, it should consist of a range of options that enable people to have a meaningful choice between contrasting alternatives, to promote a 'well informed' and 'reflective' process.[97] Yet given that the agenda does have a real impact on the final decision, the agenda should also be responsive to people's preferences and contain the positions that have most support.[98] The aim is therefore to combine the goals of responsiveness and deliberation, as with the activities in the pre-voting stage.

Whether greater emphasis should be given to either of those goals will vary according to the particular activity in question. For example, greater emphasis may be placed on the goal of responsiveness in relation to electoral activities, given the proximity to the main mechanism for aggregating preferences. By contrast, when looking at the role of the mass media, greater emphasis should be placed on supporting a well-informed and deliberative process. Despite these differences in emphasis, many activities will, to some extent, contribute to all of these different goals. For example, while responsiveness and aggregation are important in election campaigns, such activities can contribute to deliberation in providing reasons for a particular decision and can set the agenda by increasing the prominence of an issue. The different democratic theories will often value the same activities in different ways.[99]

In the account sketched above, an equal opportunity is not just about elections, but relates to political influence more broadly. Consequently, the following chapters will consider the promotion of political equality in several different contexts. In relation to elections, political parties and lobbying, the activities take place in closer proximity to the decision-making stage where the demands of equality are clearer. The other chapters will look at the opportunity

---

[96] Marmor, 'Authority, Equality and Democracy'.   [97] Beitz, *Political Equality*, p. 176.
[98] *Ibid.*
[99] For example, while an interest group pluralist will be more likely to view an activity as pressure or bargaining, the deliberative democrat is more likely to see that same action as a contribution to the deliberative process.

to influence more generally by participating in activities in public spaces and through communications in the mass media. In those contexts the demands of equality will be vaguer than in the electoral context, as such activities are not fixed within a particular timeframe on a decision. However, the principle of political equality provides an argument for addressing some of the major inequalities and securing access to the forums for communication and the mass media. Given that this broad approach combines elements from different democratic theories and primarily looks at mass politics, the focus on the core requirements of substantive political equality taken here will be consistent with various models of democracy and will be used as a standard to explain the main problems with the use of wealth in politics.

Wealth as a source of influence

So far it has been noted that wealth can be used as a political resource, and that equality in the opportunity to influence is taken as the standard for political equality. A tension arises if wealth is unequally distributed, as some citizens will have a greater chance to influence than others. However, many political resources are distributed unequally, such as time, knowledge, expertise or celebrity, but do not call for redistribution.[100] The question arises why inequalities in wealth should be targeted as opposed to other inequalities.

The first argument concerns the extent of inequalities in wealth, which, if used in politics would give the very rich much greater opportunities to influence decisions than someone on an average wage. By contrast there may be other types of inequality that are tolerated and do not raise concern or require any remedial measure because they are of a lesser scale. This suggests that the goal is not to attain perfect equality of opportunity, but to limit the most extreme inequalities. To make the point, a contrast can be drawn between wealth and spare time. While people may differ in terms of the amount of time they can devote to politics, there are at least limits on what is humanly possible when using your own spare time. A person can dedicate only so many hours in a day to a particular activity, and spare time cannot be saved up to be used on another occasion.[101] Furthermore, whether differences in time create different levels of political influence depends on what is done with that time. An hour spent delivering leaflets will generate less influence than an hour provided by a marketing executive advising a political party how to promote its policies. The difference is in terms of how the time is used, which comes down to a different type of inequality, between abilities and talents. However, those activities which

---

[100] See Justice Alito in *Davis* v. *FEC* (2008) 128 S. Ct. 2759 at 2774: 'Different candidates have different strengths. Some are wealthy; others have wealthy supporters who are willing to make large contributions. Some are celebrities; some have the benefit of a well-known family name. Leveling electoral opportunities means making and implementing judgments about which strengths should be permitted to contribute to the outcome of an election.'

[101] Verba *et al., Voice and Equality,* p. 289.

require time and no special skill, such as handing out leaflets, canvassing, taking part in a march or attending a rally, are less likely to generate vast inequalities. Differences in time alone have a natural cap, and attempts to resolve differences could possibly be addressed by ensuring that citizens have the spare time to become active in politics and encouraging people to use that time to participate.[102] This argument only goes so far. It may explain why inequalities in wealth are more problematic than inequalities in spare time alone or other measurable sources of influence. However, some sources of influence such as expertise or reputation are harder to quantify, making it difficult to show that inequalities in influence derived from such sources are less severe than those of wealth. The level of inequality cannot distinguish wealth from all other unequal sources of influence, but the fact that wealth is measurable makes the problem apparent and makes some remedial measures possible.

One response to the concern about wealth may be to argue that it is one of several different unevenly distributed political resources, such as time, expertise, contacts, celebrity and professional status, which can work to constrain one another. Under this view, wealth may provide a channel of influence for those who lack the time or expertise to devote to politics. Wealth is then seen to balance other sources of influence and other sources of influence balance wealth. Such an argument reflects the pluralist model of democracy discussed earlier, in which some groups may have greater wealth, while others may have advantages in expertise or education. The pluralist account suggested that the influence secured through a resource will vary from issue to issue; so different groups will be influential on different matters.[103] Under this view, power is dispersed and one source of power 'does not afford a group general power or automatically give it access to other sources of power'.[104]

However, this leads to a second argument why inequalities in wealth require special attention, that money is not just one political resource among many. Instead it is 'a universal transferable unit infinitely more flexible in its uses than the time, or ideas, or talent, or influence, or controlled votes that also constitute contributions to politics'.[105] An expert in energy policy is likely to have a high level of influence in his area of expertise, but is largely limited to that field. By contrast, someone with sufficient economic resources can commission a range of experts in a range of fields, as well as fund marketing campaigns. Wealth can be used to secure other political resources such as information, access to the media and publicity, and contacts. Where political resources can be bought, then advantages in the various sources of influence may become concentrated in the hands of those with sufficient spending power rather than widely dispersed. The convertibility of wealth can result in the various sources

---

[102] For example, Ackerman and Fishkin's proposal for a public holiday for deliberation would provide time off work specifically to encourage political activity, see B. Ackerman and J. Fishkin, *Deliberation Day* (New Haven: Yale University Press, 2005).

[103] Held, *Models of Democracy*, p. 202.   [104] Cunningham, *Theories of Democracy*, p. 77.

[105] A. Heard, *The Costs of Democracy* (Chapel Hill: University of North Carolina Press, 1960) p. 90.

of influence becoming aligned and reinforcing rather than constraining one another.

Similarly, when those in government also have an advantage based on wealth, then the economic resources can uphold rather than check state power. The most visible example of such a connection is in Italy, where Silvio Berlusconi, one of the country's wealthiest individuals and owner of much of its mass media, is also its Prime Minister. The concentration of political resources helps to maintain the hold on power. Yet such concentration does not have to arise in relation to one individual, and can also arise through more general alliances between wealth and officeholders. For example, where a political party in office is supported by, or has a close connection with, a media mogul or group of multi-millionaires, the economic resources can reinforce that party in power. This does not give those with sufficient wealth complete control, but it limits the extent to which other political resources act as a countervailing power.

A third reason why the influence of wealth requires special attention lies in the way it secures a greater opportunity to influence. Earlier it was stated that some inequalities in influence are tolerated and the example was given where influence arises by persuading other people of the merits of a particular view. In this sense, influence is not direct but mediated by other citizens who make a choice whether to accept or reject an argument. This argument does not, however, apply to wealth as a source of influence, as the advantages it secures do not flow from the audience's choice. It is the unequal opportunity secured by wealth that is problematic. Bernard Manin draws a similar distinction when discussing candidates for election that are articulate, persuasive or charismatic and thereby have greater chance of being elected.[106] The reason for their influence is that citizens choose to place weight on these qualities. By contrast, the argument against the influence of wealth is not, according to Manin:

> that there is something about wealth that makes it particularly unworthy to serve as a criterion for selecting rulers. It is rather that, if the advantage enjoyed by wealthy candidates (or the wealthy classes which candidates are inclined to address principally in their appeals for funds) derives from the cost of disseminating information, the superiority in wealth confers power *by itself*, and not because voters choose it as a proper criterion of selection.[107]

Under this view, if voters want to elect a candidate because she is rich or because they want to listen to the arguments of a wealthy investor on account of her experience, then that is their choice. By contrast, in securing access to the channels of communication, wealth directly determines which views will get a hearing. The allocation of time to the speaker who buys access is not mediated by the citizen's choice. There is still an element of choice for citizens to decide whether to listen to a particular speaker or channel; however, they do

[106] B. Manin, *The Principles of Representative Government* (Cambridge University Press, 1997) pp. 157–8.
[107] *Ibid.*, p. 159.

not decide which speakers or views will be funded and disseminated in the first place. The use of economic resources therefore sets the agenda and determines which views will get priority during the pre-voting stages.

The difficulty with this argument as a way of isolating wealth as a source of influence is that other inequalities, such as levels of expertise, can also determine who gets to disseminate information to a wide audience. When deciding whom to invite to brief Downing Street on an issue or whom to invite to speak on *Newsnight*, there is no need to put an established policy expert on the same footing as any other person with a vague interest in the topic. This decision is not mediated by the public, who have not chosen the expert, so it seems as if the agenda is being set for them. However, one difference is that it is the wealthy individual alone that decides to spend in order to disseminate a particular message. By contrast, the expert has to be invited by someone else, so it is not direct and unmediated; it is simply mediated by someone other than the general public. The expert holds the position because she has something to offer to the democratic process, not simply because she wants to speak and can afford to do so. The choices of public officials and controllers of the mass media of whom to invite when setting the agenda should, ideally, reflect democratic goals such as responsiveness and diversity, rather than their own partisan agenda. The official or journalist selecting an expert will often be subject to certain professional constraints. Furthermore, the opportunities afforded to experts at various stages of the process may be seen as a trade-off, as a necessary qualification of political equality in order to promote better decision-making and administration. Alternatively, the role of the expert can be reconciled with political equality in so far as it helps inform and implement democratic decisions.[108] This is not to deny that the influence secured by experts can pose a problem for political equality,[109] but rather to note that such concerns are of a different nature from inequalities in wealth and will call for a different response (if one is needed).

Finally, the arguments advanced above suggest that politics has different distributive rules to the economic sphere. In the economic sphere, rewards are distributed for reasons that are not applicable in the political sphere. As Michael Walzer explains:

> Democracy is a way of allocating power and legitimating its use … Democracy puts a premium on speech, persuasion, rhetorical skill. Ideally the citizen who makes the most persuasive argument – that is, the argument that actually persuades the largest number of citizens – gets his way. But he can't use force, or pull rank, or distribute money; he must talk about the issues at hand.[110]

---

[108] See discussion in Christiano, *The Rule of the Many*, ch. 5.
[109] Robert Dahl has argued that 'the long-run prospects for democracy are more seriously endangered by inequalities in resources, strategic positions, and bargaining strength that are derived not from wealth or economic position but from special knowledge'. R. Dahl, *Democracy and its Critics* (New Haven: Yale University Press, 1989) p. 333.
[110] M. Walzer, *Spheres of Justice: a Defence of Pluralism and Equality* (Oxford: Blackwell, 1983) p. 304.

By contrast, the economic sphere has its own distributive values and rewards behaviour aside from persuasiveness or reasons. For example, some argue that inequalities of wealth are necessary as a way of maximising the overall level of wealth, by providing incentives to individuals. Politics can be contrasted, as a process that focuses on a particular outcome or decision to which each citizen will be bound, in which some options are accepted or rejected, or some compromise reached.[111] Inequalities in the political sphere do not increase overall levels of political power that are to everyone's benefit. It might be argued that prior to the decision-making stage, inequalities can benefit others by increasing the overall levels of information. That argument suggests that inequalities in political spending on research and publicity simply lead to people being better informed. However, while the quantity of expression is an important factor, using money to get something onto the deliberative agenda and command attention is itself a form of power.[112] It helps to decide what issues will be considered and which views will be most prominent. Furthermore, it has already been mentioned that inequalities in wealth can undermine a person's status as an equal. While this was raised in relation to inequalities in wealth generally, the point is more pressing where inequalities of wealth can be used to provide opportunities for political influence. If inequalities in wealth in the economic sphere are to be accepted, substantive political equality becomes all the more important as the central expression of a person's equal status regardless of their socio-economic position.[113] The distinct values of the two spheres explain why an individual who endorses extreme inequalities in wealth as part of the economic system may see that such inequalities should not be allowed to influence political decisions. Some people may find it perfectly acceptable that Silvio Berlusconi has the wealth that he has, but believe that his wealth should not be used to promote his political career.

As a result of these differences, equality of opportunity for influence is more demanding in the political sphere. Stricter controls need to be placed on the background conditions to put people at an equal starting point. However, the language of equal opportunities generally suggests that whether a source of influence is legitimate or not will depend on whether that resource has been acquired through the individual's own choices and efforts.[114] If a person has a greater chance to influence because he or she is willing to dedicate more time to politics or to acquire skills that are an advantage, then that has arguably been something open to all individuals. This might lead to an argument that the uses of wealth in politics are unproblematic if people acquire those economic

---

[111] S. Verba and G. Orren, *Equality in America: the View from the Top* (Cambridge, MA: Harvard University Press, 1985) ch. 10. Brighouse, 'Egalitarianism and Equal Availability of Political Influence', pp. 132–3.

[112] Copp, 'Capitalism versus Democracy', p. 96.

[113] See J. Cohen, 'Money, Politics and Political Equality', in A. Byrne, R. Stalnaker and R. Wedgwood (eds.), *Fact and Value* (Cambridge, MA: MIT Press, 2001) p. 53.

[114] For discussion see Sadurski, 'Legitimacy, Political Equality, and Majority Rule', at p. 58.

resources fairly through their own efforts. However, the objection to wealth gaining political influence is not that the distribution of wealth is unjust, but that the wealth is distributed according to different values and under different conditions. For example, one person may work hard all her life to become an investment banker. Entirely through her own efforts she amasses a personal fortune, but shows little interest in politics while working at the bank. By contrast, another individual works hard to become an expert in criminology and exercises some influence on sentencing policy through the publication of papers and being consulted by civil servants. The investment banker, on retirement, decides to run her own advertising campaign to convince the public that sentencing policies are too lenient and offers a donation to any candidate sponsoring mandatory life sentences. While both have a level of influence based on their own personal choices, the investment banker's influence rests on the money and the rewards of the economic sphere. The problem is not that the distribution of economic resources is unjust, but rather that rewards granted to personal choices in the economic sphere may not be appropriate for the distribution of political power or influence.[115]

The argument so far has not been against the use of any wealth in politics, as most kinds of political activity will require some economic resources. Instead, the argument has focused on the distribution of wealth and its potential to generate unfair inequalities in the opportunities to influence political decisions. Consequently, not all large sums spent on political influence will violate the principle of political equality and some participants may be permitted to spend larger sums where those resources have been acquired in ways that fit with democratic principles. For example, if a large group decides to pool resources and build up a fund to be spent on lobbying, campaigning and advertising, that does not seem to raise the same equality concerns as one very wealthy individual choosing to spend the same amount. The former can be seen as an association of equal citizens, whereas the latter is just one citizen.

A danger with this view is that it seems to consign the chance to use more economic resources to groups that can identify their formal members or subscribers, which seems to envision one way of doing politics. It also suggests the value of the groups is in aggregating and amplifying the voice of individual citizens. However, different democratic theories may point to different roles for groups, so greater flexibility may be required. The approach taken here is

---

[115] Other approaches that seek a just distribution of economic resources, relying on criteria other than choice, may still require a different method of distribution to secure political equality. For example, under the difference principle, Rawls permits inequalities of wealth that are attained 'under conditions of fair equality of opportunity' and 'must be to the greatest benefit of the least advantaged members of society'. However, inequalities in a just distribution of wealth can still pose problems for political equality, and Rawls makes separate provision for the 'fair value' of political liberties. See Rawls, *Political Liberalism*, pp. 326–8. See also Norman Daniels, 'Equal Liberty and Unequal Worth of Liberty', in N. Daniels (ed.), *Reading Rawls* (New York: Basic Books, 1975) p. 271.

individualistic in taking each person as the primary unit against which equality is measured. However, this can be adjusted to accommodate those models of democracy that place greater emphasis on groups. For example, greater resources for some groups may be permitted if the goal is to increase minority voices in order to enhance deliberation. Under this view, there may be some scenarios where an unequal level of resources is permissible because those resources have been distributed in accordance with values relevant to the political rather than the economic sphere. The point is that permissible inequalities should be an issue of the design of the process, and should not fall wherever the wealth happens to be.

Egalitarian politics and policies

One concern with the account of political equality advanced so far is that it appeals to a particular understanding of what fairness and equality require. Concerns about the role of wealth will have a sympathetic audience with those who regard the redistribution of resources as central to the exercise of freedom in general and are less suspicious of state intervention in this domain. One criticism is that while dressed up in the language of procedure, this account of political equality is not politically neutral.[116] If arguments about democratic citizenship are merely a way of advancing political demands for greater economic equality, then it may, as Will Kymlicka writes, be 'a matter of putting old wine into new bottles'.[117] The arguments about political equality and the fairness of the democratic process echo divisions in other political debates. While the theory of political equality may reflect some political divisions, it does not mean that the outcomes of a democratic process with this model of political equality will favour any political viewpoint, any more than the universal franchise led to radically egalitarian outcomes. It may even have the reverse effect. If the existing economic system is endorsed through a process that has not been skewed by political donations, lobbying efforts and media campaigns, then that outcome may be seen as having greater legitimacy. The concern is therefore not that the model of political equality being advanced will favour particular outcomes, but that the preconditions of an egalitarian political process will themselves demand substantive programmes of wealth redistribution.

The strength of that concern depends on what measures are regarded as a precondition of political equality. One approach may be that a more even distribution of wealth in general is the only way to secure political equality. However, this would render a substantial component of democratic politics

---

[116] For example, Martin Redish argues that attacks on economic power 'may represent little more than the regulator's normative disagreement with the substance of the political and economic positions taken by the majority of economically powerful speakers'. See M. Redish, *Money Talks* (New York University Press, 2001) p. 3.

[117] Kymlicka, *Contemporary Political Philosophy*, p. 319.

redundant, namely those questions about the distribution of wealth that lie at the heart of politics. Another approach could be to democratise parts of the private sector, for example by making the exercise of private power more directly accountable to citizens. This would not simply be a system of shareholder democracy, but would rather give those affected by the decisions and actions of a particular company some say in the way it is run.[118] This approach would not guarantee that everyone has equal political resources at their disposal, but would create a wider distribution of ownership of resources that can be used to influence policy, whether through the 'privileged position' of business or direct participation in the political process. Again, like the previous suggestion, this demands that the economy be organised in a particular way, something which may impose too much of a constraint on the outcomes of democratic decision-making.

The strategy to be considered here is to find other ways of reducing the impact of economic inequalities in the political sphere. In so far as legal reforms can be used to address these difficulties, strategies to be considered will include transparency requirements, limits to the amounts that can be spent on political activities, and the redistribution of political resources. Such measures take steps towards a fair process, but do not impose too great a restriction on the possible outcomes for democratic decision-making. As conceded at the beginning of this chapter, no system of regulation is going to fully prevent inequalities of wealth from having some influence on political decisions. The steps proposed in this book may be less effective than the two alternatives suggested above, but will keep open the range of options for democratic decisions.

Conclusion

This chapter has attempted to sketch an account of political equality, which shows how the principle varies according to different theories of democracy, different stages of the democratic process and different types of activity. This discussion has not aligned itself with any specific account of democracy, but has attempted to show that when inequalities of wealth generate unequal chances to influence the democratic process, the principle of political equality is undermined. The argument advanced so far does not demand that everyone has equal influence over the process, but has sought to identify why inequalities in wealth are problematic for a democracy. Inequalities in wealth have been singled out on account of the direct and unmediated effect, the convertibility into other resources, and the basis of distribution. The approach to be considered in later chapters is whether legal or other regulatory techniques can help to insulate the opportunity for political influence from the distribution of economic resources.

---

[118] See Dahl, *Democracy and its Critics*, pp. 327–32.

This addresses only one element of political equality, and even if such strategies could succeed, many other issues for a fair process would remain. Before looking at specific areas where such a strategy may be employed, the next chapter will develop some of these arguments by looking at their implications for freedom of expression.

2

Freedom to speak and freedom to spend

Political equality has a close connection with the freedom to speak and to associate. Participation in a democracy requires that people are free to engage in political activities, such as debating, protesting and forming associations. Such freedoms are also necessary to ensure people remain well-informed and can hold government to account. A central objection to censorship is that to silence a person is to treat him unequally and to deny him a say. The political freedoms and equality therefore complement one another as central components in the democratic system.[1] Steps to promote political equality that give people the means to participate can also serve those political freedoms. For example, some subsidies for expressive activities can give more people a real opportunity to exercise the freedom to speak.

Political freedoms and political equality can, however, come into tension with one another. Two people can be made equal not just by improving the position of the disadvantaged, but also by curtailing that of the advantaged. Those attempts to promote political equality that seek to restrict the way people can spend their money or use their property are sometimes criticised for infringing political freedoms. These arguments can arise where laws limit the amount that can be spent in an election campaign, grant a person access to another's property, or require the mass media to be impartial or inclusive. This line of criticism highlights the impact of egalitarian measures on the expression of a person who wants to use his wealth for political purposes.

The tension between political equality and freedom of speech has been most prominent in the United States, where the Supreme Court has struck down measures limiting election campaign spending. However, similar legal challenges have been made in a number of other jurisdictions. For example, the European Court of Human Rights (ECtHR) has found that very low limits on political communications during an election campaign[2] and a ban on political advertising in the broadcast media[3] violate freedom of expression.

---

[1] See R (Animal Defenders International) v. Secretary of State for Culture, Media and Sport [2008] 1 AC 1312 at [49].

[2] Bowman v. United Kingdom (1998) 26 EHRR 1.

[3] VgT Verein gegen Tierfabriken v. Switzerland (2001) 34 EHRR 159; TV Vest As & Rogaland Pensjonistparti v. Norway [2008] ECHR 21132/05.

Furthermore, the European Convention on Human Rights (ECHR) does not ensure that people have the means or resources to participate. For example, the ECtHR has found that a shopping centre owner's right to exclude leafleters from its land was consistent with expression rights.[4] Freedom of expression did not require the state to secure the leafleters' access to that land. Consequently, the danger is that political freedoms can be interpreted in ways that assist those that already have the money to speak, but do less to help those without.

Commenting on the legal challenges in the United States, Cass Sunstein has asked whether freedom of speech is being treated as 'a purposeless abstraction', which is 'sometimes used to undermine democracy'.[5] The concern is that freedom of expression may be used as a barrier preventing the goal of political equality being pursued and a guarantee that those with greater wealth can speak more. The criticism made by Sunstein has much greater force in the United States, where the First Amendment provides stronger protection for free speech. While regulations affecting wealth in politics can still be challenged in the courts, the UK approach allows greater flexibility and the courts have not taken the same path as their US counterparts. Under the Human Rights Act 1998 (HRA), 'public authorities' must act compatibly with rights protected in the ECHR[6] and, where possible, legislation must be 'read and given effect in a way that is compatible' with the incorporated rights.[7] Where such an interpretation is not possible the court can make a declaration of incompatibility.[8] The right to freedom of expression is protected under Article 10 of the ECHR and freedom of association under Article 11. Neither article provides an absolute protection for the political rights. For example, Article 10(2) permits interferences with expression that serve a legitimate aim, are prescribed by law and are necessary in a democratic society. This provision allows expression rights to be subject to 'formalities, conditions, restrictions or penalties', for example to protect the rights of others, as long as the state can show the measure meets a 'pressing social need', is a proportionate response and is supported by 'relevant and sufficient reasons'.[9] When applying these tests, interferences with expression concerning politics or matters in the public interest are subject to more intense scrutiny.[10] Such heightened protection reflects the central importance of political expression to the democratic values underlying the ECHR. Unlike the American First Amendment jurisprudence, the approach under Article 10 does not provide a strict rule against interferences that are based on the content of expression.[11] However, a high burden will normally be required to justify a law or regulation that targets a particular view or message, and a measure targeting

---

[4] *Appleby* v. *United Kingdom* (2003) 37 EHRR 78.
[5] C. Sunstein, *Democracy and the Problem of Free Speech* (New York: The Free Press, 1993) p. 93.
[6] Human Rights Act (HRA) 1998, s.6.   [7] HRA, s.3.   [8] HRA, s.4.
[9] *Handyside* v. *UK* (1976) 1 EHRR 737 at [48–50].
[10] See *Lindon* v. *France* [2007] ECHR 21279/02 at [46].
[11] *Police Department of the City of Chicago* v. *Mosley* 408 US 92 (1972).

a viewpoint will be open to challenge under Article 14, which prohibits discrimination based on a 'political or other opinion'.[12]

As a result, the methodology under the Convention permits expression to be regulated where necessary to preserve the integrity of the democratic process, which broadly falls within the legitimate aim of protecting the rights of others under Article 10(2).[13] The importance of that legitimate aim is supported by the protection of free and fair elections under Article 3 of Protocol No 1 of the ECHR. So when the ECtHR found a very low limit on election spending to violate Article 10 in *Bowman*, it accepted that the limit served a legitimate aim, but objected to the level at which spending was limited.[14] More broadly, outside the context of an election, the ECtHR has accepted arguments that the legitimate aim of protecting the rights of others includes a need for 'enabling the formation of a public opinion protected from the pressures of powerful financial groups, while at the same time promoting equal opportunities to the different components of society'.[15] Furthermore, where the aim is to promote a fair democratic process, Baroness Hale has stated that the question before the court is not simply whether to allow a limited interference with expression, but 'is about striking the right balance between the two most important components of a democracy'.[16] This is not to suggest that the judicial decisions on Article 10 or 11 always strike the right balance, but the methodology places considerable weight on the need to promote political equality. The approach under the HRA therefore permits a number of measures to be taken to promote political equality that engage freedom of expression, which would not survive under the US First Amendment protection of free speech. Yet this is not a criticism of the UK system, the US jurisprudence has evolved in its distinct constitutional setting and political culture. An approach that allows some measures towards an egalitarian democratic process arguably fits with the UK political culture, which has often shown greater concern about the private power of large corporations or media moguls rather than hostility to state power.[17]

The compatibility of any measure with the rights under the ECHR will be fact-sensitive and depend on its context. The purpose here is not to determine the compatibility of any particular regulation or law with expression rights, but to explore some of the theoretical arguments supporting an interpretation of

---

[12] For an argument that a stronger rule against content based interferences should be adopted under Article 10, see I. Hare, 'Method and Objectivity in Free Speech Adjudication: Lessons from America' (2005) 54 *International and Comparative Law Quarterly* 49.

[13] *Bowman* v. *United Kingdom* (1998) 26 EHRR 1 at [36–8]. Similarly, in Canada freedom of expression can be reconciled with political equality and a fair democratic process, see *Harper* v. *Canada (Attorney General)* [2004] SCJ No. 28.

[14] *Ibid.*

[15] *VgT Verein gegen Tierfabriken* v. *Switzerland* (2001) 34 EHRR 159 at [60–2] and at [72].

[16] *R (Animal Defenders International)* v. *Secretary of State for Culture, Media and Sport* [2008] 1 AC 1312 at [49].

[17] D. Feldman, 'Content Neutrality', in I. Loveland, *Importing the First Amendment* (Oxford: Hart, 1998) p. 170.

freedom of expression that permits egalitarian measures. First, the ways that expression rights can support political equality will be considered, after which the discussion will turn to the tension between the two. In looking at these issues, reference will be made to the underlying justifications for freedom of expression and the relationship with political equality. While many measures that promote political equality do not raise significant free speech issues, the discussion will focus on those that do. In particular, reference will be made to attempts to control the use of wealth in politics by capping the amounts that can be spent or limiting the use of property. Such examples provide a useful point for discussion as limits on spending already apply in UK elections and similar measures have been a focus for attention in the US debates. The argument put forward in this chapter will be that measures that stop unlimited sums being spent in elections or prevent political debate more generally being dominated by wealthy groups need not compromise Article 10, but can go some way to advance the values underlying freedom of expression.

Engaging freedom of expression

A preliminary question is why a restriction targeting the use of money or property engages freedom of expression or association in the first place. After all, preventing a person from spending large sums of money in support of a political candidate does not stop anyone from saying something. The question is sometimes formulated as to whether 'money is speech'. The difficulty with such a direct equation between money and expression is that there are many restrictions and regulations that affect the use of money without being seen to restrict speech. Having to pay taxes limits the amount of money an individual can spend on expression, but would not be regarded as an interference with that right.[18] However, given that the distribution of economic resources does impact on the ability to engage in some types of expressive activities, there will be some connection between the two. First, wealth can be used as a direct form of expression. By sponsoring a particular project or donating money to a political party, a donor may express support for a viewpoint or institution. The act of giving money itself communicates the donor's endorsement and creates a connection with the recipient.

Second, and more common, is that wealth can be used in a way that facilitates expressive activities. This can be seen where wealth is required to access the mass media, or on a smaller scale to publish leaflets or hire a meeting hall. Controls on the use of wealth may therefore impact on the extent to which the speaker can engage in these activities, but that is not enough to say it interferes with freedom of expression. Where a law restricts the amount that can be spent

---

[18] See Justice White's dissent in *Buckley* v. *Valeo* 424 US 1 (1976) at 262–3. For a strong criticism of the equation between money and speech, see J. Skelly Wright, 'Is Money Speech' (1976) 85 *Yale Law Journal* 1001.

in an election campaign, it restricts many uses of economic resources, such as on fuel for the campaign bus, and does not single out those used to communicate.[19] Yet experience shows that the production and dissemination of expression tends to be a major expense in election campaigns, so a restriction on election spending will generally have a greater impact on the exercise of expression rights. Furthermore, while some limits may aim to keep the cost of campaigning down for a range of reasons, the purpose of such measures is often connected to expression in so far as it aims to prevent a person, group or party gaining an unfair advantage in political debate. Consequently, for the purposes of this chapter, it will be accepted that restrictions on the use of wealth in politics do engage freedom of expression.

Positive obligations

Freedom of expression has traditionally been understood as a negative protection against state interference. In that traditional understanding, freedom of expression serves equality in a formal sense, such as protecting individuals from undue discrimination by the state.[20] Yet this approach is open to the same criticisms as formal equality, discussed in Chapter 1. An absence of state censorship does not guarantee that people can in practice publish their own political material or buy advertisements. Along these lines, it is often argued that the protection of expression is of limited value if the would-be speaker does not have the resources necessary to communicate. Such a concern can be seen in statements that 'freedom of expression cannot be exercised in a vacuum',[21] or that '[f]reedom of the press is guaranteed only to those who own one'.[22] Consequently, if freedom of expression is closely linked with the economic resources that facilitate expression, then an argument can be made that the freedom is best served by supplying people with the means to speak. For example, such a provision could be secured by the state directly subsidising speakers and providing the speaker with access to the channels of communication. The argument can be taken further to suggest that freedom of expression imposes a positive obligation on the state to provide those resources. This suggests that freedom of expression and political equality are not in tension, and the former can be invoked to secure the latter.

One difficulty with a view that freedom of expression imposes a positive obligation on the state to provide resources is that the demands of such a requirement can quickly become unmanageable. Expression rights cannot mean that whenever a person wishes to speak, no matter how trivial, the state is under a duty to provide resources. To use John Rawls' example, freedom of religion

---

[19] Justice White, *Buckley* v. *Valeo* 424 US 1 (1976) at 263.

[20] See *Police Department of the City of Chicago* v. *Mosley* 408 US 92 (1972).

[21] Lamer CJ, *Her Majesty The Queen in Right of Canada Appellant* v. *Committee for the Commonwealth of Canada* [1991] 1 SCR 139 at 155.

[22] A. J. Liebling, *The Press* (New York: Ballatine, 1964) pp. 30–1.

does not require that citizens have the resources to build a temple, should they wish to do so.[23] Similarly, freedom of expression does not entail such a broad claim to resources. One strategy to deal with such a problem is to narrow down the positive obligation to support the exercise of those rights only in relation to expression that engages with the democratic process, namely political expression. Along such lines, Rawls argued that the 'fair value' of liberty should be secured only in relation to the political liberties.[24] The fair value means that the 'worth' of liberties, that is the material means to exercise those liberties, should be approximately equal.[25] Consequently, in Rawls' account, while the fair value is to be secured in relation to the political liberties, the other liberties are protected in the negative sense. That distinction between freedom and its worth also helps to separate arguments for effective freedom (focusing on the worth) from the traditional understanding of the political freedoms.[26] However, even within these more limited confines, a claim for the resources to exercise the right is still difficult to manage, for example in deciding what resources a person is entitled to and what burden should be imposed on the state to provide for the expressive purposes. These objections do not stop the state taking some measures to ensure people have some resources for expression, but show that some lines will need to be drawn to limit a judicially enforced positive obligation.

In some circumstances Articles 10 and 11 will impose a positive obligation on the state to use its resources to protect or facilitate expression. For example, the ECtHR has recognised that the state has a positive duty to protect speakers assembling in public places from a hostile audience.[27] As a result, the state is under a duty to provide some police resources to protect speakers. However, the demands can only go so far and any positive obligation must not 'impose an impossible or disproportionate burden' on the state.[28] In some circumstances those positive obligations can help provide access to important forums for expressive activities. The ECtHR has held that the state is under a positive obligation to ensure that speakers can access private land for the purpose of expression, but only where to hold otherwise would destroy the 'essence of the right'.[29] The result is that Article 10 does impose some positive obligations, but

---

[23] J. Rawls, *Political Liberalism* (New York: Columbia University Press, 1996) pp. 329–30.

[24] *Ibid.*, pp. 325–6. See also Norman Daniels, 'Equal Liberty and Unequal Worth of Liberty', in N. Daniels (ed.), *Reading Rawls* (Oxford: Blackwell, 1975).

[25] Rawls, *Political Liberalism*.

[26] Republican accounts of freedom also emphasise the need for equality in relation to political rights. Those accounts that stress freedom as non-domination do not require material equality in relation to all freedoms, but only where such material inequalities would lead to the domination of others. Inequalities in political liberties can lead to such domination in giving some people greater influence over the collective decisions to which everyone is bound. See P. Pettit, *Republicanism* (Oxford University Press, 1997) p. 117 and R. Bellamy, *Political Constitutionalism* (Cambridge University Press, 2007) p. 162.

[27] See *Plattform 'Arzte fur das Leben'* v. *Austria* (1988) 13 EHRR 204 at [32]; *United Macedonian Organisation Ilinden* v. *Bulgaria* (2007) 44 EHRR 4 at [115].

[28] *Osman* v. *United Kingdom* (2000) 29 EHRR 245 at [116].

[29] *Appleby* v. *United Kingdom* (2003) 37 EHRR 78 at [47].

this is the exception rather than the norm. Recognising that the state has some positive obligations to secure the means to speak can go some way towards protecting equality. However, the positive rights recognised by the courts tend to provide a limited threshold of resources, rather than ensuring that people have an equal chance to influence.

Given the difficult questions raised by a positive obligation to provide the resources necessary for expression, it is unsurprising that the courts play a more limited role in securing equality. However, even where the legal right to freedom of expression does not mandate such measures, there are still steps the state can take to promote political equality. Such measures serve freedom of expression by providing people with the means to speak, but are distinct from the negative understanding of freedom of expression that the courts are more commonly concerned with. The issue is more difficult when the measure to promote political equality does not simply provide others with resources, but curtails a person's use of money or property for certain expressive purposes, for example through spending limits. Here, equality comes into tension with freedom of expression in the negative sense. In resolving this tension, it is argued here that the negative right to expression should not be elevated over the goal of political equality. Instead, such measures can in some cases serve those democratic values that partly justify freedom of expression. To consider the relationship between political equality and freedom of expression further, the remainder of this chapter will consider the reasons why that freedom of expression is valued.

Justifications for freedom of expression

A number of arguments have been advanced to justify the protection of freedom of expression. One of the most prominent is that freedom of expression is essential to the pursuit of the truth. Under the version of this argument advanced by John Stuart Mill, allowing the 'the collision of adverse opinions' is most likely to lead to the truth.[30] A variation of this argument provides an account of freedom of expression as a 'marketplace of ideas', in which, Justice Holmes famously stated, 'the best test of truth is the power of the thought to get itself accepted in the competition of the market'.[31] In contrast to the argument advanced by Mill, the marketplace of ideas rests on a sceptical view of the truth. Holmes' account of the truth is that it is what emerges from the process of competition, rather than something which can be verified as true or false. Both versions of the truth argument justify the collective benefits of expression in providing something which is of value to society as a whole. By contrast, a second type of justification values freedom of expression as promoting the individual's self-fulfilment and individual autonomy.[32]

---

[30] J. S. Mill, *On Liberty* [1859] (Oxford University Press, 1998) p. 59.
[31] *Abrams* v. *US* 250 US 616 (1919) at 630.
[32] See E. Barendt, *Freedom of Speech* (Oxford University Press, 2005) pp. 13–18.

A third argument is that freedom of expression is justified as serving democracy. This argument has had the strongest support from the European Court of Human Rights[33] and from UK courts. The argument was summarised by Lord Steyn in *ex parte Simms*:[34]

> freedom of speech is the lifeblood of democracy. The free flow of information and ideas informs political debate. It is a safety valve: people are more ready to accept decisions that go against them if they can in principle seek to influence them. It acts as a brake on the abuse of power by public officials. It facilitates the exposure of errors in the governance and administration of justice of the country.

This justification has a number of elements that are closely connected with the previous two arguments. The statement above emphasises the collective value of expression in a democracy, for example by providing citizens with information and ideas. This element of expression provides citizens with what they need to make democratic choices and to become engaged and informed participants in the process.[35] To some extent, this element of the democratic justification can be compared to the marketplace of ideas outlined above. Both the marketplace of ideas and democratic justification entail an assumption of fallibility, in which decisions should be open to challenge and revision. While this relativism has been a point of criticism for the truth argument in relation to questions of fact, that objection arguably has less force in relation to the democratic justification, as there is less certainty that a political policy is correct.[36] The flaws of this position will be considered below, but the relevant point here is that the marketplace of ideas is sometimes recast as a model for political debate.[37]

This does not mean that freedom of expression serves democracy by simply giving information to a passive audience. The democratic justification also stresses the importance of expression as a channel of participation beyond an informed choice at the ballot box. It allows individuals to directly engage in the political process by advancing their own views, developing their arguments and responding to the arguments of others. Expression provides a way for citizens to actively shape the political process.

The reference to democracy alone provides little indication of how expression should be protected. Among those supporting the democratic justification, there is disagreement as to whether it applies only to political expression

---

[33] For example, *Handyside* v. *United Kingdom* (1979) 1 EHRR 737 at [49].

[34] *R* v. *Secretary of State for the Home Department ex p Simms* [2000] 2 AC 115 at 126.

[35] Often this role is emphasised in relation to the media. For example see Lord Bingham, *McCartan Turkington Breen* v. *Times Newspapers* [2001] 2 AC 277, 290–1: 'the majority cannot participate in the public life of their society … if they are not alerted to and informed about matters which call or may call for consideration and action'. *Castells* v. *Spain* (1992) 14 EHRR 445 at [43]: 'Freedom of the press affords the public one of the best means of discovering and forming an opinion of the ideas and attitudes of their political leaders.'

[36] F. Schauer, *Free Speech: a Philosophical Enquiry* (Cambridge University Press, 1982) p. 39.

[37] See C. E. Baker, *Human Liberty and Freedom of Speech* (Oxford University Press, 1989) p. 28.

or other categories of expression.[38] If it is restricted to political expression, then there is further disagreement as to how broadly or narrowly that category should be defined.[39] Furthermore, there is considerable disagreement as to whether the justification requires a very strong presumption against state interference,[40] or whether the central role of political expression permits some regulation to reflect its importance.[41] Lord Walker, in *Prolife Alliance*, noted the 'paradox' that while political speech is given 'particular importance … there may be good democratic reasons for imposing special restrictions'.[42] These questions cannot be answered without further consideration of the connection between expression, democracy and equality. In looking at that connection, the discussion will draw on arguments that justify freedom of expression more generally as well as those that specifically refer to the democratic process, and will look at justifications based on the speaker's interest and then the collective interest in expression.

The speaker's interest

The first approach emphasises freedom of expression from the perspective of the speaker. Under the speaker-based perspective, a person's freedom to say whatever they want confirms their status as moral agents whose opinions, interests and views count. Under this account, it is not for the state to tell a person what opinions or views are acceptable and to deny a person's right to speak is to deny their equal status.[43] As C. Edwin Baker summarises: 'Respect for people as autonomous agents implies that people should be viewed as responsible for, and given maximal liberty in, choosing how to use their bodies and minds to develop and express themselves; and should be given equal right to try to influence the nature of their collective worlds.'[44] This argument is separate from the democracy based justifications and is not restricted to political expression. Instead, it is the autonomy of the speaker that justifies freedom of expression. Other speaker-based accounts also emphasise the role of expression in a person's self-fulfilment, for example allowing the speaker to develop his or her own personality. These justifications do not depend on each individual expressing new ideas or even useful ones. Whatever the merits of the idea, the fact that it is held by a citizen requires that he or she be free to express it.

[38] J. Balkin, 'Digital Speech and Democratic Culture: a Theory of Freedom of Expression for the Information Society' (2004) 79 *New York University Law Review* 1; looking at free speech theory aimed at promoting a 'democratic culture'.

[39] Compare R. Bork, 'Neutral Principles and Some First Amendment Problems' (1971) 47 Ind. L.J. 1 with A. Meiklejohn, 'The First Amendment is an Absolute' [1961] *The Supreme Court Review* 245 at 262–3.

[40] See J. Weinstein, 'Campaign Finance Reform and the First Amendment: an Introduction' (2002) 34 Ariz. St. L.J. 1057.

[41] O. Fiss, *Liberalism Divided: Freedom of Speech and the many uses of State Power* (New York: Westview Press, 1996) ch. 1; and Sunstein, *Democracy and the Problem of Free Speech*, ch. 3.

[42] *R (ProLife Alliance)* v. *BBC* [2004] AC 185 at [130].

[43] Schauer, *Free Speech*, p. 62.

[44] Baker, *Human Liberty and Freedom of Speech*, p. 59.

An account that stresses autonomy may raise objections to legal measures that restrict the amount a person can spend on political expression. Under this view, different speakers may want to use varying amounts of wealth to reflect their level of interest in politics or to develop their political skills. Constraints on the amount of money a person can spend, or how he can use his property, may stop that person from engaging in such activities to the extent that he would like. The objection to limits on political spending is that it suggests only so much is required to participate. Along these lines, the concern with autonomy suggests it is not for the state to determine how much someone can put into an activity, or in what ways that activity can be pursued.

However, a ceiling on spending is not an outright limit on all political activities and people can still participate in ways that do not involve spending large sums. Furthermore, the standard of equality of opportunity would still permit the use of some economic resources, but may limit the amount a single participant can use to influence others. The spending caps will limit only the very large sums, and within those limits accommodate different levels of engagement in politics. Despite this, strategies that aim to promote equality through a constraint on the use of money or property will be in tension with justifications based on the speaker's autonomy. Such justifications are, however, strongest where the speaker pursues his or her own interest without affecting or harming anyone else. By contrast, political expression clearly relates to and affects other people in so far as it attempts to influence collective decisions. The greater spending of one person and promotion of a particular view may come at the expense of the potential influence of another. Under this view, political activities are not just another pastime, and attempts to limit political inequalities stop people exercising 'disproportionate power over the lives of others'.[45] Genuine participation in the democratic process requires citizens to engage with one another as equals, which in turn leads to a commitment to the equal opportunity to participate. The danger with a very strong or absolute protection of freedom under the speaker-focused view is that it tends to view the individual in isolation.

While the above account refers to freedom of expression in general, a variation of this approach emphasises the speaker's interest as part of the democratic justification for expression. By safeguarding the right to participate, freedom of expression respects a person's equal status in a democracy. Along these lines, Robert Post refers to freedom of speech in a democracy as an attempt 'to reconcile individual autonomy with collective self-determination by subordinating governmental decision-making to communicative processes sufficient to instill in citizens a sense of participation, legitimacy, and identification'.[46] The right to speak is thereby valued as a form of participation and engagement in the process, which grants legitimacy to collective decisions. Similarly, James Weinstein

[45] H. Brighouse, 'Democracy and Inequality', in A. Carter and G. Stokes (eds.), *Democratic Theory Today* (Cambridge: Polity Press, 2001) p. 62.
[46] R. Post, 'Meiklejohn's Mistake: Individual Autonomy and the Reform of Public Discourse' (1993) 64 U. Colo. L. Rev. 1109 at 117.

emphasises the importance of expression from the perspective of the speaker, as 'each person has a right to try to persuade others about any matter of public concern' and participate in 'public discourse'.[47] Under a broad speaker-based account, even where speech does not attempt to persuade, it provides an outlet for the speaker to signal to the world what he or she thinks. Under this view, what matters is that each person gets the chance to participate rather than the substance of what is said. Such participation can be valued as a contribution to the democratic process and can promote a person's sense of inclusion.

The speaker-based approach requires that people should be equally free to speak and provides a strong argument against state censorship, where the criminal law is used to banish certain content from political debate. Such censorship denies a citizen a chance to contribute to the democratic process and persuade others. Yet the concern with state censorship is not the same as a right to use unlimited resources. If the concern is with the legitimacy of democratic decisions, allowing wealth to generate inequalities in the chance to speak could undermine that justification underlying freedom of expression.[48] If someone is given a disproportionate chance to express his or her views, or have greater prominence than others, then it may undermine other people's sense of inclusion in the process and symbolise unequal status. For example, one citizen may have a chance to send a letter to a newspaper, but this does not mean that he feels on an equal footing with someone who has the resources to spend vast amounts on advertising on the same topic. Measure that promote equality may thereby serve democratic legitimacy. Those strategies that pursue the goal by providing subsidies to give people the resources to speak will sit more comfortably with the speaker-based approach. If participation is necessary for democratic legitimacy, the speaker-based argument may suggest that citizens should be given some resources to facilitate the exercise of the right to speak, at least to secure an adequate chance for each individual to participate.[49]

Justifying expression as a form of political participation can therefore strengthen claims that the chance to participate should be equally distributed. Under this view, the purpose of expression is more closely connected with political equality and some attempts to secure an equal chance to participate serve the values of freedom of expression; although this will depend on the specific measure in question. Yet an objection that spending limits and other measures are in tension with freedom of expression may come from another direction, the perspective of the audience. Under this view, freedom of speech is justified as a way of informing citizens, and it suggests that equality is served by helping people form their own opinions. This relationship between equality and the audience's interest is more complex and will be considered in the following sections.

---

[47] Weinstein, 'Campaign Finance Reform and The First Amendment' at 1081.
[48] *Ibid.*, at 1092–3.
[49] Barendt, *Freedom of Speech*, p. 106, referring to speaker-based claims more generally.

Collective justifications for expression rights

The collective element of the democratic justification stresses the value of expression to its audience or society as a whole.[50] This approach is most famously put forward in the work of Alexander Meiklejohn, whose theory justified expression in serving the interests of the audience by providing a diverse range of information that enables people to make considered choices relating to collective decisions.[51] Under this theory, allowing people the freedom to speak and provide information can be justified in the hope that freedom of expression will lead to better decisions and more reasoned outcomes. It can also be seen as facilitating citizen participation, as such quality of debate and information is necessary for citizens to develop political views. The point is that ideas need to be heard in order for people to decide for themselves whether they are persuaded by it. The perspective is also underlined by the provision in Article 10 of the ECHR that freedom of expression protects the 'right to receive' information and ideas, and also a number of judicial decisions in the UK and ECtHR.[52] Such an approach also has a connection with the deliberative activities discussed in the previous chapter, in so far as it emphasises expression as an activity that provides reasons and generates influence by persuading its audience.[53]

A marketplace of political ideas

It is sometimes thought that the marketplace of ideas serves the collective element of the democratic justification.[54] Under this view, an absence of government regulation allows a range of information and ideas to be disseminated from which the audience is free to choose. A simple analogy of political debate and a free marketplace, however, raises a number of difficulties. The comparison between the system of expression and a marketplace points to a view of politics as a contest between different views or interests.[55] As the previous chapter

---

[50] The interest of the audience is distinct from that of society as a whole. The latter may include the interests of bystanders, see Barendt, *Freedom of Speech*, pp. 27–30; however, while the audience has an interest in being informed, society as a whole also has an interest in so far as this promotes a fair and well-informed democratic process.

[51] A. Meiklejohn, *Political Freedom* (New York: Harper, 1960), see *Part One: Free Speech and its Relation to Self Government*.

[52] Similarly, the ECtHR has stressed the need for 'open discussion of political issues', with a particular emphasis on the role of the media in providing information and ideas. See *Lingens v. Austria* (1986) 8 EHRR 407 at [42]. See also Lord Nicholls, *Reynolds v. Times Newspapers Ltd* [1999] 4 All ER 609 at 621: 'This freedom enables those who elect representatives to Parliament to make an informed choice, regarding individuals as well as policies, and those elected to make informed decisions.'

[53] For example, Sunstein emphasises the collective interest in promoting political deliberation; see Sunstein, *Democracy and the Problem of Free Speech*, ch. 5.

[54] The marketplace could be modified to refer to political debate, rather than free speech in general. On the connection between the marketplace the collective element of the democratic justification, see Baker, *Human Liberty*, p. 28, and Schauer, *Free Speech*, pp. 39–40.

[55] Baker, *Human Liberty*, p. 28.

outlined, this approach is not shared by all democratic theories, with some emphasising political debate as a process governed by reasons that can be recognised by all citizens.[56] Similarly, Meiklejohn argued that the free speech principles do not cover private self-interested expression, which would be the norm in a marketplace.[57] Yet putting that objection aside, a marketplace model would still raise other problems. The marketplace model assumes that an absence of state regulation will create a fair competition between ideas, and fails to take account of the distribution of resources and the impact this has on the ability to communicate. As a result, the marketplace will give an advantage to those ideas and arguments that have a wealthy patron, can attract advertising revenues, or an audience willing to pay through subscriptions.[58] One consequence is that those perspectives that cannot attract sufficient funds may be excluded from the marketplace of ideas. A second consequence is that even if all the different perspectives and arguments enter the marketplace, those arguments and ideas that are supported with more resources will have a competitive advantage. The distribution of resources is one factor that led Stanley Ingber to argue that the 'marketplace has severely restricted those inputs most challenging to the status quo', with the consequence that 'resulting outputs similarly are skewed to favor established views'.[59] As a result the 'marketplace of ideas is more myth than reality' and perpetuates existing advantages.[60]

The thrust of the criticism above is that while the unregulated marketplace does produce diverse information and ideas, the process that generates the overall output is unfair. Some views will never make it into the marketplace, and those that do may be at a disadvantage compared to better-resourced competitors. The result is that the system is not the best way to ensure that citizens are fully informed about collective decisions. When considering the ban on political advertising in the broadcast media, Lord Bingham made an argument along these lines:

> The fundamental rationale of the democratic process is that if competing views, opinions and policies are publicly debated and exposed to public scrutiny the good will over time drive out the bad and the true prevail over the false. It must be assumed that, given time, the public will make a sound choice when, in the course of the democratic process, it has the right to choose. But it is highly desirable that the playing field of debate should be so far as practicable level. This is achieved where, in public discussion, differing views are expressed, contradicted, answered and debated ... It is not achieved if political parties can, in proportion to their resources, buy unlimited opportunities to advertise in the

[56] See discussion of deliberative democracy in Chapter 1.
[57] Meiklejohn, *Political Freedom*. According to this theory, private self-interested speech can be abridged as long as due process has been fulfilled.
[58] For criticism of the operation of markets in relation to the media, see E. Baker, *Media, Markets and Democracy* (Cambridge University Press, 2002); and Sunstein, *Democracy and the Problem of Free Speech*, pp. 71–3.
[59] S. Ingber, 'The Marketplace of Ideas: A Legitimizing Myth' (1984) Duke L.J. 1 at 47.
[60] *Ibid.*, at 48.

most effective media, so that elections become little more than an auction. Nor is it achieved if well-endowed interests which are not political parties are able to use the power of the purse to give enhanced prominence to views which may be true or false, attractive to progressive minds or unattractive, beneficial or injurious. The risk is that objects which are essentially political may come to be accepted by the public not because they are shown in public debate to be right but because, by dint of constant repetition, the public has been conditioned to accept them.[61]

The statement starts off expressing some faith in a process for exchanging ideas, but quickly qualifies that position by requiring a level playing field. This suggests that it is unfair if people can buy 'enhanced prominence' and implies that such a position is likely to influence the public. In the same case, Baroness Hale referred to the need for 'the free exchange of information and ideas', but also the need to prevent the 'grosser distortions' brought about through unequal wealth.[62] While those statements were made in the context of the broadcast media, which arguably raise special considerations, both make a general point about the distorting effect of wealth. Consequently, the democratic justification has been relied upon to justify and call for reforms that improve the conditions of the marketplace.[63] More broadly, some reformers argue a more equal distribution of expressive opportunities could also play a role in moving away from the marketplace metaphor altogether, to a more inclusive, robust and deliberative political debate.[64]

If the concern is with debate being skewed, it suggests the marketplace of ideas is failing to meet some standard.[65] The difficulty, however, is in attempting to identify the ideal standard for expression and deliberation that is distorted. The complaint above focuses primarily on the process and structure of the system of expression, rather than its failure to produce some independently verifiable output. One response is to seek to improve the process through a fairer distribution of communicative opportunities. However, this in turn raises the issue of what constitutes a fair process for political debate and how those opportunities should be distributed among the different speakers and views in order to level the playing field.

The difficulty is that in the context of national political debate, the commitment to equality cannot mean a complete levelling of economic resources for political use among individual citizens. While equal opportunities among

---

[61] *R (Animal Defenders International)* v. *Secretary of State for Culture, Media and Sport* [2008] 1 AC 1312 at [28].

[62] *Ibid.,* at [48].

[63] J. Barron, 'Access to the Press: A New First Amendment Right' (1967) 80 *Harvard Law Review* 1641.

[64] Sunstein, *Democracy and the Problem of Free Speech*, ch. 2; O. Fiss, *Liberalism Divided*, ch. 1.

[65] For example, when the ban on political advertising was considered in the High Court, Ousley J implied such a standard when arguing that the ban supported 'the soundness of the framework for democratic public debate'. *R (Animal Defenders International)* v. *Secretary of State for Culture, Media and Sport* [2006] EWHC 3069 (Admin) at [125].

citizens can be more easily secured in some forums, such as an open space or town centre, it is more problematic while looking at the mass media or the distribution of resources among political parties. For example, there would be little point in requiring time or space in the mass media to be evenly divided among every speaker, and such a measure would do little to inform people.[66] However, the account of political equality in Chapter 1 requires no such thing, and merely provides an argument against the opportunities following the distribution of wealth. Instead, an ideal system may seek to distribute political resources and access to the forums of communication in a way that serves the goals of responsiveness and deliberation. To illustrate this, the following section will contrast an approach of 'citizen equality' in which resources are allocated responsively to citizens' preferences, and 'equality of ideas' in which those resources seek to promote deliberative goals.[67] While there are other bases to distribute political resources and spending, these two models will be considered to contrast different goals and highlight the alternative to the opportunities being determined according to the distribution of wealth.[68] Both attempt to make the system of expression more inclusive and egalitarian.

Citizen equality

One way to define a fair process would be to establish a model of citizen equality in which resources are given to political groups or speakers in proportion to the level of support among citizens. Such an approach can be seen in some proposals for grants to political parties to be allocated according to the number of votes received in the previous election.[69] It can also be seen in the media, in which the figures in the leading political parties get the greatest amount of coverage. Such a model reflects the equality of each individual as the resources available to that speaker reflect the level of support.[70]

---

[66] R. Post, 'Equality and Autonomy in First Amendment Jurisprudence' (1997) 95 Mich. L. Rev. 1517, at 1537, criticising the references to equality in the 'collective' justification for freedom of expression on their own terms.

[67] Similar models have been used to explain the rules on the impartiality of political coverage on the broadcast media, in so far as it requires the broadcaster to include a range of relevant opinions and views, while taking into account the 'weight of opinion' holding those views. Lord Annan (Chairman), *Report of the Committee on the Future of Broadcasting*, Cmnd. 6753 (1977) at [17.10].

[68] For example, T. Christiano, *The Rule of the Many* (Oxford: Westview Press, 1996) p. 91, distinguishes between 'numerical equality' in which 'resources are distributed equally to persons' and 'qualitative equality' in which 'resources are divided equally among certain qualities of persons' such as among groups or viewpoints. For discussion of a similar distinction and its shortcomings and dangers, see Ingber, 'The Marketplace of Ideas: A Legitimizing Myth', at 53.

[69] For example, the Houghton Committee proposed a system in which state funds would be granted to qualifying political parties proportionate to the number of votes received in the previous general election. See *Report of the Committee on Financial Aid to Political Parties*, Cmnd. 6601 (1976).

[70] Christiano, *The Rule of the Many*, p. 92.

This would provide citizens with a diverse range of information and ideas and is also appropriate where the expression seeks to transmit the preferences of a particular group of citizens or apply pressure on an official. However, an approach based on citizen equality cannot provide the sole model for a fair distribution of political resources. The first problem is that it is not known how many people support a particular viewpoint. It is hard to envisage how this could be achieved unless the distribution of political resources is to be decided by some method of polling. A second difficulty is that such a standard is inappropriate to select speakers that might help to inform the audience. For example, an expert or other knowledgeable source may provide factual information, which would not normally attract supporters. However, such experts may need greater resources to communicate in order to disseminate valuable information. This is justified not by its support, but by its value to the audience.

Even where it is possible to identify the level of support for each speaker or viewpoint, a standard of citizen equality can have a circular effect. Under such a model, a person or group may have greater resources because it has more support, but that level of support may have been attained because it had more resources to gain publicity in the first place.[71] An established political party will often attract support because it has more resources to raise its profile at the outset. The system of expression therefore needs to include not just those views that are popular, but also those views that have a chance of gaining support if heard by the audience. For example, if the vast majority of individuals supports a law designed to combat terrorism, but it is strongly opposed by 5 per cent of citizens (such as members of a particular group most likely to be wrongly targeted by the anti-terror laws), such views still need to be disseminated widely even though that view is not widely held. Information and ideas that do not have popular support still need to be included to ensure that the audience's views are informed and considered.

In some cases, the level of support will be important to select which speakers will be prominent on the political agenda, but does not determine the ideal level of resources to be granted to each speaker. Once a speaker is included, then the need for a competitive debate may require resources to be split evenly between the speakers. One example is where a televised debate is organised between the major party leaders. The level of support for each party may be used to decide which party leaders are invited to participate. However, if one political party has the support of 60 per cent of the electorate and the other has 40 per cent, the allocation of time among speakers would not be divided so that the leader of the former gets six minutes to answer each question and the latter just four minutes. Instead, it seems fairer to split the time fifty-fifty. In this example, popular support decides which speakers are included in the debate, but does not determine how much each will speak.

[71] See Sunstein, *Democracy and the Problem of Free Speech*, pp. 73–4.

Equality of ideas

An alternative to citizen equality is for the collective interest in expression to be served under a standard of 'equality of ideas'. Under such an approach, the 'resources for social discussion ought to be allocated equally to each view, not to each person'.[72] The views are not selected according to the level of support, but on the contribution that will be made to the debate. This means that the agenda for political debate should not simply be responsive, but also needs to be deliberative. Such an approach is reflected in Meiklejohn's account of freedom of expression, in which: 'What is essential is not that everyone shall speak, but that everything worth saying shall be said ... the vital point, as stated negatively, is that no suggestion of policy shall be denied a hearing because it is on one side of the issue rather than another.'[73] In this approach, Meiklejohn famously compared the system of expression to a town meeting, in which the state takes the role of the moderator, deciding when people can speak, in what order and for how long. Consequently, expression may be regulated by the state to ensure that everything worth saying gets a hearing.[74] However, this model of a small-scale meeting is too simple to give a precise account of the whole system of expression and different political activities in the various forums. Instead, only an approximate analogy can be made in the context of larger scale politics, where the equivalent rules may be regulations determining how much people can spend on expression, which participants require a subsidy and some mass media regulations.[75] Such an approach has the potential to improve the rigour of the debate and analysis by ensuring that ideas and arguments are subject to serious contest. It also ensures that unpopular views or those of minorities cannot be ignored and should get serious consideration along with more mainstream views.

If equality of ideas is the standard to be applied in the distribution of political resources, a number of problems emerge. The first is that it is difficult to know what constitutes a distinct idea or viewpoint that is worthy of a hearing.[76] Most issues have multiple dimensions. For example, in the current debate on ID cards, some opponents argue that the plan would be too expensive, others that it would be ineffective in combating terrorism, and others that it could lead to the abuse of government power. The question is whether these three positions should be taken as a single idea or view (opposition to ID cards) or three distinct ideas. If the 'equality of ideas' standard is applied, then the way each of

---

[72] Christiano, *The Rule of the Many*, p. 92.

[73] Meiklejohn, *Political Freedom*, pp. 26–7.

[74] Meiklejohn argued that rules governing the order or time allocated to speakers in a debate regulated but did not abridge expression rights. See A. Meiklejohn, 'The First Amendment is an Absolute' [1961] *The Supreme Court Review* 245 at 252.

[75] For discussion, see F. Pasquale, 'Reclaiming Egalitarianism in the Political Theory of Campaign Finance Reform' [2008] U. Ill. L. Rev. 599 at 621–30.

[76] This discussion draws on the arguments set out by Christiano, *The Rule of the Many*, pp. 272–7.

these positions is characterised will determine the level of resources that will be given to arguments opposing ID cards. If they are taken to be three distinct positions, this will be advantageous to opponents, whereas taking it to be a single stance may arguably not do justice to the differences in each of the stances. A second problem is that the number of ideas is not fixed and it is difficult to structure a debate around such equality in advance. New ideas will emerge during the course of a debate, which may not fit into the agenda that has already been drawn up.

A third problem with equality of ideas is that not every idea deserves equal attention.[77] There seems little reason to give equal time and resources to ideas that are, say, self-evidently outlandish. Furthermore, given the constraints on time and attention, if a decision is ever to be made it is not possible to dedicate equal resources to every possible idea or viewpoint. Some issues and ideas need greater attention to examine the implications in detail and the political agenda needs to be constrained if deliberation is to be meaningful.[78] This becomes more pressing as a decision on that particular issue comes closer, and the leading arguments need closer scrutiny. Furthermore, if the goal is to make sure that citizens are fully informed, then it requires more than just differing viewpoints to be aired. It requires that citizens be given the tools to assess the different arguments, which will require the inclusion of analysis, critical scrutiny and expert opinion.

Consequently, it is not so simple to demand equality of ideas, as some decision has to be made to determine which topics and views will be debated and how many relevant dimensions to that issue exist. Once this is accepted, the term equality of ideas becomes misleading, as some ideas will benefit from greater resources and attention. This term really means that ideas should not be ignored or excluded arbitrarily, and that each view should be given a fair hearing or chance to gain support. The standard is therefore concerned with the quality of expression, and the task of moderating gives substantial power to shape and influence the democratic process.[79]

The discussion above highlights the difficulty in trying to establish a standard by which to evaluate the diversity of information and ideas provided to the audience in a system of expression. The standard by which debate is evaluated is not self-executing and gives the state, when acting as a moderator, considerable control over the political agenda. Along these lines, Robert Post criticises Meiklejohn's town hall model of expression, as deciding what should make it onto the agenda and which ideas are relevant 'are themselves matters of potential dispute',[80] and rejects such issues as being neutral questions

[77] Ibid., for discussion explaining why the views of different groups may not deserve equal attention.
[78] C. Beitz, Political Equality: an Essay in Democratic Theory (Princeton University Press, 1989) pp. 167–9.
[79] Post, 'Equality and Autonomy in First Amendment Jurisprudence', at 1528–9.
[80] R. Post, 'Meiklejohn's Mistake: Individual Autonomy and the Reform of Public Discourse' (1993) 64 U. Colo. L. Rev. 1109 at 1118.

of procedure: 'Meiklejohn cannot appeal to a neutral distinction between substance and procedure to justify this contraction of the scope of self government, for the procedural assumptions he wishes to enforce, no less than substantive ones, are ultimately grounded in a distinctive and controversial conception of collective identity.'[81] Post believes the town hall model, even though aiming to promote democratic values, will frustrate the assumptions on which self-government is based.[82] The question of what is actually in the interests of the citizen is potentially imposed from above, seemingly undermining the purpose of democratic self-government. While this highlights the problem of granting such broad power to the state to fix the political agenda, a similar objection can be made if those with more economic resources determine the agenda. While regulations should be approached with caution, diversity or fair treatment of ideas can still have a role to play as something to be aspired to, and in explaining why the unregulated marketplace of ideas amounts to a distortion. However, the ways of achieving this should not simply be imposed on citizens, but be open to contest with some democratic input.[83]

Combining equality of ideas and citizen equality

Both citizen equality and equality of ideas raise problems if taken as the sole ideal for the distribution of political resources. However, each of the two standards may be appropriate for different activities and different stages of the democratic process. Yet the two standards can also complement one another. If we imagine equality of ideas as a starting point for public debate, then citizen equality will become more important as the debate progresses and citizens have a greater role in deciding which ideas and viewpoints should go forward to receive more focused scrutiny.[84] Of course, political expression does not work in such a linear progression; there is no clear start and end of a political debate as new issues and concerns arise all the time. Consequently, the system requires that attempts to distribute political resources combine these different values. For example, when looking at the distribution of resources in an election campaign the emphasis will be on responsiveness (reflecting citizen equality), whereas the mass media will partly reflect the deliberative goals and include a more diverse range of views. The different standards described above do not aim to provide a precise blueprint for how such regulations could work, but at least give general points of reference when thinking about a fair system of expression and provide some basis to critique the unregulated marketplace approach.

---

[81] *Ibid.*, at 1117.
[82] *Ibid.*, at 1125. In this, Post does not oppose some state subsidised speech to improve debate or time, place and manner restrictions that coordinate public debate. Post's reservation is with the use of this model to suppress expression 'for the sake of imposing a specific version of national identity', p. 1121.
[83] Christiano, *The Rule of the Many*, p. 278.
[84] Beitz, *Political Equality*, p. 206, distinguishing the range of alternatives required when setting the agenda and during the campaign period.

Quantity, scarcity and competitive advantages

The argument pursued above suggested that certain measures securing greater equality in relation to the political uses of economic resources and property could further the values of expression from the collective perspective. However, an objection advanced by critics of the egalitarian approach is that some steps seeking to control wealth in politics limit the quantity of expression and consequently limit the information and ideas a person can receive.[85] Such a scenario may arise where the regulation attempts to limit the amount that can be spent in an election or limit the use of property for certain political purposes. While many laws might have effects that limit the quantity of expression, the objection to those controls on wealth is that the central purpose of the regulation is to reduce the quantity of expression.[86]

Such a view can be seen in the reasoning in *Buckley* v. *Valeo*, in which the US Supreme Court struck down limits on the amounts of money that may be spent on election campaigns, by stating that the First Amendment: 'was designed to secure the widest possible dissemination of information from diverse and antagonistic sources and to assure unfettered interchange of ideas for the bringing about of political and social changes desired by the people'.[87] Underlying the argument is a view that the expression generated by wealth is an extra, an addition to the diverse views, and does not take anything away from other speakers. Such an argument suggests that the criticism of the marketplace of ideas given above is misplaced, and that there is no distortion as long as people are free to accept or reject whatever is being said for themselves. Critics of an egalitarian approach therefore argue that the overall level of expression is not fixed and inequalities simply increase the quantity of expression.[88] While the US Supreme Court has on occasion softened its position on some election spending controls,[89] its stated position has been to reject equality as a ground for limiting First Amendment speech rights.

One question is whether the quantity of expression can be equated with spending. If a limit on the amount that can be spent on political advertising stops a message being repeated over and over again, the loss to the audience may be minimal.[90] Compare a situation where a wealthy group purchases a

[85] For example, see M. Redish, *Money Talks* (New York University Press, 2001) p. 102, 'Whichever value or values one believes that free expression fosters, those values inevitably are undermined by a governmentally imposed reduction in the sum total available expression'.
[86] Barendt, *Freedom of Speech*, p. 478.
[87] *Buckley* v. *Valeo* 424 US 1 (1976) at 49.
[88] Redish, *Money Talks*, pp. 107–8.
[89] See *Austin* v. *Michigan State Chamber of Commerce* 494 US 652 (1990) at 659–60; *McConnell* v. *Federal Election Commission* 540 US 93 (2003) at 150–4. However, *Austin* and the parts of *McConnell* permitting controls on corporate expenditures have since been overruled, see *Citizens United* v. *Federal Election Commission* 558_US (2010).
[90] R. Dworkin, 'The Curse of American Politics' (1996) 43 *New York Review of Books* 19 at 22, explaining that as the expression curtailed by election spending limits 'would almost certainly

one-page newspaper advertisement for five days in one week, with a situation where the same group puts up the same advert three days in one week and a rival group puts its advertisement up for just one day. In the latter situation, we have less expression in terms of quantity, in that there are only four advertisements in total rather than five, but we may still prefer that situation because it provides greater diversity to the audience. There is greater quantity in that there are more views being expressed, yet there are fewer words being printed.

The difficulty with the argument favouring the quantity of speech is that it separates expression from its political context. Under the democratic justification outlined earlier, expression is valuable because it helps determine what issues will be on the political agenda, helps to transmit citizen preferences and contributes to deliberation. The concern with quantity does not consider how expression performs these different functions or how it does so in the context of a competitive process, which will eventually influence collective decisions. It assumes that the audience is best served by the maximum amount of expression from which to choose. While permitting an unregulated marketplace has the potential to provide more information, those views backed by greater resources have a competitive advantage. Wealthier participants can use the resources to produce more information, respond to each argument in greater detail and ensure their message has a wider reach than their opponent's. The classic scenario arises in US political campaigns where most candidates can afford some television advertisements, but often a disparity exists, depending on the level of resources. Part of this relates to the cost of producing information, for example through research and polling. The other part relates to the cost of disseminating the information. The latter is often put in terms of a 'drowning out' argument in which those with fewer resources are able to disseminate their message, but the reach and the repetition of opposing views quickly dwarfs their effort and audience attention is diverted to those with more resources. The thrust of this argument is that more speech is not simply an extra, but in some way comes at the expense of other speakers.

Progressive vouchers

One response to this argument is that high spending on expression can facilitate other views being produced and disseminated. Strategies can be designed that allow unequal spending on expression, but only where that spending generates more opportunities for other speakers, including those with opposing views. Such a possibility is outlined by David Estlund's model of a 'progressive voucher scheme'.[91] Under this scheme each citizen is given an equal number of

have repeated what the candidate had said on other occasions, it seems unlikely that the repetition would have improved collective knowledge'.

[91] D. Estlund, *Democratic Authority: a Philosophical Framework* (Princeton University Press, 2008) pp. 195–8. The proposal echoes Rawls' difference principle that inequalities in wealth are 'to be to the greatest benefit of the least advantaged members of society'.

vouchers to contribute to political campaigns. However, citizens can purchase additional vouchers at a cost above the actual cash value of the voucher. For example, purchasing an extra £50 worth of vouchers will cost £88, and another £50 worth of vouchers beyond that will cost £153. The additional funds, secured by the state through charging more than the cash value of the additional vouchers, are then redistributed among other citizens. The arrangement may lead to more money being redistributed than is gained by the individual purchasing the additional vouchers. For example, where the second additional voucher costs £153, the purchaser only gains £50 worth of vouchers and the remaining £103 is redistributed. With this scheme, the gains made by allowing some inequalities are, therefore, not one-sided and can benefit those with fewer resources. One important factor to note is that this proposal is not a call for a free market in expression, and will still require considerable regulation. The case for redistributing the additional sums underlines the need to combat disparities in the use of wealth in politics.

This is a powerful argument against fixed caps on spending, but whether such a scheme is desirable depends on its particular workings and the alternatives. If the alternative were a system that creates equality among participants, but with a limit on political spending to be fixed at a very low level, then the progressive voucher scheme would have greater value in informing the public. Quantity of expression is clearly a factor to be considered, otherwise equality could be secured by an outright ban on all expression. This is reflected in the approach of the European Court of Human Rights, which permits limits on expression to be imposed, as long as an acceptable quantity of expression is allowed.[92] Under the European approach, the quantity of expression is to be considered alongside political equality. Given that arguments for equality are premised on the importance of expression in the democratic system, extremely low limits, combined with no alternative channels of communication, would in any event be in tension with the very reason why equality in the opportunity to speak is valued.[93] Equality in the opportunity to influence requires that such opportunities exist in practice.

However, the quantity of expression is just one factor and not decisive. The progressive voucher scheme may allow the high spender to maintain a competitive advantage, for example where the extra resources for poorer speakers are merely divided among a large number of citizens. In such circumstances, while slightly better off, the least well off still have a relatively insignificant voice compared to the wealthy individual. The political expression is still part of a competitive process and the resources available to influence take on importance relative to other speakers. The voucher scheme could, however, be arranged

---

[92] *Bowman* v. *United Kingdom* (1998) 4 BHRC 25 where a limit of £5 on spending to promote the election of any candidate was found to constitute a 'total barrier' to expression.

[93] T. Christiano, *The Constitution of Equality* (Oxford University Press, 2008) pp. 32–5, addressing the 'levelling down' objection.

in a different way, so that additional resources are not simply split among a wide range of people. For example, if all redistributed resources are allocated through a lottery to a particular group or speaker, then the gains to the lottery winner will be greater than those bought by the wealthy individual.[94] Yet there are still difficulties with that approach, as the chances of the less well off depend on the result of a lottery, whereas the wealthier person can guarantee an extra say through the use of this money. The progressive vouchers also have to be considered alongside other goals of equality, for example whether permitting those inequalities would be consistent with showing equal respect to each person. Versions of the progressive voucher scheme could bring about some gains to the democratic process, but that will depend on exactly how that scheme is designed and how it fits alongside the commitment to political equality.

Drowning out and scarcity

So far it has been noted that unequal spending power in politics occurs in a process where citizens' influence is relative to others, and that there is some potential for the well resourced to 'drown out' other speakers. An objection that may arise is that expression is not direct power and its influence arises by persuading other citizens. Along these lines, it may be argued that additional expression does not take away from other speakers, but just gives more for the speaker to choose from. The additional expression therefore informs the choice of the citizens. One response to this objection is that the opportunity to communicate is always subject to some constraints. Under this view, in some contexts at least, when one person speaks he takes the place of another potential speaker. As Owen Fiss has argued: 'in politics, scarcity is the rule rather than the exception. The opportunities for speech tend to be limited, either by the time or space available for communicating or by our capacity to digest or process information'.[95] This has two elements: that in some cases access to the channels of communication is limited; and where this is not the case, the audience's attention, time and ability to scrutinise the content is limited. In the former case, it may be argued that people will always have some place to speak and that the channels of communication are not scarce. However, access to those channels that command attention will generally be limited, such as media outlets with a large audience. While it is often argued that such scarcity is now alleviated by developments in technology, it is likely to remain the case that only a small number of forums will command a large audience at one time.[96] In this way the scarcity in the channels of communication quickly blurs into scarcity of audience attention, as listeners can only be in one place at one time.

---

[94] J. Cohen, 'Money, Politics and Political Equality', in A. Byrne, R. Stalnaker and R. Wedgwood (eds.), *Fact and Value* (Cambridge, MA: MIT Press, 2001) p. 52.
[95] Fiss, *Liberalism Divided*, pp. 15–16.   [96] See Chapter 8.

In terms of scarcity of the audience's attention, the more information that is available the harder it is to get anyone to listen. The difficulty with arguments focusing on scarcity of attention is that once the information is in the public domain, the audience chooses whether to pay any attention to it.[97] However, it is questionable just how much the direction of attention reflects the choice of a citizen. If a message is repeated far and wide it will naturally command a greater level of attention. It is unlikely that individuals will search out all other arguments that have made it into the public domain, and will focus on the most prominent. Where wealth is used to access those channels of communication or to gain publicity, then the citizen does not choose which views will gain prominence or decide in advance which views will be heard. Acquiring access to those channels where one can be heard is a form of power itself, which helps to decide which views, arguments and issues will be most salient in political debate.[98]

One criticism of this approach is that it is difficult to determine what quantity of expression is adequate. It is hard to identify the point at which enough information has been heard, the audience has become 'overloaded' and when further expression from that speaker will drown out others.[99] Even a repetition may allow a statement to reach new people, show strength of feeling, and signal that people still hold that view.[100] Furthermore, limiting political expenditures may stop new and important arguments being communicated. For example, in the August before the 2004 US presidential election, the famous Swift Boat Veterans for the Truth attacks on John Kerry's military record were broadcast. It is said that the Democrats did not respond to these attacks because they had accepted public funding, which limited the amount that the campaign could spend during the election. Consequently, the campaign needed to save the available resources for the later stages of the campaign. For this reason, the limit on unequal campaign spending arguably prevented the audience from hearing important arguments at the most crucial time.[101] If a strict limit is imposed on the amount of expression that can be heard, then there may come a point at which one speaker's opportunities are exhausted before he or she has put forward their best arguments.

This is not an argument against all controls on wealth, but an argument to the effect that care should be taken not to limit the resources for expression too rigidly. The concern that an important argument was not heard focuses on the quality of debate, rather than the quantity or its distribution according to wealth.

---

[97] See C. Fried, 'Perfect Freedom, Perfect Justice' (1998) 78 B.U.L. Rev. 717 at 736–8.

[98] D. Copp, 'Capitalism versus Democracy', in J. D. Bishop (ed.), *Ethics and Capitalism* (University of Toronto Press, 2000) p. 96.

[99] Redish, *Money Talks*, p. 109.

[100] *Ibid.*; K. Karst, 'Equality as a Central Principle in the First Amendment' (1975) 43 U. Chi. L. Rev. 20 at 40.

[101] For an account by one of John Kerry's advisers, see B. Shrum, *No Excuses: Concessions of a Serial Campaigner* (New York: Simon and Schuster, 2007) pp. 458–9 and pp. 468–71. While there were other channels of communication which could have been used, television commercials were seen as the most effective.

The solution to this type of concern is not simply to allow unlimited amounts of wealth to be spent on expression. Ensuring that the media give fair coverage during an election is one way to combat that type of problem, which can reduce the reliance on paid communications. Furthermore, a system in which the opportunities for communication are distributed according to wealth imposes limits on how much a person can speak. The speakers' economic resources set the limit, rather than the importance of the message. Instead, when designing a regulation it is important to ensure that new and important arguments are not closed off, but this does not mean abandoning the goal of equality.

A measure limiting the quantity of expression need not be seen as a paternalistic underestimation of people's abilities to process information. In many cases it will be rational for an individual operating under constraints of time and expertise to give greater attention to those viewpoints and ideas that have greatest prominence and reach. However, such an argument could find itself criticised from another angle, namely that it fails to respect the moral status of individuals. This line of argument, which will be considered in the next section, is distinct from the instrumental value of expression in serving the audience. Instead, the argument to be considered is that 'drowning out' arguments fail to respect the autonomy of the listener.

Listener autonomy

Listener autonomy has been advanced as a justification for freedom of expression, most notably by Thomas Scanlon in an argument against state restrictions on expression that fail to treat listeners as 'equal, autonomous, rational agents'.[102] According to this approach, the citizen is 'sovereign in deciding what to believe and in weighing competing reasons for action'.[103] Where the state seeks to restrict speech because it is persuasive and provides reasons for the listener to act, it does not treat the listener as autonomous.[104] This approach does not stop the state restricting all paternalist measures, but just those that restrict expression on the grounds that it provides a reason for others to act. For example, it does not prevent the government from requiring seatbelts to be worn, but does prevent the government from stopping a person suggesting to another not to wear a seatbelt. The argument is advanced as a justification distinct from the democratic rationale, but the two can be connected in so far as the democratic argument rests on a belief in the autonomy of citizens to decide political questions for themselves.[105]

---

[102] T. Scanlon, 'A Theory of Freedom of Expression' (1972) 1 *Philosophy and Public Affairs* 204 at 215. The theory has been subject to a number of criticisms that have been outlined elsewhere, in particular that it is both over and under protective of expression. See R. Amdur, 'Scanlon on Freedom of Expression' (1980) 9 *Philosophy and Public Affairs* 287; Barendt, *Freedom of Speech*, pp. 15–18. Scanlon himself later rejected the approach; T. Scanlon, 'Freedom of Expression and Categories of Expression' (1979) 40 U. Pitt. L. Rev. 519.

[103] Scanlon, 'A Theory of Freedom of Expression', p. 216.   [104] *Ibid.*, p. 221.

[105] For discussion of autonomy and democracy see D. Held, *Models of Democracy*, second edition (Cambridge: Polity Press, 1996) ch. 9.

While Scanlon does not refer to controls on political spending and leaves open measures that secure access to the means of communication, his line of argument could be advanced against some controls on wealth in politics.[106] For example, the theory could challenge limits on political spending on the grounds that it is based on an assumption that 'people who spend more will circulate their ideas more widely and more effectively, and will thereby convince more voters'.[107] The argument suggests that controls on wealth are really aiming to stop people from being persuaded by the expression of arguments backed by wealth. For example, arguments that some expression will be 'drowned out' or that people can be manipulated by high spending campaigns arguably undermine people's status as autonomous and rational agents. The critics' objection suggests that regulations limiting the use of wealth are based on an assumption that citizens cannot assess the information rationally for themselves.

The difficulty with the critics' argument is that such regulations do not target expression because it will persuade the listener. As has been stated, the argument for controlling wealth does not rest on an assumption that wealth generates influence, but rather that it provides an unequal opportunity. Controls on wealth do not ban a particular message, so the listener can still hear that expression and be persuaded by it. This argument will apply not only to Scanlon's account, but to more general arguments that people should be left to evaluate information for themselves. The controls on wealth are not attempting to steer the citizen towards or away from a particular view and the audience is still free to make its own mind up on that issue. In this sense, controls on political spending do not raise the same concerns for listener autonomy as a ban on cigarette advertising, for example in that the latter is attempting to direct the listener to a particular conclusion.

A more ambitious argument is that controls on wealth may enhance listener autonomy. This is secured in so far as it protects the audience from being manipulated by private sources, for example by preventing political debate being dominated by one side.[108] This is not to suggest that citizens are automatically persuaded by a one-sided debate; but that steps can be taken to secure an environment where the citizen can make his or her own choices

---

[106] The argument advanced by Scanlon is not simply to let the people decide for themselves, but is concerned with the justification for state interference. Scanlon's account of autonomy follows from a relationship between citizen and government based on a social contract. Given that autonomous persons will not 'accept without independent consideration the judgement of others as to what he should believe', such persons will not grant the power to the state to decide what to believe under the social contract.

[107] D. Strauss, 'Persuasion, Autonomy, and Freedom of Expression' (1991) 91 Colum. L. Rev. 334 at 341.

[108] Here listener autonomy is meant in a different sense from Scanlon's constraint on government, and aims to prevent citizens being manipulated by any actor, whether public or private. For comment on the differences see D. Strauss, 'Persuasion, Autonomy, and Freedom of Expression' at footnote 62. David Strauss argued that expression can be restricted consistently with the autonomy principle if it prevents a person being manipulated into making ill-considered decisions (at 357).

independently.[109] To do this, citizens need to have access to a range of different ideas, providing at least the means to assess their existing views.[110] Limiting the role of wealth may ensure that speakers compete on fairer terms, which better enables citizens to evaluate the options.

However, it will take more than just a limit on wealth to make the individual the true author of his or her choices. There will always be other background conditions that shape the person's choices, such as education, family or existing policies. Even with far-reaching controls on all these background conditions, it seems difficult to secure the conditions to ensure that the individual's choices are truly his or her own. For example, a fuller account of autonomy along these lines may also call for regulations to ensure the reliability of information.[111] One response is that controls on wealth at least help to promote autonomy even if not fully securing its conditions. Such limits may not make the listener the full author of his or her choices, but may assist the citizen in making an informed choice under conditions that are compatible with a fair democratic process.

Electoral and political expression

The argument advanced so far suggests that these considerations apply to any expression that engages with the political process. A remaining issue is whether the interference with expression to promote political equality should be permissible only when an election is proximate. On one view, there is something distinct about expression taking place within the electoral context, as opposed to a general political discussion, which makes the controls on the use of wealth more pressing.[112] For example, in *Bowman*, the ECtHR stated that as the election campaign is concerned with the expression of the people's choice of representatives, it may be necessary 'to place certain restrictions, of a type which would not usually be acceptable, on freedom of expression'.[113] Under this view, an election provides a special exception to the normal rules on freedom

---

[109] For example, Lichtenberg states that 'thinking for oneself is a matter not of coming up with wholly original ideas but rather of subjecting one's ideas, which come largely from others, to certain tests'. J. Lichtenberg, 'Foundations and Limits of Freedom of the Press', in J. Lichtenberg (ed.), *Democracy and the Mass Media* (Cambridge University Press, 1990) p. 114. Consequently, diverse viewpoints are necessary for the values of autonomy underlying freedom of expression. See also O. O'Neill, *A Question of Trust* (Cambridge University Press, 2002) ch. 5.

[110] See M. Lipson, 'Autonomy and Democracy' (1995) 104 Yale L.J. 2249.

[111] O'Neill, *A Question of Trust*, p. 87.

[112] For example, Pildes and Schauer discuss the institutional setting of an election which distinguishes it from non-electoral political expression; see R. Pildes and F. Schauer, 'Electoral Exceptionalism and the First Amendment' (1999) 77 Tex. L. Rev 1803. See also R. Briffault, 'Issue Advocacy: Redrawing the Elections/Politics Line' (1999) 77 Tex. L. Rev. 1751.

[113] *Bowman* v. *United Kingdom* (1998) 26 EHRR 1 at [43]. The emphasis on a fair process in an election is supported by the right to free elections under Article 3 of Protocol No 1 to the ECHR.

of expression. Such an approach would therefore attempt to limit spending controls in the context of an election, defined by its proximity to the polling day or the reference in the expression to a particular political actor. The line is notoriously difficult to draw, especially as decision-making in an election takes place over a longer period than the formal election campaign. While the election spending controls applicable to national political parties in the UK define the campaign period as the 12 months prior to a general election, even this extended period does not cover all of the 'long campaign'. Furthermore, opinions in an election are formed not just with reference to direct advocacy of a particular party or candidate, but also through general policy discussion. Yet such line drawing between electoral and general political discussion, however blurred, is not an insurmountable hurdle.

The arguments in this chapter have suggested that political equality is a factor that goes beyond the immediate context of an election. If there is a difference between electoral and political discussion, it is not a rigid separation of values inside and outside the electoral setting. Along these lines, while *Bowman* makes clear the election may justify special restrictions, Auld LJ, in *Animal Defenders International*, noted that the concern with distortion extends beyond the electoral period.[114] However, the way that political equality is respected will vary depending on whether it takes place in the later stages of an election, or is political in a more general sense. As an election approaches, competition among speakers and viewpoints will be at its greatest, justifying tighter controls on the use of wealth. Here the primary participants in the process, the candidates and parties, will be well defined, which enables the design of some controls on the use of wealth. While imposing controls on the amount political parties can spend during a campaign is possible, it becomes more problematic if such limits are extended to all types of political expression.[115] Outside the context of an election, or where a decision is still somewhere in the distance, the deliberative elements of political equality may be more prominent. Here the standards are harder to define and the overall agenda is more fluid. It becomes less clear what limits should be appropriate and to whom it should apply. Capping political expenditures more generally in the non-electoral context would potentially permit too many far-reaching restrictions that would be difficult to monitor and enforce.[116] However, this is not to say that equality is irrelevant in such a context. Some measures that address the greatest inequalities in wealth may be appropriate

---

[114] *R (Animal Defenders International)* v. *Secretary of State for Culture, Media and Sport* [2006] EWHC 3069 (Admin) at [80], the decision was later affirmed by the House of Lords. In *VgT Verein gegen Tierfabriken* v. *Switzerland* (2001) 34 EHRR 159, the ECtHR also accepted that 'a certain equality of opportunity between the different forces of society' was a legitimate aim without referring to elections.

[115] Christiano, *The Rule of the Many*, pp. 277–8.

[116] D. Thompson, *Just Elections* (University of Chicago Press, 2004) p. 114: 'If the principle of free choice were to require a balance of influences in politics generally, it would justify constant intervention by the government in nearly all aspects of the political process.'

outside the context of an election, such as providing some access to the forums for expression and some subsidies for speakers. While different types of control are appropriate for electoral and non-electoral contexts, the two settings are informed by the same commitment to equality.

Conclusion

In this chapter, some of the justifications for freedom of expression have been examined from both the perspective of the speaker and the audience. From the perspective of the speaker, it was argued that if expression rights are required to secure participation, this justification points to equality in the opportunities to speak as well. From the audience's perspective, things are more complex. It is in the interest of the audience to hear more information and ideas, as well as expert opinions and views from different sections of society. Equality has a role to play in determining how political resources should ideally be distributed among speakers and viewpoints. While one concern is that this may impact too greatly on the quantity of expression, it was argued that this is just one factor to be considered rather than the decisive factor. Finally, it was argued that far from undermining the autonomy of the audience, controls on wealth can enhance such autonomy.

This still leaves the concern that such controls on wealth subject political participation to too many constraints and grant too much power to those deciding what those constraints would be. A simple approach to expression, with a strong rule forbidding most government interferences, at least avoids these questions. However, any system of political debate is subject to constraints, both public and private. Furthermore, the environment for expression is itself a product of laws and government decisions, for example a newspaper depends on the law of property to protect its communicative opportunities.[117] The danger lies in allowing someone or some institution to decide what political debate should look like. The concern is with the attempt to manage and direct the system of expression. However, that will depend on the measure in question, and it is submitted that the measures discussed in later chapters do not go that far. Instead, securing an equal opportunity to influence political decisions can create a fairer process that serves the democratic values which underlie freedom of expression.

---

[117] Sunstein, *Democracy and the Problem of Free Speech*, p. 36.

3

Strategies and reforms

Various strategies can be devised to address the tensions between inequalities in wealth and political equality. Such strategies include the prohibition of certain types of exchanges or payments, the disclosure of political expenditures, limits on political spending, subsidies to facilitate participation, rights of access to public spaces and certain types of media regulation. None of these measures fully secure political equality and even with such measures in place, inequalities in wealth will remain influential in relation to the various unregulated activities. However, these strategies still have value in taking a step towards a more egalitarian system and in recognising the ideal of political equality. Many such measures are already in place in the UK, having arisen in a piecemeal fashion for a variety of different reasons. The argument here is that such measures can be connected as playing a role in promoting political equality. While the workings of each strategy will be considered in later chapters, the aim here is to provide an introductory overview and look at some of the main problems associated with each method.

The risks of state intervention

Before looking at the different strategies, it is useful to consider whether the risks associated with state interventions are so great that the impact of inequalities of wealth should be tolerated. In the previous chapter, one recurring concern was that, even if political equality is a desirable goal, there is a danger in empowering someone to decide what controls should be imposed on the use of wealth in politics. Whoever fixes the limits on political spending or distributes subsidies will have some power over the political agenda. While those arguing against the egalitarian measures point to the dangers in handing such powers to the state, the response advanced in earlier chapters was that those commanding great economic resources should not be left to decide these issues. Yet critics of the egalitarian approach argue that state power is more objectionable for a number of reasons. Under that view, state interference in political expression can be damaging and prone to abuse, even when attempting to create a fairer democratic process. The assumption of that argument is that giving the state power to regulate political participation gives rise to greater harms than the inequalities associated with private wealth. Consequently, the use of state power might be thought to distort democracy, rather than inequalities in wealth.

The concern with state power is illustrated by those approaches to democracy that stress the self-interest of political actors. One example, the 'elite competitive theory', was discussed in Chapter 1. Under that approach, the popular involvement in democracy is largely confined to voting in elections and provides a mechanism to remove bad leaders.[1] Given that goal, the danger is that a power to regulate any type of political activity will be abused by self-interested politicians who want to maintain a hold on office. They may use their power to censor critics and thereby short-circuit the very process that checks the power of the state. For these reasons, the elite competitive theory will be more committed to formal equality, seeing the state as the main threat to a fair process, with inequalities in wealth being less problematic.

A more developed objection to state controls comes from another 'realist' or economic model of democracy, which again focuses on the self-interest of political actors.[2] Under this view, politicians act in their own self-interest, rather than as agents of the electorate or a political ideology, and seek to maximise their own power and time in office. As a result, the politician will respond to people offering the greatest advantage to his re-election campaign, or other private interests. For example, he will use his powers to favour those people that make the largest donations to his election campaign. Under this account, people get involved in politics for reasons of self interest and to extract whatever benefits they can from the state. So, donations are made by those who want something from the politician. As some people or groups have more resources and greater incentive to organise, the opportunities to influence are spread unevenly.

This view of democracy suggests that politicians will grant benefits to certain people, but the costs of those benefits will be spread among taxpayers as a whole. While this theory may call for restrictions on attempts to influence officials, for example on lobbying, the argument may point to limits on state activity as the primary safeguard and demand that more decisions be left to the market. This takes a very sceptical view of arguments for state interventions to promote political equality, as politicians, acting out of self-interest, are more likely to favour regulations that will maintain their grip on power. For example, a politician may seek to enact party funding laws that work to the advantage of his party. Consequently, state regulations are likely to perpetuate the advantage of the already powerful rather than make the process any fairer.[3] In this view, state regulations and subsidies are the problem rather than the solution, and

[1] See V. Blasi, 'The Checking Value in First Amendment Theory' (1977) Am. B. Found. Res. J. 521 at 542. See discussion of elite competitive theories in Chapter 1.
[2] For discussion see J. Cohen and J. Rogers, 'Secondary Associations and Democratic Governance' (1992) 20 *Politics & Society* 393 at 397–406.
[3] R. Epstein, 'Property, Speech, and the Politics of Distrust' (1992) 59 *The University of Chicago Law Review* 41 at 56–7.

the better response is to limit the power of the state in general, so that it can sell fewer favours and leave more decisions to the market.

While this approach to democracy raises broader questions that are beyond the scope of discussion here, a number of criticisms are often advanced against this view. The first objection questions the assumptions underlying this theory, such as the emphasis on self-interest as the politician's motivation, or the various incentives that lead to the formation and organisation of a group.[4] Self-interest, it is argued, need not be as dominant as that account suggests. The second objection is to take issue with the arguably anti-democratic implications of the theory and the preference shown by some theorists for decisions to be made in the market. The third criticism is that even if the powers of the state are limited, there are still areas where the state action is necessary and those decisions should still be made under a fair process. Consequently, if the various political actors do behave strategically, then one argument is that the resources needed for people to organise and influence political decisions should be distributed equally.[5] Steps towards political equality may go some way to address concerns about politicians being more responsive to well resourced and organised interests.[6] The sceptical view of democracy is not taken here. Aside from the results it produces, the democratic process is also valued as an expression of people's equal status. However, the economic account of political behaviour described above does make an important point about the potential for regulations to serve the self-interest of political actors. When evaluating any proposals (and the process in which those proposals were developed) it is important to remember that a politician involved in a regulation will have much at stake and an incentive to design a system that is to his advantage.

Aside from the sceptical account of democracy, there are other reasons to be cautious about the use of state powers in relation to political activity. One argument is that the power of the state to distort the democratic process and undermine participation is far greater than the effects of the unequal distribution of wealth. For example, complaints about the distortion of the democratic process through the exercise of economic power sometimes arise when a private media owner refuses to grant access to a speaker holding a particular view or to cover a particular issue. However, people can generally find ways to avoid limits on expression arising from the wealth of others. For example, if a person's view is not carried on a particular television channel, people can always seek out another media organisation.[7] By contrast, if the state uses legal powers to censor

---

[4] S. Croley, 'Theories of Regulation: Incorporating the Administrative Process' (1998) 98 Colum. L. Rev. 1 at 42.

[5] R. Hasen, 'Clipping Coupons for Democracy: An Egalitarian/Public Choice Defense of Campaign Finance Vouchers' (1996) 84 *California Law Review* 1 at 16.

[6] Croley, 'Theories of Regulation', at 50–1, states 'reforms in the area of campaign finance, for one example, might go far to alleviate the problems that lead public choice theorists to call for deregulation'.

[7] C. Fried, *Saying What the Law Is* (Cambridge, MA: Harvard University Press, 2004) pp. 84–5.

or interfere with expression, there is nowhere else to turn and those restrictions can be imposed across the board. Furthermore, once the state restricts expression, it has a claim to authority and its laws and regulations will generally be followed.[8]

That line of argument is strongest where the criminal law is used to punish a particular message and much free speech theory was developed as a reaction against such legal penalties. However, the concerns with state power depend on the particular type of control at stake, rather than a general hostility to all state action. It might be argued that state and private powers are blurred to such an extent that it no longer makes sense to focus on threats from the state. Along these lines, a decision not to carry a party election broadcast on television has a similar impact on the speaker whether that decision is made by the state broadcaster, the BBC, or the privately owned ITV.[9] If we are concerned with the effects on political participation, then the state is one possible force among many. Furthermore, no area of activity is completely free of state control; for example, the property rights of a broadcaster or the owner of a public space are themselves enforced through laws.[10] These arguments suggest there is less force to general objections to the use of state power, and those uses that correct private distortions in the political process are less problematic. However, it might be objected that as we cannot precisely identify where a measure is a distortion or correction, it is better for the state not to act at all. Alternatively, the objection to state intervention may rest on a slippery slope argument, that modest interventions in political activity will be the first step towards more heavy-handed regulation. The difficulty with a strong assumption against state interferences is that it comes at too great a cost to the democratic process, and underestimates the impact of the inequalities in wealth. This does not mean the state should have a blank cheque, but that the concerns with state power need to be balanced with the need to secure a fair democratic process.

Finally, mention should be made of the risk of over-regulation of political participation. The fear raised by this risk is not that state power will be abused by an official. Instead the concern is that the various constraints on the use of wealth will generate new layers of bureaucracy and administrative barriers that make it harder for excluded groups to participate. A system that requires people to record the amounts spent in an election campaign, or to register before lobbying brings new costs to political activity. These barriers may impact on those with the fewest resources to meet those burdens, or discourage voluntary activities. Those that are already organised and well resourced, by contrast, will be better placed to employ lawyers or other professionals who can negotiate

---

[8] Blasi, 'Checking Value in First Amendment Theory', at 540.

[9] E. Barendt, *Freedom of Speech*, second edition (Oxford University Press, 2005) p. 153. O. Fiss, *Liberalism Divided: Freedom of Speech and the many uses of State Power* (New York: Westview Press, 1996) pp. 39 and 148.

[10] C. Sunstein, *Democracy and the Problem of Free Speech* (New York: The Free Press, 1993) pp. 43–6.

and exploit gaps in the administrative hurdles. An unregulated system is not, however, free from such burdens. Even without legal regulations, participants face a number of economic barriers and administrative burdens. Activities including fundraising or organising an advertising campaign require some level of administration. However, any new controls or regulations should be designed in a way that minimises additional burdens on those smaller scale political activities that raise fewer issues for political equality. For example, small donations to a political party are currently exempt from the disclosure requirements. To attempt to counter inequalities arising from the costs of compliance, measures could also be supplemented through education and other forms of support, to ensure that citizens know about any available subsidies and can deal with the administrative issues.

There are other broader issues about the use of state power that are beyond the scope of discussion here. There are objections to controls on the use of private wealth on the grounds that such measures are an undue interference with property rights. Given that the aim of some measures is to restrict certain uses of wealth, clearly there will be some limitation on such rights. Yet the argument pursued here is focused on what is necessary in a democracy and assumes that such a goal does permit some controls on property rights. The arguments made above show that there is good reason to be concerned when the state seeks to regulate political activity. However, the arguments for political equality are not a licence for the state to engage in censorship of views, which also raise concerns about equality. For example, if a law censors or unfairly disadvantages a particular viewpoint in the political process, it treats those people holding that view unequally by singling them out for separate treatment. Yet such fears can be addressed in ways other than hostility to any measures that engage expression or association rights. Along these lines, while Articles 10 and 11 of the ECHR permit the state to take measures that aim to promote a fair democratic process, measures will be scrutinised with reference to factors including the type of expression at stake, the severity of the interference, the particular aim being pursued and the alternative means to pursue that aim. The methodology fits with the argument set out above in so far as it acknowledges the need to check state power, while also allowing the state to address private power.

Insulating the democratic process

The previous section set out some of the objections and fears arising from the strategies for insulating the political process from economic inequalities. It was argued that inequalities in wealth pose a threat to the democratic process alongside the traditional concern with state power. The following sections will look at various types of strategy for promoting political equality, each of which will be discussed in their specific context in later chapters. The aim here is to give an overview outlining common themes and potential problems.

Blocked transactions and payments

The first type of strategy is the bluntest, the outright prohibition of certain exchanges or payments. It keeps the political and economic spheres separate by preventing economic resources securing political power. For example, it is a criminal offence to buy a person's vote.[11] Transactions thought to facilitate such an exchange are also sometimes blocked, such as the prohibition of paid canvassers in an election.[12] This prohibition was introduced not because canvassing was thought to be a type of power, but because payments to canvassers were a way of disguising bribes to voters.[13] Other blocked transactions include bribing a representative or public official in return for some favour or benefit. When a person makes a bribe the payment directly secures some form of power over a decision. Most arguments for blocking particular transactions and payments tend to centre on corruption, but also provide a method of keeping economic inequalities out of the democratic process in those settings where equality is most important.

Transparency requirements

A second strategy does not constrain the use of wealth in politics, but allows some level of transparency to reveal how money or property is being used to influence political decisions. This can be achieved by requiring the disclosure of political spending in certain contexts. For example, political parties can be required to disclose their sources of funding. Similarly, meetings between professional lobbyists and ministers can be disclosed, along with details of who paid the lobbyist and how much has been spent on the lobbying activities. The disclosure rules can promote political accountability, as the information allows the public to decide for itself whether a particular financial arrangement breaks ethical standards or whether a politician is too closely aligned with a particular group. Transparency can also indirectly serve political equality, as public criticism of excessive political spending or lobbying may impact on people's behaviour and make those uses of money less attractive as a way of influencing decisions. Knowing who is paying for a message or activity is also an important piece of information in itself as it can help people to assess and evaluate a particular message. For example, people may think differently about research claiming the effects of global warming are exaggerated, if they know a consortium of airlines sponsored it. Transparency requirements can thereby act as a check on manipulation or misinformation, which in turn may act as a check on some of the political advantages that can be secured through spending.

---

[11] Representation of the People Act 1983, s.113.   [12] Ibid., s.111.
[13] C. Seymour, *Electoral Reform in England and Wales* (New Haven: Yale University Press, 1915) p. 436.

There are a number of measures that already promote transparency. Members of Parliament have to disclose certain financial interests on the Register of Members' Financial Interests, and donations to political parties are published by the Electoral Commission. The Freedom of Information Act 2000, despite its limits, has gone some way to make the workings of government more accessible.[14] Yet there is still more that can be done, and some further requirements will be considered in relation to lobbying in Chapter 4.

Transparency rules do not directly limit participation, but can come with some costs. It can impose an administrative burden on some forms of participation. Disclosure rules may also promote a suspicion of wrongdoing where none has occurred. If it is known that someone met with a politician or made a donation to a political party, the temptation is to see any government action connected with that person as tainted. A further cost is in terms of privacy, where a person wants to express support for a party by giving money, or wishes to discuss a matter with a politician, and that matter becomes open to the public. These concerns can, however, be dealt with through some limited exemptions, for example in the case of confidential information. However, where someone is spending large sums to influence policy, that is something the public will normally have a right to know, both to see how decisions are being made and to check the propriety of the measure. Although transparency does not stop spending to influence political decisions, it is an important step that can help reveal the workings of government and allow the extent to which money is used in politics to be assessed.

Limits on expenditures and donations

The third strategy is to impose a limit on the amount that can be spent in relation to certain political activities. When looking at party funding in Chapter 5, limits on election spending and a possible donation limit will be discussed. Such limits may promote equality by controlling the disparity in the use of resources, but do not put people in an equal position. Within a limit on political expenditures or donations people can still spend varying sums, which may reflect economic inequalities. Furthermore, like the transparency requirements, such a strategy will also entail administrative issues, as it requires some system in which people record their spending and disclose those sums to the body responsible for securing compliance. In the previous chapter many of the issues raised by spending limits in relation to freedom of expression were discussed.

---

[14] Under the Freedom of Information Act 2000, any person can request information held by a public authority. While such requests provide a valuable tool when seeking to discover who and what is influencing the government, the Act contains some limits on access to information. In particular the duty to disclose is subject to a wide range of exemptions and ministers have the power to veto disclosures under s.53. On 19 February 2009, the Secretary of State for Justice issued the first ministerial veto, preventing the disclosure of minutes from Cabinet meetings discussing the legality of the war in Iraq.

The main objection to this type of restriction is in reducing the quantity of expression, although the strength of that argument will depend upon the level at which the spending limit is set.[15]

A spending limit also provides a fairly blunt method of control if it stops expenditure above a certain level, regardless of how that money was acquired or collected. For example, it restricts the political party funded by multiple small donations, as well as the party bankrolled by a few millionaires. The former type of spending is less problematic for political equality in so far as the spending power reflects its level of support. As noted in Chapter 1, the concern is not with all uses of wealth, but with the potential for economic inequalities to transfer into the political sphere. The case for imposing a limit, therefore, depends on the willingness to allow a restriction of the mass donor-based party in order to prevent inequalities arising through the spending by others. One solution is to focus on the source of funds to the group, for example, by limiting donations to parties, which would stop the multi-millionaires bankrolling the party in the first place. However, similar issues arise where a limit on political donations applies to all donors and would limit donations from those pressure groups that have secured their funds through small contributions from their members. When designing the system, the goal is to tailor regulations so that it targets only the spending that is in tension with political equality. These points aside, the limit on spending may also serve other goals, such as a competitive electoral system to ensure one party cannot grossly outspend another.

A general limit on spending in elections arguably poses fewer risks of abuse of power in so far as it applies to all parties and their supporters. However, spending limits do still raise difficult issues. For example, it may be seen to benefit those already in power, who receive greater media attention and do not need to spend so much on publicity. The difficulty with that argument is that the absence of the limit will help only those challengers with the additional resources to spend. Another objection to this strategy is that while a spending limit or cap on political donations may be superficially neutral, it may impact on some people more heavily than others. Yet this alone does not point to an abuse of power, or suggest that any person is being unfairly discriminated against. For example, if political donations from individuals were limited to £1,000 per year, the measure would impact more harshly on a political party that is bankrolled only by millionaires. However, in this case, rather than acting unfairly, state regulation may correct the distortion arising from the distribution of wealth.

More problematic are limits imposed selectively on one particular type of body or activity. For example, it would clearly be unfair if a law specifically limited the amount the Liberal Democrats can spend in an election or the amount people can give to that party, with no other party being subject to such a control. While that example highlights the potential for unequal treatment, some

---

[15] See Chapter 2.

selective limits have been enacted and do not raise similar concerns. In the party funding laws, political parties are subject to different spending limits than other campaigning organisations. Such a selective control does not unfairly single out or target a particular viewpoint or message, so need not raise concerns about censorship. The election spending limits are also selective in exempting the political coverage of newspapers and broadcasters. While this does not raise censorship issues or directly promote a particular viewpoint, it does give media organisations greater freedom to use their property to influence an election. Yet this might be addressed through other means, such as certain media regulations, rather than by extending the spending limits. Consequently, while laws applying limits do raise some difficult issues and require lines to be drawn, the concerns depend on the context, and such measures can play an important role in addressing the inequalities found in an unregulated system.

Subsidies

The provision of subsidies is a fourth strategy to promote political equality. Subsidies do not limit the amount of economic resources that can be used in political activities, but give people the resources necessary to participate. As a result, subsidies will merely mitigate, rather than eliminate, inequalities. Subsidies can take a variety of forms, including direct grants to political parties, the provision of a free mailing for election candidates, tax relief on some political activities, the use of public buildings and facilities, and access to the state-owned media. This approach levels up, rather than down, and in some circumstances can be used in conjunction with spending limits to ensure that there is both a floor and a ceiling in political spending. That combination allows the subsidy to compensate for other controls on the spending of private funds and helps to maintain the overall quantity of expression. For example, while political advertising in the broadcast media is not permitted in the UK, the effect of that ban is partly compensated for by providing political parties with free access to public service broadcasters.[16]

Given the numerous demands made on state resources, one question is whether such subsidies are a good use of funds. With the level of outrage following the publication of MPs' expenses in 2009, few people are likely to see a strong case for giving politicians access to more of taxpayers' money. Yet whether a subsidy is a good use depends on the particular scheme in question and the extent to which it is necessary to promote a fair political process. Beyond the competing demands on resources, a taxpayer may object to public funds being distributed to political parties or groups that he disagrees with.[17] This is one of the most common arguments made against further state funding for political parties in the UK, even though parties already receive some

---

[16] See Chapter 7.
[17] For discussion see S. Shiffrin, 'Government Speech' (1980) 27 *UCLA Law Review* 565 at 589–95.

subsidies.[18] The point is frequently made when a subsidy is granted to a speaker known to have extreme or offensive views.[19] However, subsidies do not compel taxpayers to support a particular political position. The subsidy is not an endorsement of that speaker, but merely recognises their status as a participant in the democratic process and the need to facilitate their contribution to political debate. The fact that a taxpayer objects does not distinguish state subsidised expression from any other state activity. There are many uses of state resources to which some taxpayers may object, such as going to war or providing welfare payments.[20]

Another objection to subsidies is that they may encourage people to form groups or pursue activities simply to become the recipient of state funds. For example, the provision of free time to political parties in the broadcast media during an election may encourage single-issue groups to field candidates in an election as a way to qualify for that media access. There are also dangers that subsidies will bring the private political actors more closely within the fabric of the state, potentially changing the nature of the political group. A dependency on funds from the state, as opposed to private supporters, may result in groups becoming more removed from citizens. The state-supported group has less incentive to reach out to potential donors or members. State subsidies may therefore undermine the representative function of the group and also reduce the level of participation. The other side of the argument is that at least state funds stop political groups or organisations being indebted to, or bankrolled by, wealthy private interests. There are also a number of ways the subsidy can be designed to address these concerns, such as making funds conditional on some level of engagement with citizens, or limiting funds for fixed periods to avoid longer-term dependence.

State subsidies may raise fewer concerns in relation to freedom of speech than spending limits as they increase the overall level of expression and do not stop anyone from speaking.[21] However, if economic resources do impact on substantive political equality, the power of the state to grant funds may advantage the recipients of the subsidy over others in the political process. Just as inequalities in private wealth can undermine the value of political equality, the

---

[18] Research on public attitudes to the funding of political parties noted an 'instinctive hostility' to the idea of such a use of taxpayer's money, Electoral Commission, *The Funding of Political Parties* (2004) at [2.9].

[19] Such a difficulty has arisen where candidates and parties on the extreme right have been given free time on the media and free mailings. For discussion see J. Rowbottom, 'Extreme Speech and the Democratic Functions of the Mass Media', in I. Hare and J. Weinstein (eds.), *Extreme Speech and Democracy* (Oxford University Press, 2008).

[20] For example in *Buckley* v. *Valeo* 424 US 1 (1976) at 92, the US Supreme Court rejected the argument that a scheme for state funding to political candidates must allow individual taxpayers to designate to which candidate their tax dollars must go as: 'every appropriation made by Congress uses public money in a manner to which some taxpayers object'. See also Shiffrin, 'Government Speech', at 592–3.

[21] Justice Scalia in the US Supreme Court argued in *NEA* v. *Finley 524 US 569* (1998) at 599 that state funding of artistic expression does not engage the First Amendment.

same can be said of the distribution of state resources.[22] Clearly, it would be an abuse for the political party in government to grant a subsidy only to itself and no other party. The potential for abuse is to some extent checked by legal controls. While people are not normally entitled to a particular subsidy as a right, a refusal to grant an existing subsidy on 'discriminatory, arbitrary or unreasonable grounds' or to grant the subsidy subject to 'discriminatory, arbitrary or unreasonable conditions' is open to challenge under HRA.[23] Similarly, allocation decisions by a public body will also be open to challenge through judicial review. However, the courts will normally be deferential in approaching such questions, and there are difficulties in identifying a standard to distinguish the fair allocation of funds from the arbitrary.[24]

One way to avoid the difficult questions in allocating subsidies is to decentralise the decision, so that the distribution of funds is more closely based on people's choices. In Chapter 5, reference will be made to a scheme in which each individual receives a voucher worth a certain amount of state funds, and then decides which party, group or speaker to give the voucher to, which in turn determines the allocation of state funds.[25] Other decentralised methods of allocation may arise where there is a subsidy in kind that is open to anyone engaging in a particular activity. In the UK, newspaper sales are exempt from VAT which provides a type of subsidy, but the allocation is based on people's behaviour and buying habits. Decentralisation of allocation may reduce the risk of the system becoming a stagnant cartel of insiders receiving block grants from a central agency, and help to ensure that the system remains dynamic and can still produce some surprises. However, the choice to decentralise and the criteria on which to distribute funds are themselves issues of judgement which may benefit certain participants. For example, a small political party with fewer supporters may complain that a voucher scheme stops it gaining the funds necessary to be heard.

In other circumstances, it will not be possible to devise a mechanistic way to allocate funds. For example, a publicly funded broadcaster is a resource, which is used to subsidise some political communications. However, the general coverage of political affairs cannot be divided up between every possible participant. Some judgement needs to be exercised by the broadcaster to decide which views and speakers should be included in the public broadcaster's coverage. While this involves a discretionary power and some selection, there are safeguards that can be imposed. For example, someone independent from

---

[22] However, those that are sceptical of private wealth having the capacity to drown out or distort will similarly be sceptical of the state resources having a similar effect. See F. Schauer, 'Government Speech' (1983) 35 *Stanford Law Review* 373 at 379–83.

[23] *R (ProLife Alliance)* v. *BBC* [2004] AC 185 at [8].

[24] See *R* v. *Broadcasting Complaints Commission, ex p Owen* [1985] QB 1153; in relation to the allocation of political coverage on television.

[25] For such a proposal in relation to the funding of election campaigns, see Hasen, 'Clipping Coupons for Democracy' and E. Foley, 'Equal-Dollars-Per-Voter: A Constitutional Principle of Campaign Finance' (1994) 94 *Columbia Law Review* 1204.

government can exercise the judgement in accordance with set criteria, and that criteria should be transparent and formed in consultation with all the relevant actors, and the decision should be open to challenge. Again, subsidies for certain political activities raise difficult questions, which cannot be answered in the abstract, but can at least reduce the dependence on private wealth and give more people and groups the means to participate.

Forums for communication and participation

The final type of measure to be considered concerns the forums for communication and participation. A forum can be broadly defined as 'a meeting or medium for an exchange of views'.[26] While the term 'public forum' is used in US law to describe a particular type of space, in this section it is used in its broader and more literal sense. A forum is a space where people can associate with one another, speak to a wider audience and hear different viewpoints. For the speaker, a forum provides a place to communicate with an audience and be heard. For the audience it provides a range of information and ideas, and a space for deliberation. The main examples that will be considered in later chapters will be publicly accessible land and the mass media.

Access to, or some form of inclusion in, such forums is of central importance to political equality. Part of the concern about inequalities of wealth in politics is that it secures access to the means to disseminate views and arguments. Ensuring that people have access, or that diverse viewpoints are covered in the major forums, is one way to offset those additional opportunities for political influence that are secured through wealth. Yet it might be thought that closing a forum to all people engaging in political activities treats people equally. Under this view, denying everyone the chance to speak about politics in a public space is consistent with equality. However, it would not serve the value of political equality in so far as it deprives people of the very thing that should be distributed on an egalitarian basis.[27] Equal opportunities for participation require that people have sufficient resources to participate. In any event, denying the use of forums to all political speakers would not lead to equality, as political decisions will still be made, but the lack of access cuts people off from the process. If the forums were closed, those making political decisions or influencing the decisions through other channels would have much greater power, as people would have fewer opportunities to influence that decision or hold the decision-maker accountable. This provides a reason why political equality does not lead to a levelling down below a sufficient level of resources. Here the connection between the right of access and political equality is in the provision of the resource.

Some forums are owned by the state, in which case regulating access will be less problematic. Access to a state-owned forum is a type of subsidy, which gives

---

[26] *The Concise Oxford English Dictionary*, eleventh edition (Oxford University Press, 2006).
[27] T. Christiano, *The Constitution of Equality* (Oxford University Press, 2008) pp. 32–5.

the participant a chance to speak in a particular place and potentially reach a specific audience. It raises similar issues to those considered in relation to subsidies. The first issue is identifying where a publicly owned space constitutes a forum, as opposed to property to be used in pursuing a government function. For example, one cannot demand access to a courtroom, or speak at a government press conference. The second issue is who can access the state-owned forums, which raises similar issues as the allocation of a subsidy.

Where the forum is privately owned, things are more complex. The owner of the forum is free to participate in the democratic process and can use that forum for his own purposes, for example by selectively denying access to some speakers, or using the forum to give prominence to a particular message. This often gives rise to claims of private censorship, in which people are cut off from the chance to communicate. Just like the refusal of access to the state-owned forum, it deprives people of the opportunity to persuade others that lies at the heart of political equality. However, political equality enters the equation for another reason. By virtue of owning a particular piece of property that happens to be of importance for others to participate, the forum owner has a greater chance to influence democratic decisions. Measures that regulate access to such a forum therefore amount to a redistribution, in which the resources of the forum owner are shared with other participants.[28] Not only does it facilitate the expression of others, it limits the political power of the forum owner arising from his use of property.

The difficulty with regulating the privately owned forum is that the owner has his own political rights, which are arguably undermined by regulations such as a right of access. While those excluded from the forum may complain about private censorship, the forum owner may complain that regulations securing access amount to state censorship of his speech.[29] Along these lines, requiring a privately owned forum to carry a particular speaker's message may be seen as analogous to compelled expression.[30] This is not compelled expression in the sense that it forces words into the forum-owner's mouth.[31] Instead, the complaint is that it requires the private actor to collaborate in the communication of messages not of his own choosing. The objection may also be that the owner is forced to carry views that he finds offensive, such as those of certain extremist speakers. Similar arguments can also be made that access rights amount to a compelled association. A forum is not just a place where the owner communicates to an audience, but is a place where people come together to hear and

---

[28] See J. Balkin, 'The New First Amendment: Some Realism about Pluralism: Legal Realist Approaches to the First Amendment' [1990] Duke L. J. 375, discussing access rights and redistribution.

[29] F. Schauer, *Free Speech: a Philosophical Enquiry* (Cambridge University Press, 1982) p. 122.

[30] See M. Redish, *Money Talks* (New York University Press, 2001) pp. 174–80.

[31] For example, the US Supreme Court has held that requiring school children to salute the American flag constitutes compelled expression, *West Virginia State Board of Education* v. *Barnette* 319 US 624 (1943).

exchange different views. A right of access affects the right of association by forcing a particular speaker onto the participants within that forum. In some cases, however, access will only be a limited infringement of the association rights, as it requires only that people can use a particular resource, rather than be accepted or welcomed into the association. Furthermore, the expression of the visitor is unlikely to be confused with that of the forum owner if made clear that it is being carried pursuant to a right of access.

Where the forum is owned and maintained for reasons other than communicating political expression, the right of access is less problematic. An open space that is maintained for public leisure, such as a park, can be utilised for public meetings without severely infringing the political rights of the owner.[32] Here access does not interfere with the expression of the forum owner. It may be argued that the right of access interferes with the other functions of the forum, for example if the frequency of public meetings means that a park can no longer be used for recreational purposes. However, such concerns can be dealt with through managing the right of access so it does not unduly interfere with other uses.

The objections to a right of access are stronger where the forum has an 'expressive' purpose, where communication is one of the central purposes of the forum, for example in the case of a newspaper. Where the forum has an expressive function, the argument against a right of access is that it will distort or 'change the message' of the forum.[33] Its purpose will be undermined if the viewpoint advanced by or within the forum has to be followed by an opposing view.[34] Similarly, where there is an expressive purpose, the association claim becomes stronger and the forum should be free to define who can participate within the forum and form part of the association.[35] This objection to the right of access is that it does not merely redistribute resources, but changes the terms on which people can participate, combine and express themselves.

Once again, the tension lies between the participation rights of those excluded and those of the forum owner. However, it is argued here that the strategy to resolve the tension will depend on the nature of the forum and the function it performs. In some cases, a right of access or some requirement of inclusion may

---

[32] For example, in *Pruneyard Shopping Center* v. *Robins* 447 US 74 (1980), a right of access to a shopping mall did not violate the First Amendment as the shopping centre did not have an expressive purpose. In his concurring opinion, Justice Powell explained, at 99, that the 'selection of material for publication is not generally a concern of shopping centers'.

[33] *Roberts* v. *United States Jaycees* 468 US 609 (1984) at 628.

[34] Schauer, *Free Speech*, p. 128.

[35] *ASLEF* v. *UK* [2007] ECHR 11002/05 at [39] 'Where associations are formed by people, who, espousing particular values or ideals, intend to pursue common goals, it would run counter to the very effectiveness of the freedom at stake if they had no control over their membership'. In the United States see *Dale* v. *Boy Scouts of America* 530 US 640 (2000). See also A. Gutmann, 'Freedom of Association: an Introductory Essay', in A. Gutmann (ed.), *Freedom of Association* (Princeton University Press, 1998) p. 11: 'Any meaningful right to free speech must protect associations whose primary purpose is expressive from political interference in their membership policies insofar as that interference is directly related to its expressive purposes.'

be the appropriate response where the forum is a resource that provides a central means by which to reach different people. In those circumstances, the forum acts as a place where different sections of society come together and can be a primary point where people obtain information and hear diverse views. This type of forum is most clearly seen where it has a monopoly or dominant position, resulting in a lack of alternative spaces to reach people. Examples include a private actor owning common land or a large media outlet, where people simply have few other places to potentially reach a particular audience. Such forums play an important function as a source of information and outright exclusion can deprive people of the chance to communicate with a broader audience, or participate on equal terms.

By contrast some forums function as a place for speakers to deliberate and communicate around a particular viewpoint, set of interests, or areas of expertise. These forums allow people to participate with others who have similar interests, allowing the development of an idea or viewpoint in greater depth before it is put to the test and assessed alongside competing views.[36] An obvious example is a newsletter produced by a political party or pressure group, or space for members of a pressure group to meet. Rights of access are a much greater interference where the forum is associated with a distinct political outlook or viewpoint. If a person wants to issue a pamphlet on the virtues of socialism, it would be unfair to require him to water down his message with the views of free marketers.[37] The concern is not just that a right of access will prevent the communication of a clear message to the outside world, but that it will undermine its internal debate and deliberation. In this context, the concern with inequality and exclusion would be better served by ensuring that more people have the resources to set up their own forum.

Conclusion

This chapter has looked at some of the main strategies aiming to promote political equality. None will fully attain that goal, but can take an important step towards a more egalitarian system. Each of these strategies raises difficult questions about the impact on political rights, the response to which will depend on the specific measure being proposed and its context. There are also problems of loopholes, where people merely modify their behaviour to avoid whatever controls are imposed. However, the concerns outlined above should not lead to a presumption against any state regulations or the abandonment of strategies that seek to promote political equality. Such a presumption would come at too high a price, in so far as it allows inequalities in wealth to influence the democratic

---

[36] While highlighting the dangers of polarisation within homogenous groups, Sunstein also highlights that such 'deliberative enclaves' can serve as a place for otherwise suppressed voices and views to be developed and heard. C. Sunstein, *Designing Democracy: What Constitutions do* (Oxford University Press, 2001) pp. 45–7.

[37] Redish, *Money Talks*, p. 183.

process. Yet the discussion highlights a number of issues and concerns that need to be assessed in relation to each measure in question.

The various strategies to promote political equality will be appropriate at different stages of the process and for different activities. For example, the limits on spending will be more suited to the electoral setting, where the scope of the controls can be defined and as the voting stage approaches. By contrast, the need to secure access to the forums is a continuing goal, relating to the deliberative stages of the political process. While the various strategies arise in different areas, for example in relation to the media, to public land and to political parties, such policies can be seen as part of an attempt to secure the same objective in promoting political equality. The following chapters will take up the issues discussed in this and earlier chapters, and examine the ways of insulating politics from the inequalities in wealth in relation to these specific areas of activity.

4

Access, influence and lobbying

The chance for people to influence legislative and executive decisions is not limited to elections. At other times people can influence political decisions through contact with a range of officials, in the legislature, executive, or the various administrative and regulatory bodies.[1] Not every person or group can participate equally in the decision-making process. The official taking the decision has considerable freedom to choose which people to meet with and listen to; a choice that gives varying opportunities to different people. Yet such decisions take place within the political framework, either with MPs acting as representatives, or officials performing certain public functions. Given this setting, political equality is important, in so far as the chances to influence the official should not depend on the wealth of the individual or group in involved. However, there are a number of ways that inequalities in wealth can impact upon the decision-making process, the most obvious being corrupt payments to officials to secure a benefit or favourable treatment. Aside from corrupt payments, more common ways to influence ministers, MPs or civil servants include lobbying, which is sometimes associated with techniques that appear to give privileged access to those willing to pay.

A number of factors have led to the growth of lobbying as a professional activity. Constitutional changes mean there are more points of entry for lobbyists. The devolved assemblies, as well as the institutions of the EU, provide targets for those seeking to influence policy beyond Westminster and Whitehall. The decline of corporatism in the UK, in which relations between the main groups and government were more formally structured, means that many groups rely more heavily on lobbying to gain access and influence decisions.[2] Alongside this trend, an increase in the number of pressure groups means there are more organisations engaging in such practices.[3] These provide a selection of reasons why lobbying has become a more prominent

---

[1] The focus will be on national politics, looking at contact with Members of Parliament (MPs), government ministers and civil servants. For ease of discussion, the term 'officials' is used to refer to MPs, ministers and civil servants.

[2] P. Norton, *Parliament in British Politics* (Basingstoke: Palgrave, 2005) p. 204, on how the decline of the corporatist model encouraged groups to lobby Parliament.

[3] *Ibid.*, p. 203.

feature of political life and a common way to influence those in Parliament and government.

The term lobbying often raises suspicion, conjuring images of MPs and government officials making backroom deals with outside interests. The regular controversies reported in the media help to perpetuate this image. In January 2009, a newspaper alleged that several members of the House of Lords were willing to use their parliamentary powers to advance the interests of clients, if paid a retainer by a lobbying firm.[4] In the late 1990s, the so-called 'lobbygate' affair highlighted the role of professional lobbying firms in providing outside interests with inside information and access to Ministers and senior civil servants.[5] In that controversy, one paid lobbyist claimed to be 'intimate' with the most important members of the government, and could facilitate contact with those people for his clients.[6] Before that, during the Major government, concerns arose about MPs receiving payment for tabling questions in the House of Commons, in the 'cash for questions' affair.[7] Earlier still, in the John Poulson affair in the 1970s, an architect was found to have paid civil servants and elected politicians to secure public contracts. Poulson was later convicted of corruption offences, but the scandal led to calls for stronger controls on the ways outside interests can influence political decisions.[8] The list of controversies goes on and at the centre of each is the sense that, one way or another, money has secured political influence. Most of the episodes have been followed by attempts to reform the system and stop such abuses arising again. As a result, the laws and regulations that control lobbying and the relationship between external groups and officials are a patchwork that has developed gradually with each responding to a particular controversy.

Lobbying is a difficult area to examine for a number of reasons. One problem is in acquiring the information necessary to assess the extent of lobbying, such as when a public official met an outside interest and what was said or agreed in the meeting. It is also hard to know whether lobbying is influential and the extent to which the actions of the official are attributable to the lobbyist's efforts. Finally, difficulties arise in drawing the boundary to decide where such activities are unethical, or where it is merely an exercise of a citizen's right to communicate with government. In addressing the final question a distinction can be drawn between those methods of influence that clearly fall foul of any ethical standards, where the person attempts to use wealth to purchase some form of official action, and those methods which expend resources as part of an effort to

---

[4] See House of Lords, Committee for Privileges, *The Conduct of Lord Moonie, Lord Snape, Lord Truscott and Lord Taylor of Blackburn* (HL 88 2009).
[5] For an account by the journalist that broke the story, see G. Palast, *The Best Democracy Money Can Buy* (London: Constable and Robinson, 2002) ch. 7.
[6] *Ibid.*, p. 283.
[7] See House of Commons Select Committee on Standards and Privileges, *First Report* (1997 HC 30) and *Eighth Report* (1997 HC 261).
[8] See *Royal Commission on Standards in Public Life*, Cmnd. 6524 (1976).

persuade the official. As will be seen, the line is not watertight. However, before looking more broadly at the various methods and techniques for lobbying, the next section will look at the former types of influence, the direct payments that bribe the official.

Cash for favours, access and corruption

The most objectionable use of wealth to influence political decisions is the 'cash for favours' scenario, where payments are made to an official in exchange for an action, decision or omission. Making a gift to an officeholder in return for the use of public power to grant a favour or benefit is a classic example of a corrupt deal. Such deals were seen in the Poulson affair and since then in a number of bribery cases involving local government officials. Yet similar concerns also arise in the controversies surrounding political donations, where allegations have been made (but not proven) that money to a political party secured a contract or honour.[9] Such deals do not just entail cash payments, but can take the form of any type of advantage or benefit, such as an offer of employment for when the official leaves office. Where such a corrupt exchange takes place, the ordinary procedures for decision-making are bypassed. The use of wealth has a direct impact on the decision or action, and the official action is based neither on its merits, nor its popular support.[10] Such direct exchanges face similar objections to vote buying where influence is not secured through persuasion, but secured through payment. 'Cash for access' is slightly different, as it does not suggest that the decision has been purchased by an outside interest, but that the official agrees to meet or listen to someone in return for payment. The payment therefore helps to set the official's agenda and gives the payer a stronger chance to put their case to the official and to acquire information about government policy. In practice, it may be difficult to distinguish 'cash for access' and 'cash for favours' as it is hard to tell whether the financial inducement has merely secured access, or has influenced the mind of the decision-maker.

When such payments are discovered, allegations of 'sleaze' will often impose a heavy political price on the politician. To combat the most blatant ethical breaches, laws and rules restricting bribery and corruption are an

---

[9] There has been speculation that donations to political parties have been used as part of strategy to secure honours, government contracts and favourable planning. For example, in relation to planning decisions, property developer Minnerva's plans were approved by a government minister and two of the company's chairmen had made large donations to the Labour Party, see 'Prescott caught in loans row', *Sunday Times*, 26 March 2006. In another example, Powderject was awarded a contract to supply a smallpox vaccine, after the Chief Executive made donations to the Labour Party. However, the National Audit Office, *Procurement of Vaccines by the Department of Health* (HC 625 2003) and the Public Accounts Committee, *Procurement of Vaccines by the Department of Health* (HC 429 2004) found no connection between the donations and the contract. On the award of honours to Labour Party donors, see House of Commons Public Administration Committee, *Propriety and Peerages* (2007 HC 153).

[10] See Chapter 1, contrasting aggregative and deliberative accounts of democratic decision-making.

important feature of any democratic system. However, defining corruption and pinpointing the instances where an official has breached an ethical standard is a more difficult task. Activities thought to generate some undue influence are sometimes hard to separate from the legitimate business of the official, who needs to maintain contact and relations with a range of outside groups. A starting point for addressing these issues is to look at the definitions of corruption and how it relates to a more general concern with the influence of wealth and political equality.

Political corruption and political equality

There are a number of ways to define political corruption, two of which will be considered here: a 'norms of office' approach and a public interest approach.[11] Under the former definition, a corrupt act occurs where a person holding office deviates 'from norms binding upon its incumbents' for personal or private gain.[12] To decide whether an arrangement is corrupt therefore requires the identification of those norms that are binding on the officeholder. In some cases there may be a set of rules stating precisely the duties and obligations to which the official is subject. This definition does not tell us what standards the official is expected to live up to and takes as a given the existing rules that bind the officeholder, which themselves may have been the product of political decisions.[13] While therefore providing some flexibility by allowing the definition of corruption to change as the norms governing the office change, the question whether an action is corrupt refers back to the rules or expectations governing that particular office.

The second definition of corruption moves away from the norms of the public office and looks to the 'public interest', in which a payment to an official for a favour is corrupt when it is damaging to the public interest. This brings the normative questions into the open and provides a way of thinking about whether an action should be thought of as corrupt. The major difficulty with this definition is in determining whether an arrangement is detrimental to the public interest. For example, providing a knighthood to reward someone for donating millions of pounds to a charity is arguably in the public interest for promoting a good cause, yet to others looks like a corrupt sale. Deciding

---

[11] When looking specifically at the public sector, 'norms of office' is sometimes recast as a 'public office' approach. Other leading approaches include the public opinion and market approaches. The former refers to public opinion to determine what should be regarded as corrupt. The difficulty is that it provides a subjective definition, and where there are differences in public opinion it does not tell us which opinion should be preferred. James C. Scott, *Comparative Political Corruption* (New Jersey: Prentice-Hall, 1972) p. 4. The market definition primarily looks at the incentives on the various actors to engage in corrupt actions, but does not itself provide a definition of corruption. It takes an existing definition of corruption and looks at the incentives and consequences of such acts. See Arnold J. Heidenheimer (ed.), *Political Corruption: Reading in Comparative Analysis* (New Brunswick: Transaction, 1970) pp. 4–5.
[12] Heidenheimer, *Political Corruption*, p. 4.   [13] Scott, *Comparative Political Corruption*, p. 6.

what is in the public interest is open to debate. Consequently, a public interest definition does not provide answers as to whether lobbying activities, beyond the most obvious scenarios, should be regarded as corrupt.

Under these definitions, the difficult questions of when an action should be regarded as corrupt refers back to a broader question, such as how one decides the norms of a public office, or when the public interest has been damaged. This should come as no surprise, as the term corruption suggests a deviation from an ideal standard for official conduct.[14] As Mark Philp explains, the difference between the public office and public interest definitions is really a difference as to 'how to derive the standard for identifying the naturally sound condition from which corrupt politicians deviate.'[15] Consequently, to decide whether something is corrupt requires some standard to determine the naturally sound condition.

Along these lines, it has been suggested that there is a close connection between corruption and political equality, in so far as the latter plays a role in defining the standards from which the public official deviates. For example, if the norms regulating the official or the standard of the public interest are drawn from democratic theory, then the 'basic norm of democracy' is that 'every individual potentially affected by a decision should have an equal opportunity to influence the decision.'[16] This standard will be applied in different ways to different offices. For example, MPs acting as representatives are expected to be responsive to citizens. By contrast, while the executive official may not be as responsive to the people as the MP, the civil servant holds a position of trust and political impartiality, which is broken when responding to those with an ability to pay.[17] If an egalitarian model of politics is accepted, then the reason why payments to an official are regarded as corrupt is because he has deviated from the standard required by that model.[18]

If this approach is taken, then the term corruption begins to have a broader meaning and more general arguments about equality and the influence of wealth shape the understanding of corruption. For example in *Austin v. Michigan State Chamber of Commerce* a majority in the US Supreme Court upheld a statute, which prohibited the use of corporate funds to make independent election campaign expenditures.[19] Justice Marshall stated that even if the regulation did not restrict explicit deals between the donor and official, it still served the goal of preventing corruption: 'Michigan's regulation aims at a different type of corruption in the political arena: the corrosive and distorting

---

[14] *Ibid.*, p. 3.

[15] Mark Philp, 'Defining Political Corruption' (1995) 45 *Political Studies* 436 at 445.

[16] Mark E. Warren, 'What Does Corruption Mean in a Democracy?' (2004) 48 *American Journal of Political Science* 328 at 333.

[17] *Ibid.*, p. 335.

[18] For discussion of the relationship between corruption and equality see B. E. Cain, 'Moralism and Realism in Campaign Finance Reform' (1995) U Chi Legal F 111, and David Strauss, 'Corruption, Equality and Campaign Finance Reform' (1994) 94 Colum. L. Rev. 1369.

[19] (1990) 494 US 652.

effects of immense aggregations of wealth that are accumulated with the help of the corporate form and that have little or no correlation to the public's support for the corporation's political ideas.'[20] While the Supreme Court has since moved away from this position,[21] it points to an account of corruption as a distortion of an ideal way of doing politics. Under this view, the electoral process is corrupted by the political spending of the corporations. This does not suggest that the criminal law of bribery should apply to such spending, but rather that arguments based on corruption start to blend with political equality, and both are rooted in a common concern.

Despite this connection, corruption in the more traditional sense can be distinguished from equality, as corruption normally relates to the behaviour of the officeholder. From the perspective of political equality, the corrupt deal is particularly problematic in that it shows a strong causal link between economic resources and the political outcome. The ordinary methods of making the decision have been bypassed. However, the concern with political equality is less focused on whether the official has breached a duty, but looks at the overall process leading to the decision. For example, concerns about equality arise when a group spends vast amounts of money to hire a lobbying firm, to pay for research and advertising to get the official's attention, but the official's behaviour is not corrupt. The advantage is arguably unfair, but not corrupt as it has not induced or attempted to induce the official to act contrary to his public duty. Similarly in the case of the American electoral expenditures considered in *Austin*, the aggregations of wealth allow the campaign to spend vast amounts of money to persuade the public, but the voters persuaded by those messages do not breach their civic obligations in the way those selling their votes do. The money is spent in an effort to convince others that voting a particular way is part of their duty. A similar point can be made when individuals go to court and one party can afford a gifted lawyer, but the other cannot. The process may be unfair and there is an inequality, but the judge has not taken a bribe or been induced to make a biased decision.

In so far as the concern with corruption is specifically focused on the official, or an attempt to influence the official, it is distinct from a concern solely about equality.[22] Arguments against corruption also go beyond concerns about inequalities in wealth. For example, offering a policy in return for sexual favours, or awarding government jobs to friends, is seen as corrupt, as the decision is based on an irrelevant consideration. There are factors other than equality that define the official's duties. Furthermore, even if all wealth was distributed equally and people had an equal chance to buy favours, there are good reasons not to auction off government policies. While anti-corruption measures play

---

[20] At 659–60. See also *McConnell* v. *Federal Election Commission* (2003) 540 US 93.

[21] *Federal Election Commission* v. *Wisconsin Right to Life* (2007) 551 US 449. The US Supreme Court overruled *Austin* in *Citizens United* v. *Federal Election Commission* 558 US (2010), rejecting the 'anti-distortion' argument.

[22] See T. F. Burke, 'The Concept of Corruption in Campaign Finance Law' (1997) 14 Const. Commentary 127 at 136.

a considerable role in limiting the influence of wealth, such controls will not address all the concerns that lobbying raises for political equality. The arguments based on corruption are distinct from and narrower than those looking at the political equality in the broader decision-making process.

Criminal law controls

Even with the narrower view of corruption, difficulties of definition still arise, which can be seen by looking at some of the problems commonly found in relation to bribery laws. At the time of writing, the government is proposing a new statute on the law of bribery, which aims to clarify and unify the law. To date, the laws of corruption and bribery in the UK have been a patchwork of statutory and common law offences.[23] For example, there is a common law offence of bribery and further bribery offences under two statutes. The bribery offence under the Public Bodies Corrupt Practices Act 1889 applies to servants of public bodies other than the Crown,[24] whereas the Prevention of Corruption Act 1906 applies to those in a principal/agent relationship. Other statutes cover more specific instances of corruption, such as buying honours[25] and paying voters at an election.[26] To complicate matters there is some uncertainty whether MPs are subject to the offences as they are not agents under the 1906 Act and Parliament itself is, arguably, not a 'public body' under the 1889 Act.[27] Further uncertainties arise as to whether the common law offence applies to MPs.[28] There are also questions as to whether parliamentary privilege under Article 9 of the Bill of Rights, which prevents parliamentary proceedings being questioned in a court, would inhibit the prosecution of an MP for bribery.

It is hoped that the new legislation will clarify these matters, but given that the law is in a state of change, detailed discussion will not be undertaken here. Instead some common problems of definition will be considered. As a result of these problems, such laws tend to control only the most direct uses of economic resources to influence decisions. Several issues in bribery laws illustrate these

---

[23] The common law of bribery comprises several specific offences, but can be broadly defined as: 'the receiving or offering [of] any undue reward by or to any person whatsoever, in a public office, in order to influence his behaviour in office, and incline him to act contrary to the known rules of honesty and integrity.' *Russell on Crime* (twelfth edition, 1964) p. 381, cited in the Law Commission, *Reforming Bribery* (2008 HC 928) at [2.4]. In addition to bribery, an official exercising public power who responds to payments may also commit the common law offence of misconduct in public office. See *Attorney General's Reference (No 3 of 2003)* [2004] EWCA Crim 868.

[24] See *R v. Natji* [2002] EWCA Crim 271, interpreting the Public Bodies Corrupt Practices Act 1889 s.7 and the Prevention of Corruption Act 1916, s.2 and 4(2). For guidance on the meaning of a public body, see *R v. Manners* [1978] AC 43.

[25] Honours (Prevention of Abuses) Act 1925.

[26] Representation of the People Act 1983, s.113 and 114.

[27] For an argument to the contrary on the 1889 Act, see G. Zellick, 'Bribery of Members of Parliament' [1979] *Public Law* 31 at 33–4.

[28] The uncertainty is whether an MP holds a 'public office' for the purposes of that offence. However, see A.W. Bradley, 'Parliamentary Privilege and the Common Law of Corruption' [1998] *Public Law* 356.

problems. First, establishing that a payment was made; second, that it was made to induce or reward the conduct of the recipient in their official capacity; and, finally, that the inducement was corrupt or improper.

The first issue concerns establishing that a payment was made. Many corrupt deals do not involve a blatant payment of cash to an official and the types of financial inducement vary; for example, payments could be made to a friend or relative. Payments may also be made to a third party, such as a political party or lobbying firm. To count as an unlawful bribe, the payment need not enrich the official personally. This reflects the harm of corruption, that the official has been induced by some private (not only personal) gain, contrary to the standards of office.[29] In any event, the line between a personal enrichment and one to another party is not clear-cut. For example, a donation to a political party does not give money for the official to use as she wishes, but may enhance a politician's career prospects and thereby provide some personal benefit.[30] However, this only means that payments to third parties do not automatically fall outside the bribery laws, once that payment is established it still has to be shown that it was made corruptly to induce or reward the official.

A second difficulty is in determining whether the payment sought to influence the official in the performance of his public function. Not every payment to an official is unlawful, and it is 'only unlawful if there is a link between the payment and him doing something in pursuance of his public duty'.[31] The question is then whether the official's conduct relates to the performance of the public function.[32] For example, a donation to a political party may not secure a favour, but it can be effective in securing access. If the politician wants to secure a large donation from a group or individual then it seems inevitable that some personal contact will be made.[33] It is not clear whether the donation has induced or rewarded any action relating to the official's public duties. The payment may not have resulted in any favourable outcome and, even if it has, it is not clear whether this is a result of the payment or a result of the merits of what has been said in the meeting. However, it is arguable that in some circumstances, arranging a formal meeting is itself an action relating to a public duty. The law of bribery could, therefore, cover some 'cash for access' arrangements, if a payment is made to arrange a formal meeting on a policy issue.[34]

---

[29] The 1889 Act s.1(1) covers payments made to third parties. The 1906 Act s.1(1) is less clear as it does not require the official to personally benefit from the payment, but does require that the official be the recipient of the payment and leaves open the potential for evasion through payments to third parties. The bribery offences under the Draft Bribery Bill 2009 will also apply to payments to third payments.

[30] Strauss, 'Corruption, Equality and Campaign Finance Reform', at 1373.

[31] R. v. *Leslie Charles Parker* (1986) 82 Cr. App. R. 69 at 73, Purchas LJ approving the direction of the trial judge.

[32] The Draft Bribery Bill 2009 also applies to payments inducing an improper performance of a 'function of a public nature'.

[33] A. Nownes, *Total Lobbying* (Cambridge University Press, 2006) p. 215.

[34] D. Lowenstein, 'Political Bribery and the Intermediate Theory of Politics' (1985) 32 *UCLA Law Review* 784 at 828.

In other cases the meeting will not be arranged in exchange for the donation; it will be incidental to some other purpose. For example, if a person donates money to a minister's government project and is invited to an event to present the cheque, that occasion may provide an opportunity for the donor to make their case to the minister, or request a further meeting, without access being purchased.

The scope of official functions also raises questions where an official is paid in the hope that it will secure some favourable treatment, but not through the exercise of her official power. This could arise where the official is induced not to perform their own function, but to persuade another official to do so. For example, such a scenario could arise where an MP is induced to persuade a councillor on a particular matter.[35] Another example arises where a minister is induced to write to a foreign government to make a case on behalf of a multinational company, but that matter is not within the minister's remit or powers. While it is the status as an official that provides the position of influence and attracts the payment, it is not clear under the current law whether this would amount to doing something in pursuance of a public duty, as it is not an exercise of official power.[36] Such ambiguity points to a grey area that potentially undermines the purpose of the law of corruption.[37] The difficulty is in extending the law to cover such scenarios, without unduly restricting the politician's freedom to associate and communicate with outside people and organisations that are regarded as legitimate.

Finally, not every payment made to an official will be unlawful, so most laws have some additional requirement that the payment must be made 'corruptly', or, under the common law that payment must be 'undue'.[38] In most cases once it is established that the payment has been made with the intention of influencing some official action, the corrupt or improper element will be self-evident. However, the requirement imposes some limit on liability to prevent the criminal law intruding on legitimate activities.[39] It prevents the provision of hospitality from an organisation seeking to promote its agenda, for example being caught under the criminal law offence. However, the difficulty is in determining what types of payment or support are legitimate and which are corrupt, on which the case law provides little guidance. In *Cooper* v. *Slade*, the

---

[35] See *ibid.*, and Zellick 'Bribery of Members of Parliament', at 42–4.
[36] See D. Lanham, 'Bribery and Corruption', in P. Smith (ed.), *Criminal Law: Essays in honour of JC Smith* (London: Butterworths, 1987) pp. 95–6, on the relationship between the bribe and the official's duty, comparing the narrow approach of *HM Advocate* v. *Dick* (1901) 3 F. (J.) 59 with the broader approach of the Privy Council in *Attorney General of Hong Kong* v. *Ip Chiu* [1980] AC 663. See also *Morgan* v. *DPP* [1970] 3 All ER 1053.
[37] See Lowenstein, 'Political Bribery and the Intermediate Theory of Politics', at 817.
[38] Similarly, under the Draft Bribery Bill, the payment must either be made to secure the 'improper' performance of a public duty or be made in circumstances where receipt of the payment would be 'improper'. Improper is then defined as whether a person under a duty of impartiality, good faith or in a position of trust breaches a relevant expectation.
[39] Lowenstein, 'Political Bribery and the Intermediate Theory of Politics', at 831.

term 'corruptly' was defined as 'not "dishonestly", but purposely doing an act which the law forbids as tending to corrupt'.[40] While this definition has been followed in more recent cases,[41] it has also been criticised for its lack of clarity, in so far as it begs the question of when an act is 'tending to corrupt'. While new legislation can provide some further guidance, if the law is not to be too rigid (and thereby open to evasion), grey areas will inevitably emerge.

The discussion so far has highlighted some of the limits and uncertainties in corruption laws. This is not to criticise those laws, as limits to the application are to be expected given the heavy penalties associated with the criminal law. However, as a result of these difficulties, even in situations where a bribe or corrupt purpose cannot be established, there can still be a perception of corruption. The presence of a payment from an outside interest may be enough to taint the decision in the eyes of the public, even if it cannot be shown that either party has acted in a way that is corrupt. Consequently, additional restrictions attempt to prevent conflicts of interest arising in order to avoid the situation where a payment could be a factor influencing the decision. One strategy to prevent a conflict of interest is to forbid the official from receiving certain payments. For example, a local government official is prevented from receiving payments 'under colour of his office or employment' from other sources, regardless of whether it may be corrupt.[42] Another strategy is to regulate a particular type of payment or activity. For example, a cap on political donations would, arguably, reduce the scope for a conflict of interest. However, it would be impossible to restrict all payments that could potentially influence the decision-maker. Instead greater reliance will be placed on controls on the conduct of the official, for example in disclosing any potential conflicts of interest.

The law of corruption plays an important role in blocking the purchase of political power. Bribery offences are targeted at the most extreme cases, and provide just one part of a broader strategy to protect the integrity of the decision-making process. In addition to the criminal law, MPs, ministers and civil servants are subject to additional rules to avoid improper influence and to prevent conflicts of interest. Yet most attempts to influence public officials through the use of economic resources stop short of corrupt practices. Economic resources tend to be deployed in lobbying strategies, which rely on a number of techniques. Before looking at the possible controls on lobbying, it is important to say more about what these activities entail and what the possible objections to lobbying are.

Lobbying

Lobbying describes several different activities 'used in an effort to influence the policy process'.[43] Such a broad definition covers most forms of political activity

---

[40] *Cooper v. Slade* (1858) 6 HL Cas 746.   [41] *R. v. Godden-Wood* [2001] EWCA Crim 1586.

[42] For example, see the Local Government Act 1972 s.117(2).

[43] F. Baumgartner and B. Leech, *Basic Interests: the Importance of Groups in Politics and in Political Science* (Princeton University Press, 1998) p. 34.

and can be narrowed by focusing on those activities that are directed at a public official. This distinguishes lobbying from electoral activities targeting voters and focuses on just one part of an organisation's strategy to promote a particular position. However, the strategies can be connected. In addition to targeting officials, the lobbying organisation may target newspaper columnists and journalists, or run media campaigns on a particular issue. The different strategies may be difficult to distinguish in practice, for example when an interest group targets a newspaper columnist, or engages in 'grassroots lobbying' by encouraging members of the public to write to their local MP, in the hope that this places indirect pressure on the politician. However, if taken to refer to attempts to influence an official, lobbying still refers to a wide range of activities of a large number of organisations including public relations firms, businesses, charities, interest groups and trade unions.

Despite the various controversies involving some lobbying firms, most seek to persuade the official, rather than provide a financial inducement to act. As part of such a strategy, a personal meeting with an MP, minister or civil servant is particularly valuable. In the meeting, the lobbyist can ensure the information is received by the relevant person. The lobbyist also has the chance to listen to the views of the official and refine his arguments accordingly.[44] Such meetings provide a chance for statements to be made off-the-record without public scrutiny and also allow the case to be made more forcefully and persuasively. The meeting is just one example; other techniques of lobbying include the provision of written information and research. These lobbying activities do not require a financial link with the official and in such circumstances the decision-maker will not normally have any conflict of interest or personal benefit at stake.

The question of whether lobbying, using this term in its widest sense, is beneficial or detrimental to the democratic process will vary according to the particular model of democracy. Pluralist accounts give a central role to pressure groups and their lobbying activities, viewing politics as a competition among various external groups. Other models take the view that pressure group activities are detrimental to democratic decision-making, for example where the lobbyist extracts a benefit or favour at the taxpayer's expense. Alternatively, another concern is that lobbying tends to promote sectional interests in decision-making and diverts attention away from the broader public interest.[45] However, the account of the democratic process taken here does not require such a sceptical approach and accepts external groups can perform a valuable function when contacting and communicating with officials. The issue here is whether that activity is consistent with political equality.

Inevitably, not every group will be able to access or make their case to an official. Officials are likely to develop links with particular groups and tend to

---

[44] Nownes, *Total Lobbying*, pp. 213–15.
[45] See G. Jordan, 'The Professional Persuaders', in G. Jordan (ed.), *The Commercial Lobbyists* (Aberdeen University Press, 1991) p. 28.

consult with some more frequently than others. For example, the government will invite particular representatives or individuals to sit on taskforces or take part in consultations and form policy networks and communities.[46] Inequalities also arise from organisational barriers. Some groups will already be organised and have the administrative machinery to facilitate lobbying, such as established interest groups that have the contacts and know the best ways to persuade officials. Incentives can also play a role in determining which groups are organised and which are heard. Those groups subject to state regulation whose profits may be affected by a decision will have a strong incentive to put their case to the official. There are also inequalities in access to information, as some groups will work in that area of policy, or may have closer links with government. These inequalities are beyond the scope of discussion here, but all raise questions about the fairness of the process to influence decisions. Instead, the specific issue here is whether the techniques associated with lobbying provide more scope for inequalities in wealth to impact on the chance to influence legislators and government.

Professional lobbyists

One important factor that impacts on the cost of such activities is the growth of lobbying as a professional activity. A distinction can be drawn between two types of professional lobbyist, the in-house and the multi-client firm. Sometimes a company or organisation will have its own professional lobbying staff (in-house lobbyist) specifically employed to monitor policy and maintain political contacts. Alternatively, services can be secured by hiring a firm. A professional multi-client firm does not represent its own interests to an official, but acts on behalf of its clients. The services of such firms to clients include the provision of information, making representations or requests on their behalf, and preparing documents to submit to an official. Much of the work of the lobbyist is in monitoring policy, knowing exactly what changes are being proposed and how this will affect clients. In providing such guidance, the lobbying firm trades on its expertise or inside knowledge of the policy-making process. For example, the firm can explain which officials to target, how the arguments should be presented, and what types of language or evidence will appeal to the particular decision-maker. Sometimes the firm will have established contacts with existing officials or employ former officials, which can provide advantages in both information and in securing meetings. While lobbying firms are most commonly public affairs or public relations firms, other types of company such as law firms, accountants and management consultants may provide lobbying in addition to their core services to clients.

Reliance on a professional lobbyist is not a guarantee of success. Under some accounts, the professional lobbyist is regarded as an unnecessary expense that

---

[46] See W. Grant, *Pressure Groups and British Politics* (Basingstoke: Palgrave, 2000) pp. 48–51.

has little impact on the final decision.[47] By contrast others see the lobbyist as a well-connected person of dubious ethics who can convert clients' pounds into policy. Sometimes the latter view is promoted by lobbyists themselves who claim to have influenced a decision that would have been made in any event. Both accounts have probably been true on some occasions without accurately characterising all lobbyists. The lobbyist cannot work miracles and much will vary according to the political landscape at the time and strength of the case being advanced.[48] Yet hiring a lobbyist can offer some advantages and, in the right circumstances, influence policy.[49] Under this view, hiring a lobbyist is like hiring a lawyer in that it does not guarantee success, but a good one is a major advantage.

The standard justification for the lobbyist's work is that they offer a number of benefits to the decision-making process. At the most basic level, lobbying provides the official with expert information. Those private actors that have worked in a particular area can tell the official about the implications of a policy, or the best ways to facilitate a policy. This view is promoted, unsurprisingly, by lobbying firms themselves.[50] Such an account paints a picture of lobbying as a fairly benign activity, which assists the legislative and policy-making process. It also suggests a very narrow view of lobbying as the provision of information and data. Such information may, however, reflect one particular perspective or the experience of one group. Furthermore, lobbying seeks to influence as well as inform. The information will often be advanced strategically to steer the official towards a particular result. Whether this is seen to be beneficial will depend on the view taken of the proper relationship between officials and outside interests, and whether the process is sufficiently accessible to all those wishing to influence the official.

Hired guns and privileged access

Contrary to the relatively benign view of lobbying, there are a number of concerns about the impact of lobbying on the democratic process. The first is that some lobbying activities border on corruption, or at least cross some ethical boundaries. Many of the lobbying scandals in the press have centred on this line of argument, suggesting that there is some impropriety involved. For example, in the 'lobbygate' affair, no official received a payment. The concern was that

---

[47] For an overview of the debate see S. John, *The Persuaders: When Lobbyists Matter* (Basingstoke: Palgrave, 2002) ch. 1.

[48] *Ibid.*, p. 201.   [49] *Ibid.*

[50] For example, such an argument has been advanced by the Chartered Institute of Public Relations, arguing that lobbying 'enables legislators to have access to expert opinion; allows policy proposals to be "reality checked"; and allows those with a legitimate interest in the political process to provide comment on proposals which affect them'. See House of Commons Public Administration Committee, *Lobbying: Access and Influence in Whitehall* (2009 HC 36) vol. II Ev 146 ('Public Administration Committee, *Lobbying*'). See also *US v. Harriss* 347 US 612 (1954) at 625.

employing a lobbyist could help secure access to the official and that where the lobbyist has a close link with the government or MPs, she may gain access to information that is not publicly available. Other examples are where the politician receives some benefit from a lobbying firm or its client, such as a donation or a loan of staff, raising possible questions about whether such payments influence the work of the official. Under this view, even if such activities do not constitute bribes under the criminal law, they have a potentially corrupting effect.

The second concern is with the equality and opportunities to access the official.[51] While, as mentioned earlier, the process of group representation will consist of many inequalities, the professionalisation of lobbying has the potential to emphasise the advantages open to those with more economic resources. Most obvious are the expenses required to hire a lobbying firm. In addition to this are the costs in developing research and information to persuade the official. Other ways a lobbying organisation can use money is by sponsoring another entity, such as a think-tank, to produce detailed analysis and information, giving their arguments an appearance of expertise and independence. Those with economic resources are also in a better position to provide staff to an MP, sponsor an event or make a donation, all of which may gain the official's attention.

Unlike the direct purchase of political favours described above, such a use of wealth does not secure power over an outcome, but provides an opportunity to persuade the official. Persuasion is not, however, limited to those with sufficient wealth. Many groups without substantial resources can present a well-researched argument, especially one based on its own experience and expertise, without requiring a major investment. Furthermore, the presence of resources is not a guarantee of success.[52]

The concern, however, is that the professionalisation of lobbying makes influencing officials a more capital-intensive activity. Pressure groups always had to spend money, but now hiring a lobbyist is an expected part of the process for some major players. As a result, wealth increases in its importance, and is not just one resource among others. A further concern is that even if advantages in wealth can be countervailed by other organisations' activities, hiring the right firms and spending alone should not be sufficient to get a place at the table or command the attention of the official. A related complaint is that 'increased activity by lobbyists creates "noise," swamping MPs so that worthwhile causes are washed away by the sheer size of the tide'.[53] Given that most lobbying seeks to persuade a particular official on a particular decision or outcome, the ability of one group to command the attention of an official potentially diverts

[51] Public Administration Committee, *Lobbying*, at [4].
[52] John, *The Persuaders*, p. 199.
[53] C. Grantham and C. Seymour-Ure, 'Political Consultants', in M. Rush (ed.), *Parliament and Pressure Politics* (Oxford University Press, 1990) p. 77.

attention from another.[54] However, the employment of a lobbyist does not always reflect inequalities in wealth. For example, a group funded by a number of small donations can hire a lobbyist and, in such a case, the firm helps the voice of that group to be heard, especially where that group cannot afford its own in-house lobbyist. Therefore the objection relating to equality does not apply to all lobbying, but there is concern about the general tendency to make the process for influencing government more expensive.

A third concern with lobbying is with the lack of transparency and its secretive nature. This concern is not specifically with the professional firm, but with lobbying more generally. As people do not know what is said when a representative or group meets with an MP or minister, there is an image of backroom deals. In such circumstances, lobbying activities may lead to a suspicion that influence is exerted not just through persuasion, as the private meeting provides a setting where pressure can be applied on the official away from public scrutiny. For example, if a wealthy individual threatens to move assets or businesses out of the country if taxes are increased, it does not provide an argument on the merits of the policy but attempts to force the official to reach a particular conclusion. Similarly, it is sometimes thought that representatives from the media can influence government policy by promising negative or favourable coverage in response to a decision.[55] The complaint is not against lobbying itself, but that it provides an avenue for such threats to be made in private and to amplify the voice of the already powerful. Such pressure may be harder to apply if there is greater openness and scrutiny. While tactics such as threats seem unlikely if the lobbyist or client wants a long-term relationship with the official,[56] with such little knowledge about the process, suspicion is likely to arise.

Lack of transparency is not just a concern for the public, but also for the official. Sometimes she may not be fully aware of whose interests are being represented by the lobbying firm. This can arise where representations are made without the official knowing who the clients are. Furthermore, sometimes front organisations are set up to give the impression of being a representative or expert group, which is really sponsored by a particular interest.[57] Such efforts are problematic because when evaluating the merits of the presentation, the official will need to know whether there is some vested interest paying for the

---

[54] As Greg Palast told Sixth Report of the Committee on Standards in Public Life, *Reinforcing Standards* (2000) Cm 4557 at [7.7], 'When Government gives special access to business interests, the rest of the public is left outside the door'.

[55] For example, a Freedom of Information request revealed that Tony Blair and Rupert Murdoch spoke over the phone on three occasions in the nine days before the war in Iraq leading to the speculation that the views of the media owner were influential; see *Independent*, 19 July 2007. For discussion see House of Lords Communications Committee, *The Ownership of the News* (2008 HL 122) at [194–7].

[56] John, *The Persuaders*, p. 43.

[57] For example, in 2006 one MP expressed dismay at becoming involved with a group campaigning for access to drugs to treat cancer, without knowing that the group was wholly funded by a pharmaceutical company, see 'Support for Cancer Group Naive, says MP', *Guardian*, 20 October 2006.

campaign. With such information, the official can factor in the potential of bias when assessing the arguments and representations made, which potentially helps to check the inequalities.

A variation of this theme arises in relation to 'grassroots' lobbying, which aims to show an official that a particular position is widely supported. The letter-writing campaign to an MP is a classic example of such lobbying. However, in some cases lobby groups invest resources in campaigns to give the appearance of public support, so-called 'astroturfing'.[58] For example, in 2008 a number of MPs were persuaded to support a motion opposing proposals to restrict the display of cigarettes in shops after being sent a large number of cards from local shop-owners in their constituencies arguing the proposals would have a severe impact on their businesses. However, the campaign was funded and orchestrated by the tobacco industry, a fact that some MPs claimed to be unaware of.[59] If such 'front organisations' for wealthy interests lack genuine popular support, then it has the effect of misleading the decision-maker. Furthermore, such an impression may also distract attention from those groups that genuinely do have widespread support.

However, the line between such 'astroturfing' and genuine 'grassroots lobbying' is not clear-cut, as the industry-funded letter-writing campaign may still require individual citizens to sign up to its activities. In so far as the group does have genuine support, the activities should not be dismissed as fake. The difficulty is in determining how far the individual has passively put their name to an industry-drafted letter or petition, or whether that individual has reflected on the issue and genuinely supports the stance. While such questions will be difficult to determine, this could be dealt with through greater transparency requirements for the lobbying group, showing its industry connections in communications to decision-makers, for example. Once it is shown to be funded and orchestrated by the industry, the official is in a better position to assess the campaign.

Having outlined some of the concerns commonly associated with lobbying, the following sections will consider strategies for addressing those concerns while preserving people's right to communicate with and influence public officials. The first type of control to be considered is on the conduct on the official. The second strategy is to look at ways of opening up the decision-making process to offset any advantages secured by hiring professional firms. The final method of control will be rules requiring greater transparency in relation to lobbying.

[58] However, those communications to the public may be subject to marketing regulations. For example under the Privacy and Electronic Communications (EC Directive) Regulations 2003, reg. 23 direct marketing via email must not conceal the identity of the person sending the message or on whose behalf it is sent.

[59] 'MPs Fall Foul of "Dirty" Tricks by Tobacco Giants', *Observer*, 14 December 2008. Similarly, it was reported that a student organisation opposing proposals to raise the legal age for buying alcohol in Scotland received funds from the drinks industry, *Sunday Herald*, 12 October 2008.

Lobbyists, Parliament and the executive

MPs, ministers and civil servants are subject to additional rules regulating their contact and relationship with outside interests. These rules primarily aim to avoid corruption and its appearance, and prevent conflicts of interest. Given those aims, the restrictions provide a further barrier on the influence of wealth, but do not aim to secure equality in the chance to influence more generally. Furthermore, in attempting to preserve the freedom to associate with outside groups, the rules have limitations and often leave open other methods for a lobbyist to seek privileged access.

Members of Parliament

The rules governing MPs attempt to balance the freedom to associate with outside interests with the need for propriety in such relations. Given the role of the MP as a representative, it is essential that they can communicate with and hear the views of external groups. Exactly how one thinks the MP should relate to those groups depends on the view taken of the representative's role, invoking broader debates about whether the MP should act as a delegate or trustee.[60] If the representative is seen as a delegate, meeting with outside interests performs a way for constituents to transmit their preferences to their MP. By contrast, under the trustee approach such activities provide the MP with the information necessary to form his independent judgement on a particular issue. In practice, the MP is largely free to decide how to relate to constituents, subject to the constraint of an election. However, given the MP's role, the democratic arguments about fair opportunities for access will be particularly strong. Under any of the approaches to representation, the responsiveness or judgement of the MP should not be based on payment, or on his own financial interests.

There are longstanding rules forbidding payments to secure activity in the legislature. In 1695, a resolution provided that the payment of money or any other advantage to an MP to promote any matter in Parliament was 'high crime and misdemeanour'.[61] Bribery of an MP is also a contempt of Parliament.[62] Since 1947 paid advocacy by MPs has been banned. The rule still stands in modified form and that rule, at the time of writing, provides that no MP shall act as a paid advocate during proceedings in the Commons.[63]

---

[60] For classic discussion, see H. Pitkin, *The Concept of Representation* (Berkeley: University of California Press, 1967). For discussion in relation to the US law of bribery, see Lowenstein, 'Political Bribery and the Intermediate Theory of Politics', at 831–7.

[61] See Committee on Standards in Public Life, *MPs, Ministers and Civil Servants, Executive Quangos* Cm 2850 (1995) at [24]. This resolution was a response to the Speaker of the House of Commons, Sir John Trevor's acceptance of a bribe of £1,100 from the City of London.

[62] House of Commons Code of Conduct (2005) at [11].

[63] See House of Commons Code of Conduct (2005) at [89]. Similar provisions are contained in a separate Code of Conduct for the House of Lords.

This means that MPs cannot initiate or participate in parliamentary proceedings 'to confer benefit exclusively upon a body (or individual) outside Parliament, from which the Member has received, is receiving, or expects to receive a financial benefit, or upon any registrable client of such a body (or individual)'.[64]

This arrangement blocks the most direct ways to purchase political influence. However, the MP can still receive money or other benefits from outside interests and can still act on matters that relate to that body, as long as that interest is declared. The ban provides the MP cannot act *exclusively* for the benefit of the body making the payment.[65] This raises the question of when the MP acts 'exclusively' for that outside interest, or when the matter is merely relevant to that interest. Obviously, this does not mean the MP can use his position primarily to benefit a particular company in which he has an interest, and claim that the benefit is not exclusive because it also has a beneficial effect on the wider economy.[66] However, the ambiguity provides the MP with some freedom to pursue the causes of outside interests that are paying him, and the rules are designed to preserve the MP's freedom. For example, if MPs were forbidden from initiating proceedings on any matter affecting an interest that had paid them, it might prevent MPs returning from a fact-finding trip, paid for by the host country, initiating proceedings based on the information that had been acquired on that trip.[67] Furthermore, one argument against stricter regulations is that the MP's expertise may lie in the area where he has a financial interest and, under that view, the rules should allow the MP to contribute to those proceedings in that area. The difficulty is identifying those actions and arrangements that give the outside interest some undue influence and those that are merely assisting the MP in his job and acquiring expertise.

The rule discussed above prohibits the MP from acting on a payment, but does not prohibit payments to him. As long as the payment is not for advocacy, an MP can still receive financial and other benefits from outside organisations, the most obvious example being donations to an MP's political party, which will be discussed in the next chapter. There are a number of other ways that outside organisations can use their resources to gain access to the MP and information. Three examples will be mentioned here: first through the employment of an MP, second through the MP's staff and, finally, through All Party Groups.

---

[64] *The Guide to the Rules relating to the Conduct of Members*, HC 735 (2009) at [96].
[65] *Ibid.* at [96].
[66] See the House of Commons Committee on Standards and Privileges, *Conduct of Mr Tony Baldry* (2005 HC 421) at [11–14]. Compare the ruling on the similar ban on paid advocacy in the Scottish Parliament in the Standards and Public Appointments Committee, *Complaint against David McLetchie MSP* (2005 SP Paper 419).
[67] Sixth Report of the Committee on Standards in Public Life, *Reinforcing Standards* (2000) Cm 4557 at [3.85].

The first way an outside organisation can use its resources to gain access to an MP is through employment. MPs are currently permitted to have second jobs, including working as consultants that give political advice to firms and other clients, as long as such arrangements are disclosed and the MP does not engage in paid advocacy. The work of MPs as paid lobbying consultants was a high pro-file issue in the 1990s,[68] and while the rules have since been tightened,[69] many MPs continue to have second jobs. Figures published in July 2009 show that several MPs were making over £100,000 a year through second jobs. For exam-ple, while an MP, Patricia Hewitt earned an estimated £45,000 as a consultant to Alliance Boots and a further £55,000 as an adviser to Cinven,[70] and is reported to have received another £75,000 per year as a director of BT.[71] In 2009, former Conservative Party leader and frontbench spokesman William Hague had sev-eral sources of extra income including £45,000 a year as a parliamentary adviser to the JCB Group.[72] This is just to give two examples, and some change to the rules on second jobs is possible following the general concerns surrounding MPs' expenses.

Such employment arrangements highlight the way that outside interests can use their economic resources to gain privileged access and some connection with Parliament. These issues are clearest where the MP provides a parliamen-tary consultancy, but can be made about second jobs more generally. By employ-ing such a person, the company can gain knowledge of what is happening in the legislature and receive advice on policy matters. More broadly, it provides a channel of access in so far as the company has its own person in Parliament. Such arrangements are, however, defended as a way for MPs to gain greater knowledge and expertise from the outside world. The difficulty with that argument is that it suggests that the MP's political views are to some extent shaped by the experi-ence gained in that second job. So while there is no paid advocacy, the chance to influence that MP's views arises more generally, by providing a link to and par-ticular perspective on the outside world. Furthermore, the additional knowledge secured by the MP through such employment could be acquired through other means such as expert evidence, or meetings with external groups. The contro-versy with the second jobs highlights the tension between the MP's freedom to associate with outside interests and the need to prevent any advantages in influ-ence being bought. The MP is free to choose which groups or people to associate with and how to acquire information, but the danger with second jobs is that it allows economic resources to secure a link with Parliament.

A second way to seek access is not through a financial link with the MP, but through the staff working for the MP. For example, some companies, such as

---

[68] For example, see M. Hollingsworth, *MPs for Hire* (London: Bloomsbury, 1991) ch. 6.

[69] Furthermore, two of the self-regulatory bodies for multi-client lobbying firms, the Association of Professional Political Consultants and the Public Relations Consultants Association provide that their members cannot employ MPs. See Public Administration Committee, above n. 50 at [46].

[70] *Register of Members' Financial Interests*, 21 July 2009.   [71] *Independent*, 27 June 2009.

[72] *Register of Members' Financial Interests*, 21 July 2009.

accountancy firms, second staff to MPs' offices, to assist with research. Such arrangements are permissible if the sponsorship is disclosed on the MPs' Register of Financial Interests. Yet this provides a donation in kind, which creates a link by having employees work with an MP, find out about policy and potentially contribute to that policy. Where the staff member is not seconded by the outside interest, sometimes MPs' staff members have other jobs, which create a link with some other outside interests. To deal with such potential conflicts of interest, those working for MPs with passes to Parliament have to disclose other employment and gifts received. While researchers may need other sources of income or part-time jobs, some entries on the register have shown that people employed by MPs also work for lobbying firms and consultancies.[73] In these circumstances, the concern is that the professional lobbying firm gains a connection inside Parliament, which can offer some advantages to clients.

The House of Lords had no similar register for holders of passes or staff members until 2008.[74] Prior to that, some members of the House of Lords were reported as providing parliamentary passes to people working as lobbyists or for other companies. Here the concern was that the resources provided by the pass would be abused to advance the interests of clients, for example by using the Parliament library and the opportunity to meet other officials.[75] While such arrangements in the Lords are now subject to a greater level of transparency, concerns have still arisen about peers' staff also working for lobbyists.[76] On the other hand, some argue that it may be beneficial for some MPs and peers to benefit from the knowledge of someone with outside experience, and this can extend beyond the employees of large firms, for example where a staff member works for a charity. Again the tension lies between the benefits of having outside interests building links with a member of the legislature and the potential to generate privileged access.

The third way that a lobbyist may seek a connection with Parliament is through unofficial parliamentary committees known as All Party Groups (APGs).[77] These are groups of MPs and peers set up to consider a particular area of policy, which also provides a point of contact between external groups and MPs. Some APGs are sponsored and receive administrative support from an external body, including lobbying firms. One concern is that sponsoring organisations may have considerable influence over the proceedings of such committees and there have been allegations that sponsors have drafted the committee reports.[78] The complaint is that the sponsor can thereby shape the proceedings and output of the committee. However, the APGs are subject to some transparency requirements. The sponsors of the committee have to be

---

[73] 'Now MPs are drawn into the row over access to Parliament', *The Times*, 18 July 2007.
[74] House of Lords Committee for Privileges, *A Register of Interests of Members' Research Assistants and Secretaries* (2007 HL 140).
[75] *Independent*, 26 June 2008.   [76] *Financial Times*, 27 January 2009.
[77] Norton, *Parliament in British Politics*, pp. 127–8.
[78] 'How business pays for a say in Parliament' *The Times*, 13 January 2006.

disclosed, and where the services of the sponsor are made at the 'request of a client', or with that client's financial support, the identity of the client also has to be disclosed.[79] A gap was subsequently found as lobbying firms sponsoring such committees do not have to disclose the identity of their clients who do not directly pay for the sponsorship, but do have an interest in the area of policy. Consequently, the concern was that MPs were unaware of some clients of the sponsor that had interests in the area discussed by the APG.[80] Since those complaints, the House of Commons Standards and Privileges Committee has recommended a modification to the rules so that lobbying firms providing support of over £1,500 to the APG are expected to publish a list of clients on its website, or provide such a list on request.[81] Again the problem is that the freedom to associate with outside interests opens up another channel for privileged access.

The three examples show some of the different ways in which outside interests have been known to develop closer connections with parliamentarians, either for their own benefit or on behalf of paying clients. Not all such arrangements are part of lobbying campaigns, or even problematic, but these avenues provide an opportunity for those that do wish to lobby. The discussion here is not comprehensive but merely raises three of the most prominent examples of ways in which resources can be used to gain a link with legislators.

More broadly there are a number of transparency requirements governing the relationship between MPs and outside interests. Pecuniary interests have to be disclosed on the Register of Members' Interests.[82] This includes details of any employment taken, so if an MP is employed by a lobbying firm, then he must also disclose any clients of that firm to whom he has personally provided services.[83] MPs also have to register all gifts, benefits and hospitality given in relation to their position as an MP, which have a value of more than 1 per cent of the annual parliamentary salary.[84] MPs are also required to declare any relevant interests, including those from the recent past or expected in future, before participating in parliamentary proceedings. Consequently, this approach does not ban financial links with outside interests, but merely attempts to ensure that such arrangements are open to public scrutiny and that any conflicts of interest can be avoided. This openness is certainly beneficial in that it facilitates the scrutiny of the ethics of the arrangements, allowing the public to form its own view on the propriety of the relationships with outside interests.

Where a breach of the transparency or paid advocacy rules is found, the House of Commons Privileges and Standards Committee can recommend penalties including reprimand, loss of salary, suspension and expulsion from

---

[79] House of Commons Committee on Standards and Privileges, *Lobbying* and *All Party Groups* (2006 HC 1145) at [50–6].

[80] 'How Business Pays for a Say in Parliament', *The Times*, 13 January 2006.

[81] House of Commons Committee on Standards and Privileges, *All Party Groups* (2009 HC 920) at [11].

[82] See the Guide to the Rules relating to the Conduct of Members, 735 (2009).

[83] *Ibid.*, at [27].   [84] *Ibid.*, at [16].

the House.[85] Final say, however, rests with the House of Commons as a whole, which can reject the conclusions of the Committee. In relation to the equivalent code in the House of Lords, it had been previously thought that there were fewer sanctions and that there was no power to expel or fine a peer, and breaches could only be brought to the attention of the House.[86] The more relaxed framework made the House of Lords more attractive to lobbyists. However, its shortcomings were highlighted in 2009 after allegations that peers, were willing to use parliamentary influence to promote the interests of paying clients[87] and the Lords Privileges Committee stated that it has the power to suspend peers 'for a defined period not longer than the remainder of the current Parliament'.[88] Furthermore, legislation introduced in 2009 will provide for the expulsion of peers, which will allow a tougher sanction for serious breaches of the Code.[89]

The current rules, which attempt to preserve the freedom of the MP while limiting the influence of payments from outside interests, face a number of difficulties. In particular, it is difficult to separate instances where the payment or provision of resources to an MP is made in pursuance of a legitimate activity, from attempts to use payments or benefits to influence him or secure privileged access. The two can overlap. One response may be to ban MPs from taking second jobs or contracts completely; prevent outside interests providing staff and services to assist MPs; and prevent lobbying firms sponsoring APGs.[90] The case for such measures would depend on whether the loss to the MP in terms of the freedom to associate and to acquire assistance and information would be outweighed by the benefits of transparency. A more limited step would be to ban specific employment arrangements, for example preventing the MP from working for a multi-client lobbying firm.[91] Such arrangements are generally thought more likely to generate a conflict of interest and prohibited by two of the lobbyists' self-regulatory bodies. MPs in the UK have traditionally enjoyed considerable latitude in their relations with outside bodies, a level of freedom which reflects their status as members of the sovereign lawmaking body and is a legacy from an earlier era in which the judgements of politicians were accorded greater deference. Yet even

---

[85] Following the disclosure of details of MPs' expenses and the abuses of that system, legislation was quickly enacted in the Parliamentary Standards Act 2009, providing for an Independent Parliamentary Standards Authority. However, at the time of writing, it is envisaged that the non-statutory Parliamentary Commissioner for Standards will continue to investigate breaches of the MPs' Code of Conduct.

[86] House of Lords Committee for Privileges, *The Code of Conduct: Procedure for Considering Complaints against Members* (2008 HL 205) at p. 11.

[87] House of Lords, Committee for Privileges, *The Conduct of Lord Moonie, Lord Snape, Lord Truscott and Lord Taylor of Blackburn* (2009 HL 88).

[88] House of Lords Committee for Privileges, *The Powers of the House of Lords in Respect of its Members* (2009 HL 87).

[89] Constitutional Reform and Governance Bill, introduced in Parliament in July 2009.

[90] Sixth Report of the Committee on Standards in Public Life, *Reinforcing Standards* (2000) Cm 4557 at [7.64] discussing that option.

[91] See Committee on Standards in Public Life, *MPs, Ministers and Civil Servants, Executive Quangos*, Cm 2850 (1995) at [55].

if the rules are tightened up, it would attempt to prevent corrupt transactions, conflicts of interest and provide some level of transparency, but would not seek to secure a fair process for outside interests to influence the MP. Stricter controls on the representatives would stop the use of economic resources to secure some link with an MP, rather than promoting greater equality between outside interests.

The executive

While the relationship between Parliament and outside interests raises high-profile controversies, lobbyists will often have a stronger incentive to target ministers and civil servants rather than MPs. Targeting the executive allows the lobbyist to influence the formation of policy in its early stages, and also to secure smaller technical changes to a particular policy.[92] Yet like MPs, ministers are political figures who will be expected to have associations with certain outside interests. When devising policies, drafting legislation and deciding how to apply existing policies, the minister will be expected to listen to outside interests in order to acquire information and expert opinions, and also to find out how different interests will be affected. However, given their broader powers and responsibilities, ministers are subject to stricter controls in their conduct, which aims to reduce such conflicts of interest.

Ministers are subject to a separate set of rules over and above those applying to MPs, which are set out in a non-statutory Code of Practice. Under the Code, ministers can retain gifts of a value up to £140, but anything of a higher value is to be handed over to their department and published in an annual list.[93] In 2009, a list of ministers' private interests was published for the first time.[94] The Ministerial Code also provides that government ministers must ensure that there is no conflict between their public duties and private interests, and must not accept any gift that might reasonably appear 'to compromise their judgement or place them under an improper obligation'.[95] While the Code aims to provide a set of general principles rather than detailed guidance, the type of obligation that is 'improper' remains ambiguous and gives the minister considerable room for manoeuvre. That the Code is ultimately enforced by the Prime Minister has also raised concerns that the provisions do not provide a robust check on such influence. While there is now an Independent Adviser on Ministers' Interests to advise and investigate potential breaches of the Code, investigations can only be made at the request of the Prime Minister and, in the event of a breach being found, the Prime Minister will decide what sanction, if any, should follow.[96] The process is therefore one of internal self-regulation.

Unlike ministers, civil servants do not have a representative role, are politically neutral, and are therefore subject to stricter controls to regulate their relations

[92] Grant, *Pressure Groups and British Politics*, p. 64, and John, *The Persuaders*, p. 186.
[93] *Ministerial Code* (2007) at [7.22]. The Code can be found at www.cabinetoffice.gov.uk.
[94] The register was first published in March 2009 and includes a broader range of information than the register for MPs' interests.
[95] *Ministerial Code* (2007) at [1.2].
[96] See Public Administration Select Committee, *Investigating the Conduct of Ministers* (2008 HC 381).

with outside interests. In addition to the corruption laws, civil servants are subject to a code similar to that applied to ministers, which provides that civil servants must not 'be influenced by improper pressures from others or the prospect of personal gain'[97] or accept 'gifts or hospitality or receive other benefits from anyone which might reasonably be seen to compromise your personal judgement or integrity'.[98] Furthermore, under their obligation of impartiality the civil servant must not 'act in a way that unjustifiably favours or discriminates against particular individuals or interests'.[99] The controls on civil servants go beyond those merely concerned with preventing private gains or conflicts of interest and place a stronger obligation on the civil servant not to be swayed by sectional interests in ways that compromise their obligation of neutrality. The stricter duties of impartiality and political neutrality make it harder for possible financial links with outside interests to be justified under the cover of a legitimate political association.

The provisions discussed so far concern financial links with outside interests while the civil servant or minister is still in office. However, another technique that may be used to influence the official is to offer employment for when he leaves office. The process is known as the 'revolving door' in which the former ministers and civil servants later lobby the government they once worked for, or advise others on how to do so. Such a practice raises a potential conflict of interest where the official may be tempted to make decisions while in office for the benefit of the future employer, or the employment may be seen to reward past favours. Furthermore, the entity offering that employment will then benefit from the former official's expertise and network of contacts. Under the current rules such employment is not prohibited, but ministers and senior civil servants must take advice from an advisory committee in relation to employment or appointments to be taken up in the two years after leaving office.[100] The committee can advise that certain appointments only be taken if the person does not engage in lobbying. However, the difficulty with this procedure is that lobbying is not consistently defined. Sometimes it refers only to attempts to influence particular departments or advocacy, whereas in other cases it is defined more broadly as giving advice on securing contracts.[101]

The executive is also constrained by the potential for legal challenge under judicial review proceedings. For example, if a minister takes an administrative decision based on irrelevant considerations, such as some form of threat or undue pressure applied by a lobbyist, then such a decision could be

---

[97] *Civil Service Code* (2006) at [8]. The Code can be found at www.cabinetoffice.gov.uk.

[98] *Ibid.*, at [6]. See also *Guidance for Civil Servants: Contact with Lobbyists* (1998). Such an obligation also applies to special advisers, temporary civil servants with a political attachment who advise ministers, and often provide a point of contact for political groups seeking to make their case to a minister; see *Special Advisors' Code* (2007) at [5].

[99] *Civil Service Code* (2006) at [12].

[100] The Ministerial Code requires that ministers taking up an appointment or employment within two years of leaving office must consult with the Advisory Committee on Business Appointments. *Ministerial Code* (2007) at [7.25].

[101] Public Administration Committee, above n. 50, at [89–118].

quashed.[102] If the minister effectively delegates his power to a lobbyist, so that the lobbyist in practice takes a decision, that would also be unlawful.[103] Where the official has some pecuniary or personal interest, the decision would be open to challenge on the rules against bias.[104] In some circumstances parties have procedural rights to be included in the decision-making process, such as where the group has an expectation to be consulted or to be given the chance to make a representation. For example, if the government undertakes to hold a public consultation, the court can intervene if that process is flawed or unfair.[105] Furthermore, the courts will give considerable leeway to the executive to choose with whom to consult, and will tend to intervene where it is clear that the lobbyists' influence has been improper, or the decision-making process has been biased or unfair. The laws of judicial review are complex, will vary according to the types of decision and are beyond the scope of the present discussion. However, judicial review provides one avenue to challenge some decisions where the executive has been too reliant on lobbyists or unfairly excluded some people from the process.

To summarise, the various methods of control outlined above all attempt to regulate the conduct of the official. However, the rules do not operate as a complete bar to the use of wealth to influence an official. It is often difficult to ascertain when an arrangement is improper, and the standards by which conduct is evaluated will depend upon the public official in question. This will be most problematic in relation to those MPs that are elected and politically accountable, where considerable freedom to engage with outside interests is central to their work. This raises the question of whether it is preferable for stricter controls to be imposed, which may arguably control some legitimate activities, for the sake of reducing the chance of any undue influence. The controls discussed above are important in limiting the most objectionable uses of wealth that short-circuit the decision-making process. However, these controls do not prevent all arrangements that raise ethical questions, nor do they address broader concerns about the impact of lobbying where there is no financial or other direct connection with the official.

A participatory process

An alternative strategy is to offset any advantages or influence secured through professional lobbying by making the policy-making process more accessible to

---

[102] In some exceptional circumstances, the courts will still give the official discretion to comply with those threats. For example, the Director of the Serious Fraud Office discontinued an investigation into allegations that corrupt payments were made by BAE to a Saudi official, after threats had been made by representatives of the Saudi government to end negotiations on a valuable contract between Britain and Saudi Arabia and to stop cooperating on counter-terrorism. See *R (on the application of Corner House Research and others) v. Director of the Serious Fraud Office* [2008] UKHL 60.

[103] *H Lavender and Son Ltd v. Minister of Housing and Local Government* [1970] 3 All ER 871.

[104] *Dimes v. Grand Junction Canal* (1852) 3 HL Cas 759.

[105] *R (on the application of Greenpeace) v. Secretary of State for Trade and Industry* [2007] EWHC 311 (Admin).

groups, regardless of wealth. Such openness in government could help groups to find out what policy proposals are being considered, and make research and evidence more widely available. The government can also offer advice to those external organisations that wish to communicate with an official, but cannot afford a lobbying firm. Such an approach follows arguments that the commitment to political equality means that people should have a more direct say and the chance to participate in executive decisions.

The government has taken steps towards greater openness and inclusiveness in policy-making and examples of these steps include the use of citizen juries and various web-based projects. Another notable example is the increased level of formal consultation in the policy-making process. Under these exercises, members of the public are invited to respond to the publication of government proposals and draft legislation, and to provide evidence for parliamentary committees.[106] These processes allow individuals and groups to put forward their views; they also provide people with greater information about potential changes in policy. This may be seen as opening up the lobbying process to a wider range of organisations and ensuring that information is not just shared with a select few. However, the extent to which consultations have this effect is questionable. The best time for outside interests to influence policy is at the earlier stages of the process, before the publication of the consultation document. Once the draft policy has been published and the government has shown some commitment to a particular policy, the chances of changing the government's position are more limited. Consequently, those with insider contacts may be more influential at the earlier pre-consultation stages of the process than those responding to the consultation itself.

Some high-profile examples also bring into question the extent to which the public can fully contribute to the process. In 2007, the High Court found a consultation process on the role of nuclear power as an energy source to be seriously flawed.[107] While the government had promised the 'fullest public consultation' prior to making a decision, the consultation paper provided an inadequate level of information and detail for a considered response to be given. The consultation contained no specific proposals, and some relevant information was published only after the consultation had closed. The process was therefore unlawful as it breached the claimants' expectation for a full consultation, as had been promised. While this is just one ruling, it fuels the sceptics' view that consultations can be arranged in ways that do not give people a genuine chance to participate in policy-making. Critics also point to a consultation on a third runway at

---

106 For discussion of consultations see J. Morison, 'Models of Democracy: From Representation to Participation?', in J. Jowell and D. Oliver (eds.), *The Changing Constitution*, sixth edition (Oxford University Press, 2007) pp. 150–5.

107 *R (on the application of Greenpeace) v. Secretary of State for Trade and Industry* [2007] EWHC 311 (Admin). Judicial oversight of the consultation process provides a limited safeguard, and the courts will intervene on an issue of policy where something has gone 'clearly and radically wrong', see [46]. For discussion of grounds for judicial oversight of the consultation process, see P.P. Craig, *Administrative Law*, sixth edition (London: Sweet and Maxwell, 2008) pp. 732–9.

Heathrow Airport and have alleged that it included misleading data, was skewed to promote the government's favoured stance and was influenced by lobbying from the airport company BAA.[108] As a result, sceptics doubt whether the responses to consultations really influence policy and view the process as a public relations effort that gives officials advance notice of potential criticisms.[109]

These cases provide just two examples and the benefits of consultations should not be dismissed. Putting the worst-case scenarios aside, the new opportunities for people to participate in the process take place alongside, but do not balance, the more traditional types of lobbying. Furthermore, some government departments show a preference for informal off-the-record meetings with outside interests. Government departments see benefits in having discussions behind closed doors and away from public scrutiny.[110] For example, such meetings can be used as a testing ground for policy ideas and exchange of views. Consequently, the more traditional techniques to lobby officials remain, giving those with access to government a chance to exercise influence over and above the formal consultations. Under this view, a two-tier system can emerge in which certain activities are widely accessible, but some privileged access remains.

Strengthening transparency

The primary remedy generally advanced when discussing lobbying is to improve transparency, so that people know who is lobbying whom and how often. Such controls may be hoped to discourage corruption and help to detect it.[111] Disclosure requirements can inform the official about the identity and sources of funding of those seeking to persuade her. Transparency rules can also inform the public and other interest groups, allowing them to know how a decision was reached and which groups may have been influential. Such transparency rules do not secure a greater level of political equality. It does not help interests that are not organised, nor does it impact on what is said in a meeting with an official. Transparency allows problems to be diagnosed without providing a solution. Yet such rules may have some indirect benefits for equality. The information provided about the decision-making process may mobilise some groups into action.[112] Being open to political scrutiny may make some interests more wary of lobbying, although that may discourage a range of

---

[108] 'Evidence Fix led to Third Runway being Approved', *The Times*, 9 March 2008.

[109] See A. Brazier, S. Kalitowski, G. Rosenblatt and M. Koris, *Law in the Making* (London: Hansard Society, 2008) p. 178.

[110] For example, in addition to formal consultations, the Department for Business, Enterprise and Regulatory Reform arranges informal bilateral meetings, such as away-days, discussions and dinners, with representative bodies. For an account see the decision of the Information Tribunal in *The Department for Business, Enterprise and Regulatory Reform* v. *Information Commissioner and Friends of the Earth* (29 April 2008), Appeal Number: EA/2007/0072.

[111] See R. Briffault, 'Lobbying and Campaign Finance: Separate and Together' (2008) 19 *Stanford Law & Policy Review* 105 at 116–17.

[112] As the Information Tribunal explained in *The Department for Business, Enterprise and Regulatory Reform* v. *Information Commissioner and Friends of the Earth* (29 April 2008) Appeal

lobbying organisations and not just those relying on wealth. It may encourage the official to hear a range of different sources in order to appear fair, but this is not guaranteed either. Nevertheless, it does provide a first step in acquiring information, and disclosure requirements are preferable to an absence of knowledge about the relationship between officials and outside interests. Greater transparency can be achieved in two ways, through stronger obligations on the official or on the lobbyist, each of which will be discussed in turn.

Disclosure by the official

Some transparency rules already apply to MPs and ministers, such as the register of interests. However, these disclosure requirements reveal only the stronger and more formal connections. A more stringent requirement is for the official to disclose which external organisations he has met with to discuss an area of policy. For example, an earlier version of the Ministerial Code required ministers to record meetings with lobbyists and outside interest groups, setting out the reasons for the meeting and the names of those attending and the interests represented.[113] In October 2009, the government committed itself to voluntarily publishing records of ministerial meetings with outside interest groups on a quarterly basis.[114] The measure will only reveal the contacts with ministers and will not include those with senior civil servants.[115]. It would be harder to require such a publication scheme for MPs, given the sheer numbers of appointments and the issues of privacy relating to constituents. However, for ministers, for such a record to be kept and published provides a starting point for transparency. The difficulty is that such a measure may inform the public about who is meeting a minister, but would say little more about the interests being represented.

Regulating the lobbyist

An alternative is to establish a system for the registration of lobbyists and disclosure of their clients. While a number of jurisdictions have a register of lobbyists, there has been a reluctance to regulate the lobbyist in the UK. House of

---

Number: EA/2007/0072, at [177]: 'there is a strong public interest in understanding how lobbyists, particularly those given privileged access, are attempting to influence government so that other supporting or counterbalancing views can be put to government to help ministers and civil servants make best policy. Also there is a strong public interest in ensuring that there is not, and it is seen that there is not, any impropriety'.

[113] *Ministerial Code* (2005) at [8.16].

[114] House of Commons Public Administration Committee, *Lobbying: Access and influence in Whitehall: Government Response to the Committee's First Report of Session 2008–09* (2009 HC1058) p.10.

[115] The government stated that to publish details of all high-level meetings 'would involve collating a huge amount of information and divert significant resources within departments,' *ibid.* However, details of other meetings can still be obtained through Freedom of Information Act requests.

Commons committees considered and rejected such proposals for lobbying Parliament in 1969, 1975 and 1985.[116] Similarly, the Committee on Standards in Public Life has rejected a registration and disclosure regime twice. On the first occasion, the Committee concluded that it is 'the right of everyone to lobby Parliament and Ministers', and expressed a preference for regulating the conduct of MPs and ministers in various codes, rather than interfering with those citizens' rights.[117] Several years later when the same Committee considered the issue following the 'lobbygate' controversies, it concluded that 'the weight of evidence is against regulation by means of a compulsory register and code of conduct' as any useful information about the decision-making process 'would not be proportionate to the extra burden on all concerned of establishing and administering the system' and it gives the impression that only registered lobbyists have 'an effective and proper route to MPs and Ministers'.[118] Instead, the regulation of lobbyists has been left to the self-regulatory bodies.[119]

However, there is by no means a consensus against such regulations. In 1991, a House of Commons Committee proposed a compulsory register for lobbying firms targeting MPs; a code of conduct; and the disclosure of lobbying firms' clients.[120] More recently, in 2009, another House of Commons Committee proposed a mandatory register for lobbyists that seek to influence ministers and civil servants. The 2009 proposal would apply not only to multi-client lobbying firms, but also to organisations lobbying on their own behalf.[121] Such a register would provide not just details about meetings with the minister, but also additional information about any clients represented by the lobbyist and whether the lobbyist previously held public office.[122] Such an approach would provide more extensive information, which could help inform the official about the lobbyist. However, where such registers are created, common difficulties include deciding what constitutes lobbying; defining a 'lobbyist'; and what level of detail must be registered. The dilemma is between an over or under-inclusive register.

The first issue is in defining what is meant by lobbying. The obvious definition is to cover communications made directly to an official or his staff on some matter in connection with a public function, for example where trying to influence a particular policy or legislative vote. The Canadian laws define lobbying as making direct communications with the public official in respect of a policy,

---

[116] Select Committee on Members' Interests (Declaration) (1969–70 HC 57); Select Committee on Members' Interests (Declaration) (1974–5 HC 102); Select Committee on Members' Interests (1984–5 HC 408).

[117] Committee on Standards in Public Life, *MPs, Ministers and Civil Servants, Executive Quangos*, Cm 2850 (1995) at [72].

[118] Committee on Standards in Public Life, *Reinforcing Standards*, Cm 4557 (2000) at [7.28].

[119] Public Administration Committee, above n. 50, at [44–6]. Since the Public Administration Committee's report, the lobbyists' self-regulatory bodies have proposed to collaborate on a voluntary register of lobbyists and to establish a UK Public Affairs Council in 2010. While similar questions may arise in relation to self-regulation and legal controls, the discussion here will focus on the proposals for a mandatory statutory register.

[120] Select Committee on Members' Interests, *Parliamentary Lobbying* (1991 HC 586).

[121] Public Administration Committee, above n. 50, at [188].   [122] *Ibid.*, at [35].

legislation, regulation, grant or contract, or to arrange a meeting with an office-holder.[123] If the definition is restricted to those who communicate with an official, it will not cover those lobbyists who advise others how to persuade the official, but have no contact with him themselves.[124] A further question is what type of communication or contact constitutes lobbying, for example whether a telephone call would be sufficient.[125] Even with a very broad approach, there is still the potential for other opportunities for contact to fall outside the definition, such as informal or social meetings at which the minister or civil servant can discuss policy with the lobbyist.

A second question is who should be required to register. One starting point is for anyone engaging in lobbying activity to register. However, not every attempt to influence government should be subject to such administrative requirements. One alternative is to take a narrower definition and require only professional lobbyists to register. However, if this were restricted to multi-client lobbying firms, it would exclude those employing their own in-house lobbyists.[126] The register could therefore be extended to those organisations with an in-house professional lobbyist, namely an employee who spends over a certain proportion of time engaging in lobbying activities.[127] However, that definition would also fail to cover much activity by other lobbying entities, for example those for whom lobbying takes up a small proportion of time, but who nevertheless have considerable influence. There are other ways to refine the definition to ensure that smaller groups are not deterred from participating. For example, the register could apply to those seeking to influence the official only on a regular basis,[128] or those spending above a certain amount of money on lobbying activities. For example, the US federal law takes such an approach by imposing registration requirements only on lobbyists that receive more than $3,000 from clients or spend over $11,500 on their own behalf over a quarterly period.[129] The danger is that the narrower the range of people or organisations subject to the requirements, the more lobbying activities that will remain off the radar and the greater potential for evasion.

The central issue is what should be disclosed under a lobbyists' register. One approach is to require disclosure of the lobbying organisation and any

---

[123] In Canada, the Lobbying Act 1985 (R.S.C. 1985, c. 44 (4th Supp.)), as amended in 2008, requires a return to be filed by anyone that 'for payment, on behalf of any person or organization … undertakes to communicate with a public office holder' about legislation, its amendment, the development of policy, appointments or awarding contracts, or anyone 'a meeting between a public office holder and any other person'. See s.5(1), and for in-house lobbyists see s.7.

[124] M. Rush, 'The Canadian Lobbyists Registration Act' (1998) 51 *Parliamentary Affairs* 516 at 518.

[125] Committee on Standards in Public Life, *Reinforcing Standards*, Cm 4557 (2000) at [7.38].

[126] Public Administration Committee, above n. 50, at p. 72 notes this criticism of the Australian Lobbying Code of Conduct.

[127] Along these lines the Lobbying Disclosure Act 1995, 2 U.S.C. 1602, in the United States targets professional lobbyists, namely those 'employed or retained by a client for financial or other compensation for services that include more than one lobbying contact' and the definition of a lobbyist excludes individuals 'whose lobbying activities constitute less than 20 percent of the time engaged in the services provided by such individual to that client over a 3-month period'.

[128] Public Administration Committee, above n. 50, at [170].

[129] US Lobbying Disclosure Act 1995, s.4 (2 U.S.C. § 1603).

clients being represented, or with an interest in the lobbying effort. Further information may include not only details of the communication or meeting between the official and lobbyist, but also the subject matter of the communication or meeting.[130] This approach was proposed by the House of Commons Public Administration Committee in 2009, which at least ensures the public has some knowledge and that the official is informed about the group.[131] However, such transparency will be met with some objections about the impact on the free discussion with officials. As disputes under the Freedom of Information Act highlight, some lobbyists argue that the prospect of disclosure deters the provision of frank advice, and that some space is needed to air their views and exchange ideas informally. Such arguments are less convincing if only the fact of the meeting, the people present and topics discussed are recorded.[132] That level of detail will provide some transparency, but give little indication of whether the lobbyist influenced a decision, or how that influence was attained. Provision could also be made for an exemption where disclosure would amount to a breach of confidence.

A broader requirement is to disclose some financial details of the lobbying activities. For example, under the voluntary register for those lobbying the European Commission, firms provide details of their turnover that is linked to their lobbying activities and list their clients in order of each contract value. The US federal law requires the filing of reports, with estimates of the income received from a client for lobbying activities, and for in-house lobbyists to provide an estimate of the amounts spent on those activities. Further requirements also include details of political donations.[133] In the UK, the Public Administration Committee expressed doubts about getting reliable spending figures and was concerned that such detail would unduly burden the lobbyist.[134] However, if it is possible, such figures would provide an important starting point to assess how much wealth is used to impact on the decision-making process, and the extent to which it makes the process less egalitarian.

The transparency requirements could also be extended to ensure that those lobbying make clear their sources of funding. This would prevent the transparency requirements being evaded through the establishment of front organisations that pose as citizens' associations, or expert bodies, but are funded and supported by a well-resourced interest. Such an approach is taken under

---

[130] For example, the Canadian lobbying laws require the lobbyist 'to identify the subject-matter in respect of which the individual undertakes to communicate with a public office holder or to arrange a meeting'. Lobbying Act, s.5(2) and s.7(3).

[131] Public Administration Committee, above n. 50, ch. 6.

[132] The Information Tribunal has ruled that such an impact is unlikely, especially given only those details that are recorded are disclosed. Furthermore, the Tribunal ruled in the same case that there is a public interest in transparency in meetings with lobbyists, so that the public can understand the process of decision-making and can be sure there was no impropriety. See *The Department for Business, Enterprise and Regulatory Reform* v. *Information Commissioner and Friends of the Earth* (29 April 2008) Appeal Number: EA/2007/0072 at [117] and [124].

[133] Lobbying Disclosure Act 1995, s.5 (2 USCS § 1604).

[134] Public Administration Committee, above n. 50, at [166].

the US rules, which require the disclosure of the identity of other organisations providing more than $5,000 per quarter to fund the lobbying activities
and taking part in the planning, supervision or control of those activities.[135] A
similar approach in the UK could be taken to require the disclosure of those
contributing funds to a particular lobbying group. The difficult questions
would be deciding what level of donation would trigger the disclosure requirement, and determining when a donation is given to a group to support a lobbying activity, as opposed to a donation to its more general funds. Again, all these
questions represent an attempt to mediate between a regime that is not easily
evaded, while not burdening every group that seeks to influence government
or the legislature.

A further item that could be disclosed is whether the lobbyist has engaged
in grassroots campaigning. The US laws do not extend to 'grassroots lobbying'
in which an organisation persuades members of the public to write to a representative, which is often seen as a significant gap in the law.[136] By contrast,
under the Canadian law, the registered lobbyist must also disclose details of
any attempts to persuade the public directly 'to place pressure on the public
officeholder to endorse a particular opinion'.[137] The inclusion of such details
can help to prevent the officeholder being misled by any potential astroturf
campaigns.

Even if a register is introduced for Westminster and Whitehall, there will
always be attempts by lobbyists to resort to activities that fall outside the legal
definition, leading to never-ending demands for the law to be tightened. A
register is unlikely to restore trust by itself, and it does not indicate which
groups or lobbyists have been influential. Simply revealing that an official
met with various groups does not tell us which were persuasive or changed
a decision. Instead of quenching the thirst for information about lobbying activities, disclosure may simply raise further questions and demand
more far-reaching reporting requirements. The result may be an area which
becomes ever more complex and potentially bureaucratic.[138] Furthermore,
a register does not secure a fairer or more equal system of representation
and some fear it would create a perception that only registered lobbyists can
access an official. Consequently, a register on lobbying should be considered alongside other efforts to make the process more open and accessible to
other groups.

Finally, restrictions on lobbying are thought to raise some issues of freedom
of expression, especially where the influence of the lobbyist rests on its capacity

---

[135] The US Lobbying Disclosure Act 1995, s.4(b) (2 USCS § 1603(b)).
[136] C. Thomas, 'Interest Group Regulation in the United States' (1998) 51 *Parliamentary Affairs* 500
at 509.
[137] See Canadian Lobbying Act, s.5(2)(j).
[138] For example, Allard notes the complexity in applying the rules preventing an official having
meals bought by a lobbyist, see N. Allard, 'Lobbying is an Honourable Profession' (2008) 19
Stanford Law & Policy Review 23 at 57–9.

to persuade or inform.[139] Under this view, lobbying activities engage not only the right to speak, but also to petition government.[140] This view is not shared by everyone, especially in relation to professional lobbyists. In his account of free speech serving self-government, Alexander Meiklejohn argued that the principle applies to expression that contributes to a public discussion, rather than pursues a private interest. Consequently, he distinguished 'a paid lobbyist fighting for the advantage of his client' from 'a citizen who is planning for the general welfare'.[141] Under this view, the professional lobbyists' activities do not fall within the free speech principle, as they do not constitute a contribution to public discussion. The difficulty in taking such an approach is in distinguishing public discussion from private speech and determining whether the lobbyist can always be characterised in such a way, especially where a firm is not hired. Yet Meiklejohn's argument does point to the question of whether professional lobbying serves the democratic process that underlies his account of freedom of speech. The approach taken here accepts that lobbying can engage freedom of expression; but that its restriction should be permissible in so far as it serves a fair democratic process. The regulations discussed have a more limited effect on the right to communicate with government. For example, registration requirements do not stop people advancing their views and need not burden the activities of smaller groups. Instead, such requirements help to promote the values of expression in so far as they help inform the public about the policy-making process.

Conclusion

Lobbying makes a difficult case study when looking at the use of wealth as a source of political influence. This is partly because the term applies to a diverse range of activities of different entities seeking to influence different officials, making any general rules hard to formulate. The approach taken here has been to look at a small selection of activities to illustrate some of the problems and possible responses. It is also difficult to formulate a standard for the fair distribution of lobbying opportunities. Unlike the right to vote, there is no right to be heard by an official.[142] Different people and groups will inevitably have varying levels of access. Instead, the various external actors should have at least an equal

---

[139] For example, the public affairs firm Bell Pottinger told the Public Administration Select Committee '[p]reventing certain groups of people or a particular type of organisation from talking to Government would be ... a restriction on freedom of speech' and would mean officials 'have less access to the information they need to make informed decisions'. See Public Administration Committee, above n. 50, vol.2 Ev 174.

[140] For example, see the US Supreme Court in *US* v. *Harriss* 347 US 612 (1954). See also Justice Blackmun in *Regan* v. *Taxation with Representation of Washington* 461 US 540 (1983).

[141] A. Meiklejohn, *Political Freedom* (New York: Harper, 1960) p. 37.

[142] Briffault, 'Lobbying and Campaign Finance: Separate and Together'.

chance to lobby, in the sense that access should not rest on the ability to hire professional lobbyists or spend vast sums on a campaign.

In terms of the range of lobbying activities to be regulated, blocking corrupt transactions will limit the scope for wealth to be used to bypass the normal decision-making procedures and secure a particular outcome. Other controls could block those arrangements that are most problematic, for example where MPs work for or rely on staff from lobbying firms. However, this still permits the use of wealth in other lobbying activities that attempt to access or influence the official. Given that such methods are difficult to distinguish from those communications that are legitimate parts of the political process, rather than imposing limits or blocking all such arrangements, the approach may be to call for greater transparency and for officials to be under a duty to seek out a wider range of views. One difficulty is that for all the administration entailed, registration and disclosure is unlikely to secure equality in the chances to participate and merely provides more information about the activities. It does, however, provide a starting point in revealing who influences decisions and how, and exposes some of the inequalities in influence that arise in that process.

5

Beyond equal votes: election campaigns and political parties

Recent years have seen a succession of scandals and controversies surrounding the funding of political parties and election campaigns. The high-profile controversies have tended to focus on wealthy individuals providing funds to political parties, as in the 'loans for peerages' affair in which a number of individuals nominated for a place in the House of Lords had been found to have donated and loaned money to the Labour Party.[1] As with lobbying, the concern is often that payments to politicians and parties influence decision-makers or secure favours from the politicians. This chapter will argue that party funding raises broader issues about the potential use of wealth to influence the choices voters make at the ballot box. The influence of wealth arises not only in the attempt to secure privileged access or favourable treatment from politicians, but in the use of economic resources to persuade others. The issue is not just one of corruption, but also concerns the equal opportunity to influence an election and participate in political parties.

Party funding and election spending provide a context where controls on the influence of wealth are most likely to be called for, devised and implemented. The central targets for regulation, namely candidates and political parties, are defined and provide a focus for the controls. Such controls apply to specific activities in a limited period of time, an election campaign, rather than regulate the influence of wealth in general. Some controls on election spending have also been a longstanding and accepted feature of politics in the UK. While such factors may suggest the regulation of party funding is less problematic than the regulation of the activities discussed in other chapters, the experience so far points to a range of difficulties. Disagreements arise as to the justification, extent and method of controls on party funding. Political actors themselves have also shown a tendency to look for loopholes and ways to evade the law. No matter how much regulation is imposed, new ways for money to generate influence seem to emerge. This area therefore provides an important case study, providing lessons that will inform the regulation of wealth in politics in other contexts.

---

[1] For background see K. Ewing, *The Cost of Democracy* (Oxford: Hart, 2007) ch. 6.

Background

Concern about the influence of money in elections is nothing new. The legal approach to election finance in the UK can be traced back to the nineteenth century, when corrupt practices, such as bribing voters and treating, were widespread.[2] During that century and as the concern with corruption grew, a number of legal reforms attempted to combat such practices. For example, those constituencies deemed to be most corrupt were gradually disenfranchised.[3] The Corrupt Practices Act of 1854 strengthened the definitions for corruption offences and established election auditors to record the sums spent by each candidate in an election.[4] In 1868, the courts were given the power to decide election petitions.[5] The secret ballot, established by the 1872 Ballot Act, made it harder for bribers to ensure that voters cast their ballot the way they had been paid to, although that did not eliminate the practices of bribery and treating.[6]

Despite these measures, corrupt practices continued. In the 1880 election, candidates' high spending included indirect payments to voters through treating and sham employment arrangements.[7] The concern following that election led to the enactment of the Corrupt and Illegal Practices Act 1883, which imposed tougher penalties for corruption offences and closed some loopholes in the law. For example, the Act prohibited the payment of canvassers, which had previously been used as a mechanism to make payments to voters. Most significantly, the Act imposed a limit on political spending by candidates during an election campaign, a framework that is still followed today, albeit in modified form.[8]

The aim of the spending limits in the 1883 Act was to prevent corrupt offences, such as bribing and treating voters, by limiting the supply of money available from candidates in an election. The Act thereby addressed the problem of corruption by constraining those candidates willing to spend large sums on a growing electorate.[9] This was not the sole aim of the Act; Attorney General Sir Henry James set out a broader justification for election spending limits

[2] 'Treating' refers to a practice where voters are provided with food, drink or entertainment to corruptly influence their votes, see the Representation of the People Act 1983 (RPA), s.114.
[3] For example, the Redistribution Act 1885. See H. J. Hanham, *Elections and Party Management* (Sussex: Harvester Press, 1959) p. 281.
[4] Although such a provision was easily evaded by submitting returns that 'appeared to be reasonable and not mentioning the money spent on illegal activities', see W. Gwyn, *Democracy and the Cost of Politics* (London: The Athlone Press, 1962) p. 84.
[5] The Election Petitions and Corrupt Practices Act of 1868. Petitions had previously been heard by parliamentary committee.
[6] Hanham, *Elections and Party Management*, pp. 274–5.
[7] See C. Seymour, *Electoral Reform in England and Wales* (New Haven: Yale University Press, 1915) pp. 436–8. Eight Royal Commissions were established to investigate the corrupt practices, reporting in 1881, C. O'Leary, *The Elimination of Corrupt Practices in British Elections, 1868–1911* (Oxford: Clarendon, 1962) p. 159.
[8] For the current spending limits on expenditures in support of a candidate see the Representation of the People Act 1983, ss.75–6. Under the same statute, it is an offence to bribe, treat or exert undue influence over voters, ss.113–15.
[9] Seymour, *Electoral Reform in England and Wales*, p. 420.

when introducing the first version of the legislation in Parliament in 1881: 'The mere fact that a candidate is called upon to provide an extravagantly large sum for his election is in itself a great evil. It prevents men of great mental capacity from entering the field. Such men have to yield their places to others who possess the one virtue of wealth, and that alone.'[10] Under that view, the chance to become an MP should not rest on the ability to pay. The logic of this argument extends beyond a concern with corrupt payments and applies whenever electoral activity becomes so expensive that it excludes potential candidates. The justification for the measure was not solely about corruption, but introduced a concern with the fairness of the process and attempted to limit inequalities between candidates.

The controls enacted in 1883 reflect both justifications. The expenditure limit restricted the supply of funds from which corrupt payments could be made. However, the legislation limited all funds used by a candidate, and thereby restricted not just money used for bribery or treating, but also restricted the amounts that could be spent on materials to persuade voters. Its effect was therefore to restrict the non-corrupt as well as the corrupt payments. As a result, the measure was controversial and raised concerns that the limit might outlaw legitimate campaign activity and set the limit on expenditures at too low a level,[11] a concern echoed by critics of current election laws. Despite this, the method of regulation introduced by the 1883 Act created a level of fairness between the candidates in an election.

Parliament did not enact the reforms primarily in response to the concerns about corruption among the general public, or a popular democratic movement. In the early part of the nineteenth century, the public tolerated corrupt practices, which were seen not as a 'crime' but as a 'venial offence' considered in 'the same light as smuggling or poaching'.[12] While public attitudes to corruption changed over the course of the century,[13] the momentum for change came primarily from the politicians themselves, many of whom felt pressured to fund the corrupt payments during an election.[14] It was the candidates standing for election who had to meet the high costs and payments demanded by the corrupt voters. Consequently, the nineteenth-century reforms were not a result of a grassroots democratic movement, but were part of a programme of top-down

[10] Parl. Deb., vol. 257, ser. 3, col. 265, 7 Jan 1881.
[11] Seymour, *Electoral Reform in England and Wales*, pp. 446–7.
[12] *Ibid.*, p. 194. Similarly, Gwynn writes that prior to and in the early stages of the reform era, the electorate 'could not see anything very wrong about selling their votes' and 'corrupt voters continued to look upon their suffrages as means of making a little money or receiving free food and drink'. Attitudes towards those making the payments were also lenient and 'a man was not considered immoral for making a travesty of the electoral process by buying his way in to the House of Commons'. Gwyn, *Democracy and the Cost of Politics*, pp. 68 and 72.
[13] By the 1880s, bribery, 'like drunkenness, was coming to be looked on as a social evil'. O'Leary, *The Elimination of Corrupt Practices*, p. 178.
[14] See Gwyn, *Democracy and the Cost of Politics*, pp. 73–6, on the pressures faced by candidates to pay for corrupt practices.

reforms governing political life.[15] Given that the reforms were a product of the political classes, it is unsurprising that the reform aimed to create some level of fairness between those members of the political class that were the principal participants in the process, the candidates themselves.

Following the enactment of the 1883 legislation, the number of petitions alleging corruption declined. It is hard to pinpoint a precise cause for this decline, and a number of reasons can be advanced: the difficulties in paying an increasingly large electorate; the tougher sanctions; and the more comprehensive controls in the 1883 Act.[16] The decline in corruption can also be attributed to a change in public opinion and moral attitudes that developed as democratic participation increased.[17] As part of that trend, the 1883 Act played a role in shaping public attitudes towards corruption. Whatever the cause of these developments, the 1883 Act is generally viewed as an initial success in changing the conditions for election campaigns and controlling the amounts spent by candidates in an election.[18]

As the techniques of campaigning transformed in the twentieth century, the candidate spending limits imposed in 1883 became less effective in controlling the cost of elections. The Act limited spending by candidates, and the controls were later extended to cover spending by third parties in support of a candidate.[19] The controls did not, however, restrict money spent in support of political parties that came to characterise election campaigns in the twentieth century. The limits of the controls were confirmed in the *Tronoh Mines* decision in 1952, which concerned a newspaper advertisement urging the electorate to oppose the Labour Party and save 'the country from being reduced, through the policies of the Socialist government, to a bankrupt "Welfare State" '.[20] When the company placing the advert was prosecuted for breaking the election spending controls, McNair J, in the Central Criminal Court, found that the advertisement fell outside the election spending limits, as those controls applied to expenditures made in support of 'a particular candidate in a particular constituency', as opposed to expenditures supporting or opposing a political party 'generally in all constituencies'. This reading of the controls enabled political parties and

---

[15] For an account of this trend, see D. Marquand, *Britain Since 1918: the Strange Career of British Democracy* (London: Weidenfeld & Nicolson, 2008) pp. 27–37. The 'general feeling' among the public that something had to be done after the 1880 election helped to enable the enactment of the stricter legislation in 1883, see Hanham, *Elections and Party Management*, p. 273.

[16] See Gwyn, *Democracy and the Cost of Politics*, pp. 90–2; Seymour, *Electoral Reform*, p. 449.

[17] Gwyn, *Democracy and the Cost of Politics*, p. 92.

[18] See Seymour, *Electoral Reform*, pp. 448 and 454.

[19] The limit was first introduced in the Representation of the People Act 1918, s.34, and can now be found in the RPA 1983, s.75.

[20] *R* v. *Tronoh Mines Ltd.* [1952] 1 All ER 697. The decision concerned third party spending which was then governed by the Representation of The People Act 1949, s 63 (1). The approach was confirmed in *DPP* v. *Luft* [1977] AC 962 in which the House of Lords held that the controls applied to expenditures to prevent, as well as to promote, the election of a particular candidate or candidates.

other groups to spend freely on general party political communications that did not promote or oppose a particular candidate. Consequently, the controls were ineffective in limiting most of the campaign spending taking place during a general election. Election spending at the national level could therefore increase and the controls first imposed in the Victorian era provided little constraint.[21] By the late 1990s the high spending was causing increasing concern. In the 1997 general election the Conservative Party spent an estimated £28 million and the Labour Party £26.8 million nationally.[22] Shortly after that election, the newly elected Labour government asked the Committee on Standards in Public Life chaired by Lord Neill to consider the funding of political parties.

When the Committee published its report (the Neill Report), it concluded that the legal framework had become outdated[23] and recommended that the controls should be extended to spending by and in support of a political party in an election. While there was talk of corruption, this was not simply an old problem resurfacing; the nature of the problem had changed since 1883. Parties now spent money on billboard advertisements and communications to voters, rather than on vote buying or treating. Candidates no longer had to be personally wealthy to bankroll their campaigns as those costs were met by the political party, but the party now had to attract funds from donors. Instead of voters being corrupted by bribes from politicians, the concern was that politicians themselves would be influenced by the donations to the political party. These fears were highlighted shortly after the Labour government was elected and prior to the Neill Report, when newspapers revealed that Formula One chief Bernie Ecclestone had donated £1million to the Labour Party and the government had subsequently proposed to exempt motor racing from a planned ban on tobacco advertising at sporting events.[24] The controversy led to speculation that, by making the large donation, Ecclestone had gained access to the government and influenced a change in government policy.

Another justification advanced by the Neill Report for extending the controls had a closer link with the rationale for the 1883 Act. Just as the 1883 Act showed a concern for fairness between candidates, the Neill Report noted the need for fairness between political parties. The high spending on national campaigns gave the impression that a party needed a large reserve of funds to seriously compete in an election, echoing the concern voiced by politicians

---

[21] Professor Pinto-Duschinsky argues that overall party expenditures have remained constant in the long term, when party spending at both the local and national level are taken into account. However, Professor Pinto-Duschinsky accepts that 'spending by constituency parties fell while the expenditures of central party organisations increased', a shift which has been permitted by the regulatory framework. See M. Pinto-Duschinsky, *Paying for the Party* (London: Policy Exchange, 2008) p. 6 and ch. 6.

[22] The Fifth Report of the Committee on Standards in Public Life, *The Funding of Political Parties in the United Kingdom* Cm.4057-I (1998) ('the Neill Report'), at Table 3.10, p. 43.

[23] *Ibid.*, at [10.16–10.17].

[24] See D. Osler, *Labour Party Plc* (Edinburgh: Mainstream Publishing, 2002) ch. 5; A. Rawnsley, *Servants of the People* (London: Hamish Hamilton, 2000) ch. 6.

over a century before that it was unfair to require candidates to be wealthy to stand for Parliament. The point was that political parties should not have an advantage simply because they have money or can attract the wealthy donors.[25] While the old corrupt practices had stopped, new methods of campaigning meant the concern with wealth in elections remained. To address this, the Neill Report made a number of recommendations, most of which were enacted in the Political Parties Elections and Referendums Act 2000 (PPERA). While this legislation provided the most significant overhaul of the election funding rules since 1883, the concerns about money in elections remain and since the enactment of the PPERA, a number of reports and committees have called for further reform.

Spending limits

The Political Parties, Elections and Referendums Act (PPERA) imposes a cap on spending in support of a political party during an election campaign. The cap is proportionate to the number of seats contested by that party in the election.[26] Limits are also imposed on third-party election spending, to prevent the evasion of the limits imposed on political parties through the electoral activities of independent groups or individuals.[27] As a result of the legislation, election spending is now governed by a complex two-tier system of regulation: the first tier is the longstanding candidate spending limits which remain in place; the second is the political party spending limits, imposed by the PPERA. By creating a second tier of limits, the PPERA seeks to create a level of fairness between the competing political parties. This goal shows how the rationale underlying the Victorian era reforms has had an enduring legacy, as, like the 1883 Act, the election spending controls in PPERA focus on fairness between the principal political actors contesting the election.

Since the enactment of the PPERA, a number of methods to avoid the spending limits have been used. One such method exploited the differing definitions of the campaign period under the two tiers of regulation that distinguish

---

[25] Neill Report, above n. 22, at [2.17]. However, some members of the Committee did not accept this justification for the restrictions, see [10.28].

[26] See Political Parties Elections and Referendums Act 2000 (PPERA), Schedule 9 Part II. The amount will be varied periodically. In the 2005 general election, the spending limit for the major political parties was £18.8 million; see Ministry of Justice, *Party Finance and Expenditure in the United Kingdom* (2008) Cm 7329 at [3.11]. Such sums pale into insignificance when compared to the $730 million spent by Barack Obama for the 2008 US presidential election and the $333 million spent by John McCain, according to the figures from the Center for Responsive Politics, www.opensecrets.org/pres08 (accessed 11 February 2009).

[27] See PPERA Part VI. Under the current provisions, if a third party wishes to spend more than £10,000 in England or more than £5,000 in Scotland, Wales or Northern Ireland in support of a political party during an election campaign, it must register as a 'recognised' third party, see s.94(5). Under Schedule 10 of the Act, a recognised third party spending in a general election is limited to £793,000 in relation to England, £108,000 in relation to Scotland, £60,000 in Wales and £27,000 in Northern Ireland.

between spending in favour of a party and spending to promote a candidate. The controls on expenditure by the party, but not the candidate, under the 2000 Act apply twelve months prior to a general election.[28] By contrast, the candidate spending limits are in place for a shorter period of time, normally beginning with the dissolution of Parliament (just weeks before the election).[29] As a result, the two-tier spending limits provided an incentive to make expenditures in support of a candidate in the twelve months before an election, but prior to the dissolution of Parliament. Such spending fell outside the party spending controls but were incurred before the candidate spending controls were in force. In the 2005 general election this strategy was most notably pursued by Lord Ashcroft, who donated money to the Conservative Party through his company, Bearwood Corporate Services, to be spent in key marginal constituencies in support of the candidates. The spending was not covered by either the party or the candidate spending limits. While the candidate limits still apply, an amendment enacted in 2009 attempts to address this problem by imposing an additional limit on spending in support of a candidate in the months prior to the dissolution of Parliament, which can apply to expenditures before the person has officially become a candidate.[30]

Even if that amendment succeeds in closing the loophole, a similar tendency to spend outside the controls is likely to continue. Controls on election spending are manageable because the electoral setting gives some definition of the targets for regulation; the controls focus on specific activities by political actors in a fixed timeframe. However, this focus brings costs in terms of the effectiveness of the regulation. For example, looking at the regulated activity, the spending limits apply only to election expenditure, which excludes costs such as staff wages and day-to-day administrative expenses.[31] Such spending can, however, still contribute to the party's election effort, create a demand for large donations and allow disparities between political parties to continue. In relation to the fixed timeframe, by imposing limits for a defined campaign period the political party has an incentive to spend its resources before the controls are in place, during the 'long campaign'. Such spending can be very effective given that preferences are often formed in the longer period in the years prior to an election, rather than in the shorter formal election campaign that is subject to regulation. If party spending controls apply only to electoral activities, then parties will spend additional

[28] PPERA, Schedule 9 s.3(7).   [29] RPA, s.118A.
[30] Under the amendment, once the life of the Parliament has run for fifty-five months, a £25,000 cap on candidate expenditures is applied in the period prior to the dissolution of Parliament. However, such controls would not apply to early expenditures when Parliament is dissolved less than fifty-five months into its life. RPA 1983, s76ZA, inserted by the Political Parties and Elections Act 2009.
[31] The Constitutional Affairs Committee found that the vast majority of party expenditures over a five year period were on routine rather than campaign activities; see House of Commons Constitutional Affairs Committee, Party Funding (2006 HC 163) at [40–1].

funds on costs that are defined as non-electoral, but which can nevertheless help their election efforts.

A blurring between electoral and non-electoral expenditures is difficult to eradicate, and any limit on the scope of election spending controls presents the potential for a loophole to emerge. The desire to close off the channels for evasion will potentially result in an ever-expanding definition of electoral activities to broaden the scope of the controls. Such a response can be seen in recent proposals to reduce the scope for evasion through a limit on all party spending over the life of Parliament, a maximum of five years.[32] This proposal would extend the controls in two ways: it would broaden the range of activities covered by the spending limits, and extend the period of time in which those limits are in place. The appeal of such a proposal will depend on how far the activities of a political party are seen solely as electioneering.[33] One objection is that political parties spend money on activities other than election campaigning, such as conducting research or providing a forum for political debate. As such non-electoral activities can be carried out by think-tanks and pressure groups without any spending limit, the concern is that extending the controls on parties could create unfairness relative to these other groups. The think-tank could spend as much as it likes on a report criticising a particular policy, but, under proposals for an extended control, a party could spend only a limited amount on a reply to that report.[34] A further effect of such a restriction is that it may in turn encourage the channelling of political funds to independent organisations and pressure groups, which are subject to the more limited third-party regulations on election spending. Such an imbalance could enhance the relative influence of those political actors, such as pressure groups, whose activities fall outside the regulations.

To prevent the channelling of political funds to third parties, an extension of third-party spending limits could accompany any extension of those limits applicable to political parties. The most far-reaching way to prevent such evasion would be to impose an overall limit on the money spent on political, not just electoral, expression by think-tanks and pressure groups each year. Such a measure would clearly be too far-reaching and likely to fall foul of freedom of expression under Article 10. It would also be impossible to monitor and enforce such limits on all actors, and would impose substantial burdens on political

---

[32] *Ibid.*, at [89].

[33] In evidence to a parliamentary committee Jack Straw MP stated: 'The notion that there are fallow periods for political parties when they are not using their money for electioneering is, I think, incorrect. The truth is that almost all parties' active spending is for election purposes. Obviously, they have to have an infrastructure, but that is also for election purposes' (Constitutional Affairs Committee, *Party Funding*, vol. II at Ev. 38).

[34] Think-tanks that are registered charities cannot engage in party political activity. However, reports produced on areas of policy may touch on areas that are of interest to the political party, on which the party may wish to comment. Furthermore, despite the non-partisan requirements for charities, some think-tanks are seen to have a close relationship with a political party, for example acting as a testing ground for policy ideas.

activity. The government has already made clear that even a modest extension in the time period covered by third-party election spending would be going too far.[35] The influence of wealth outside the context of an election can be problematic, but calls for a different regulatory response. The methods considered in the other chapters provide ways of limiting wealth as a source of influence outside the electoral context. As an election requires separate controls to reflect the decision-making stage of the electoral process,[36] a line has to be drawn to define the electoral sphere. While expanding the definition of electoral spending has the potential to reduce evasion, there will come a point in which the election spending controls are too intrusive. Whichever way the line is drawn, there is a risk that channels for evasion by spending outside the legal definition of an election will emerge.

The final point on the spending limits is the compatibility with freedom of expression and association.[37] In the United States, the courts have struck down attempts to cap election spending on the grounds that such controls limit the quantity of expression. While Article 10 of the European Convention permits spending limits, such a restriction may violate freedom of expression if it is set too low. In *Bowman*, a limit of £5 on third-party expenditures in support of candidates was successfully challenged by an anti-abortion campaigner in the European Court of Human Rights.[38] Consequently, a restriction on campaign spending needs to be fixed at a level which permits a sufficient amount of communication. However, *Bowman* looked at a particularly severe limit, but did not indicate what level of spending is necessary to provide an adequate amount of expression. Given that the current limits on political parties are at a much higher level than those in *Bowman*, some would say too high, a strong argument can be made that the regulations are consistent with Article 10.[39] The limits imposed on third-party expenditures in support of a candidate, which were the subject of the challenge in *Bowman*, have been raised to £500 in a general election and £50 in a local government election. While the third-party expenditures in support of a candidate are set at a low level, so far no legal challenge has been made. While the Article 10 jurisprudence seems to prohibit only the most severe restrictions, care has to be taken when fixing or adjusting the spending limits to ensure a sufficient quantity of expression.

[35] Ministry of Justice, *Party Finance*, Cm 7329 (2008) at [3.69].
[36] The view that special controls on information are required during an election campaign can also be seen in the stricter rules imposed on broadcasters when covering politics once Parliament has been dissolved, for example prohibiting the broadcast of opinion poll results on the day of the election; see Ofcom, *The Ofcom Broadcasting Code* (2009) section 6. In another example, s.106 of the RPA 1983 makes it a criminal offence to publish 'any false statement of fact in relation to the candidate's personal character or conduct', thereby imposing a restriction separate from defamation laws in the context of an election.
[37] See Chapters 2 and 3.   [38] *Bowman* v. *UK* (1998) 26 EHRR 1.
[39] For discussion, see J. Marriott, 'Alarmist or Relaxed? Election Expenditure Limits and Free Speech' [2005] *Public Law* 764, pp. 779–83.

While US free-speech doctrine is most hostile to limits on campaign spending, the US courts have upheld legal caps on donations to parties and candidates. By contrast, UK laws to date take a relatively light touch when it comes to donations to political parties. Individuals and institutions can donate as much they like to a political party. The regulatory system in the UK is the reverse of that in the United States: the US limits donations but allows unlimited spending; whereas the UK limits spending but does not restrict donations. The UK system has thereby allowed a number of high-profile large individual donations: Lord Sainsbury has made several donations of £2 million or more to the Labour Party;[40] Lakshmi Mittal has made two donations of £2 million to the Labour Party;[41] in 2007 Lord Laidlaw donated £2.9 million to the Conservative Party;[42] in 2001 Sir Paul Getty gave £5 million to the Conservative Party in a single donation;[43] Lord Ashcroft's company Bearwood Corporate Services has made a series of cash and non-cash donations of over £5 million to the Conservative Party.[44] While calls for a cap on donations have been made on several occasions, there has previously been a reluctance to accept such a measure. The Neill Committee rejected calls for a cap with an appeal to freedom: that 'individuals should have the freedom to contribute to political parties, and the parties should be free to compete for donations'.[45] In 2004, the Electoral Commission also rejected a cap on donations, on the more pragmatic ground that large donations were necessary to ensure that parties are well funded.[46] However, the tide seems to be turning with more recent reports on party funding such as the Sir Hayden Phillips Review and the House of Commons Constitutional Affairs Committee supporting a donation limit in principle. The following sections will look at the case for, and methods of, regulating donations.

Political donations

Donations and political favours

The most common concern with political donations in the UK is the perception that influence is being bought. By imposing a limit on political spending, the PPERA hoped to cap the demand for money and make it less likely for parties to develop 'an unhealthy reliance on a handful of wealthy donors'.[47] By limiting

---

[40] According to the Electoral Commission register, such sums were accepted on: 31 July 2008; 10 September 2007; 10 March 2005; 1 March 2003; 13 January 2002.
[41] According to the Electoral Commission register, such sums were accepted on: 13 July 2005; 22 January 2007.
[42] According to the Electoral Commission register, the donation was accepted on 27 November 2007.
[43] According to the Electoral Commission register, accepted on: 11 June 2001.
[44] Data from the Electoral Commission shows £1.6 million in cash donations and £3.4 million in non-cash donations were given to the Conservative Party between February 2003 and September 2009.
[45] Neill Report, above n. 22, at [6.7].
[46] The Electoral Commission, *The Funding of Political Parties: Report and Recommendations* (2004).
[47] Hansard, HC, vol. 342, col. 36 (10 January 2000).

the amount needed to contest an election, the hope was for parties to raise sufficient funds without depending on very wealthy donors, making politicians less vulnerable to corrupt practices. The controls do not completely limit the demand for funds as parties still need money for non-electoral activities that are not capped by the statute. However, even if the controls successfully limit the demand for money, the spending limit can arguably increase the relative influence of the wealthy donor. For example, if a party can only spend £15 million on its campaign, then three wealthy donors providing £5 million each could bankroll the full campaign cost. Where election costs are limited, the £5 million donation covers a higher proportion of the overall campaign expenditure than under a system where the party is free to spend more. While the party need not rely on the wealthy donor and can turn elsewhere for financial support, it remains easier for fundraisers to turn to regular large donors to write a cheque than engage a much broader base of smaller donors.[48]

The other way the PPERA deals with concerns about corruption is through a range of transparency requirements. Donations of over £7,500 to the party HQ and donations over £1,500 to a constituency party have to be disclosed to the Electoral Commission, and are then published.[49] While the prospect of publicity will deter some potential donors, it has not stopped the controversies surrounding large donations.

The transparency requirements have also been evaded through a number of gaps and loopholes. Most notably, the loans for peerages affair highlighted a loophole in which a number of wealthy individuals loaned money to political parties. Lending the funds on supposedly commercial terms provided a way to avoid the disclosure requirements, as such commercial arrangements did not count as donations. Another method of evasion that emerged was through the use of intermediary organisations, which are funded by wealthy donors, to give money to political parties. If the intermediary organisation acts as an agent of the wealthy individual, for example where a donor gives money to the organisation on the understanding that a specified sum will go to a political party, then the original source of the funds must be disclosed to the Electoral Commission.[50] However, if an individual donates money to the general funds of an organisation, and the organisation then donates money to a political party, then only the name of the organisation has to be disclosed to the Electoral Commission. The boundary between an organisation acting for itself or as an agent provides a potential loophole. For example, controversy surrounded donations made to the Conservative Party by the Midlands Industrial

---

[48] See Lord Levy, a Labour Party fundraiser, in Constitutional Affairs Committee, *Party Funding: Oral Evidence* (2007 HC 988-i): 'Sometimes it is easier for a person to write out a cheque for £100,000 than for someone to pay a subscription or a membership due of, perhaps, £25[…] the cost element against bringing in large gifts is very, very small – it is minimal in actual fact – whereas the cost element in bringing in grass roots donations is very substantial.'

[49] These requirements are not limited to the election period, although donations must be reported more frequently during the election campaign; see PPERA ss.62–3.

[50] PPERA, s.54.

Council, an organisation backed by a number of wealthy donors whose identity and financial support did not have to be disclosed.[51] Through such an arrangement, the sources that fund the intermediary organisation, and ultimately the party, were not transparent. To combat these concerns, a number of loopholes have been closed. The law was amended in 2006 to require commercial loans to be disclosed.[52] An amendment to the PPERA made in 2009 will require people or organisations making contributions above £7,500 to make a declaration stating whether money has been provided by any other person or body in connection with the donation.[53] While such amendments attempt to address the specific loopholes, more broadly these episodes show the tendency for political actors to exploit grey areas in a way that goes against the spirit, if not the letter, of the law.

The transparency requirements aim to provide details about the funding of political parties, which allows the public to make a judgement on the propriety of a donation.[54] The rules facilitate a channel of political accountability. As with lobbying, the fact that a politician disclosed a donation does not provide a defence to an alleged wrongdoing or provide any proof of the acceptability of a financial arrangement. Instead, disclosure opens the discussion of the propriety of the funding arrangement. While transparency requirements are an important step in providing information about the sources of funding, it does not provide any mechanism to resolve questions about the ethics of a donation. Such resolution will come from the controls on the politician, such as the law of corruption or the ministerial codes.[55] Information revealed under the transparency requirements can highlight a possible breach of such rules, and in some cases trigger an investigation. However, there remain difficulties in establishing a link between a political donation and a specific favour, so speculation and suspicion about the influence of a donation can continue, even where an official investigation makes no finding of a wrongdoing.[56] An alternative way to deal with corruption is to go beyond controls on the official and to cap donations at a level so low that the sum given to the party is unlikely to secure any political favours. This would not, however, stop corrupt payments being made through

---

[51] According to data from the Electoral Commission, the Midlands Industrial Council donated over £1.5 million to the Conservative Party between April 2003 and November 2007, and made further donations to a regulated donor, the Constituency Campaigning Services Board. Those providing financial support to the Midlands Industrial Council included Conservative Party donors Anthony Bamford and Robert Edmiston. The Electoral Commission was reported to have found such donations did not violate the transparency rules, *Guardian*, 6 October 2008.

[52] See PPERA Part IVA, inserted by the Electoral Administration Act 2006.

[53] PPERA, s.54A, inserted by the Political Parties and Elections Bill 2009. To combat the same problem, the 2009 amendment also provides that unincorporated associations that donate over £25,000 to a party in a year have to disclose any gifts it receives of over £7,500; see PPERA, s.140A.

[54] For example Dominic Grieve MP in the Standing Committee debates on the PPERA, opposed a cap on donations because 'if there is transparency the public – the electorate – make the judgement', Official Report of Standing Committee G, *Political Parties, Elections and Referendums Bill*, col. 130, 27 January 2000.

[55] See Chapter 4. [56] See pp. 80–7.

other channels, so transparency requirements and controls on the decision-maker remain the primary safeguard against corruption. A cap on donations could supplement these safeguards to address the specific concerns that donations are an easy way to influence an official.

One difficulty with this approach is that it restricts not only the corrupt donations, but also those merely intended to express support for a particular candidate. However, the argument in favour of a cap on donations is that whenever a donation is made above a certain level, there will be a suspicion that it is aiming to secure influence. Such influence can potentially arise, even where the donor's purpose is merely to express support. For example, where an individual, known to have strong views about an area of government policy, makes a donation of several million pounds to show his support for a political party, that party may feel under pressure to adopt a policy that will ensure the donor's continued support. The same pressure applies whenever something affecting the large donor's interests is considered by the government. Consequently, the concern is that the large donation gives rise to a conflict of interest in which the donation could be one of several factors that influence the decision-maker.[57] Controls on the politician can deal with some conflicts of interest, for example requiring a minister not to make a decision where she has a personal interest. The difficulty with political donations is that the whole party in office will have an interest, so other potential decision-makers will have a similar conflict of interest. A cap on donations helps to avoid this conflict of interest.

Donations and political equality

As with lobbying, the prevention of corruption is just one justification for regulating donations. Aside from this concern, political donations raise questions about the distribution of political resources and the opportunities to exert influence. The level of funding secured by each political party will determine which parties will command attention and have the capacity to compete in an election. The ideal distribution of funds should therefore reflect a number of competing goals, in particular ensuring that the distribution of funds is responsive to the citizens' choices; that there is diversity of choice at the ballot box; and the system is sufficiently competitive to ensure that the various policy proposals are rigorously debated.

The limits on party spending during an election do not address all these goals and merely aim to secure a level of fairness between political parties and candidates by preventing one party or candidate outspending another by unlimited amounts. Within the limits there is still considerable disparity in resources between the parties. However, a fair system does not require that every political party or candidate have equal resources to contest an election.[58] The ability of larger political

---

[57] See D. Lowenstein, 'The Root of All Evil is Deeply Rooted' (1989) 18 Hofstra L. Rev. 301 at 322–9.
[58] Neill Report, above n. 22, at [2.20].

parties, whether Labour, Conservatives or Liberal Democrats, to outspend less well-known rivals arguably reflects the level of support for those parties, and ensures that elections are focused on the leading options and are competitive. The goal is not for each party to have equal resources, but to ensure that any differences in resources are fair and justified.

Leaving political donations largely unregulated does not guarantee that the inequalities between parties will be fair. Some parties that are popular and offer a new perspective on political issues may be relatively under-funded, whereas another party may be able to spend more because it receives a small number of very large donations. Yet large donations are not essential. Parties do not need wealthy patrons to compete, and in an unregulated system a party can still secure sufficient funding through a large number of small donations.[59] However, the possibility for any party to compete in an election simply because it has a wealthy supporter is the problem. Under this view, it is unfair for a well-supported party with a broad base of donors to find itself on an even footing, in terms of resources, with a party that has far fewer, but much wealthier, supporters. Consequently, the question about fairness between parties is not just a matter of limiting the spending differences, but rests on the way that those parties came to acquire their funds. For a political party to compete in an election and gain attention simply because it has a smaller number of wealthier patrons, undermines the equal status of those individuals supporting an opposing party, but who cannot donate as much. In a system where large donations are permitted, the support of the latter group of individuals counts for less. By framing the issue in this way, a connection is made between fairness among parties and political equality among individuals.

A limit on political donations could help to address such problems. The aim of such a limit would be to remove the distribution of political funds from the hands of the very wealthy and give greater say to a broader range of citizens, thereby making the distribution of resources responsive to citizens. Under this view, the goal of the regulation is not just to secure fairness between parties and candidates, but between individual citizens. A donation is then seen as a method of expressing support for a political party, analogous to other methods of participation, such as volunteering for a campaign or voting. A view of donating as an act of citizenship is reflected in the requirement that donors have a stake in UK politics, thereby barring foreign nationals from donating to a political party, and allowing only those companies or organisations based in the UK to donate.[60]

Along these lines, if political resources are distributed evenly, a policy pledge made by a politician in the hope of attracting a greater number of donations is similar to a pledge aiming to win votes or to please a particular group of voters.

[59] Such a strategy has been seen in Barack Obama's presidential campaign in which large sums were raised through small donations made via the Internet; for discussion see Chapter 8.
[60] Neill Report, above n. 22, at [5.16]: 'those who live, work and carry on business in the United Kingdom should be the persons exclusively entitled to support financially the operation of the political process here'.

There are still objections to the politician's attempt to secure donations. For example, that it encourages the politician to pander to popular views rather than make decisions on principle, or that it will distract the politician from the discussion of substantive issues. Such objections depend on whether one thinks such responsiveness is a desirable part of the democratic process and goes beyond the concern with political finance. Whatever the side effects, a distribution of political funds that responds to citizens as equals is preferable to one that responds to a small number of wealthy individuals.

The account given above draws an analogy between donating to a party and casting a vote. While the 'one person, one vote' standard of citizen equality does not provide a template for political equality in relation to all political activities, it has stronger appeal as a model of distribution for party funding. First, political donations have a close link with the electoral process. By making donations, individuals are casting a type of 'vote' that helps to set the electoral agenda and decide which parties or candidates the voters can choose from in the election. The right to vote provides the most basic expression of political equality, but can be undermined if the competition between candidates and parties prior to the vote is unfair. Limiting the capacity of citizens to outspend those with less wealth helps to preserve the integrity of the electoral process.

Second, a donation to a political party is distinct from other types of electoral expression as it does not attempt to persuade people directly, but gives a party the resources to persuade others. A donation registers a decision in a distinct institutional setting as to which parties will have the resources to campaign. This distinction is not watertight and a donation can be used to directly express the donor's support for a political party, which may in turn persuade others who value the donor's views. However, given the limited amount of information conveyed by a donation, such statements of support can still be expressed within the confines of a donation limit.[61] A person does not need to give tens of thousands of pounds to register their support for a party. While a cap may prevent wealthy individuals showing the full intensity of support through a very large donation, the donor can express that intensity through other political activities where the opportunities to participate are more evenly distributed.

Finally, it is easier to imagine how an analogy with voting and donating would work in practice. One-person-one-vote could provide a template for political funding in which each individual has equal sums to donate to a political party. Donations provide a measurable unit that can be given to a specific entity against which the equal chance to influence can be defined.

Such an analogy between voting and donating is only approximate. Donating has its own qualities, in that it allows people to express support outside the context of an election, show strength of feeling, and allow participation without

<hr>

[61] More problematic are instances where a third party engages in a direct form of persuasion, but this is coordinated with the party and counts as a donation in kind. Here the third party does engage in persuasion so it has greater similarities with other types of expression. However, to protect such expression, such communication could be made as a third-party campaign.

joining a particular political association.[62] While donating can be a solitary activity, it can also be exercised by institutions and associations, such as trade unions, companies and pressure groups. Attempting to distribute political funds like votes would make the system responsive to citizens, but ignores other goals of the system including diversity and competition among the parties. Yet despite these differences, a broad analogy between donating money and voting provides a starting point. A cap on donations can provide a step towards such a model, not by giving people equal sums to donate, but by limiting the disparities in the amount that any person can give to a political party.

Setting a limit

Whether a cap on donations would serve citizen equality depends on the level at which the limit is fixed. Under most proposals, substantial inequalities will persist within the donation limit. Even if the cap on donations were limited to £1,000 per year, a figure much lower than in any of the recent proposals, the maximum contribution would be beyond the reach of most individuals. Such a limit would not guarantee each person equal say in deciding which parties should be well resourced. If a donation limit aims to make political parties responsive to citizens as equals, the cap on donations would have to be fixed at a very low level. The most recent proposals in the UK have been to limit donations to £50,000 a year.[63] Under such a limit, a single donation may be less likely to influence a decision-maker than a donation of £5 million. However, £50,000 is still a substantial sum and could be seen to put some pressure on elected officials. Consequently, such a high limit would not address concerns with corruption, let alone equality.

A cap of £50,000 would change political fundraising, but whether the effects are an improvement is open to question. While this measure would restrict the very large donations, it raises difficulties of its own. For example, imagine a political party requires £15 million to contest a general election and that, for the sake of ease, each party wishes to get these funds from the smallest possible range of large donors. Under the present system, a political party could secure those funds through fifteen wealthy supporters that can give £1 million each or even through a single donation from one person of £15 million. By contrast if a donation cap is set at £50,000, then a party will need to attract at least 300 supporters that can each give the maximum amount to fund the campaign. The latter situation may be preferable in so far as it removes such influence from the super-rich. A cap of £50,000 helps to ensure that super-rich donors cannot buy their way into becoming a party grandee.

The influence of wealth will still be felt with a £50,000 limit, but less visibly. To get the maximum funds, the party will seek to appeal to a broad range of

---

[62] D. Strauss, 'Corruption, Equality and Campaign Finance Reform' (1994) 94 Colum. L. Rev. 1369 at 1373–5.

[63] Constitutional Affairs Committee, above n. 31, at [99].

people with £50,000 to spare. Rather than appeal to the specific wishes of a super-rich individual, the party will need to appeal to some common denominator among a sufficient number of wealthy individuals. The party will have an incentive to make policies that appeal to, or at least do not alienate, people with a high enough income to make the maximum donation. Such a strategy is not essential, as the party could seek a larger number of small donations. However, the framework would provide an incentive for parties to cultivate a wider range of high earners. The parties thereby become more responsive, but still only to a very narrow section of society.[64]

It is sometimes thought that if there is a cap on donations, then a limit on election spending by parties will no longer be needed.[65] Under this view, differences in resources between parties will be roughly dependent on levels of support. However, the concerns discussed above show why it is important to keep a cap on campaign spending by parties and candidates. Even with a cap on donations, inequalities persist and the cap on election spending at least limits the advantage that can be gained by attracting a smaller number donating the maximum amount. A cap on spending also allows the system to remain competitive by preventing a single party getting so far ahead in fundraising that its campaign effort will dwarf other parties' campaigns. Spending limits reduce the incentive for loopholes in the donation limit. To cap donations while having an unlimited demand for money will provide a strong incentive for a party to look for ways around the regulations, so that it can raise the maximum amount possible. Consequently, the cap on spending would complement a regime of limited donations.

A donation limit, however, raises the problems of loopholes. For example, it may encourage the channelling of money to organisations other than political parties. While a donation limit could be extended to money given to registered third parties that wish to make substantial electoral expenditures, such a limit could not be extended more generally to groups engaging in non-electoral political expression. Aside from concerns about freedom of expression, such a measure would be burdensome on such groups and difficult to monitor. As a result of these difficulties, a cap on donations may lead to political funds flowing into non-electoral political expression. The experience with the spending limits and transparency requirements suggest that further regulation will be met with avoidance strategies.

State funding

A strict limit on donations will restrict the flow of funds to political parties and potentially reduce resources to a level that cannot support the existing activities

---

[64] The point applies to any high donation limit, and not just one of £50,000. For example, with a limit of £25,000 or £10,000, the maximum would be out of reach for most people. While all parties would be free to adapt to the regulatory, the objection is that through such a strategy the parties would be more responsive to those on higher incomes.

[65] See for example, R. Hasen, 'Justice Souter: Campaign Finance Law's Emerging Egalitarian' (2008) 1 Alb. Gov't L. Rev. 169 at 189–90.

of the parties. In 2008, the Ministry of Justice estimated that a donation cap set at £50,000 'would produce a shortfall of £5–6m for each of the two largest parties compared with the amount they would be expected to receive if there were no limits on the amounts they could raise'.[66] The consequence is not inevitable and the parties would change fundraising strategies to compensate for the loss of other sources of funds. Such a change in behaviour is one of the main arguments for a donation limit. If the parties do struggle to find alternative sources, a legally imposed cut in the supply of funds would be likely to prompt demands for greater state support for political parties. However, a case for state support does not automatically follow from a donation limit, except in so far as the regulation would increase costs of compliance and administration. The basis for a donation limit is to prevent parties gaining funds in a way that most blatantly undermines political equality. If the reliance on large donations is unfair, parties cannot demand state funds to compensate for the loss of that unfair advantage.

Instead, the argument for increasing state funds must be based on a view that political parties perform a public function, such as informing the public and providing a vehicle for participation. In its report on party funding, the Sir Hayden Phillips Review expressed such a view: 'Healthy parties are, in themselves good for democracy. It is in our interest that they prepare robustly researched policies, that they consult widely, and that they train people in the skills needed to be effective in public office.'[67] The argument for state funds is that the democratic functions performed by political parties make them worthy of financial support, even if the private sources cannot fund a sufficient level of activity.

This is already recognised in the different types of state funds that political parties in the UK receive. Opposition parties in Parliament receive funds to support their work in scrutinising the government.[68] The Electoral Commission can award policy development grants from an annual fund of £2 million to political parties for research and development of policies for the election manifesto.[69] Under the current scheme, each eligible party receives an equal share of the first £1 million of the available funds. The second £1 million is then divided between the parties at variable rates, so parties receive different sized grants depending on whether they have representatives in England, Scotland, Wales or Northern Ireland. In addition to such grants, parties also receive subsidies in-kind. Parties contesting at least one-sixth of the seats up for election are eligible for free time on the broadcast media, and candidates in parliamentary elections are entitled to send an election address to voters in the mail free of charge.[70] There are other ways that state funds go to political parties without a direct subsidy. For example, councillors and MPs may dedicate a percentage of their salary to the local political

---

[66] Ministry of Justice, *Party Finance*, Cm 7329 (2008) at [4.21].

[67] The Review of the Funding of Political Parties, *Strengthening Democracy: Fair and Sustainable Funding of Political Parties* (March 2007), at p. 17 ('Sir Hayden Phillips Review').

[68] Known as 'Short Money' in the House of Commons and 'Cranborne Money' in the House of Lords.

[69] PPERA, s.12.   [70] RPA 1983, s.91.

party, which may be seen as a way of channelling state funds to a party. These examples show that political parties receive a range of subsidies that are distributed on different criteria. The question is whether parties require additional support and how any extra funds should be distributed.

There are a number of arguments that state funding could work to undermine the democratic functions performed by the parties. While state funds may relieve parties from the pressure of fundraising, it could also provide less incentive to engage with citizens. This latter concern emphasises the voluntarist tradition in the UK and was a reason for refusing a major extension of state funds when enacting the PPERA in 2000. As the then Home Secretary, Jack Straw, explained: 'The health of democracy is better served if parties are principally reliant on their own efforts to secure adequate funding. Such an approach compels parties to engage with their members and supporters.'[71] To some extent, this objection can be met by distributing funds in a way that encourages parties to interact with citizens, which will be considered later.

Another objection is that making parties dependent on state funds generates greater scope for abuse of power. Political actors, who have their own vested interests, will draw up the criteria for allocating funds. Consequently, a danger emerges that the main parties will collude to lock themselves in as the main contenders for power, in effect creating a cartel.[72] The major political parties already enjoy the benefits of office, with the support and media attention that entails, and such parties could design the state-funding system to further entrench those advantages.

Yet there are limits for any scope for abuse. First, grants can be awarded on a fixed criterion, making reference to factors such as votes received, seats in Parliament or seats contested in an election. It is not a general discretion in which an official simply chooses who is deserving of funds. By allocating funds according to such fixed standards, a criterion that benefits a party one year could work against it the next, although in practice it may tend to benefit the major political parties. A second factor is that such criteria will be transparent and published before any funds are distributed. In such circumstances, it will normally be clear when the rules are most likely to benefit a particular party. As a result, any self-interest when deciding the criteria for allocating funds can be detected, and would leave the system open to criticism and potential legal challenge. A third factor is that responsibility for the allocation of funds can be delegated to an independent body, the Electoral Commission. Finally, deciding the basis for allocating the state funds should be a process that includes all the different political parties, giving the smaller parties a chance to raise any concerns.

---

[71] Jack Straw MP, Hansard, HC, vol. 342, col. 34 (10 January 2000).

[72] See R. Katz and P. Mair, 'Changing Models of Party Organization and Party Democracy' (1995) 1 *Party Politics* 5. A criticism of the Sir Hayden Phillips Review of the funding of political parties, was that he attempted to seek a consensus among the major political parties on the system, which included how state funds should be distributed; see Constitutional Affairs Committee, above n. 31, vol. II at Ev 18–19.

Before looking at the method for distributing the funds, a number of preliminary issues need to be considered. The first is deciding which political parties should be eligible for any state funds. The goals in setting the electoral agenda do not require that every registered party receive funding. Furthermore, to give every party funding would be costly and potentially encourage pressure groups to register as parties in order to gain additional resources.[73] The difficulty is in finding some basis for deciding which parties should be included, without unfairly excluding some smaller parties. Previous proposals have generally focused on whether the party is represented in Parliament, the number of seats contested in an election, or the number of votes received. However, by looking at the popularity, or existing level of activity of the party, the potential to exclude smaller and newer parties still remains.[74]

A further question is whether state funds should supplement private donations to parties or completely replace private funding. The latter is the more radical, and will increase the stakes associated with the question of distribution and eligibility for state funds. However, in the UK, existing state support supplements private funding and previous proposals for reform have assumed this will remain the case. A further consideration is whether parties would receive state funds subject to certain conditions. Such conditions could specify the permissible uses of the funds or require the party to conduct its internal affairs in a particular way. For example, one proposal is for a political party to receive state funds on the condition that its members have greater say in running the party.[75] While there are arguments in favour of such measures, state funds with conditions attached raise problems in ensuring compliance with those conditions. The conditions also raise concerns about the state interference with political freedoms, in particular for those parties depending on state funds, while giving a freer hand to parties with sufficient resources to reject that support. All of these points show that care needs to be taken in designing a system of state funding, but the main issue for the current discussion is, once eligibility has been satisfied, on what basis state funds should be distributed.

Making subsidies responsive

The case for state funding discussed so far does not centre around political equality, but on the need to sustain a level of party activity. That goal can

---

[73] Such a problem arises under the existing subsidies. By fielding candidates in an election, a single-issue group can gain free access to the broadcast media through a party election broadcast, see *R (ProLife Alliance)* v. *BBC* [2004] 1 AC 185.

[74] For example, regulations governing political parties in Canada have been challenged for discriminating against smaller political parties, see *Figueroa* v. *Attorney General of Canada* [2003] 1 SCR 912. For a similar point in relation to UK broadcasters, *R* v. *BBC, ex parte Referendum Party* [1997] EMLR 605.

[75] Ewing, *The Cost of Democracy*, pp. 246–8, proposing a Charter of Members' Rights in return for additional state aid.

be connected with political equality by distributing funds in a way that is responsive to citizens' choices. Under this approach, state funds provide parties with a form of state subsidised donations from individuals. Allocating the funds in a way that reflects citizens' preferences also has the advantage of decentralising the decision and arguably gives politicians an incentive to engage with the public. To assess the benefits and difficulties of such a scheme, the next sections will explore three approaches to a responsive distribution of state funds.

Electoral support and membership

The first approach is to distribute funds on a level proportionate to the party's support in the previous election, a method that has been considered several times in the UK.[76] The appeal of this model lies in its simplicity, as that data is already available. Given that an election tends to be the political activity involving the largest number of people, it ensures the maximum level of participation in the decision on the distribution of funds. However, in terms of giving politicians an incentive to engage with citizens, this proposal adds the least, as at the time of an election a politician will already seek to win over voters.[77] It also potentially entrenches the status quo. Not only will the leading elected parties benefit from all the advantages of office, but will also secure additional funds. Those parties with fewer or no seats in Parliament may need the funds most in order to get a hearing.

An alternative proposal is to distribute state funds based on the number of members in each political party. This proposal is an equivalent to parties increasing subscription costs, with the state subsidising the additional cost to members. Such an approach would encourage parties to make membership more attractive, for example by offering members greater input into policy-making, and thereby engage with citizens as participants rather than as voters. However, many people, including those supporting a particular party, may not have a strong attachment to a single party and be more reluctant to formally join a party. Consequently, such individuals may be willing to show support by joining informal networks of party supporters, for example signing up for a supporters' group on a social networking site, attending some meetings or by making an occasional donation. A method of distributing funds based on membership would not be responsive to, or subsidise, the activities of those more informal party supporters.

---

[76] The Houghton Committee proposed to distribute state funds to parties that saved deposits in six constituencies, had two MPs returned, or had one MP returned plus 150,000 votes. Under the scheme, parties would receive five pence for each vote received in the previous election. See Report of the Committee on Financial Aid to Political Parties, Cmnd. 6601 (1976). See also Sir Hayden Phillips Review, above n. 67, at p. 19.

[77] As Sir Hayden Phillips argued, this method of distribution is 'based on public support' rather than 'public engagement', see Sir Hayden Phillips Review, above n. 67, p. 18. However, it would be expected that the two are connected, in so far as engagement is necessary to gain support.

State funds following donations

Another way to make state funding responsive to citizens is to distribute the money in a way that reflects the pattern of private donations. Along these lines, the Neill Committee and Electoral Commission have proposed tax relief on political donations. This means that political parties would receive an additional sum, equivalent to the basic rate of tax, for each private donation. Those making private donations to parties would thereby determine the distribution of state funds. Such a scheme may encourage people to make a donation and could be administered in the same way as tax relief on donations to charities.[78] However, the scheme would have to be devised in such a way that does not give those on higher incomes and paying more tax greater incentive to donate than other individuals. For example, granting full tax relief on a donation of £10,000 would use state funds to amplify the voice of the wealthy donor with that amount of money to spare.[79] Imposing a limit on the value of the donations benefiting from tax relief would address such a concern. The scheme would also have to accommodate those who do not pay tax, but wish to donate money.[80] Rather than granting tax relief on donations, the state can provide a level of funding directly to a party to match amounts received in private donations.[81] Under such a scheme of matching grants, if a private donor gives £10 to a party, then the state would also provide £10. Again, to avoid increasing the influence of the large donor, state funds should match only a small value of private donations, such as the first £10 or £50 of each donation.

Advocates of such schemes see it as a way of encouraging parties to seek a wider range of smaller donors.[82] While it is currently more convenient for parties to seek large regular donations, such additional funding may change these incentives. However, the problems of tax relief or matching grants would mirror those associated with private donations. Many individuals may not be in the habit of donating to a political party, and it may be thought that those from a particular socio-economic background or with a higher income are more likely to make a donation. If this method is to be taken seriously as a channel for securing responsiveness, the scheme will require some promotion to ensure greater take-up of its benefits. However, it is not clear how effective such encouragement would be and, even with the limits to the scheme outlined above, the scheme may amplify the voice of those already in the habit of donating.

[78] See The Electoral Commission, *The Funding of Political Parties* (2004) at pp. 98–101.

[79] To avoid this, the Electoral Commission proposed limited tax relief to donations up to the value of £200. *Ibid.* at [6.50].

[80] While a similar scheme for charitable donations allows donors paying above the basic level of taxation to claim relief on the extra tax paid, such a provision would potentially give greater incentive to those on higher incomes to donate.

[81] For example, in 1981, the Hansard Society proposed matching grants of £2 for each individual that donated £2 or over, *Paying For Politics: the Report of the Commission upon the Funding of Political Parties* (London: Hansard Society, 1981).

[82] Neill Report, above n. 22, at [8.15–8.22].

Voucher schemes

One of the most interesting and innovative ways to distribute state funds is through voucher schemes. Under such a scheme, each individual has an equal number of vouchers representing a fixed value of state funds, and give, their vouchers to a political party of their choice. Political parties then receive state funds reflecting the value of the vouchers donated. The proposal attempts to permit the benefits of a system of donations while ensuring an even distribution of the opportunities to contribute. In 2006, the Power Inquiry proposed a simple example of such a scheme, in which individuals would choose which party he or she wishes to allocate £3 of state funds to while casting the ballot.[83] While it has some merit, this system is similar to the allocation of funds according to the number of votes received, given that it is responsive to those who vote in an election.

More complex voucher schemes have been proposed by scholars in the United States in which individuals can contribute vouchers outside elections, and to pressure groups as well as parties.[84] The difficulty with this type of proposal is that it would potentially be complex to administer. It is also questionable whether it really would encourage politicians to engage with citizens. The politician may instead hire a firm or organisation to collect vouchers for the party in return for a fee, just as companies collect signatures in US ballot initiatives.[85] Given that the vouchers come to the individual at no cost and require no other form of commitment to the party, the citizen may be all too ready to give the vouchers away. If distributing funds on the basis of membership of a political party requires too much commitment from an individual, the counter-argument is that the voucher scheme potentially requires too little.

None of the methods of making state funds responsive are perfect and all come with potential drawbacks. One way to address the various concerns is to combine the different methods of distribution. For example, parties could receive some funds based on votes received in an election, complemented by additional funds through matching grants or vouchers.[86] Given the flaws shown in the criteria for allocating funds, no single method should determine how all the state funds are distributed. The hope is for the combination of criteria to ensure that any unfair consequences or flaws in one distributive criterion are

[83] The Report of Power: an Independent Inquiry into Britain's Democracy (London: Power Inquiry, 2006) pp. 211–13.
[84] B. Ackerman and I. Ayres, *Voting with Dollars* (New Haven: Yale University Press, 2002); R. Hasen 'Clipping Coupons for Democracy: An Egalitarian/Public Choice Defense of Campaign Finance Vouchers' (1996) 84 *California Law Review* 1; E. Foley 'Equal-Dollars-Per-Voter: A Constitutional Principle of Campaign Finance' (1994) 94 Colum. L. Rev. 1204.
[85] See D. Lowenstein, 'Voting with Votes' (2003) 116 *Harvard Law Review*, 1971 at 1990.
[86] Both the Sir Hayden Phillips Review and the Constitutional Affairs Committee proposed a mixed basis for allocating funds, with the funds distributed according to votes cast for that party in the previous election and through a matching grant scheme. See Sir Hayden Phillips Review, above n. 67, p. 18; Constitutional Affairs Committee, above n. 31, at [131].

offset by another. Under this view, a party with fewer votes or members could still attract funds through matching grants. The existing methods of state support, including policy development grants, election broadcasts and free mailings, all rely on different criteria and such a mixture of approaches could provide a model for any additional state funds.

Responsiveness and other democratic goals

The approach sketched above seeks to limit the role of wealthy donors and establish a framework that has responsiveness to citizens as its central criterion for distributing funds. However, a system based on responsiveness arguably overlooks the other goals of the democratic system. Such a system does not ensure that parties have a stable source of funds, as its resources will fluctuate with public opinion. A responsive system does not directly ensure that the system is deliberative, or offers the electorate a diverse and meaningful choice. Nor does it ensure that the elections are competitive, as a responsive system could allow one party to acquire a much higher share of public funds. While a responsive distribution of political funds may support a diverse and competitive system, there is no guarantee it will have this effect. Instead, that system could reinforce the advantage of the leading parties, which gain more resources and in turn can spend more to attract further support.[87] Just as some parties currently have more resources to campaign for votes, the well-resourced parties will have more resources to campaign for donations and maintain the financial advantage.

Under a system of unrestricted donations, there is at least the hope that there would be enough super-rich donors to bankroll different parties. For example, one wealthy individual might have a strong ideological commitment and make donations to a party that would otherwise struggle to find funds. An unregulated system of donations may not be responsive, but can provide some level of diversity. For example, some smaller parties have benefited from wealthy patrons, most notably Sir James Goldsmith's support of the Referendum Party in 1997. The difficulty with this argument is that such support is the exception rather than the norm, and the very large donations tend to go to the major parties. In any event, where small parties do attract large donations, the difficulty is that the diversity of parties is not the product of a fair process. There may be a number of small political parties with a wider range of support, lacking a wealthy supporter and in a financially weaker position. The diversity of parties should not depend on or reflect the pet projects and whims of a handful of wealthy people and groups. However, it is important to acknowledge that something might be lost by capping donations and limiting the capacity for wealthy patrons to support voices that might not otherwise be heard.[88]

[87] See Chapter 2, p. 48.
[88] Consequently, if diversity among parties is valued as a goal, then the solution may be to provide greater support for small political parties, rather than to preserve the status quo.

While responsiveness is an important element in political funding, it should not be the sole basis for distributing resources. A purely responsive approach may work to keep small political parties on the margins without having a chance to attract new supporters. While it is not a requirement that small political parties have funds equal to the more popular parties, it is still important to ensure that the views and interests represented by that party get a hearing in the electoral process. One way around this would be to permit small political parties that are not eligible for state funds to opt out of the donation limits.[89] The difficulty with such a proposal is that it would benefit those political parties with a wealthy patron without giving much support to those without. Instead, state funds should be granted to some smaller parties in recognition of the value of the diversity added to the electoral process. For example, a block grant could be given to some small parties to fund a minimal level of activity. However, not every party can demand state support, so some eligibility threshold will be unavoidable, which will normally be based on a level of activity or support. Once such a threshold is met, each eligible party could receive an equal basic grant to support the goal of diversity, a method which is partly reflected in the current scheme for Policy Development Grants. Other regulations also allow responsiveness to be supplemented with other democratic goals. Measures such as a cap on election spending or a limit on the maximum amount of state funds awarded to any single party, could help maintain a competitive system and prevent any party having a runaway advantage.

While responsiveness should not be the sole criterion, there is a strong argument for saying that responsiveness should be the main criterion in the distribution of political funds. In so far as the funds are used largely for electoral activity, they are engaged in the part of the democratic process that is responsive to voters. Even aside from the concern with elections, party funding provides a channel to give citizens greater say in the political agenda. The agenda is often set by a range of other actors such as the media, experts and other political actors, rather than through direct input from citizens. Giving citizens greater say on the distribution of political resources among parties can provide a point of entry for citizens in shaping the political agenda, which helps to balance the role of elites in other contexts.

Institutional donations

So far it has been assumed that the funding for political parties will come from individual donations. However, the traditional approach in Britian has been for political parties to receive funds from institutions, in particular companies and trade unions, rather than individuals. The difficulty lies in deciding how

---

[89] See Sir Hayden Phillips Review, above n. 67, at p. 19. Such an argument was also made by the Conservatives to Constitutional Affairs Committee, above n. 31, at [121].

such a tradition could fit with a cap on donations, if such a limit were enacted. Limiting the amount institutions can donate would deprive UK political parties of a major source of funds. Yet to leave institutional donations unregulated would allow large donations to come from a single source.

The issue is also politically sensitive. Given the tradition for trade unions to contribute towards one side of the political spectrum and companies to the other, the issue has high stakes for the main political parties.[90] For example, a limit on union donations will result in a substantial cut to the Labour Party's funds.[91] While Labour will be resistant to such a limit, other parties are less likely to agree to more lenient rules for unions that do not apply to companies and pressure groups. Both sides will argue that it is unfair to regulate funding in a way that impacts on one party more than another. That the political actors all have their own interests at stake when designing the system makes agreement on this issue particularly difficult and for one party in government to unilaterally impose such a control would raise concerns that the measure discriminates according to viewpoint.[92] For these reasons, institutional donations have been one of the issues preventing the major political parties coming to an agreement on a donation limit, and thereby maintaining the status quo.

Even putting the political context to one side, the issue remains problematic in so far as it raises the question of what role institutions and associations should play in distributing funds to a political party. At one extreme lies the view that there is no role for institutional donations. Given that companies, trade unions and pressure groups do not have a vote, this line of argument calls for a ban on institutions giving money to a political party. Under this view, '[e]lectoral politics should primarily be a matter for individuals, not well-heeled pressure groups, trade unions or corporations'.[93] This argument suggests that associations and institutions have a role in elections by informing the public, but not in distributing funds to political parties.[94] Even with a ban on institutional donations, trade unions, pressure groups and others can still play a role by acting as a facilitator of individual activity, encouraging people to join a party.[95] This would allow the party and institution to maintain a relationship,

[90] Although that is to make a generalisation, as the Labour Party also attracts company donations. However, trade unions remain a substantial source of funds for the Labour Party.

[91] The Labour Party was founded in 1900 by the trade unions in order to field their own candidates. The connection has continued and a number of trade unions pay to affiliate to the Labour Party and are consequently represented on the Party's decision-making bodies. For background on the link see K. Ewing, *Trade Unions, the Labour Party and the Law* (Edinburgh: Edinburgh University Press, 1982).

[92] See Chapter 3, p. 72.

[93] A. Tyrie, *Clean Politics* (Conservative Party, 2006) pp. 8–9. The Conservative Party's proposals for reform published in 2006, argued that a donation cap should apply to institutions in the short term, but eventually such donations should be phased out.

[94] See T. Christiano, *The Rule of the Many* (Oxford: Westview Press, 1996) p. 257, on the role of interest groups.

[95] The Canadian law was amended in 2003, banning donations from a trade union, company and other associations. While trade unions can no longer contribute to a political party in

but those individuals associated with the institution would provide funds to the party.

The difficulty with an outright ban on institutional donations is that it would be in tension with freedom of association, in so far as it prescribes the way individuals can combine and participate in the democratic process. It takes the analogy between voting and donating to an extreme and requires the political party to adopt a particular type of relationship with individuals. By contrast, some political parties may prefer a model in which institutions affiliate to the party, and individuals are represented indirectly through those institutions. For example, the Labour Party started out as a 'federation' of affiliated organisations. Individuals could not join the Party as members until 1918.[96] The model of affiliated organisations may provide a structure that allows individuals to participate through activities within the affiliated institution. The point is not to compare the relative benefits of the affiliate organisation or individual membership model, but to note the different ways a party can organise. Yet freedom of association is not absolute.[97] Parties should be free to organise in diverse ways, but not in ways that undermine political equality. For example, a decision by three multi-millionaires to bankroll a political party would be an association, but would raise problems for a fair democratic process. Consequently, the goal is to ensure that parties have flexibility in the methods of organisation, while respecting each individual's equal chance to influence.

Along these lines are alternative approaches that allow some institutions to finance political parties. For example, if the distribution of political funds is to be primarily responsive to citizens, then institutions that represent citizens may deserve a more lenient approach. Representative institutions mediate between the individual and the political party. One approach is therefore to exempt such representative institutions that fulfil certain criteria (such as some channel of accountability to its membership) from any donation limits that are applicable to individuals and permit those institutions to make large donations. If a donation limit were enacted, institutions could be subject to a cap at a level proportionate to its overall number of members. While such an approach moves away from the individual as the sole political actor, it arguably respects citizen equality and the distribution of funds is roughly responsive.

If such an approach is granted to representative groups, there is a danger of duplication of representation, in which citizens give money to a range of different pressure groups and organisations, which in turn donate money to

Canada, it can still affiliate on the basis of union members that are full members of a party. This arguably gives the trade union an incentive to persuade members to join the party. See Constitutional Affairs Committee, above n. 31, at [105]. For background see Ewing, *The Cost of Democracy*, ch. 9.

[96] S. Fielding, *The Labour Party: Continuity and Change in the Making of 'New' Labour* (Basingstoke: Palgrave, 2003) pp. 119–21.

[97] For example, see *Parti Nationaliste Basque – Organisation Régionale D'Iparralde* v. *France* (2008) 47 EHRR 47, upholding a restriction on donations from foreign political parties, despite its impact on a small regional party.

the political party. A similar concern is that the institution making the large donation might be a front organisation for a wealthy individual. To avoid these difficulties further measures could secure compliance with an individual donation limit, including the institution keeping a record of its sources of funding;[98] and a limit on the amount any individual can contribute to the institution that will be used to make a political donation. To fulfil the latter requirement, the institution would have to establish its own political fund from which donations are made, separate from its general funds. Payments into the institution's separate political funds could then be capped. Finally, some criteria would have to be devised to determine whether the institution itself is representative and deserving of the more lenient donation limit.

The debate about trade union donations to the Labour Party highlights the difficulty in agreeing criteria necessary to show when the institution is representative. Trade union donations are subject to a number of legal requirements, but there is debate as to whether such measures go far enough, or too far. Under the current law, if a trade union wishes to make any political expenditure, it is required by statute to ballot its members first, and then make such expenditures out of a separate fund.[99] Individual members can opt-out from paying into the political fund, ensuring that no members are forced to fund political messages.[100] Critics of the arrangement see this as offering a minimal form of representation and emphasise the limits of the members' input. Some argue that the opt-out provision means that payments into the political fund are a sign of members' inertia rather than approval of the political expenditures.[101] Critics may regard an opt-in provision as a better way to ensure the payments into the political fund are voluntary. Furthermore, union members are merely consulted about establishing a political fund and the union leadership can decide what donations to make out of that fund. Given that union members do not directly control the spending of the political funds, the critics argue that union donations are not truly responsive to individual members.

When looking at the issue in 2007, the Sir Hayden Phillips Review proposed to limit trade union donations to a level equal to the costs of affiliating each union member to the political party.[102] Under the proposal, a union with one million members could make a donation equivalent to the individual affiliation fee multiplied by one million. While the arrangement would allow unions to give more money than an individual donor, it would restrict donations above the cost of affiliation. The limit to affiliation fees was proposed on the basis that it must be 'possible to trace payments back to identifiable individuals'.[103]

---

[98] The Sir Hayden Phillips Review, at p. 11, proposed that third parties should identify who is providing funding to them, prior to making political expenditures.

[99] Trade Union and Labour Relations (Consolidation) Act 1992, Chap. VI, esp. ss.71–3.

[100] *Ibid.*, s.84.

[101] V. Bogdanor, *Power and the People* (London: Gollancz, 1997) pp. 152–3.

[102] When affiliating to the Labour Party, trade unions pay a fee of a few pounds for each member paying into the political fund.

[103] Sir Hayden Phillips Review, above n. 67, at p. 10.

The Review also stated that trade union decisions on donating must be 'clearly transparent' and that union members should be reminded of their rights in relation to the political fund. While still seeming to prescribe a particular method of organisation, the proposal at least attempts to accommodate a role for the institution.

Given the emphasis on responsiveness, representation is a strong argument to permit larger institutional donations. However, as stated above, responsiveness is just one goal and the focus on the representative nature points to an individualistic view of the institution in which it is valued by reference to the number of people it represents.[104] Instead, some institutions are valued not because of the number of citizens they represent, but because they speak for a distinct section of society or set of interests. Such institutions may argue that they should donate higher sums to give a voice to those sections of society. If there is to be a higher donation limit for certain institutions, the difficulty is in deciding which interests or sections of society need to be heard and would be subject to the more generous donation limit.

The view of institutions representing interests rather than citizens may suggest a continuing role for donations from for-profit companies. While companies require a resolution from company members authorising political expenditures over a four-year period before any donation can be made,[105] this alone does not make the for-profit company a representative interest group.[106] Instead, the argument for such company donations is to allow some level of advocacy of corporate interests. This, however, justifies only limited donations from such non-representative groups. The wide range of for-profit companies allows such a sectional interest to be widely represented even with a low cap on donations. Finally, it is questionable whether such groups should influence party funding at all, when channels such as lobbying already provide opportunities for political influence to such non-representative institutions. For these reasons, it is argued that only those institutions that represent larger numbers of individuals should benefit from any higher cap on political donations.

The enactment of a donation limit would make the role of institutions problematic. A continuation of the status quo would sit uneasily with a donation limit on individuals and allow large donations to continue from institutions. However, imposing a donation limit on individuals and institutions alike would potentially reflect a particular understanding of politics and limit the contribution made through associative activities. The political context also needs to be considered. As stated earlier, a relatively high donation limit of £50,000 would

---

[104] B. Cain, 'The Democratic Implications of Voting with Dollars' (2003) 37 U. Rich. L. Rev. 959, at p. 973, criticising Ackerman and Ayres voucher scheme for treating groups as 'the sum of equal individuals'.

[105] Companies Act 2006, s.366.

[106] While some pressure groups are organised as companies, it is the presence of subscribing members that makes it representative, which does not arise in the case of the for-profit company.

privilege the highest earners, yet a similar limit on institutional donations would cut off contributions from those groups that traditionally represent those on lower wages. Donations from representative groups arguably offset the political advantages that a cap on donations would give to those with the money to donate the maximum sum possible within the limit. Distinguishing between the types of institution (such as the representative and the non-representative) may therefore provide an appealing route to avoid these difficulties. However, such a distinction raises the question of what type of institution should be permitted to donate and at what level, and then deciding which institutions fulfil those criteria.

Conclusion

While making a case for controls on party funding, the discussion in this chapter highlights a number of hazards and difficulties with legal reform. Abstract arguments of equality may point to further reform, but no system of legal control is likely to create a perfect system of equality. For example, within the amounts permitted by donation and spending limits, a range of inequalities based on wealth can persist. Furthermore, making one area of activity more egalitarian may do little to advance political equality if the effect is for people to channel money to other less regulated political activities. Yet these concerns are not arguments against further control, but merely warn against complacency if further controls are introduced.

In the UK party funding laws, fairness between competing parties and candidates has been the traditional goal. The complaint in 1883 was that the unregulated system was unfair as only richer candidates could stand for election. However, fairness does not require that every party or candidate can compete on equal terms with the same resources. The difficulty lies in identifying where differences in funding treat parties unfairly. Consequently, it has been argued here that the focus of the law should move away from fairness between candidates and parties, towards equality among citizens. Under this view responsiveness to individuals is a central goal by which to assess the fairness of the distribution of funds to parties. Differences in the amounts parties can spend are fair when those differences reflect the levels of support for the party, but not when they reflect the wealth of the party's supporters. The concern with a fair process for parties and candidates is rooted in the value of political equality.

Party funding laws are often greeted with scepticism that loopholes and methods of evasion will always emerge, and the experience in the UK provides some support for that view. However, as a counter to the sceptics, a new system of party funding would not simply constrain politicians from practising old habits, but could define new expectations in public life. Just as political morality changed following the legislation in the latter half of the nineteenth century, new legal controls can set the ethical standards against which conduct should be judged and have an impact on the behaviour of political actors. The concerns discussed above show that care should be taken when thinking about new restrictions on party funding and these difficulties need to be addressed in the design of the regulations. For all the limits and hazards, reforms in party funding could take an important step towards political equality.

6

Public spaces, property and participation

Many forms of political activity, such as lobbying, contributing to a political party and using the mass media, require substantial resources. This chapter will, however, look at assemblies and other expressive activities in public spaces, forms of participation thought to be accessible regardless of wealth. These forms of participation include marching through the streets, static assemblies, handing out leaflets or collecting signatures for a petition. They have had a long tradition as a vehicle for large-scale political dissent in the UK, with examples ranging from the Chartists in the nineteenth century, to the more recent campaigns against the war in Iraq, the ban on fox-hunting and the anti-capitalist movement. Such activities perform a range of functions, which include showing strength of feeling, gaining publicity, collecting signatures for a petition and distributing information.

Expressive activities in public places have qualitative differences from other types of political participation, for example by facilitating face-to-face contact.[1] While a newspaper report may convey information and opinions, face-to-face communications allow people to see those affected by a particular policy and those holding a particular view. This contact can emphasise how some issues are close to home. For example, if a town council closes a facility, then a peaceful protest on nearby land can remind people of the impact of that decision on the local community. The transparency of assemblies, where the audience can see the individuals participating, makes fake 'astroturfing' campaigns more open to detection.[2] Certain types of public space can also be of central importance to the effectiveness of the expressive activity.[3] For example, speakers seeking to influence a legislative vote will choose a location most likely to get lawmaker's attention, which explains why restrictions on speakers in Parliament Square have been so controversial. Similarly, assemblies promoting a boycott of a particular store will choose a location most likely to reach that store's potential customers. Other types of activity may be symbolic, choosing spaces closely connected to the message of the assembly.[4]

---

[1] See M. Kohn, *Brave New Neighbourhoods* (London: Routledge, 2004) pp. 3–4. T. Zick, *Speech Out of Doors* (Cambridge University Press, 2008) p. 16.

[2] Zick, *Speech Out of Doors*, p. 18.   [3] *Ibid.*, pp. 105–13.

[4] *Tabernacle v. Secretary of State for Defence* [2009] EWCA Civ 23 at [37].

Most significantly for the argument here, access to public space provides a cheap means of communication. While resources may be necessary to organise an assembly and publish leaflets, the economic barriers to this type of activity tend to be lower. Consequently, the capacity to gain attention and influence does not derive from wealth, but from the number of people involved, the nature of the message, or the inventiveness of the organisers. That is not to say that everyone participates equally. It may be that the same small group of people participate in street protests on a regular basis, but broadly speaking the opportunity is open to all regardless of wealth. Consequently, accessing public places to communicate can offset some of the inequalities found in other channels of political influence.

In so far as there are more equal chances to participate, such activities are particularly important in serving the individual's interest in communication and participation. The chance to participate need not be valued on account of the speaker's expertise or capacity to enlighten the audience, but as a reflection of her equal status as a participant. For this reason, measures aiming to promote the rational style of debate sometimes associated with a deliberative democracy are less appropriate in this context. The equal opportunities to participate make such activities suitable for applying pressure, or registering numerical support for a policy, both of which can have an aggregative function.

Such activities can also serve the audience interest in receiving information. Expressive activities in public spaces confront people with views they were not aware of and often disagree with. While sometimes a nuisance, such activities can inform, even if it merely shows that an issue is of concern to some people. Assemblies in public places can thereby help counter the increasing opportunities for individuals to filter and control the information they receive. However, there are limits on the extent to which it serves the audience's interest in receiving diverse information. In so far as people in a particular locality have easy access to the public space, the messages expressed may tend to emphasise the interests of those already living in that area. As a result it may provide a stronger voice to Nimbyism or opposition to new developments. For example, a town centre may provide a forum for opponents of a proposed airport development in that area, yet the advocates of the airport from outside the locality seem less likely to use that space. However, the meetings that inform the government on town planning and regional economic strategy provide a separate forum in which the developers and other interested parties can make the case for the project.

Public spaces and a shrinking subsidy

The more equal chance to participate afforded by public spaces is not inevitable and follows from the decisions about the ownership and management of the land. Expressive activities and assemblies require resources, in terms of access to land. The provision of public land can be seen as a form of subsidy to permit expressive activities. This 'public space subsidy' arises in so far as people are allowed to use the land to communicate with others and thereby make use of a resource that facilitates certain political activities. The subsidy is not just in terms of providing space, but also in the local services, which may have to tidy up after the assembly and police the event. The European Court of Human Rights has held that the right to assemble includes positive obligations, such as the provision of police to ensure hecklers or counter protestors do not suppress speakers.[5] The obligation is not to provide unlimited resources,[6] but the police cannot silence a speaker simply because it is cheaper than policing the activity.

If access to public spaces is seen as a subsidy, it is one that raises fewer problems than other speech-related subsidies, such as the state funding of political parties. For the most part, it avoids the difficult administrative question of who should qualify for the subsidy. Whoever wishes to speak in the public space will be able to do so, subject to regulations that accommodate the other uses and users. However, when a large-scale assembly is planned, where a public space is particularly busy, or where more than one speaker wishes to occupy the same space, then decisions about allocations arise. Such decisions are normally made through the powers to regulate the assemblies to preserve public order. The extent and increasing range of statutory controls on assemblies, including public order laws, harassment laws and police stop-and-search powers, have caused considerable concern among scholars and commentators about the limited scope for freedom of assembly.[7] However, in so far as the use of public spaces facilitates expression, such powers raise two specific issues of concern here.

The first concern is that some of the powers used to manage the public space, such as those of breach of the peace or under the Public Order Act 1986, give a broad discretion to the police.[8] The danger exists that the police use the broad discretion in ways that discriminate against some speakers based on the viewpoint expressed. The police discretion is not unfettered and is subject to judicial oversight, so any such intentional abuse of that power would be unlawful.[9] However, it will often be difficult to detect such abuses and the courts will place

---

[5] In *Plattform 'Ärzte für das Leben' v. Austria* (1988) 13 EHRR 204, the European Court of Human Rights stated at [32–3] that Article 11 is not solely a negative right and it 'sometimes requires positive measures to be taken, even in the sphere of relations between individuals, if need be'. However, in fulfilling any positive obligation states will 'have a wide discretion in the choice of the means to be used'.

[6] *R v. Chief Constable of Sussex, ex parte International Trader's Ferry Ltd.* [1999] 2 AC 418.

[7] See D. Feldman, *Civil Liberties and Human Rights in England and Wales* (Oxford University Press, 2002) ch. 18; Joint Committee on Human Rights, *Demonstrating Respect for Rights* (2009 HC 320, HL 47).

[8] For a definition of a breach of the peace, see *R v. Howell* [1982] QB 416 at 427.

[9] See *Redmond-Bate v. DPP* [1999] Crim LR 998 and *R. (on the application of Laporte) v. Chief Constable of Gloucestershire* [2007] 2 AC 105.

considerable weight on the judgement of the police where difficult public order issues are present.[10] Consequently, the broad discretion coupled with the limits of judicial scrutiny raises a danger of unfair discrimination against certain people, which restricts their use of the public space subsidy.

The second concern is that the more legal powers there are to regulate expressive activities in public, the greater the potential to devalue or limit the subsidy provided through access to public spaces. Given the importance of such activities as a form of 'cheap speech', the effects of such restrictions will impact most on those speakers who cannot access the other channels of communication. Such concern arises not only where speakers are silenced, but also where there are regulations on the time, place or manner of the speech aiming to protect other users. The decision in *Brehony* illustrates the tension between public order laws and the purpose of an assembly. In that case, a group of people took part in a long-running weekly assembly to promote a boycott of a particular store. In the weeks before Christmas, the police moved the group to a location half a mile away from that store, in order to accommodate shoppers and other users of the space at that busy time of year.[11] The case therefore highlights the difficulties in managing the competing uses of the public space. Yet given the importance of the location to the success of the message, a decision that gives priority to the use of the land by local shoppers over the assembly can undermine the effectiveness of the assembly and its capacity to reach the target audience.

Neither of these concerns suggests that there should not be any public order controls. Police and those managing public spaces cannot avoid decisions on the various uses. Furthermore, managing the competing uses can work to the benefit of some speakers. For example, use of police powers to ensure protests are peaceful and not intimidating to others can make the space more attractive to visitors. Keeping the space as an inviting place can enhance the value of the 'subsidy' that public places provide by making sure the space remains popular and that speakers using that area can reach a wide audience. Police powers need to be exercised carefully to fulfil these goals, while ensuring that they do not shrink the public space subsidy or allocate it according to the views of the speaker.

Other trends erode the availability of public spaces for expressive activities. The remainder of the chapter will look at controls arising from the prerogatives associated with land ownership. In considering the effects of these different controls on the equal chance to participate, the focus will be the peaceful activities that attempt to persuade others on political issues. Although activities such as direct action have important political implications, they raise broader issues, which are beyond the scope of this chapter. The examples of peaceful activities are sufficient to highlight the importance of access to public spaces for political equality.

---

[10] *Austin v. Metropolitan Police Commissioner* [2009] UKHL 5.
[11] *R (on the application of Brehony) v. Chief Constable of Greater Manchester Police* [2005] EWHC 640 (Admin).

Access to state-owned property

Controls on activities in public spaces come from the landowners' powers as well as public order laws. Under the traditional rules of property, access to land for the purposes of political expression and association is normally at the discretion of the owner or possessor of land.[12] Not only can the landowner decide who to let on her land, but can also grant access to visitors subject to conditions, or limit entry for a specific purpose.[13] As a result, the owner of the land can refuse access to speakers or grant access on the condition that the visitor agrees not to speak or distribute leaflets. This position has traditionally applied to publicly owned property as well as private landowners. The general rule is that public bodies can exclude speakers from land like any other landowner,[14] although that power is subject to the legal qualifications. Unless provided for elsewhere in the law, there is no general right to access publicly owned spaces and public bodies have the discretion to permit or refuse access for expressive activities.

The right to exclude is not absolute and is subject to a number of statutory and common law restrictions. For example, where a public right of way runs through land, the landowner's permission is not necessary for access. Such a right of way provides a limited opportunity to assemble on the land following a House of Lords decision in 1999 upholding the use of highways for reasonable and non-obstructive assemblies.[15] The decision was a significant alteration to the common law, which traditionally limited the public's right to use a highway for passage and re-passage and activities incidental to that purpose.[16] As a result of the decision, assemblies on a highway do not always constitute a trespass. The use of the highway for expressive purposes can arise where the right of way runs through privately owned land.[17] The impact of the decision is, however, limited. The right applies only where there is an existing highway, and even where there is, the House of Lords only found assembles that are reasonable and non-obstructive to be consistent with the use of the right.

While the common law definition of property does not draw a sharp distinction between private and public ownership, publicly owned spaces are more likely to be subject to legal controls that lead to greater access. The highways described above provide one example. There are also a number of statutory controls that regulate access to publicly owned property. A very specific

---

[12] For the sake of simplicity, the term 'owner' will be used to refer to the holder of the right to exclude. However, this right will be held by possessors of land, which are often not owners.

[13] *Perth General Station Committee* v. *Ross* [1897] AC 479.

[14] For example in *Ex parte Lewis* (1888) 21 QBD 191 the Divisional Court held that there was no right to hold political meetings in Trafalgar Square.

[15] *DPP* v. *Jones* [1999] 2 AC 240. See also *Westminster City Council* v. *Brian Haw* [2002] EWHC 2073.

[16] *Harrison* v. *Duke of Rutland* [1893] 1 QB 142.

[17] Although Lord Irvine and Lord Hutton suggested that where the highway runs through privately owned land, the assembly is more likely to be an unreasonable use. See *DPP* v. *Jones* [1999] 2 AC 240 at 256 and 293.

example grants candidates in an election campaign the use of a schoolroom for the purpose of holding a public meeting.[18] More generally, specific statutory powers and duties such as those regulating public parks or universities curtail the public body's powers of ownership. A public body's exercise of its powers of ownership is also open to challenge through judicial review, for example where a decision to exclude a group or person from property is contrary to the principles of administrative law. In *ex parte Fewings* a decision by a council to use its statutory powers to exclude a group of hunters from publicly owned land was unlawful, because the councillors based their decision on personal objections to hunting.[19] When exercising its statutory powers the council had to pursue public duties rather than their personal beliefs. Where the power to own land rests on the Crown's residual non-statutory powers, decisions to exclude are also subject to judicial review on similar grounds.[20]

In addition to judicial review, excluded speakers can challenge a public authority decision under the Human Rights Act 1998 (HRA). Prior to the HRA, freedom of assembly had traditionally been a residual liberty in which assembly was permitted in so far as it was not unlawful.[21] The position has since changed with the enactment of the HRA, as the ECHR provides for a right to assemble under Article 11 and for freedom of expression under Article 10, both requiring that restrictions serve a legitimate aim and are 'necessary in a democratic society'.

There are strong reasons in principle why the state's powers as an owner of land should be subject to stricter controls.[22] Broadly speaking, property owned by the state is not for public officials to use in accordance with personal preferences, but to pursue public duties and the public interest.[23] As the example in *ex parte Fewings* shows, the council could not exclude individuals based on a personal objection to the activity in question. The principle extends more strongly still to exclusions based on the council's dislike of the speaker's message. By

---

[18] Representation of the People Act 1983, s.95–6.

[19] *R* v. *Somerset CC, ex parte Fewings* [1995] 3 All ER 20 at pp. 28–9.

[20] See P. P. Craig, *Administrative Law*, eighth edition (London: Sweet and Maxwell, 2008) pp. 535–6. For discussion of the residual power see B. V. Harris, 'The "Third Source" of Authority for Government Action Revisited' (2007) 123 LQR 626. Some accounts have questioned whether the government should be able to rely on such powers without legal authority and that in any event such powers should only be used for limited purposes to pursue the public interest. See Laws J in *R* v. *Somerset CC, ex parte Fewings* [1995] 1 All ER 513; and *R (Shrewsbury & Atcham Borough Council)* v. *Secretary of State for Communities and Local Government* [2008] EWCA Civ 148 at [48]. Other authorities have suggested a broader approach where such powers can be used as long it does not conflict with other laws or individual rights. See *Malone* v. *Metropolitan Police Commissioner* [1979] Ch 344; *R* v. *Secretary of State for Health, ex p. C* [2000] 1 FLR 627.

[21] *Duncan* v. *Jones* [1936] 1 KB 218 at 222.

[22] See discussion in J. W. Harris, 'Private and Non-private Property: What is the Difference?' (1995) 111 LQR 421 at 433–7; and D. Feldman, 'Property and Public Protest', in F. Meisel and P. Cook (eds.), *Property and Protection* (Oxford: Hart Publishing, 2000).

[23] See Laws J in *R* v. *Somerset CC, ex parte Fewings* [1995] 1 All ER 513, 'A public body has no heritage of legal rights which it enjoys for its own sake; at every turn, all of its dealings constitute the fulfilment of duties which it owes to others; indeed, it exists for no other purpose.' For a more recent statement by Laws LJ on similar lines see *Tabernacle* v. *Secretary of State for Defence* [2009] EWCA Civ 23 at [38].

contrast, a private landowner is free to use the property for her own purposes, whether that is for personal profit or political beliefs. The private landowner can discriminate and exclude speakers because she disagrees with the political views being expressed. The private owner can also use the property to advance her own political beliefs by putting a poster up in the window of her home during an election campaign, but such a move would not be acceptable in a government office. Decisions from public bodies to exclude are therefore subject to a greater level of legal accountability.

While judicial review and the HRA allow decisions to exclude a person from land to be challenged, neither guarantee access. There are occasions where the public body may have a good reason to exclude speakers from a particular place, such as where the assembly interferes with the performance of a government function. Along these lines, Chief Justice Lamer in the Canadian Supreme Court stated that as the state administers its properties for the benefit of the citizens as a whole, 'it is the citizens above all who have an interest in seeing that the properties are administered and operated in a manner consistent with their intended purpose'.[24] Consequently, in *ex parte Fewings*, the council could have excluded the hunters from public land if the decision was to pursue the purpose of the statute, rather than to advance the councillors' personal preferences. Similarly, the state may exclude speakers from assembling at a courthouse or outside a prison, if it threatens to disrupt the administration of justice.[25] The obvious point to emerge is that assemblers cannot utilise all publicly owned property. Instead it depends on the particular property in question and the state's reason for the exclusion.

This raises the question of how to determine which publicly owned areas should be accessible and used by the public for expressive activities. In the United States, public forum doctrine provides a framework to address the issue.[26] The term 'public forum' describes publicly owned land open to use for expressive activities. There are two categories of public forum: property the public has always used for expressive and associative activity; and property designated for such activity. In the latter category, the state is under no obligation to keep the facility open to the public, but for as long as it is open it is subject to the same standards as the public forum. To survive scrutiny under the First Amendment the state must show that any content-based restriction on expressive activity in a public forum 'is necessary to serve a compelling state interest and that it is narrowly drawn to achieve that end'.[27] However, the state may also regulate the time, place and manner of the activity. Finding

---

[24] *Canada* v. *Committee for the Commonwealth of Canada* [1991] 1 SCR 139 at 156–7. Lamer CJ concluded that the access should be permitted only where consistent with the state's use of the property.

[25] *Adderly* v. *Florida* 385 US 39 (1966).

[26] For background on this concept see H. Kalven, 'The Concept of the Public Forum: Cox v. Louisiana' [1965] *Supreme Court Review* 1; G. Stone, 'Fora Americana: Speech in Public Places' [1974] *Supreme Court Review* 233.

[27] *Perry Education Association* v. *Perry Local Educators' Association* 460 US 37 (1983) at 45. Although at footnote 7, the Supreme Court found that a designated public forum 'may be created

state-owned property to be a public forum therefore creates 'an exception to the government's right of ownership' and its discretion to exclude.[28]

The public forum analysis has been subject to widespread criticism.[29] Dorsen and Gora argue that the criteria for deciding whether a space constitutes a public forum takes attention away from the expression right at stake, placing questions of ownership centre-stage.[30] Not only is the right of access dependent on the property being publicly owned, but access is determined by looking at the past use or dedication of the land in question, rather than a balance between the interest of the owner and expression right at stake. Justice L' Heureux Dube in the Canadian Supreme Court argued that a focus on past use fails to consider the dynamics of expressive activity: 'The list of sites traditionally associated with public expression is not static. As means of locomotion progress, people shall begin to gather in areas heretofore unknown. Hence the "traditional" component of the public arena analysis must appreciate the "type" of place historically associated with public discussion, and should not be restricted to the actual places themselves.'[31]

The public forum doctrine potentially creates an approach where all or no expressive activities are permitted, depending into which category the publicly owned land falls. However, as habits change, new locations can take on greater importance as a space for communication. Places that were not visited widely before may become more popular and play a more central role in reaching a particular group of people. Different spaces also have varying importance for differing speakers and groups. For example, there is normally little need to access land near a publicly owned power station for the purpose of expressive activities, but a stronger claim for such access arises if the speakers wish to protest about the harm caused to the environment by that particular power station. The connection between the message and space makes access important for that particular speaker, even though it had little past use as a space for expression.

The structure of the First Amendment partly explains the US approach, in so far as it provides less scope for balancing the right with other competing considerations. The public forum doctrine determines the reach of the expression right by focusing on the type of land at stake. If it is found to be a public forum, then the expression right receives greater weight, whereas expressive activities in a non-public forum are more open to regulation.[32] Consequently, balancing

---

for a limited purpose such as use by certain groups' implying some permissible distinction between speakers.

[28] *Canada v. Committee for the Commonwealth of Canada*, [1991] 1 SCR 139 at 150.

[29] For a summary of the criticisms see T. Dienes, 'The Trashing of the Public Forum: Problems in First Amendment Analysis' (1986) 55 *George Washington Law Review* 109.

[30] N. Dorsen and J. Gora, 'Free Speech, Property, and the Burger Court: Old Values, New Balances' [1982] *Supreme Court Review* 195 at 231.

[31] *Canada v. Committee for the Commonwealth of Canada* [1991] 1 SCR 139 at 205–6.

[32] In a non-public forum 'the State may reserve the forum for its intended purposes, communicative or otherwise, as long as the regulation on speech is reasonable and not an effort to suppress expression merely because public officials oppose the speaker's view', *Perry Education Association v. Perry Local Educators' Association* 460 US 37 (1983) at 46.

the expression right with other considerations largely takes place through the prior categorisation of the land. By contrast, the constitutional framework in the UK does not require such a category-based approach, as the court can weigh up the competing interests on the merits of the particular case. Without the strict rules on content neutrality, there is less need to decide in advance the circumstances where those rules apply. Instead, under Articles 10 and 11 the courts can assess an exclusion or restriction of expression on public land with reference to the government's aim and the proportionality of the measure. The normal use of the land will be a factor in deciding whether the exclusion or restriction is proportionate, but will not be decisive. There are some advantages to the public forum approach, as it provides speakers with clear notice as to the areas in which they will receive stronger protection, and helps define the public space subsidy. While some judicial decisions have arguably taken a step towards such an approach, there is not yet a clear equivalent of the public forum doctrine in the UK.[33] However, while the approach taken in judicial review and the Human Rights Act do not create a right of access to a public space, it at least mediates between the public body's rights as a landowner and the right to assemble, providing a potential inroad into the public body's right to exclude.

Private management of publicly owned spaces

The state is not the only actor that can control behaviour on publicly owned land, as private actors have an increasing role in managing such spaces. Examples of such public/private partnerships include policies of Town Centre Management and Business Improvement Districts (BIDs). The government modelled BIDs on programmes of the same name in the United States and Canada and enacted legislation introducing the scheme in England and Wales.[34] The scheme is a partnership between local authorities and businesses, which allows businesses in commercial areas, such as town centres and business parks, to provide services in addition to those provided by the local authority. To establish a BID, businesses in the area must approve the proposed scheme by a vote. If approved, those businesses pay for additional services through a compulsory levy, which is collected by the local authority and then transferred to the body responsible for implementing and managing the BID scheme. That body is often an independent not-for-profit company, with its board of directors drawn from local businesses and also including some members of the local authority. BIDs can provide a wide range of services, including additional cleaning of an area and security patrols by the police or private security firms. Through such services, the scheme can bring many benefits in making the space more attractive for retailers, visitors and other investors.

[33] Feldman, *Civil Liberties and Human Rights in England and Wales*, p. 1015.
[34] The Local Government Act 2003. For the Scottish BIDs see the Planning (Scotland) Act 2006.

While the BIDs programme gives the private sector a say in the management of the publicly owned spaces, it does not give businesses powers equivalent to that of a landowner. The BID therefore has fewer legal tools to control or restrict a speaker. Despite this, the US experience shows that BIDs can have an impact by allowing the interests of local businesses to define the area and emphasise its commercial purpose over other uses.[35] For example, if the BID employs private security firms to police the area, there is a concern that speakers with dissenting views, or irritating to shoppers, will be likely targets for the patrols. In the United States, reports that private security patrols used aggressive techniques to move on the homeless in the Grand Central BID in New York provide some evidence for these fears.[36] While it is still early days for the programme in the UK, critics of the scheme express similar concerns about the use of such methods by private security firms.[37] Even if no aggressive tactics are used, such private security patrols may be primarily concerned with promoting the commercial interests of the levy payers. The impact of the BID can also be subtle, changing the tone of an area in a way that makes assemblies and other political activities seem inappropriate. While BIDs may 'create an atmosphere similar to that of suburban shopping malls' and make town centres feel safer for visitors,[38] the primary function of the public space transforms to serve consumers rather than to provide a communal area that can accommodate political speakers. The UK BIDs have some differences from their US counterparts and how far such concerns will arise here remains to be seen.[39]

If such concerns do arise and the services do impact on the right to assemble, the question arises as to what those people affected can do to protect those rights. The local authority, in so far as it is connected with and has some powers over the BID, provides the most obvious channel for accountability and provides an indirect way to influence or change the BID's activities. The legal accountability of the BID to the public is less clear. The obligations of the HRA do not apply to everyone, but only to a 'public authority'. One strategy may be to argue that some BIDs are subject to the HRA as a 'public authority'. However, public/private partnerships raise some of the most difficult questions in defining a 'public authority' and the courts generally take a narrow definition.[40] The test for a public authority is based on a number of factors that the court applies

---

[35] Under the scheme in England and Wales, representatives from outside the business community may be appointed to the board of the BID, so to ensure that a broader range of interests are considered. However, given that such board members will be appointed by the business community and the additional services will be paid for by those non-domestic rate payers, it is not clear how much of a safeguard it will provide.

[36] Kohn, *Brave New Neighbourhoods*, p. 86. See also L. Staeheli and D. Mitchell, *The People's Property* (London: Routledge, 2008) pp. 67–70.

[37] A. Minton, *Ground Control* (London: Penguin, 2009) pp. 49–50.

[38] F. Vindevogel, 'Private Security and Urban Crime Mitigation' (2005) 5 *Criminal Justice* 233 at 250.

[39] On the differences, see S. Hogg, D. Medway and G. Warnaby, 'Performance Measurement in UK Town Centre Management Schemes and US Business Improvement Districts' (2007) 39 *Environment and Planning* 1513 at 1525–6.

[40] For discussion see S. Palmer, 'Public, Private and the Human Rights Act 1998: an Ideological Divide' (2007) 66 *Cambridge Law Journal* 559.

on a case-by-case basis. There are arguments on either side as to whether the company managing the BID could be subject to the obligations under the HRA in relation to some of its functions.[41] However, even if it is subject to those obligations, the board of the BID itself is unlikely to develop policies or sanction practices that violate Articles 10 and 11. The impact of the BID on speakers is more likely to be subtle, with no identifiable decision or action that interferes with the right or which can be challenged in the courts. For example, a decision to hire a private security firm may create an environment less conducive to expressive activities without interfering with the right in question.

There is also the question of whether the actions of a private security firm could be subject to the obligations under the HRA. The answer will depend on the powers exercised by the security staff. Such a firm could be subject to the HRA as a public authority if it has been 'accredited' by the police and can exercise some police powers that are not available to the ordinary citizen.[42] In such a case, the use of those police powers will be challengeable in the courts where the power interferes with a fundamental right. However, in most cases, private security guards only have those powers held by any other citizen, and will not be subject to the HRA. Unlike the police, the private security guard will not be under any duty to provide positive protection against a hostile audience. Like any other citizen, the security guard may be criminally liable for using force to restrict a speaker. Yet in most cases the security guard will use more subtle methods that rely on the consent of the individual concerned, such as asking the speaker to move on.[43] The presence of a uniformed patrol may be enough to move on a speaker, without any interference with the individual's expression right.

There are other channels for private sector management of the public space and BIDs provide just one example. None of this is to dismiss the benefits that such partnerships can bring, especially in regenerating urban areas. However,

[41] On the test for a public authority, see *YL* v. *Birmingham City Council* [2008] 1 AC 95 and *R (on the application of Weaver)* v. *London & Quadrant Housing Trust* [2009] EWCA Civ 587. The bodies managing the BIDs are often independent companies and the services provided are in addition to rather than replacing the local authority's established public functions. While those factors point to it being a private body, some other factors suggest the BID performs public functions. In particular, BIDs are the product of legislation, receive funds from a statutory compulsory levy, and are to enable projects 'for the benefit of the business improvement district or those who live, work or carry on any activity in the district'. See Local Government Act 2003, s.41. While the company managing the BID is independent, it is normally run on a not-for-profit basis. Furthermore, the activities are closely connected with the local authority, as the authority will normally be involved in drawing up the proposal, have representatives on the board of directors, and has the power to veto the BID proposal in some circumstances.
[42] Under the Police Reform Act 2002, private security guards that have been designated or accredited by the chief police officer may exercise powers that were traditionally exercised by the police. See D. Ormerod and A. Roberts, 'The Police Reform Act 2002 – Increasing Centralisation, Maintaining Confidence and Contracting out Crime Control' [2003] Crim L. R. 141. On the significance of these factors to the definition of a public authority, see *YL* v. *Birmingham City Council* [2008] 1 AC 95 at [102] and [28].
[43] M. Button, *Security Officers and Policing* (Aldershot: Ashgate, 2007) pp. 31–2.

such techniques highlight the blurring between publicly and privately run spaces and how the management of public spaces can affect its potential to become a forum for communication. While the public authority is subject to more traditional avenues of political and legal accountability, the position is less clear in relation to the private managers. The controls that arise may not amount to a direct denial or restriction of the public space to the speaker, but point to erosion, where expressive activities have a lower priority compared with other uses. While publicly owned lands were characterised earlier as a subsidy for political speech and assembly, the potential to use that space is affected by both the direct legal controls and the softer, less visible, methods of managing land use.

Public spaces and private land

The trends discussed so far concern restrictions on the use of publicly owned spaces. Private owners of publicly accessible spaces potentially have broader powers to control expression, given that the right to exclude is subject to fewer legal qualifications than publicly owned land. The discretion is not absolute, as it may be subject to statutory and common law limits such as the public rights of way. However, private owners are not generally subject to the same level of constraint as public bodies that own land.

Two trends have increased the private ownership of public spaces. The first is a policy of selling off public spaces to the private sector. In so far as those policies reduce the number of spaces that are accessible to the public without permission, the effect is to limit the subsidy provided by the state to facilitate expressive activities. The second trend is the increasing importance of spaces that become publicly accessible while under private ownership. Under this latter trend, the private owner does not buy land from the local authority, but develops his own land for a new function, which in turn becomes important as a publicly accessible space. Such privately owned places become popular for visitors and are consequently a significant location to reach a diverse range of people. The out-of-town shopping centre or business park are obvious examples, in which the privately owned space acquires importance as a result of its function and the number and frequency of visitors. These trends highlight the importance of the 'quasi-public places' which people can normally access freely, but which are privately owned. These changes raise the difficult question as to whether such properties are different from any other privately owned land, and if so how can one identify a quasi-public space. However, it is argued here that the identity of the owner, whether a public body or private company, does not determine the public nature of a space.

The shopping centre is the classic example of the tension between private ownership and the right to assemble and speak, and was at the centre of the dispute in *Appleby* v. *UK*.[44] In that case, a group of people sought to collect

---

[44] *Appleby* v. *UK* (2003) 37 EHRR 38.

signatures and distribute leaflets in a privately owned shopping centre in the town of Washington, Tyne and Wear, to oppose local authority plans to build on a nearby park. The centre had been owned by the local authority, but was later sold off to a private company. Although the owner granted access to the centre to a number of other campaigns and groups on previous occasions,[45] that company refused to give access to the leafleters. Before the European Court of Human Rights (ECtHR) the group argued that the state failed in its positive obligation to protect the speakers' Article 10 and 11 rights, as it had not secured access to the centre for the speakers. The ECtHR rejected the claim, while acknowledging that rights of expression and assembly may require the state to provide access to private land in circumstances where the denial of access would destroy the essence of the Convention right. However, the Court found that in this case the refusal of access did not destroy the essence of the right because the group had the chance to exercise their expression rights through other means, such as assembling on property outside the shopping centre and using the local press.[46] From the Court's reasoning, Articles 10 and 11 will require a right of access to private land only where the exclusion has extreme consequences for the speaker.

The decision in *Appleby* gave limited weight to the importance of the location to the message and placed the opportunity to speak on such property at the owner's discretion. In his dissent, Judge Maruste forcefully expressed such concerns and argued that the state should not be able to divest itself of responsibility through privatising land, and that under the majority's approach 'property rights prevailed over freedom of speech'.[47] Furthermore, a number of features of the case gave the speaker a much stronger claim for access: the local authority previously owned the shopping centre; it housed some public services; and other groups had permission to use the centre for expressive purposes on prior occasions. Yet despite these features, the decision in *Appleby* preserved the prerogatives of the owner even in large-scale publicly accessible developments.

Appleby is not a unique case, as the earlier case of *CIN Properties* v. *Rawlins* upheld the right of the owner of a shopping centre in Wellingborough to exclude a group of young men.[48] The policies of other large-scale shopping centres highlight the trend, such as Bluewater in Kent, which famously banned people wearing hooded tops in the Centre, and also bans people distributing leaflets without permission from the owner.[49] Local newspapers and websites sometimes report the exclusion of speakers from privately owned shopping centres, yet aside from such anecdotal evidence the extent to which such policies exclude and deter speakers remains unknown.

---

[45] *Ibid.*, at [20–1].   [46] *Ibid.*, at [48].   [47] *Ibid.*

[48] *CIN Properties* v. *Rawlins* [1995] 39 EG 148; upheld by the the European Commission on Human Rights in *Anderson* v. *United Kingdom* (1998) 25 EHRR CD172.

[49] The Bluewater Code of Conduct provides that: 'Leafleting, canvassing or the conducting of third party interviews or surveys' are not permitted 'unless authorised by Bluewater Centre Management', see www.bluewater.co.uk/content.aspx?urlkey=cu_guestconduct.

While the shopping centre has long been the focus for the tension between private ownership and public space, the scale of such developments has increased in recent years. It is becoming more common to see vast centres housing not only a wide array of shops, but also cafes, restaurants, cinemas and other leisure activities. The best known examples of these larger-scale centres include the Bluewater Centre in Kent, the Metrocentre in Gateshead, and the Trafford Centre in Manchester. As they are often located outside the traditional town centre, provide parking and have everything the visitor needs under one roof, there may be little need for the visitor to step on any neighbouring land, whether publicly or privately owned. This self-contained quality of the space in turn limits the alternative opportunities for people to leaflet or collect signatures on nearby land. The growth of the larger-scale shopping centres may increase the importance of access, if the speakers are to reach their target audience.

The increase in the private ownership of public spaces goes beyond the shopping centre. Sometimes a single company will own large publicly accessible developments with office complexes, shops and living spaces. Canary Wharf in London's Docklands, owned by a public limited company, is an early example. The potential for such a development to impact on people's capacity to communicate was highlighted in 2005, when campaigners against the low pay of cleaners employed at Canary Wharf were forced to cancel a march through the development after the owner refused to grant access and gained an injunction to stop the protest.[50] This type of development is also found in town centre spaces, such as Liverpool One, in which a single company has a 250-year lease of a 42.5-acre site in central Liverpool.[51] Such schemes can bring major benefits to an area. By leasing land for development to a private company, the area attracts private investment that helps to pay for the regeneration of urban areas previously in decline. However, with such developments come concerns that owners will follow the shopping centre model of control, with limits on access and rules on behaviour.[52] Like the shopping centres, such areas will generally employ private security firms to ensure such rules are followed. Not all such owners will attempt to follow the shopping centre model and some may be more tolerant of expressive activities. Yet this provides limited support for the speaker if the owner has discretion to revoke permission. As Lord Irvine stated in *DPP* v. *Jones*, 'mere toleration does not secure a fundamental right'.[53]

These developments raise a number of issues. Critics express concern about the dedication of public spaces to consumerism, leading to a lack of authenticity and making most town centres look the same. Defining the area in this way

---

[50] *Guardian*, 9 October 2004.
[51] See Minton, *Ground Control*, ch. 2. In email correspondence, Liverpool City Council confirmed that there are no public rights of way over Liverpool One.
[52] *Ibid.*   [53] *DPP* v. *Jones* [1999] 2 AC 240 at 258.

may be enough to signal that some speakers will not be welcome.[54] It also raises issues about exclusion, such as the 'hoodies' at Bluewater, or the lack of space for the homeless. However, the concern from the perspective of political equality is that it denies people access to an important forum and gives property owners a disproportionate opportunity to influence democratic decision-making. The first way such influence arises is through the direct political power that comes with ownership of an important public place. Like the media owner or the company threatening to take assets out of the UK, the owner of a major business or retail development will be important to the local economy. As a result, the local authority is likely to give considerable weight to the views of the owner. The second way it provides a disproportionate chance to influence is through the control of public space as a forum for expression. The owner can use the property to advance a particular viewpoint, or to limit opportunities for others to do so. While it is unlikely that a corporate owner of a public space will seek to advance the political views of its directors, the exclusion of speakers may be the result of commercial pressures, for example where some shoppers will oppose the speaker's message, or where that message upsets the businesses and other tenants on that land.[55] The concern arises not only where the owner uses this power selectively against groups with less popular views, but also where there is a blanket ban on all such expressive activities, rendering the public space largely free of political discussion. The decision in *Appleby* is therefore disappointing in preserving the owner's ability to use property in a way that shapes political debate and curtails the opportunities for others to communicate.

Rights of access

To counter the privatisation and increasing controls on public spaces, the strategy proposed here is a right of access to certain types of private property. A right would give people a legal entitlement to access property for reasonable expressive and associative purposes, and would require the landowner to show some good reason to justify an exclusion. Such a measure would promote political equality by ensuring that people can use the public space as a forum to communicate with others. As assemblies are the classic type of 'cheap speech', access to this type of forum is particularly important in a democracy. In so far as access to land is a subsidy, a legal right places that subsidy on a firmer ground and seeks to compensate for the privatisation of certain spaces. Earlier, the provision of space as a subsidy was discussed in relation to publicly owned land, whereas here the right of access relates to privately owned land. In this sense, it can be seen as a redistribution of a particular political resource.[56] A legal right does not just promote equality by securing a resource that is necessary for assembly, but

---

[54] Button, *Security Officers and Policing*, pp. 48–9.
[55] See A. Wakefield, *Selling Security* (Cullompton: Willan, 2003) pp. 76–8.
[56] J. Balkin, 'Some Realism About Pluralism: Legal Realist Approaches to the First Amendment' (1990) Duke L. J. 375.

seeks to strengthen people's position relative to the wealth of the owner of that land. A right of access imposes a limit on the owner's use of the land in so far as it curtails the extent of his or her discretion and may prevent the owner dedicating the whole space to a particular viewpoint. However, it does so in a way that increases the quantity of expression. Given that public spaces can usually accommodate different points of view, a right of access can avoid many of the difficult questions of allocation, such as monitoring how much time and space to give each speaker, aside from the public order issues discussed earlier.

Before considering the legal basis of such a right, it is necessary to distinguish between two types of access right: a general right of access and an equal right of access. Under the latter type of right, if the owner allows access to one group of speakers, then she should similarly grant access to other people speaking on that topic or issue. As a result, allowing a group of pro-life activists access to a shopping centre would trigger a group of pro-choice leafleters right of equal access to that centre. In this example, the pro-choice group's access right is contingent on the pro-life group's earlier activity. By contrast, a general right of access would allow access for expressive activities regardless of the owner's previous choices about permitting speakers on the land. The general right of access aims to supply speakers and groups with the necessary resources for effective communication. An equal access rule has a more modest goal in eliminating arbitrary discrimination between groups, rather than levelling the playing field in a more general sense.

A difficulty with a rule providing equal access is in determining what should trigger the right. Difficult questions arise in selecting a comparator with whom others can demand equal access. It is not clear if granting access for any expressive purposes, or only to those speaking about a related political theme, will suffice to trigger the right. If the latter is taken, it is not clear what views have a sufficient connection with those seeking to access the property. For example, would a group selling poppies in a shopping centre be enough to trigger a right of equal access for those protesting against a war?[57] While the problems of definition and allocation associated with the equal treatment of viewpoints are not insurmountable and can be addressed in other contexts, the difficulties in formulating a standard will be more problematic for a right of equal access that is legally enforceable.

A further problem with a right of equal access is that it would still base the right on the landowner's discretion. The initial decision to grant access to a speaker, that in turn triggers the equal access right, is the unfettered choice of the landowner. The landowner could avoid an equal access claim by refusing access to any speakers. While that appears consistent with equality, the distinctive role of those public spaces that act as a forum provides a reason against that

---

[57] In *Lloyd* v. *Tanner* 407 US 551 (1972), the right of access was limited to where expression was connected with the operations on the property. In his dissent, Justice Marshall argued that the expressive activities of other groups on that land helped to define what the operations on the mall were.

approach. Shutting off the space from all speakers would deprive people of the very resource that needs to be equally distributed. Furthermore, in practice denying access to all assemblies or speakers to that space would have unequal effects. For example, one group may voice their position in a newspaper, but the public space may provide the most suitable or affordable place for another group to reply to that message. Even if the landowner acts even-handedly and refuses access to any speaker, the latter group is at a disadvantage in the overall chances to communicate. This argument views the public space as more than a private resource with political uses, but as an important forum to which speakers need access to participate and offset inequalities that lie elsewhere. A general right of access would, by contrast, give the speaker freedom to act independently of the landowner's discretion. For these reasons, the approach considered here will be a general right of access, which could be secured in a number of different ways.

One method of securing access is for a public body to use existing powers to create rights of way when it sells off land, for example through a walkways agreements or the creation of a highway. The landowner may have little reason to agree to such a right of way and many local authorities may have little incentive to secure such rights when seeking to sell land. The presence of a right of way may reduce the value of the land and weaken the local authority's bargaining position in relation to the overall transaction. In any event, the rights of way are not the same as access for expressive purposes. While speakers and assemblies can make reasonable use of the highways for expressive purposes, such a use is less likely to be reasonable where the highway passes through privately owned land.[58] Furthermore, the purpose of a right of way is primarily to allow people to pass over land. Consequently, such rights are normally limited, for example applying only to certain parts of the property, and not to all those parts that are publicly accessible. The creation of a right of way provides some limited access to land, but the chance to speak or assemble on that property will still largely be at the landowner's discretion. Instead, the following sections will look at a separate right of access to some privately owned spaces and the potential to create such a right through the common law, through the application of the ECHR, or through statute.

A common law right of access

The first way to develop a right of access is through the common law. A common law right of access would entail some redefinition of private property to restrict the right to exclude, in areas where the owner has made the land publicly accessible and, therefore, a 'quasi-public space'. Under this approach, by opening up the property to the public, the owner grants a licence to the visitors that cannot be restricted without reasonable cause.[59] Along these lines, a common law right would qualify the law of trespass, so that the owner can exclude visitors to such spaces only on

[58] *DPP* v. *Jones* [1999] 2 AC 240 at 256 and 293.
[59] See *Uston* v. *Resorts International Hotel* 89 NJ 163 (1982).

objectively reasonable grounds. To support such an approach, Gray and Gray draw on the history of property law to argue that the right to exclude has previously been subject to similar qualifications,[60] and that a further qualification of that right would develop property law in a way that takes into account the 'unprecedented changes in the social, demographic and urban structure of contemporary life'.[61] Under this view, the power of the landowner to exclude and rely on the law of trespass should vary according to the nature and function of the property. As Laksin CJ argued in a dissent in the Canadian shopping centre case, *Harrison* v. *Carswell*, '[t]he considerations which underlie the protection of private residences cannot apply to the same degree to a shopping centre in respect of its parking areas, roads and sidewalks' and that such 'amenities are closer in character to public roads and sidewalks than to a private dwelling'.[62] Consequently, the right to exclude in its traditional form in property law should not apply to all privately owned land, but should vary according to the nature of the space.

Despite the merits of this approach, it does raise a number of broader issues in property law. Requiring reasonable cause to exclude visitors would go beyond a right of access for political expression, and would create a general right of access for other purposes such as social activities. This is not to reject the common law solution, but rather to recognise that it raises a wider range of issues than the equal chance to influence democratic politics. A further concern is the suitability of the courts to undertake this task in developing the common law. Such a concern is not shared by Gray and Gray, who argue that public law values have begun to 'infiltrate the heartland of private law' and consequently see the courts as well placed to revise the law of property to accommodate a 'reasonable access rule' for certain spaces.[63] However, in making an inroad into existing property rights, such a rule requires the court to balance competing rights and interests in deciding when the exclusion has been made with reasonable cause. Such a methodology is arguably unsuited to a private law context, which is concerned with different goals and places greater emphasis on legal certainty than is found with public law.[64] In so far as it amounts to a redistribution of resources, such a measure is arguably better suited to the elected branches of government rather than the courts.[65] In any event, so far the courts seem unwilling to take such a step. Despite arguably moving in that direction in *DPP* v. *Jones*, when such an argument has been put before them, the courts have been reluctant to develop a licence for the general public to access private property.[66]

---

[60] K. Gray and S. Gray, 'Civil Rights, Civil Wrongs and Quasi-Public Space' [1999] EHRLR 46 at 85–9.

[61] *Ibid.*   [62] [1976] 2 SCR 200 at 207–8.

[63] Gray and Gray, 'Civil Rights, Civil Wrongs and Quasi-Public Space', at 101.

[64] See Feldman, 'Property and Public Protest', pp. 57–8.

[65] R. Moon, 'Access to Public and Private Property under Freedom of Expression' (1989) 20 *Ottawa Law Review* 339 at 386.

[66] *CIN Properties* v. *Rawlins* [1995] 39 EG 148. In a subsequent appeal, the European Commission on Human Rights found there was no interference with the applicants' rights of association, *Anderson* v. *United Kingdom* (1998) 25 EHRR CD172.

While the courts will not modify the common law in such a major way on their own, as a public authority the courts are required to act compatibly with Convention rights under the Human Rights Act.[67] Given that this duty has influenced the development of some common law doctrines, particularly in relation to restraints on the publication of private information, in the future it could impact on property law. In this view, the courts are under a duty to interpret laws consistently with ECHR rights, which could in turn lead to the law being developed in a way that limits the right to exclude. However, what is required by the courts under the duty to act compatibly with Convention rights remains unclear and at present it seems unlikely the courts will rely on the duty to protect speakers from exclusion.[68] Following the decision in *Appleby* that the state is not under an obligation to provide access to privately owned land, Articles 10 and 11 do not require the courts to develop a right of access. However, even if the court did go down this path and develop the common law to take greater account of expression rights, there are still the objections about the private law concepts being ill-suited to handle the public law issues and the potential lack of clarity as such a body of law develops. Furthermore, the courts would have to take into account the privacy and property rights of the owner, so it is not clear that they would come down on the side of the expression right. Consequently, the duty on the courts under the HRA at present seems unlikely to spur the development of a common law right of access and, even if it did, it would arguably provide limited assistance to speakers.

A public authority under the Human Rights Act

Another possible method to create a right of access arises where the private owners of public spaces are directly subject to the provisions of the Human Rights Act and are required to act compatibly with Convention rights on the grounds that it is a 'public authority' under s.6 of the HRA. As with publicly owned land, such an approach would not guarantee access to the land, but would allow the challenge of any exclusions by the landowner that interfere with freedom of expression or association. Such an approach would sidestep the limits of *Appleby*, as the issue would not be whether the state is under a duty to secure access to private land. Instead, the landowner would be subject to a negative obligation not to interfere with assembly or expression rights.

Under the HRA, 'public authorities' are subdivided into two categories: 'core' and 'hybrid'.[69] The core public authority must act compatibly with Convention rights in all its actions. By contrast, hybrid public authorities have mixed public and private functions; only in relation to the former must the hybrid public authority act compatibly with the Convention right. While emphasising that no universal test exists as to whether a function is public, the House of Lords in

---

[67] See *Campbell* v. *MGN* [2004] 2 AC 457 at [132–3].
[68] In the obligation to act compatibly, the courts are not under a duty to create any new cause of action, *Campbell* v. *MGN* [2004] 2 AC 457 at [132–133].
[69] Human Rights Act 1998, s.6.

Aston Cantlow outlined some factors that indicate whether a body is a hybrid public authority, including whether a function is publicly funded, backed by statutory powers, takes the place of a local authority or government activity and whether it provides a public service.[70]

If the private landowner is to be covered by the HRA at all, it is most likely to be a hybrid public authority. However, given the generally narrow definition of a hybrid public authority taken by the courts, relatively few private landowners will come within the HRA's coverage. There could be some circumstances where the private landowner is deemed to be such a body, for example where a public body sells part of a town centre to a private company and the company is subject to public duties or holds special powers. Where the private landowner is a hybrid public authority, it will be subject to the HRA only in relation to those acts that are of a public nature, as opposed to its private actions.[71] It will not always be clear whether the landowner is acting in its public capacity when it excludes speakers from property, or whether such exclusion is an exercise of the private rights of the landowner unrelated to the public function.

The attempt to bring privately owned public spaces under constitutional constraints has parallels in the US doctrine of 'quasi public property'. The US Supreme Court developed that doctrine in *Marsh* v. *Alabama,* where Justice Black upheld the First Amendment right to distribute leaflets in a privately owned company town, where that property was the functional equivalent of a state-owned town.[72] The rationale of *Marsh* was extended in *Logan Valley* beyond a privately owned town to a shopping centre.[73] The Supreme Court held that a landowner could not invoke state trespass laws to exclude picketers from a shopping centre parking lot. Four years later in *Lloyd* v. *Tanner,* the Court began its retreat from this position and limited the reach of the doctrine to scenarios where a speaker's message relates to the shopping centre's operations and there are no alternative means of expression.[74] Finally, in *Hudgens* v. *NLRB,*[75] the Supreme Court overturned *Logan Valley,* largely freeing the private landowner from constitutional constraints. *Marsh* still stands, but only as a narrow exception to the general rule in the case of a company town. The Court's position possibly reflects not only a change of judicial priorities, but also the difficulties faced by a court in deciding where such a right applies and who is entitled to access when applying expression to privately owned land.

Despite the limits of the quasi public forum doctrine in *Hudgens,* US states are still free to grant a right of access to private land under state law.[76] An example of this can be found in New Jersey, where the State Supreme Court upheld a right of

[70] *Aston Cantlow and Wilmcote with Billesley Parochial Church Council* v. *Wallbank* [2004] 1 AC 546, Lord Nicholls at [12]. Lord Hope at [63]–[64]; Lord Hobhouse at [88]–[89].
[71] *YL* v. *Birmingham City Council* [2008] 1 AC 95 at [130–1].
[72] *Marsh* v. *Alabama* 326 US 501 (1946).
[73] *Food Employees Union Local 590* v. *Logan Valley Plaza* 391 US 308 (1968).
[74] *Lloyd* v. *Tanner* 407 US 551 (1972).
[75] *Hudgens* v. *National Labor Relations Board* 424 US 507 (1976).
[76] *Pruneyard Shopping Center* v. *Robins* 447 US 74 (1980).

access to distribute leaflets on a privately owned shopping mall under the state constitution.[77] In deciding whether there is a right of access to private land, the New Jersey courts consider the normal use of the property, the extent and nature of the public's invitation to use the property, and the purpose of the expressive activity in relation to the use of the property.[78] Consequently, a broad invitation to the public to enter the shopping mall changes the nature of the land, distinguishing it from other types of private property. For a right of access to arise, the court does not demand that the private land be the functional equivalent of the state. Instead, any analogy between the private landowner and the state provides evidence of a stronger claim to access, but it is not necessary to establish the right. In this approach to the issue of access, the New Jersey Supreme Court balances the strength of the right to exclude with the right to speak or participate and applies the same questions regardless of whether property is owned by the state or by a private body. Rather than expanding the definition of a public body or the state, it allows the application of the political rights to transcend the division.

This is not to say that the New Jersey decision has had this far-reaching effect. In *New Jersey Coalition Against the War*, Chief Justice Wilentz of the NJ State Supreme Court emphasised the limits of the right of access. The landowner could impose reasonable time, place and manner restrictions.[79] The right of access protects only expression relating to political and societal, as opposed to commercial, issues and permits only the least disruptive forms of expression, such as leafleting.[80] Furthermore, the Chief Justice indicated that the right of access would apply to a very limited range of properties.[81] In this, he suggested a cautious approach when applying the balancing exercise, mindful of the potential inroad being made into traditional property rights. Such an approach was open to the New Jersey courts, as the protection of freedom of expression under the New Jersey State Constitution does not require state action. By contrast, the Human Rights Act applies only to public authorities and could not apply to private bodies in the same way. However, the New Jersey model for access rights could provide a template for a possible statutory right of access.

A statutory right of access

Aside from any Convention obligations, a right of access established through statute could provide a wider distribution of political resources and chances to speak. Under this approach, legislation could create a presumption of access for political expression to certain privately owned properties. An initial question

---

[77] *New Jersey Coalition Against War in the Middle East* v. *JMB Realty Corp* 138 NJ 326 (1993).
[78] As set out in the test in *State* v. *Schmid* 84 NJ 535 (1980), in which access to a university campus was granted.
[79] *New Jersey Coalition against War in the Middle East* v. *JMB Realty Corp* 138 NJ 326 (1993) at 377–8. See also *Green Party of New Jersey* v. *Hartz Mountain Industries* 164 NJ 127 (2000).
[80] *New Jersey Coalition against War in the Middle East* v. *JMB Realty Corp* 138 NJ 326 (1993) at 374.
[81] *Ibid.*, at 373.

is to decide which properties it should apply to and to define a public space. One option is to delegate this task to the courts, applying the criteria on a case-by-case basis and creating a statutory balancing test similar to that in *New Jersey Coalition Against the War*. The court would then assess the strength of the claim to exclude the speakers alongside the right to expression. The criteria could consider the nature of the property; how far that property is normally open to the public; the manner of expression; the possible alternative means of communication; and the importance of the location to the message. Such factors would consider both the rights of the owner, as well as those of the speaker. The difficulty with a balancing test would be the ad hoc nature in which the claim of the speaker and the landowner remain uncertain until resolved by a court. Greater certainty may arise as more case law develops, with the courts giving an indication of when such rights will apply and of what its limits will be.

An alternative approach is to designate the public spaces through delegated legislation or an agency ruling, applying similar criteria. Legislation designating property for expressive activities may create a rigid categorisation of land and thereby overlook the dynamic relationship between location and expression, a problem with the public and quasi public forum analysis discussed earlier. Allowing the categorisation of public spaces to be periodically updated could avoid such a static approach arising. A further danger is that the official making the designation would be subject to lobbying pressure from the owners of the largest spaces, which is an important consideration when deciding who should have that power. However, under such a statutory scheme a politically and legally accountable official would decide on which private property the expressive activities take place. It would also create greater certainty than a vague balancing test. While statutory formulas based on the designation of land or a general balancing test have merits, the important point is that the legislature would sanction the limit on the property rights independent of ECHR obligations or common law doctrines.

The rights of the owner

Against such a right of access are concerns that it would constitute too great an interference with the rights of the landowner. To accommodate these concerns, the suggested criteria for deciding whether a right of access applies will take into account the impact on the owner and the use of land. This will provide a safeguard from major interferences with the owner's rights. The legislation could also provide further safeguards, such as requiring the speakers to give advance notice and allowing the owner to impose time, place and manner conditions on speakers seeking access. However, even with this qualification, the right of access still amounts to a significant change in the owner's power to use his property. The following section will consider the strength of these objections, looking at arguments that a right of access is a disproportionate interference with the owner's freedom of speech, privacy and property.

The owner's freedom of expression

A right of access could potentially conflict with the expression rights of the landowner. As was discussed in Chapter 3, the landowner may find the views of those seeking access morally repugnant, or fear an association with views he does not hold. The latter concern should not be overstated as, if the right of access is known, little chance arises for third parties to confuse the views of those with access with those of the owner.[82] However, the right of access may still undermine any political message that the landowner seeks to advance through the use of his property. This does not mean the landowner's freedom of expression should prevail simply because it is backed by property ownership.

The strength of the objection will depend on the use of the land. Large public spaces such as shopping centres or business parks are normally engaged in commercial activities, rather than seeking to persuade the public on any particular political message. In such circumstances, the right of access curtails the power to exclude speakers, but does not dilute any message the landowner seeks to advance. It only curtails the decision to dedicate the site to commercial uses, rather than impacting on the owner's political views. However, there could be instances where the owner and tenants establish a public space, which does seek to promote a particular message. One example is where a landowner establishes an ethical shopping centre in which all the retailers agree to sell only fair trade and environmentally friendly products. The owner of the centre decorates it with pictures of famous environmental campaigners and with posters explaining the risks of global warming. A right of access could undermine the purpose of the centre if it requires the owner to allow a pressure group into the centre to persuade people of the need to deregulate environment laws and abolish the minimum wage, which, this group argues, are crippling local businesses. In this example, the space has more than just a commercial use and the right of access will interfere with the message of the owner.

The owner's use of the space should not, however, be decisive. The owner's wish to use property to promote his viewpoint does not elevate his speech right above those seeking access. The owner's activity raises the very concerns about equality and the use of economic power that the right of access seeks to address. A stronger claim to exclude will arise where people choose to visit a centre (such as the 'ethical shopping centre') because they agree with its political message. Here it is not simply the owner imposing his own view, but that the centre amounts to an association of like-minded people. Such a claim will be more convincing where the centre is one among many from which people can choose, rather than a focal point for the community as a whole. These claims will depend on the circumstances and need closer examination. For example, the choice of visitors to go to the 'ethical shopping centre' may not signal

---

[82] As the landowner is free to put up signs dissociating him or herself with the views of the speakers, see *Pruneyard Shopping Center v. Robins* 447 US 74 (1980) at 2043–4.

approval of the message, but may be the result of a lack of competitors in the locality, or of convenience. In such circumstances, the power to exclude may arise again from its commercial and economic power. If that is the case, a right of access is not an imposition on the other visitors' freedom of association and may actually help balance the views being promoted by the landowner. In any event, even where every visitor consents and agrees with the political views of the centre, it is not clear that the right of access undermines the purpose of the centre. Visitors can still ignore the views being advanced by the interest group and continue to shop there. The strength of right to exclude also depends on the presence of some alternative spaces to reach other people. Where the alternatives are limited, the access rights can serve deliberative goals by ensuring the centre's visitors hear diverse views.

Privacy and the home

Different considerations arise when people seek to assemble and speak in a primarily residential area. The concern is not just that the assembly will obstruct others or create disorder, but that it will undermine the interest in privacy closely associated with the home. Reflecting this view of the home, Chief Justice Burger stated in the US Supreme Court that while 'we are often "captives" outside the sanctuary of the home and subject to objectionable speech', the right of the speaker 'stops at the outer boundary of every person's domain'.[83] Residential areas do not function as a general meeting place or forum like the town centre, and the interest in privacy is clearly a factor that can justify exclusion.

Residential areas can, however, still be important for freedom of expression. Communicative activities will often take place in streets around people's homes, although a wider range of restrictions may be thought permissible in such a location. Difficult issues arise where a privately owned housing development, or a gated community, has a rule excluding political speakers, or selectively permitting access only to speakers with a particular political outlook.[84] Assuming all the residents of the complex agree to such a rule, the question is whether the rights of owners and residents should prevail over the expression of the outsiders. While it may seem equivalent to a resident putting a sign on the door stating 'no canvassers', the impact is broader in so far as it excludes speakers not just from the doorstep, but the privately owned street. The strength of the claim here will depend on the extent to which the speaker has any alternative means to access those residents. Furthermore, a difficulty is that the residents are depriving themselves of information, raising the question of whether the residents

---

[83] *Rowan v. United States Post Office* 397 US 728 (1970), upholding a statute requiring names to be removed from mailing lists when requested by the addressee. See also *Frisby v. Schultz* 487 US 474 (1988), in which the Supreme Court considered picketing in a residential area, and Justice Frankfurter's dissent in *Martin v. Struthers* 319 US 141 (1943) at 152–3.

[84] For example, the New Jersey Superior Court affirmed a right of access to a gated residential community to distribute political leaflets, *Guttenberg Taxpayers and Rentpayers Association v. Galaxy Towers Condominium Association* 297 NJ Super. 404 (1996).

give informed consent to the rules excluding a particular political viewpoint.[85] While the right of access discussed earlier would not apply to residential spaces, such areas can still be important to the opportunity to communicate.

The concern with privacy also arises with non-residential property, where the concern is not for the privacy of the owner but of the visitor. Such issues have been most prominent with pro-life campaigners assembling outside abortion clinics, where the concern is for the patient's privacy, or with animal rights activists campaigning outside laboratories. In such circumstances the strength of the claim of the speaker to access the space will partly depend on the specific nature of the activity, and whether it is seeking to persuade rather than intimidate or harass. In the UK, harassment or public order laws regulate such activities,[86] whereas in the United States the establishment of 'buffer zones' restricting speakers in vicinity of an abortion clinic attempts to protect the rights of visitors.[87] While such controls are sometimes regarded as censorship, the approach taken here is not hostile to the limitation of expression rights where necessary to protect competing rights. Instead the imposition of any limits should depend on the interest of the visitor and the nature of the land in question, rather than on the discretion of an owner of a large plot of land. If there is a concern with the privacy of the visitor, that concern will be just as pressing no matter who owns the land.

Property rights

A further objection to a right of access is that it would interfere with the property rights of the owner. Along these lines Justice Reed, in his dissent in *Marsh*, compared the right of access to commandeering property without compensation.[88] Such an argument could also rely on Article 1 of the First Protocol to the ECHR, which guarantees the individual 'peaceful enjoyment of his possessions'. However, a right of access would not amount to a 'deprivation' of property, but would merely regulate the use of the property, to which more lenient standards apply under Article 1.[89] Such regulations and controls on property are permitted when 'in accordance with the general interest' and the interference achieves a fair balance 'between the demands of the general interest of the community and the requirements of the individual's fundamental rights'.[90] A right of access would fall within this provision, as the promotion of political expression and assembly rank not only as an objective in the general interest, but also as one

---

[85] For discussion of a similar point in relation to religious communities, see Kohn, *Brave New Neighbourhoods*, pp. 105–7.

[86] For example, in *DPP* v. *Clarke* (1991) 94 Cr App Rep 359. See also the Protection from Harassment Act 1997.

[87] See *Hill* v. *Colorado* 530 US 703 (2000).

[88] *Marsh* v. *Alabama* 326 US 501 (1946) at 515. See also Justice Black's dissent in *Food Employees Union Local 590* v. *Logan Valley Plaza* 391 US 308 (1968) at 330.

[89] In *Chassagnou* v. *France* (1998) 7 BHRC 151, a requirement to let hunters onto private land was deemed to be a 'control' rather than a deprivation of property.

[90] *Ibid.*, at [75].

of the primary aims of the Convention itself. In determining the fairness of the balance, the courts will look at whether the right of access is proportionate to the aim being pursued, although the courts will normally show respect to Parliament's judgement.[91] In considering this issue, the limited nature of the right of access must be stressed. It would permit only reasonable and peaceful activities, and could be subject to conditions on the way the right is exercised. The extent to which the access right strikes a fair balance will also depend on how far it limits the use of property or imposes burdens.

A statutory right of access imposes additional burdens if the owner has to pay to tidy up after the speakers, employ additional security guards, or make the property safe for the visitors.[92] Whether such costs will arise depends on the land in question. Where the space is already open to the public, such as a shopping centre or business park, the owner will be likely to incur such costs in any event, and it is not clear how much of an additional burden this will be.[93] If the right of access were to apply to places less frequently visited by the public, then a number of strategies could address this. For example, state services could provide some support where necessary, such as policing or security. Alternatively, any legal liabilities of the owner for visitors to the property could be limited by statute, so that the visitors or the state take on the risks of entering the property.

Even if the additional burdens are minimal, the owner will still face costs in so far as the right of access affects the value of the land. In *Appleby*, the UK government suggested that a requirement that local authorities include a contract term permitting a right of access when selling property to a private buyer would weaken an authority's bargaining position and lead to a sale at a lower price.[94] While such an argument rests on an assumption that a right of access would reduce the value of the land, such a loss is not an inevitable consequence. In large spaces that are open to the public, it need not prevent the use of land continuing to be profitable. Requiring access does not limit the primary use of the property or drain it of commercial value.[95] If such an effect could be shown, it could be dealt with through some compensation. The First Protocol does not normally require compensation when the state merely controls the use rather than deprives the owner of the property, although in some cases such a payment may help point to a fair balance being struck.[96] Even though compensation to the landowner is unlikely to be required under the ECHR, it could provide a

[91] *R (Countryside Alliance)* v. *Attorney General* [2008] 1 AC 719 at [47] and [129].
[92] See Justice Garibaldi's dissent in *New Jersey Coalition against War in the Middle East* v. *JMB Realty Corp* 138 NJ 326 (1993) above, at 403.
[93] *Ibid.*, at 342.
[94] *Appleby* v. *UK* (2003) 37 EHRR 38 at [37].
[95] In the US case of *Pruneyard*, the court concluded that allowing access to a shopping mall to distribute leaflets would not drain ownership of its value, *Pruneyard Shopping Center* v. *Robins* 447 US 74 (1980) at 2041–3.
[96] For discussion see *R (Trailer and Marina (Leven) Ltd)* v. *Secretary of State for the Environment, Food and Rural Affairs* [2005] 1 WLR 1267 at [56–8].

way of addressing concerns about losses where it can be shown that the right of access would diminish the value of the land.

Aside from the cost objections, the right of access would arguably interfere with the owner's use and enjoyment of the property, in so far as the owner loses the choice whether to exclude the speaker from the property. This argument overlaps with freedom of association as the right forces the owner to tolerate the presence of speakers she may oppose. A similar issue arose in *Chassagnou* v. *France* where a legal requirement that landowners, who were ethically opposed to hunting, permit hunters onto their land violated Protocol 1.[97] That case is distinguishable from the right of access being proposed here, as the right requires the landowner to permit only the advocacy of views she opposes taking place on the property, rather than the act itself. In other words, a right of access for expressive purposes may require some owners to tolerate the advocacy of hunting, but would not require the owner to tolerate the actual hunting on the land against her will. Given that the types of space subject to the proposed right of access would already be publicly accessible, the impact on the enjoyment of land would be limited.

Conclusion

Access to public spaces for expressive purposes is an important part of political equality. The provision of such space helps to subsidise effective communication in a way that most sections of society can utilise. It therefore provides a channel of participation that not only helps to provide information, but also serves the individual's interest in participation. Yet several trends have highlighted how this resource has come under pressure through legal controls on the right to assemble, private management of publicly owned spaces and the increasing importance of privately owned publicly accessible places. The public order controls on the right to speak and assemble potentially reduce the value of the 'public space subsidy' to the speaker and have particular impact on those without the resources to speak elsewhere. In privately managed spaces, the concern is that commercial goals receive greater priority at the expense of other uses of the land. The private ownership of public spaces raises similar points, but access to the land is largely at the discretion of the landowner. The owner therefore has greater say in the uses of the public spaces, while the opportunities for others to communicate are potentially reduced.

The solution proposed here has been to place the right of the speaker on firmer ground, to ensure that reasonable access can be secured whether the space is publicly or privately owned. The presence of the speaker would no longer be at the tolerance of the landowner, and the right of access would redistribute political resources in a way that partly offsets the impact of the privatisation of public spaces. It also avoids some of the more difficult managerial

---

[97] *Chassagnou* v. *France* (1998) 7 BHRC 151.

questions found when attempting to extend a right of access to other forums for communication, such as the mass media. Like all the measures discussed in other chapters, it is merely a step towards political equality rather than its full achievement. Yet qualifying some of the prerogatives associated with private land ownership, one of society's most prized assets, will help to demonstrate the strength of the commitment in law to the democratic values of equality, expression and participation.

7

The mass media: democratic dreams and private propagandists

The mass media play an essential role in a democracy. The virtues of a free press have long been stressed as a way of holding the government to account and maintaining an active and informed citizenry. Yet a tension exists between the mass media and equality. It is not possible for every individual or group to have equal resources to speak to a mass audience. The mass media implies a level of inequality in which a few people communicate with many.[1] The inequality is unproblematic if an idealised account of the media is taken, in which newspapers and broadcasters merely serve the needs of citizens and amplify their concerns. However, in practice, the idealistic accounts of the media often give way to a more sceptical view, that far from empowering citizens, the media exerts political power on behalf of its owners, staff or advertisers.

Concerns about the power of the media are not new. In 1931 Prime Minister Stanley Baldwin famously complained that newspaper owners exercise 'power without responsibility'.[2] The view of the media as wielding political power does not just come from disgruntled politicians. The media sometimes encourages such a view, boasting of its ability to determine an election outcome.[3] The concern may not be novel, yet the power of the media is seen to be in the ascendancy, playing a more central role in public life. As one commentator wrote in 2004, '[t]he media are more pervasive, seeping everywhere into the vacuum left by the shrinking of the old powers'.[4] While the potential influence of the media impacts on politics in a number of ways, this chapter will look at its impact on political equality. In particular it will focus on ways to prevent the media being used to privilege those with greater wealth in political debate, in the hope that such constraints can promote the more idealistic account of the media in a democracy.

Before looking at these issues in greater depth, it is necessary to say what is meant by terms such as 'media power'. Normally this does not mean direct

---

[1] C. E. Baker, *Media Concentration and Democracy* (Cambridge University Press, 2007) p. 10.

[2] Baldwin's statement was made in a speech on 17 March 1931 in support of a Conservative Party candidate, Duff Cooper. Lord Beaverbrook's Empire Party fielded an opposing candidate in the same constituency.

[3] After the Conservative Party victory in the 1992 General Election, the *Sun* published the headline on 11 April 1992, 'It's the Sun wot won it!'.

[4] A. Sampson, *Who Runs This Place?* (London: John Murray, 2004) p. 354.

power over a particular decision, but rather a chance to influence. The first and most common channel of media influence is through the capacity to communicate with a mass audience. The mass media plays a major role in deciding which people, arguments and viewpoints will be heard, and which issues will be prominent. It both sets the agenda and contributes to political debate. This is not to suggest that the media will always have an effect on its audience or political decisions.[5] Assertions that any newspaper delivered an election should be treated with scepticism. Nor will the political issues selected by the media automatically determine a legislative programme or voter's priorities. What is of concern here is the distribution of the opportunities to communicate. Media coverage may not be sufficient to secure a result, but having the chance to reach a mass audience will often be necessary to persuade the public.

The opportunities for the media to use its resources to influence the public have special protection in election campaigns. When a political party, candidate or any other actor attempts to use its resources to influence an election, the amounts it can spend during the campaign are limited by law.[6] However, coverage and comment on an election campaign in the broadcast media and the press (other than advertisements) are exempt from party funding laws.[7] Consequently, while the law stops a wealthy individual from spending unlimited sums to support a party or a candidate in an election, there is nothing to stop a media owner using his property to endorse a party, or provide favourable coverage, even if the value of this coverage exceeds the spending limits that apply to non-media entities.[8] The concern with the media therefore overlaps with the arguments about inequalities arising through election spending. Furthermore, by limiting the expression of everyone except the media, the election spending laws increase the relative influence of the latter.

The second way that the control of the mass media can bring about political influence follows from the first. The power (or perceived power) to communicate and potentially shape public opinion gives those controlling the media an advantage in securing the attention of politicians and decision-makers.[9] Attention from politicians is to be expected in relation to some areas of policy, given that media entities are important actors in the economy. However, the influence through such lobbying can go beyond the media controller's area of expertise, or contribution to the economy. The prospect of favourable coverage

---

[5] For discussion of the research on the impact on the political preferences of the electorate in Britain see R. Kuhn, *Politics and the Media in Britain* (Basingstoke: Palgrave, 2007) pp. 255–62.

[6] See Chapter 5.

[7] Representation of the People Act 1983, s.90A (on candidate election expenses); Political Parties, Elections and Referendums Act 2000, s.87 (excluding newspaper and periodical reports from controlled third-party expenditure).

[8] For discussion of this issue in relation to the media exemption from restrictions on corporate campaign spending in the United States, see R. Hasen, 'Campaign Finance Law and the Rupert Murdoch Problem' (1999) 77 *Texas Law Review* 1627.

[9] For an account of the media's lobbying role, see D. Freedman, *The Politics of Media Policy* (Cambridge: Polity Press, 2008) ch. 4.

provides a bargaining tool that can be exploited in the lobbying process. The relationship between Rupert Murdoch and Tony Blair has been the subject of much speculation, with Freedom of Information Act requests revealing conversations between the two men at the time of key government decisions,[10] as well as government attempts to assist Murdoch's business interests in Europe.[11] One former aide to Tony Blair famously described Murdoch as 'the 24th member of the Cabinet'.[12] Through these means, control of the mass media can secure a place on the inside of the decision-making process.

The opportunities for lobbying that follow from control of the media were considered in Chapter 4. The focus of this chapter will be the first channel of influence, the power to shape political debate, not just in elections but in politics more generally. Before looking at the ways that economic resources shape the distribution of communicative opportunities in the media, the next section will look at the ideal view of the mass media in a democracy.

The mass media and democracy

The mass media is a resource that provides opportunities to influence both the public and democratic decision-making. One reason why the use of wealth in politics is such a concern is because it buys access to the main forums for communication. The term 'mass media' implies an inequality, in which the mass of people form an audience whose attention is focused on a relatively small number of speakers. Not everyone can speak to a mass audience on a regular basis, and to attempt to give everyone a chance to do so would do away with the mass media altogether. Yet no one would argue for such an outcome in the name of a fair democratic process. For example, it is uncontroversial that people with expertise, journalists skilled in research and representatives from pressure groups have more time or space in the media than the average citizen. By contrast, where the opportunities to communicate are distributed solely on the basis of wealth or property ownership, the problems with political equality arise. The goal is therefore to ensure that the different opportunities to communicate in the mass media at least serve democratic values in a way that respects political equality. One approach is to view the mass media as a representative, responsive and accountable institution and that its coverage reflects the views held by its audience, and can therefore be reconciled with the standard of citizen equality.[13] A second view is that the mass media informs and educates its audience by delivering diversity in content, and thereby respects equality by providing the means for people to form their own views and engage with others. A model of the media combining elements of both these standards will be discussed later. The important point is that it shows that political equality does

---

[10] *Independent*, 19 July 2007.   [11] *Guardian*, 1 November 2008.

[12] L. Price, 'Rupert Murdoch is effectively a Member of Blair's Cabinet', *Guardian*, 1 July 2006.

[13] See Chapter 2. See discussion in Baker, *Media Concentration and Democracy*, pp. 10–13.

not require that everyone can speak in the media, but that the opportunities to communicate in the media are distributed in a way that respects democratic values, and are not determined by the distribution of wealth.

This way of thinking about the media explains why media freedom and freedom of expression are often distinguished.[14] When looking at individual freedom of expression in Chapter 2, it was argued that expression rights are partly justified from the perspective of the speaker. By contrast, media freedom places much greater emphasis on the audience's interest. The mass media is valued for the function it performs in a democracy, in particular in serving its audience or citizens as a whole. Consequently, the freedom accorded to the mass media is valued not because it gives people such as Rupert Murdoch or Jeremy Paxman a platform to pursue their political goals, but because it serves the audience. This approach means that the mass media may be open to some restrictions that are consistent with its democratic functions, which, if imposed on an individual citizen, would violate freedom of expression. Under this approach, media freedom is closely related to freedom of expression, but it needs to be considered separately from an individual's expression rights. Arguments based on media freedom tend to refer to those democratic functions that justify its potential influence.

There are a number of democratic functions that are often assigned to the media. The European Court of Human Rights has stressed the role of the press to 'play its vital role of "public watchdog"' and 'impart information and ideas'.[15] Under the 'public watchdog' function, the media holds the government to account and exposes abuses of power. The mass media are in a position to put aside time and resources to investigate the activities of government, in a way that is beyond most people. This role of the media in checking government power requires that it remains free from government censorship, but says little about the overall distribution of communicative resources.

The second function of the mass media is in facilitating democratic debate. The courts have stressed the role of the media in imparting diverse information and ideas to ensure an informed citizenry.[16] At its most basic, this will include the delivery of information and the explanation of complex political issues. Here the function of the media is like that of an expert in the communication of

---

[14] For discussion of the distinction see J. Lichtenberg, 'Foundations and Limits of Freedom of the Press', in J. Lichtenberg (ed.), *Democracy and the Mass Media* (Cambridge University Press, 1990); E. Barendt, *Freedom of Speech* (Oxford University Press, 2005) pp. 419–24; G. Marshall, 'Press Freedom and Free Speech Theory' (1992) *Public Law* 40; O. O'Neill, *A Question of Trust* (Cambridge University Press, 2002) pp. 92–5. The courts in England have traditionally equated media freedom with freedom of speech, see *Attorney General* v. *Guardian Newspapers (No 2)* [1990] 1 AC 109 at 183. In developing a public interest defence in defamation cases, the courts protect expression that is the product of activities associated with professional journalism. The courts do not distinguish the media freedom, as the defence is available to anyone performing those activities. See *Seaga* v. *Harper* [2009] AC 1 at [11].

[15] *Observer and Guardian* v. *United Kingdom* (1992) 14 EHRR 153 at [59].

[16] *McCartan Turkington Breen* v. *Times Newspapers* [2001] AC 277 at 290.

political affairs. Beyond this, the mass media provides a range of other functions that can facilitate participation. Sometimes it campaigns on particular issues, applies pressure to politicians, and advocates parties and candidates in an election. However, particular importance is placed on the role of the media in serving the deliberative element of democratic politics. In the words of John Thompson, the mass media provides

> the principal means by which individuals acquire information and encounter different points of view on matters about which they may be expected to form personal judgement. They also provide individuals with a potential mechanism for articulating views which have been marginalized or excluded from the sphere of mediated visibility. The cultivation of diversity and pluralism in the media is therefore an essential condition in the development of deliberative democracy.[17]

With this function in mind, the media should, as Meiklejohn argued, be inclusive of different views and perspectives to ensure that each gets a hearing.[18]

These functions can be performed through different methods, which can be illustrated by contrasting two models for organising the media in a democracy.[19] The first model allows each media entity to pursue whatever political viewpoint or stance it wishes. While this is sometimes described as a 'partisan',[20] 'pluralist'[21] or 'polarised'[22] media, the latter term will be used in this chapter. In this model the media can be openly biased and partial in its political coverage and each media entity criticises and debates with one another. In this way, each media entity is a form of association in which people come together to hear like-minded speakers. The polarised media are political actors who communicate the views of a section of society and mobilise their audiences over various causes and issues.[23] In so far as each relevant political grouping has its own media outlet, this sector is participatory. At the same time, the audience is served with diverse information and ideas when looking at the range of media outlets as a whole, a form of external pluralism. A wide range of polarised sources will add up to give the citizen a more complete picture.

There are limits to the polarised model. There are no guarantees that citizens will look at a cross-section of sources, each with a different political

---

[17] J. Thompson, *The Media and Modernity* (Cambridge: Polity Press, 1995) p. 257.

[18] See Chapter 2.

[19] The account of different functions assigned to the media and the distinction between public service and polarised media draws on the work of James Curran, see 'Reinterpreting the Democratic Roles of the Media' (2007) 3 *Brazilian Journalism Research* 31; and C. Edwin Baker, see *Media, Markets, and Democracy* (Cambridge University Press, 2002) chs. 6–8. For a survey of a broader range of media models, see D. McQuail, *Media Accountability and Freedom of Publication* (Oxford University Press, 2003) ch. 3.

[20] Curran, 'Reinterpreting the Democratic Roles of the Media', p. 31.

[21] Baker, *Media, Markets and Democracy*, pp. 135–8.

[22] D. Hallin and P. Mancini, *Comparing Media Systems* (Cambridge University Press, 2004) ch. 5. While the authors use the term in an account of the media in southern Europe, elements of this are found in the British press, pp. 211–12.

[23] *Ibid.*, pp. 132–3.

perspective. If each media entity's audience is primarily composed of citizens with a similar outlook, it may simply be preaching to the converted rather than serving citizens with new and challenging views. A polarised media could fragment citizens into groups where their existing views are reinforced. Under this view, people with right-wing views may focus on sources with a right-of-centre slant, and people with left-wing views may rely on left-of-centre media sources. Such a fragmented approach could lead to each group developing more extreme political positions and result in a more polarised political discourse.[24] Even if such fragmentation does not take place and people rely on a range of sources, the media landscape would simply hand the citizen a wide range of conflicting views, with little chance to evaluate the competing arguments.[25] The polarised model does not provide a place for mediation between the competing views.

A second model of the media's democratic functions aims to provide a common forum for citizens to hear different views and speakers, and to engage in debate. This model can be described as a 'public service' media, which does not itself act as an advocate for any particular political stance, but rather provides a space for different views to be heard alongside one another.[26] As James Curran puts it, public service media is a place 'where people come together to engage in a reciprocal debate about the management of society' and such a media entity 'reports the news with due impartiality, and gives space to different views'.[27] The public service media is not simply a passive conduit; it can take an active role in mediating and critically analysing competing views. Furthermore, the public service media can provide a platform for diverse speakers advocating specific political views, without endorsing those views. The function being performed is clearly distinct from that of an individual citizen participating in the democratic process. However, there are also limits to this model, as there is clearly a need for some media entities to act as advocates and develop a distinct political voice.

While there are many variations of the democratic functions of the media, the polarised and public service models have been contrasted here to show the different methods of pursuing these goals. Different political systems sometimes place greater emphasis on a particular model, with some having a predominantly polarised media and others having a media aspiring to be objective and impartial.[28] However, a combination of elements of the public service and polarised models helps to ensure the democratic functions are performed in different ways. The polarised media provides a space to develop specific political stances, and the public service media provides a place for those views to get

[24] See C. Sunstein, *Designing Democracy* (Oxford University Press, 2001) ch. 1.
[25] See O'Neill, *A Question of Trust*, ch. 5.
[26] J. Lichtenberg, 'Foundations and Limits of Freedom of the Press', p. 123.
[27] J. Curran, *Media and Power* (London: Routledge, 2002) p. 245, looking to the German broadcasting model as an example. See also Baker, *Media, Markets, and Democracy*, pp. 148–9.
[28] Hallin and Mancini, *Comparing Media Systems*, ch. 4.

a hearing, for debate and mediation. The co-existence of the two models can complement the virtues and compensate for the limits of the other.[29]

Promoting political equality is not only consistent with such functions, but can enhance the media's performance. The polarised model only serves the democratic goals where there are a wide range of media entities, each offering its own distinct views and speakers. If the chance to communicate in the mass media is largely determined by economic resources, then some less wealthy groups or viewpoints may be excluded. By contrast, a largely marginal view may receive undue prominence simply because it has sufficient economic resources supporting it. Similarly, the public service media is egalitarian in so far as it informs citizens and is inclusive, responsive and diverse. However, the media is less likely to perform this function if only those with sufficient resources can access it, or if its coverage is skewed in favour of the views or interests of its owner or sponsor.

The democratic functions should not provide a fig leaf to legitimise a system where access to and control of the media reflects inequalities in wealth. Instead, attempts to control the influence of wealth may help the media fulfil its democratic goals and serve the values underlying media freedom. Having set out an ideal account of a democratic media, the next section will identify the ways in which economic resources can determine who gets to access to and can speak in the mass media. After this discussion, the possible strategies for limiting the influence of wealth will be considered. Each of these strategies will be considered alongside the potential to enhance the media's performance of its democratic functions.

Inequalities in wealth and the mass media

Paying for access

The most obvious way that economic resources determine the chance to speak is where access is sold. Paid advertising openly provides access according to the ability to pay, the difficulties of which will be considered later. Aside from paid advertising, economic resources can indirectly determine access in so far as they help to get the attention of journalists and commentators. For example, those with the resources to organise a high-profile event or publicity stunt may have an advantage in attracting headlines. Outside interests can lobby those working in the media; for example, targeting an influential columnist may provide a way to raise the profile of a particular issue. Given the pressure to produce content for the increasing quantity of media output and to keep up with the twenty-four-hour news cycle, journalists are thought to be more dependent on external sources and consequently more vulnerable to manipulation from outside

---

[29] For a similar argument for different regulatory regimes according to the function of the media, see Curran, *Media and Power*, ch. 8, and L. Bollinger, 'Freedom of the Press and Public Access: Toward a Theory of Partial Regulation of the Mass Media' (1976) 75 Mich. L. Rev. 1.

interests.[30] The danger is that if journalists become increasingly willing to be fed press releases from organisations and external research, the economic resources needed to produce such information will have a significant role in shaping the media coverage.[31] However, it seems difficult to use any legal method to target this, except to hope that professional standards within the media will treat such communications with suspicion and subject them to critical scrutiny.

Media owners

A second way in which wealth can have an impact is through media ownership. The media owner can use his property to promote a political issue, viewpoint or speaker. For example, if a newspaper runs an editorial endorsing a political party, this may not cost the newspaper owner anything, but an external group would be permitted to access those pages only with the owner's permission, or through paid advertisements. Powers associated with media ownership also reflect inequalities in wealth in so far as substantial economic resources are necessary to acquire or start a media entity. Similarly, substantial resources are also required to run such an entity, which will normally be supplied through the owner's economic activity. More will be said about the latter point below; here the concern is the more basic one that, through media ownership, inequalities associated with the economic sphere can be influential in the political. However, to some, the concern is misplaced. Former *Sunday Times* editor Andrew Neil told the House of Lords Communications Committee in 2008 that a newspaper owner 'puts up the capital to buy it, takes all the risks, pays the bills and deals with any fallout for what an editor gets up to' and given this responsibility, the argument 'that a proprietor should have no say on the direction of content of the newspaper seems to me to be crazy'.[32] This makes sense when viewing the media as an item of property, which the owner can use as he wishes. From the perspective of democracy, Neil's argument does little to justify the additional opportunities to influence, or explain how that influence relates to the media's democratic functions. The fact of ownership points to no credentials or expertise to suggest that his input will serve democratic needs.

The image of the dominant media owner dictating the editorial stance is commonly associated with the press barons of an earlier era, such as Lords Northcliffe, Rothermere and Beaverbrook. Beaverbrook famously told the Royal Commission on the Press that he ran his papers 'purely for the purpose of making propaganda'.[33] Yet the editorial influence of a proprietor both pre-dates that era[34] and has continued since. While the era of the press baron can be

---

[30] N. Davies, *Flat Earth News* (London: Chatto & Windus, 2008) ch. 5.
[31] Kuhn, *Politics and the Media in Britain*, p. 230.
[32] House of Lords, Select Committee on Communications, *The Ownership of the News* (2008 HL 122) vol. 2, at p. 338 ('House of Lords Communications Committee (2008)').
[33] Royal Commission on the Press 1947–1949, Cmd 7700 (1949) at [87].
[34] J. Seaton and J. Curran, *Power without Responsibility*, sixth edition (London: Routledge, 2003) p. 43.

seen in Lord Rothermere's continued ownership of Associated Newspapers, it is now more common for newspapers and broadcasters to be owned by companies. This may make it harder to identify a particular individual as its owner. In some cases, a dominant individual can still be found, for example where there is a mogul who owns a substantial proportion of the media company's shares.[35] Even where there is no single owner within a company, final control will rest with the board of directors who are under a duty to further the interests of the company.[36] The directors appoint the executives responsible for day-to-day decisions, who will act in accordance with those interests. In such companies, senior appointees, such as an editor or chief executive, are sometimes the dominant figure rather than the owner.[37] In this case the individual does not owe her position to her own wealth or property, but it stems from the decision of the owner or directors of that company. The chief executive is constrained by the terms of appointment, which will require her to pursue the goal of profit, or other interests of the company. This can, in turn, give the executive scope to influence content, for example to prevent stories being published which could hurt the other investments held by the media company. Even with the duties and obligations owed to the company, the directors and executives still retain considerable discretion over the media company and have the power to influence the media content in a similar way to a traditional proprietor.

The owner may have a number of reasons to interfere with the media content including the ideological, the promotion of other business interests, or profitability. However, there will be numerous limitations on the potential to influence content. In particular, national newspapers and broadcasters are complex organisations that employ a vast number of individuals and receive content from a range of sources. Their organisation brings together a number of different professionals, all facing competing pressures and possibly with their own political agendas.[38] Given the constraints on time and expertise, no owner can dictate the stance on every issue, or prescribe how events must be reported. The mass media entity should not be viewed simplistically as the voice of its owner. However, where an owner seeks to influence content there are a number of ways this can be done.

In some cases there can be direct interventions. An owner of a newspaper can dictate its line on a particular issue, for example that a political party will be endorsed, or to oppose the UK joining the euro. Here the instruction is simple and specific, leaving the journalists and editors to get on with their job in other areas. Influence is direct and limited to those areas of most importance to the owner. The extent to which these interventions arise is unknown, but

[35] See J. Tunstall, *Newspaper Power* (Oxford University Press, 1996) ch. 5.
[36] Companies Act 2006, s.170–7.
[37] Tunstall, *Newspaper Power*, pp. 89–94, with the example of David Montgomery as Chief Executive of Mirror Group Newspapers.
[38] P. Golding and G. Murdock, 'Culture, Communications and Political Economy', in J. Curran and M. Gurevitch (eds.), *Mass Media and Society*, third edition (London: Hodder, 2000) p. 83.

instances of such incidents have been reported. In 2008, the House of Lords Communications Committee noted Rupert Murdoch's claims to set the editorial stance of the *Sun*, and heard evidence of direct interventions by owners including Robert Maxwell, the Barclay Brothers, Richard Desmond and Lord Black.[39] Direct proprietorial influence has been and remains a feature of the media in the UK, even if the frequency remains unknown.

If done blatantly to serve the owner's own interest, direct interventions can backfire and undermine the credibility of the media. For example, Tiny Rowland's interventions in the *Observer* in the 1980s to promote his business interests in Africa were widely criticised as a cynical use of his newspaper ownership.[40] To avoid a backlash, even interventionist owners will allow opposing views some space in their media outlets. This gives an appearance of balance, which may maintain credibility, even if the overall coverage favours a particular stance. For example, while Silvio Berlusconi may include his critics on his television stations, their views seem unlikely to get a fair hearing overall and are unlikely to extend to devastating criticisms.[41] However, the appearance of balance through the inclusion of some opposing views muddies the waters and makes the influence of the owner harder to detect.

The views and interests of an owner can influence content in other subtle ways. Without any instruction, employees within the media will have the owners' known views in the back of their minds when writing or selecting a story. For example, if the owner has a strong view on the UK joining the euro, the journalist or editor may feel the pressure to conform to that stance without any instruction. Similarly, a journalist will know of the owner's other businesses and take great care when handling a story that may undermine those interests. In turn this can lead to a form of self-censorship, whether or not it is done consciously. Owners can also exert pressure when distributing resources to different departments in a media organisation.[42] This form of control can help set the tone for a media entity, for example, by deciding to invest more in investigative journalism and less into regional offices. Such an allocation can be a way of setting the priorities for the newspaper or broadcaster and deciding what is important, without dictating a specific line.[43]

Another important channel of influence comes through the appointment of staff. A media owner can appoint those with a similar political outlook. This may also influence the content being produced by those journalists seeking promotion within that media organisation. Whether the owner wishes to

[39] House of Lords Communications Committee, above n. 32 at [123–8].
[40] The *Observer* was then owned by Rowland's company Lonrho. See Greenslade, *Press Gang* (London: Macmillan, 2003) pp. 389–92, and Seaton and Curran, *Power without Responsibility*, pp. 81–3.
[41] See P. Ginsborg, *Silvio Berlusconi: Television, Power and Patrimony* (London: Verso, 2004) pp. 112–15.
[42] See T. Gibbons, 'Freedom of the Press: Ownership and Editorial Values' (1992) *Public Law* 279 at 287.
[43] House of Lords Communications Committee, above n. 32, at [145–6].

interfere in these ways will depend on the personalities of all those involved, with some owners being much less interventionist than others.[44] However, even if such interference occurs infrequently, the potential for it to happen at all is a challenge to political equality.[45]

Market pressures

One of the concerns with the use of wealth, discussed in Chapter 1, is that inequalities that are generated in and relevant to the economic sphere transfer into the political sphere. Normally, when a for-profit company, for example an investment bank, wants to use its general funds to make a political expenditure, such a transfer visibly takes place. Funds acquired through its economic activity are used to influence political decisions. The difficulty with a for-profit media company is that political expression is part of its business. There is no simple line separating the economic activity from the political.[46] Under this view, the media is not simply the political tool of its controller or owner, but exists to make a profit and its continued existence will depend on this. This in turn imposes a check on the dominant owner, who cannot simply use the media as a vehicle for her political views for fear of losing the audience or advertisers.[47] Such pressures may be thought to make the media responsive, delivering the political content demanded by the audience. However, the concerns about political equality remain in relation to the commercial media. While space precludes a detailed assessment of the overall effects of market pressures, there are several commonly made arguments that such pressures allow inequalities in wealth to shape media content: namely the need to attract subscribers and advertisers and to make a profit.[48]

The first type of pressure is to produce content that is favourable to the interests of advertisers who provide financial support. That source of funding may discourage the criticism of advertisers, or their products. A newspaper, for example, may feel the need to produce content that encourages the consumption of the advertisers' products, which may entail avoiding certain political issues.[49] Consequently, the advertiser is not buying space to put across a

[44] Lord Thomson, as owner of *The Times*, is seen as less interventionist, treating the newspaper as a business rather than a source of power. However, the neutrality of his position has still been questioned, see K. William, *Get Me a Murder a Day!* (London: Arnold, 1998) pp. 230–1.

[45] Baker, *Media Concentration and Democracy*, p. 21. Along similar lines, as was argued in Chapter 6 at p. 156, mere tolerance from a landowner is not the same as a right to speak.

[46] See Chapter 1.

[47] British regulators have placed some faith in this constraint on media ownership. When considering takeover offers for *Mirror Group Newspapers*, the then Monopolies and Mergers Commission concluded that there were 'very strong commercial reasons for maintaining *The Mirror*'s left-of-centre political stance, given the absence of other tabloids in that market niche'. *Trinity/Mirror Group*, Cm 4393 (1999), at [2.25].

[48] For a robust argument that such pressures work to 'filter' mass media content, see E. Herman and N. Chomsky, *Manufacturing Consent* (London: Vintage, 1994) pp. 3–18.

[49] D. McQuail, *Media Accountability and Freedom of Publication* (Oxford University Press, 2003) p. 238.

political message, but can indirectly influence the media's political content.[50] There have also been occasional reports of companies threatening or actually withdrawing advertisements as a response to the media's content.[51] However, in most instances, constraints are more likely to be self-imposed and less specific. For example, the dependence of some newspapers on property advertisements provides a possible reason why the media did not investigate the difficulties with the property market prior to the credit crunch in 2008.[52] While not responding to any specific demand, the media may be reluctant to criticise the sources of its own funding.

Given that the decision to advertise has a direct and immediate impact on the media's resources, a newspaper or broadcaster may be more responsive to advertisers than its audience.[53] A separation of the editorial and advertising departments may help insulate the content from such pressures and is an important feature of a media organisation. However, given the need to remain profitable, it is difficult to impose a watertight barrier that prevents advertiser pressure influencing content.[54] It is, of course, difficult to determine how often the media feels such pressure and most media entities will be quick to deny such influence. That such pressure can arise highlights the way in which markets can make the media responsive to those advertisers supplying a steady stream of income.

Advertising funding also places pressure on the media to attract an audience with whom advertisers want to communicate, requiring the media to produce content that people will choose to see, rather than to advance its own agenda. In this view, the media is responsive to the demands of its audience.[55] However, these effects can arise in a number of ways and whether this pressure impacts on media content raises difficult questions. In some cases, advertisers with a mass-market product will target a wide audience consisting of those on lower incomes. There are concerns that a media entity needing a large audience may produce content that is uncontroversial, appeals to the lowest common denominator, or avoids politics altogether so as not to alienate a wide audience.[56] In this way, the media serves commercial rather than democratic needs. Where the media produces more specialised material aimed at a smaller audience,

---

[50] For discussion of such a constraint see Curran and Seaton, *Power without Responsibility*, at pp. 29–34 and pp. 185–92. The pressure can come not only from those advertising on that particular media entity, but also from those advertising on another entity owned by the same person or company.

[51] For example, in 2005 it was reported that Marks and Spencer withdrew advertising from the *Daily Mail* following critical reports, see *Independent*, 4 March 2005; in 2003 the *Guardian* website reported that MG Rover had withdrawn £3 million worth of advertising from Express Newspapers following a report that the car manufacturer was about to close, see www.guardian.co.uk/media/2003/jan/08/advertising.dailyexpress, 8 January 2003.

[52] D. Schechter, 'Credit Crisis: how did we miss it?' (2009) 20 *British Journalism Review* 19.

[53] McQuail, *Media Accountability and Freedom of Publication*, pp. 237–8.

[54] Baker, *Media, Markets, and Democracy*, p. 40.

[55] Although responsiveness to citizens is just one element of the democratic media; instead, the media has to tell people not only what they want to hear, but also ensure people are challenged with different views and see their own views subjected to critical analysis.

[56] Baker, *Media, Markets, and Democracy*, p. 27.

it will have an incentive to produce content that appeals to those with greater disposable income to spend on the advertisers' products.[57] The extent to which political content is influenced should not be overstated, as an audience composed of those with higher incomes may contain a diverse range of viewpoints. However, the point is that not all members of a potential audience are equal in the eyes of the market driven media.[58] The inequalities in wealth among the audience can impact on the constraints and pressures imposed through the market.

The effect and extent of the market pressures on the media will depend on the market in question and the other sources of income available to the media. For example, if the market is not competitive and a company has a monopoly or dominant position, then that media company will be shielded from the pressures discussed above. Given the changes in media markets, it is also unclear how the economic pressures will continue to impact on the provision of media content. There is concern as to whether the market can support a range of media, given the decline in advertising revenues and the unwillingness of consumers to pay to cover the media's full costs. It is not yet clear whether new business models will emerge, whether there will be fewer commercial media entities, or whether those surviving entities will feel the market constraints more than ever. The point is that market pressures do not alleviate concerns about media influence as they have the potential to influence media content in a way that is responsive to the distribution of economic resources.

Owner interference and market pressures

The arguments given above provide two contrasting views of the relationship between the mass media and economic power. The earlier argument suggests the media is an instrument of the owner's will, whereas the latter provides an account of the media as constrained by the market.[59] It is easy to focus on the former and portray the dominant newspaper proprietor as a villain, whose influence generates the greatest alarm among the public and commentators, given that the influence of wealth is visible. However, if the power of the media owner is taken out of the equation, there is no longer a specific demand or face behind the newspaper, but the media is still likely to find itself responding to those with higher incomes due to market pressures. The issue

---

[57] See discussion in Seaton and Curran, *Power Without Responsibility*, pp. 96–7, on advertisers' reluctance to pay to reach an audience outside the market for their products and how increases in circulation to those outside that market may impose significant costs on the media entity. Similar issues arise where the media derives its income from subscriptions, rather than advertisers. To offer a sufficient profit the media needs a mass audience paying smaller sums, or a smaller audience that is willing to pay higher subscriptions.

[58] Curran, *Media and Power*, p. 230; McQuail, *Media Accountability and Freedom of Publication*, p. 242.

[59] See Hallin and Mancini, *Comparing Media Systems*, p. 89, contrasting the structuralist and instrumentalist approaches.

needs to be approached with caution and limiting the super-rich media owners who provide a face for the influence of wealth will not eradicate the problem. Instead, the market pressures are seen by some as the greater threat to the media's democratic functions. Sometimes this makes commentators nostalgic for the days of the press baron who at least had an interest in political coverage and would be willing to bankroll controversial and unusual stances. While providing the greatest affront to equality, arguably, the media baron at least provided an investment in political coverage and possibly some diversity of views.

Although the two accounts of the media appear to contradict one another, in practice the two co-exist, with neither providing a complete account of media behaviour. The first reason why the two can co-exist is that different media entities have different ownership structures and goals. While some media companies may be under pressure to make a profit, others may be sheltered from market pressures and thereby more open to direction from the owner. For example, some newspapers may be owned to give prestige to a company, or act as a platform for promoting that company's other business interests. There may also be scope for a media entity to be cross-subsidised, where the owner has other companies or sources of income. For example, throughout its history *The Times* has made losses and required subsidy from the owner's other enterprises.[60] In 2008, the *London Evening Standard* was bought by a Russian billionaire, Alexander Lebedev, who claimed that the purchase was not made with profit in mind and was an 'act of public service' for which he would be willing to lose £30 million in total.[61] This is not to comment on the merits of this situation, but rather to note that some privately owned media entities are sheltered from the market pressures.

Even where the media is subject to the market constraints, there will still be an area of discretion.[62] The owner can influence or intervene in the media content where such intervention will not turn away subscribers or readers who are valuable to advertisers, or where any changes brought about by the intervention gain as many readers or subscribers as it loses.[63] For example, a change in a newspaper's political slant from left to right may attract as many right-wing readers as it loses from the left. Furthermore, the extent of such constraints will depend on the conditions of the market and the other choices available to the audience. For example, if there is a national newspaper that attracts a wide audience through its left-of-centre political stance, the owner will have considerable discretion in deciding what issues to cover, what angles to emphasise and what tone to take. If it is the only left-of-centre title, its readers have less scope to punish the owner's interventions where there is no alternative in that market. So while the audience may not approve of the owner's actions, it may prefer that newspaper to the available alternatives.[64]

---

[60] See Tunstall, *Newspaper Power*, p. 96; J. Eldridge, J. Kitzinger and K. Williams, *The Mass Media and Power* (Oxford University Press, 1997) p. 42.

[61] *The Times*, 7 February 2009.

[62] For discussion see Baker, *Media Concentration and Democracy*, pp. 88–96.

[63] *Ibid.*, p. 92.

[64] Curran, *Media and Power*, p. 271, noting that one can only choose from the available alternatives.

A further limit of the market relates to the distinction between citizens and consumers. In so far as the market makes the media responsive to its audience, the media responds to their wishes as consumers. The two may overlap, but a consumer's choice about what to watch or read at any moment may be distinct from what he thinks would be best to equip him as a citizen participating in a democracy.[65] For example, many newspaper readers' purchasing habits may be unrelated to the paper's political allegiance. People may purchase the *Daily Mirror* not just because it is a left-leaning paper, but because of its sports coverage, the gossip from the '3am Girls', or just out of habit or brand loyalty. Even if the market forces the media to respond to consumers in relation to some content, the owner can still retain much discretion over the political content. This discretion may be all the greater in relation to the more subtle forms of owner influence, such as resource allocation or appointments, that are less visible to the audience and less likely to provoke an immediate response.

Finally, the view that the market constrains the actions of the owner assumes that the audience's political views and preferences are fixed and that the media is merely responding to them. However, the content of the media may help to shape the political preferences of the audience, rather than vice versa, leading to problems of circularity. This is not to suggest a crude model in which an audience passively accepts whatever propaganda the media disseminates, but rather that it may play a role in shaping the audience's views. So if a traditionally left-of-centre newspaper began to adopt more centrist editorials, the newspaper may not lose all its left-leaning readers, but may persuade some to consider centrist positions. Again, this highlights the democratic function of the mass media beyond the representation of and responsiveness to citizens, emphasising its role in informing and providing a forum for debate.

This discussion has highlighted several ways in which the media can provide a vehicle for inequalities in wealth to impact upon political communications. For all these reasons, arguments that newspapers are representative of their readers should be treated with scepticism.[66] Although the extent to which the owner or advertiser influences content will depend on the particular media entity and its organisation, this section has argued that it is possible for these channels of influence to co-exist. Having considered the sources of influence, the following section will consider some methods of reconciling the media with political equality. Several strategies will be examined. The first will be controls on media ownership, which aim to prevent too many media outlets coming under the control of one person or company. The second is to control the media owner's conduct, which secures the independence of editorial staff. The third strategy is to subsidise certain media outlets, which attempts to give more speakers and viewpoints a media outlet of their own. That strategy aims to give more people a chance to communicate and more views to be heard, while also

[65] C. Sunstein, *Democracy and the Problem of Free Speech* (New York: The Free Press, 1993) pp. 72–3.
[66] See Curran, *Media and Power*, pp. 227–31.

allowing the subsidised media to challenge the power of the privately owned media. Finally, controls that impact on the output of a media entity will be considered, including rights of access to the media and rules requiring the media to be impartial in its coverage. The different strategies will be appropriate for the different media sectors.[67] For example, controls on ownership and conduct, and subsidies will be suited to the polarised media sector, where the aim is to have a wide range of media outlets promoting a particular political perspective. By contrast, subsidies, access rights and impartiality rules are more closely associated with the public service sector, where the media aims to provide a forum for different views and perspectives to be heard.

Media ownership and concentration

Ownership limits and democratic goals

The first method of control is to limit the amount of media any individual or company can own. If ownership of the mass media is shared among a wider range of people and bodies, an individual media owner will be just one voice among many, with less scope to influence public opinion and less leverage with lawmakers. Controlling media ownership does not prevent the media owner from using her property as an instrument of her own views, but seeks to limit that influence relative to other speakers. However, the controls can indirectly impact on the ability of the media owner to intervene in editorial decisions. If the mass media is largely concentrated in the hands of a few owners, then editors and reporters will have fewer potential sources of employment,[68] which may weaken their bargaining position in the event of a dispute with the owner. By contrast a less concentrated media may provide more opportunities to work with other owners. This first goal of measures to prevent media concentration is, therefore, to limit the level of control that one person or company can have over communicative opportunities, ensuring a wider distribution of the media as a political resource.

Given that the mass media by definition cannot provide each person with an equal chance to speak, the next best thing is to make media ownership itself representative of the different groups in society, a second goal of ownership limits.[69] This does not mean that media ownership has to be formally allocated to different groups, but that a less concentrated media ownership makes it more likely that each major group will have its own media outlet. Such an argument for an 'egalitarian' 'distribution of expressive power' is advanced by C. Edwin Baker, as a way to provide groups with their own media 'to debate their views internally among themselves, receive information relevant to their interests and views, rally support for their groups, and finally present their views to the world

---

[67] Baker, *Media, Markets and Democracy.*
[68] L. Hitchens, *Broadcasting Pluralism and Diversity* (Oxford: Hart, 2006) p. 135.
[69] Baker, *Media Concentration and Democracy*, p. 73.

at large'. [70] This argument does not suggest that a diversely owned media will create diverse content. Instead it aims to ensure that whatever content is produced by the mass media is itself the product of a fair process and distribution of political resources.

Controls on ownership alone are, however, unlikely to make the media more representative.[71] Compare a scenario in which Rupert Murdoch owns three national newspapers, with a scenario in which there are three national newspapers that are separately owned by Murdoch, the Barclay Brothers and Richard Desmond. In the latter, media ownership is more fragmented in so far as there are three rather than one multi-millionaire owner. The latter may be preferable in potentially reducing the political influence of a single media owner, but not because it makes the media more representative. While the response to this example is that the media needs to be fragmented much further before it comes close to being representative, it seems difficult to imagine this ever being possible with the national mass media. The market may not be able to finance a system in which every group has their own media outlet in the way suggested above. To make the media representative, some additional measures may be required to ensure communicative opportunities are fairly distributed, such as subsidies to enable traditionally excluded groups to establish their own media.

A third goal for media ownership controls is not based on a desire to make the media representative, but in the hope that greater media plurality will produce more diverse content.[72] The justification is distinct from the previous argument as it focuses on the effect of ownership on content, rather than the distribution of communicative power. Under this third goal, diverse ownership does not aim to empower the various groups with their own media, but to ensure that the audience receives different views.

While diverse ownership and diversity of content are distinct, the goals are related.[73] There are some obvious reasons why diverse ownership might be expected to produce diverse content. If the influence of the owner can seep into editorial decisions, then diverse ownership subjects the media as a whole to a more varied range of influences. This can lead to changes in style and tone, and the selection of stories and opinions. Even where those owning the leading newspapers share largely similar political views, it may be hoped that there will be some differences of opinion that manifest themselves in the content. Furthermore, a concentrated media is in a better position to suppress a particular story. By contrast, competition among a more fragmented media may encourage flaws in one newspaper's reporting to be exposed by another and it

---

[70] *Ibid.*, pp. 15–16.   [71] *Ibid.*, p. 191.

[72] This has been a goal of concentration controls in the United States; see Hitchens, *Broadcasting Pluralism and Diversity*, p. 134.

[73] For discussion of the concepts of pluralism and diversity, see Freedman, *The Politics of Media Policy*, pp. 71–8. For a criticism of the focus on content diversity, see Baker, *Media Concentration and Democracy*, pp. 15–16.

will be harder to stop a truly important story being disseminated.[74] While it is easy to assume diverse ownership will lead to diverse content, there are, however, a number of difficulties with such an assumption.

One difficulty with the account given above is that it portrays each media outlet as a separate voice. In practice the matter is not so straightforward, some media entities may produce content whereas others may distribute that content.[75] For example, among UK broadcasters, ITV and Channel 4 provide alternative news programmes, but the same external company, ITN, produces the content for both. Consequently, there may be instances where those media entities distributing content are diversely owned, but there are relatively few producing content. If a diversely owned media struggles for income and faces strong competitive pressures, rather than invest in its own content it may rely more heavily on the same external sources as other media entities. By contrast, a concentrated media may be more willing to carry diverse content as it has the resources and audience that enable making such an investment and taking a risk. Consequently, diverse ownership of outlets distributing content may have limited effects if the production of content remains concentrated.

A second difficulty is that controls on ownership may make the media responsive to different owners, but the diversely owned media may be subject to other constraints that influence content. For example, where those working in the media are constrained by the same professional values and training, it may lead to similar content choices in different media entities.[76] The diversely owned media can also be subject to the same market pressures, such as those from advertisers.[77] Along these lines, the rival media entities may produce similar content in so far as it targets the same audience. Furthermore, a diversely owned media may be more vulnerable to the pressures from the market. If more media companies compete for advertising, advertisers may have more leverage and the media will have further pressure to produce content that will attract certain advertisers. By contrast, a concentrated media may be in a better position to stand up to such pressures and take greater risks, without the fear of upsetting either advertisers or the audience. None of these outcomes are certain, but there are problems in assuming that plural sources will lead to diversity in content.[78] To avoid this, there is a need not only to ensure media ownership is not concentrated, but also to ensure that there are different sources of funding and organisational structures, in the hope that the diverse media entities are not all subject to the same pressures.

Even if diverse ownership is likely to result in diverse content, it may not be the best way to serve the deliberative goals. The arguments for a diversely

---

[74] Department of Trade and Industry, *Consultation on Media Ownership Rules* (2001) at [1.7].

[75] See Kuhn, *Politics and the Media in Britain*, pp. 107–8.

[76] Baker, *Media, Markets, and Democracy*, p. 178; Hitchens, *Broadcasting Pluralism and Diversity*, p. 135.

[77] Baker, *Media, Markets, and Democracy*.

[78] For a discussion see G. Doyle, *Media Ownership* (London: Sage, 2002) pp. 24–6.

owned media are most closely associated with the polarised model of the media, in which there are many different media entities advancing a particular political outlook. However, while a large dominant media entity may raise concerns about the owner's power, it can have some democratic benefits. It can provide a common forum for people to hear viewpoints and ideas other than their own, and ensure that political debate is focused on a similar agenda.[79] The fragmentation of the media may work to frustrate this goal if it simply polarises groups without hearing competing arguments.

Three goals for media ownership laws have been considered so far: limiting the power of the owner, making the media representative, and producing diverse content. All these arguments have to be considered alongside other goals. Media ownership is also an economic issue, which has been an important priority for policy-makers.[80] Those within the industry seeking deregulation have often stressed the efficiencies that can arise by allowing media mergers, which allow the sharing of some facilities and knowledge.[81] Given the current stories of the economic pressures being faced by media companies, it seems likely that fresh calls will be made from within the industry for deregulation to allow further mergers and concentration. The extent to which concentration enhances efficiency has been questioned by Doyle, who argues that it has been too readily assumed by policy-makers without serious investigation.[82] While such assertions of efficiency should be treated with scepticism, the economic arguments provide countervailing considerations that need to be considered aside from the democratic goals.

The discussion so far has looked at the case for controls on media concentration and the limits of such a strategy. In particular, it has been argued that diverse ownership alone is unlikely to make the media representative, or its content diverse. Any limits on ownership may be accompanied with further measures that will be considered later. Having set out and qualified the argument for such controls, the remainder of this section will look at the methods for controlling ownership.

Methods of limiting ownership

Two approaches to limiting media ownership can be contrasted. The first is to devise fixed rules that limit the number of media entities that can be controlled by one person or company. The second is to impose a discretionary control requiring approval of media mergers.[83] The first strategy has been used

---

[79] While making a strong case for a fragmented ownership, Baker also highlights this point, *Media Concentration and Democracy*, p. 193.

[80] Doyle, *Media Ownership*, p. 42.

[81] *Ibid.*, ch. 3. There are other efficiencies that may arise through media firms merging, such as greater scope for innovation and risk taking, and reducing transaction costs.

[82] *Ibid.*, ch. 5 on cross-media concentration. See also House of Lords Communications Committee, above n. 32, at [177].

[83] Hitchens, *Broadcasting Pluralism and Diversity*, p. 86.

to regulate the ownership of the commercial broadcast media in the UK. For example, until 2003 no one holding a licence to broadcast on Channel 3 could hold a Channel 5 broadcast licence and vice versa, a measure designed to ensure some diversity of ownership in the main television channels.[84] Similar fixed rules have been applied in the case of cross-media ownership, limiting the potential for a newspaper and certain channels to come under common control. For example, a company controlling one or more national newspapers with a total 20 per cent market share can only acquire a maximum 20 per cent interest in a company holding a Channel 3 licence, and a Channel 3 licence holder is precluded from having more than a 20 per cent interest in a national newspaper.[85] The '20/20' rule explains why Rupert Murdoch's television company BSkyB purchased a 17.9 per cent stake in ITV in November 2006.[86] Even though the acquisition later fell foul of the competition laws, anything much above that level would have been automatically prohibited under the fixed cross-media ownership rules.

An approach based on fixed rules provides a level of certainty with a numerical standard formulated in advance of any takeover, even if it can be difficult to apply in practice. However, critics argue that such inflexible rules cannot keep pace with the changing media system and potentially limit the capacity for media companies to expand and compete internationally.[87] While the fixed rules characterised the UK's approach to broadcasting in the early 1990s, the regime has been gradually liberalised. Instead, greater emphasis is now placed on discretionary merger controls, and what is left of the fixed rules on broadcasters provides a minimal safety net to promote plural media ownership.[88]

The second strategy for controlling media ownership, discretionary controls on mergers, already occurs through competition laws that apply in any commercial sector. Such laws will serve the democratic goals in so far as they prevent any single entity dominating a particular market and thereby limit the power that can be acquired by a media owner. As result, there have been calls to make the ordinary competition laws the sole control on the number of media entities any person or body can own.[89] The difficulty with such an approach is that without fixed rules deciding the ideal level of diverse ownership, a substantive criterion has to be devised to determine whether the merger should

---

[84] The restriction was repealed under the Communications Act 2003 s.350. It is an offence to broadcast in Britain without a licence from the communications regulator Ofcom, Broadcasting Act 1990, s.13.

[85] Communications Act 2003, Schedule 14.

[86] Rupert Murdoch's News Corporation has a controlling interest in the satellite broadcaster BSkyB. News Corporation's subsidiary News International owns the *Sun*, *The Times* and the *News of the World*.

[87] For an account of the arguments advanced by the British media industry see Doyle, *Media Ownership*, ch. 7.

[88] See Hitchens, *Broadcasting Pluralism and Diversity*, pp. 268–80.

[89] For example, see the written evidence of the Newspaper Society in the House of Lords Communications Committee, above n. 32, vol. 2, p. 104.

go ahead. In competition law the criteria focuses on economic goals, namely whether the merger would create a substantial lessening of competition in a particular market.[90] The goal is to prevent any company gaining a dominant position that can be abused or used to prevent competitors entering the market. Competition laws might have effects that are beneficial to a democratic media, but such effects are not guaranteed. A media market can be economically competitive without the pattern of ownership being representative or the content produced by the media being diverse. Furthermore, the increase in competition can also increase market constraints on the media.

Given the limits of competition laws, the regulations provide for an additional public interest test to be applied to mergers involving a newspaper or broadcaster.[91] This provides a check on media mergers over and above the competition laws, allowing the democratic goals to be considered separately. Those supporting the public interest test in Parliament justified the test by reference to those democratic goals. Lord McIntosh stated that 'it would be dangerous for any person to control too much of the media because of his or her ability to influence opinions and set the political agenda'.[92] Lord Putnam argued that a public interest test would help inform citizens by ensuring 'a range of competing voices'.[93] Under the public interest test, where a merger raises one or more of the public interest considerations specified in the statute, the relevant minister has the discretion to intervene and refer the merger to the regulators for investigation. The impact of the merger on the public interest is then considered by the communications regulator Ofcom. If Ofcom finds that public interest concerns are present, that matter is then referred to the Competition Commission for a full investigation. Once the Commission makes its conclusion and recommendations, the matter is sent back to the minister to decide what action if any should be taken. If the merger is found to be detrimental to the public interest, the minister has the power to block the merger completely, give approval, or allow the merger subject to certain conditions being met.

This method of control comes with a number of limits. The process is lengthy, placing the media entity under investigation in a position of uncertainty for a considerable period of time. To address this concern, the government has stated that public interest interventions will be made rarely.[94] While a policy of limited intervention may enhance commercial certainty, it limits the efficacy of the test as a democratic safeguard. Furthermore, intervention at the time of the

---

[90] The Enterprise Act 2002.
[91] See the Enterprise Act 2002, s.42, 58 and 59. The Communications Act 2003 amended the Enterprise Act to include the special considerations for media mergers. The provision was introduced in the House of Lords as the Communications Act 2003 was passing through Parliament to provide an extra safeguard to compensate for the relaxation in media ownership rules in that statute.
[92] Lord McIntosh of Haringey, Hansard, HL, vol. 650, col. 912–13 (2 July 2003).
[93] Hansard, HL, vol. 648, col.1432 (5 June 2003), quoting Dr Kim Howells MP.
[94] Department of Trade and Industry, *Guidance on the Operation of the Public Interest Merger Provisions Relating to Newspapers and other Media Mergers* (May 2004) at [6.3] and [8.2].

merger may take place too late in the day for any realistic alternative. For example, where the media entity being acquired is already in financial difficulties and will otherwise close, approving the merger may be the least bad option.[95]

Another limit arises from the discretionary nature of the merger control. The safeguard to protect the public interest is initiated and concluded by ministerial discretion. While this provides greater flexibility than the fixed rules approach described earlier, the use of ministerial discretion can raise the suspicion that the decision is motivated by political considerations. Through lobbying, the minister can be vulnerable to pressure from media owners when exercising that discretion. Such suspicions were aroused when, under an earlier regulatory regime, the Conservative government did not refer Rupert Murdoch's purchase of *The Times* and *Sunday Times* to the Monopolies and Mergers Commission,[96] and when the Labour government did not refer Richard Desmond's takeover of the *Daily Express*. Whether or not there is anything to justify these claims, it has certainly given rise to a strong suspicion that political motivations, such as receiving favourable coverage, influenced the ministers' decision not to intervene.

When the House of Lords Communication Committee looked at the issue in 2008, it proposed that the communications regulator Ofcom be given the power to initiate the public interest proceedings. While this would provide a safeguard, the proposal would not remove the ministers' final say in deciding whether to block, approve or attach conditions to the merger,[97] and would provide much scope for political considerations to enter the equation at the final stage. However, the problem of political considerations arises wherever the control is based on discretion, whether exercised by a minister or independent regulator, rather than fixed rules. Whoever exercises the discretion can be lobbied, or can abuse that power. However, for a sensitive question on the distribution of one of the most valuable political resources, there is a strong case for limiting the role of the minister to avoid conflicts of interest or political considerations entering the equation.

Where an intervention is made, the regulators have to look at the impact of the merger on the public interest, according to the criteria set out in the Enterprise Act 2002. For example, where a merger takes place between newspapers, three public interest considerations are to be taken into account: first, the accurate presentation of news; second, the free expression of opinion in the newspapers; and third, the plurality of views.[98] These factors do not take a fragmented media ownership to be a goal in itself, but instead look at the effects of the merger on the content and internal organisation of the media entity.

---

[95] P. Humphreys, *Mass Media and Media Policy in Western Europe* (Manchester University Press, 1996) p. 101.

[96] See R. Greenslade, *Press Gang* (London: Macmillan, 2003) pp. 377–8; B. Page, *The Murdoch Archipelago* (London: Simon & Schuster, 2003) pp. 256–78.

[97] House of Lords Communications Committee, above n. 32, at [261–4].

[98] s.58 (2A) and (2B) of the Enterprise Act 2002.

Looking at such factors on a case-by-case basis, it will be difficult to see when a specific merger will raise one of these public interest considerations. For example, the provision on the free expression of opinion in the newspaper raises the question of whether a merger will have a detrimental impact on editorial autonomy. To assess this, the regulator will hear allegations of past interferences with editorial freedom by the new owner.[99] However, given the subtlety with which the owner can apply pressure to staff, described earlier, such interference will often not be discoverable, or established conclusively.

Difficulties also arise in assessing the impact of a merger on the 'plurality of views'. The regulators do not have a clear standard to determine what level of plurality is desirable, and consequently will assess plurality with the status quo as the baseline. The question is then whether the merger departs from the existing levels of plurality. In any event, where the merger would have an impact on the plurality of views, there is little the regulator can do. Where a newspaper is being sold to a businessman who will take an interest in its political coverage and possibly change its direction, the merger cannot be made subject to the condition that the newspaper will maintain a particular political outlook. While controls on mergers are generally thought to raise fewer free speech issues, such a blunt direction on political content would be a much greater intrusion into media freedom. An alternative measure, such as blocking the merger, will only be a last resort.[100] This is not to suggest that plurality of views is too vague as a goal for other purposes. Chapter 2 provided an abstract sketch of an ideal approach to the distribution of political resources among viewpoints, which can guide the design of some regulations. However, it is difficult for regulators to apply such a standard on a case-by-case basis as mergers arise, with no further criteria.

The statute requires slightly different considerations to be taken into account where the merger involves a broadcaster: first, the impact of the merger on the plurality of persons with control of media enterprises; second, the impact on the quality and breadth of content; and third, on the ability to meet the broadcasting standards set by statute. The first standard refers to the number of people controlling the media, which, unlike the newspaper merger criteria, focuses on the distribution of ownership rather than any specific effects on content.[101] The regulators thereby have to consider what level of plurality is sufficient.[102] The difficulty lies in deciding what level of plural control is sufficient, which, again, will normally be assessed by reference to the status quo rather than any ideal standard.

The controls on media mergers provide an important safeguard against excessive concentration of ownership. However, only those mergers that can

---

[99] For example, see *Johnston Press plc/Trinity Mirror plc*, Cm 5495 (2002) at [2.122–2.135].

[100] See *George Outram/The Observer*, HC 378 (1980–81) at [8.28–8.29]; *Trinity/Mirror Group*, Cm 4393 (1999) at [2.70].

[101] House of Lords Communications Committee, above n. 32, at [245].

[102] *BSkyB* v. *Virgin Media, the Competition Commission and Secretary of State for Business, Enterprise and Regulatory Reform* [2010] EWCA Civ 2 at [78–123].

be shown to have the clearest detrimental impact on the public interest are likely to be regulated. When coupled with the government's policy to intervene only on rare occasions, this suggests that the public interest test provides only a minimal check on media concentration. Furthermore, these rules are applied only to newspapers and broadcasters and, therefore, allow mergers outside those media sectors, such as the online media, to escape the application of the public interest test.[103] While there are ways in which the existing process could be strengthened, there will still be limits as to what ownership controls can achieve. The problem is not simply that the regulations are too weak or not properly enforced, but that the controls have limited ambitions. Media ownership regulations are not a panacea, but just one part of a broader strategy to ensure the power of the media serves democratic goals.

Safeguarding editorial and journalistic autonomy

A second strategy to prevent media ownership securing political influence is not to limit the amount of media any person or body can control, but to limit the power of the media owner to interfere in editorial decisions within that media entity. One example is the establishment of an independent board of directors charged with safeguarding editorial independence and holding formal powers, such as approving the appointment or dismissal of an editor. A similar control is to require the owner to give undertakings to respect editorial independence.[104] The adherence to the professional Code of Conduct produced by the newspapers' self-regulatory body, the Press Complaints Commission, is also often included in a newspaper editor's contract of employment. All these arrangements attempt to limit the potential for the owner to pressure employees, and to constrain the conduct of the owner.[105] By giving greater independence from proprietorial interference, such measures transfer the final say over media content from the owner to the editor. Although one may ask whether such a transfer is likely to be an improvement, the appeal lies in the fact that the editor will only have a say over one particular media entity, whereas the owner may control several. For example, where five different newspapers are all owned by a single person or company, there will ideally be five separate editors, one for each title. Giving final say to each editor of a range of newspapers can thereby fragment the control over content, even where those papers are owned by the same person. Furthermore, the choices over content exercised by an editor may show a greater commitment to the professional journalistic values, rather than pursuing the political agenda of the owner – although this will depend on the individuals in question.

---

[103] House of Lords Communications Committee, above n. 32, at [252–3].

[104] Such arrangements have sometimes been imposed as a condition of approving a merger under the public interest test; see *George Outram/The Observer*, HC 378 (1980–1).

[105] McQuail contrasts controls on 'conduct' from those on media content and ownership, see McQuail, *Media Accountability and Freedom of Publication*, p. 101.

The capacity for such an arrangement to constrain a dominant media owner is subject to a number of limits, highlighted by the past failures of this type of safeguard.[106] The first limit is that the owner can exert influence over the media entity in ways that do not break any undertakings given, or which are beyond the powers and supervision of the board of directors. For example, if an owner provides a guarantee of editorial independence, pressure can still be exerted by criticising an editor's competence as a manager rather than any content decisions. Such criticisms may mask the owner's true objectives, which may be to do with editorial policy.[107] By dressing the criticism with references to matters that are a legitimate concern to the owner, such as management, it is harder for the board of directors to detect any pressure that is contrary to the commitment to editorial freedom.[108] Similarly, while the decision to dismiss an editor can be removed from the owner and given to an independent board, the owner can use other methods to achieve the same result. For example, to protect editorial freedom, an independent board of directors was agreed prior to Rupert Murdoch's acquisition of the *Wall Street Journal* in 2007. However, within months the sitting managing editor resigned and was replaced by a long-term Murdoch employee. While the terms of the *Wall Street Journal* agreement prevented the editor from being dismissed by the owner, the editor was effectively 'demoted' when Murdoch appointed his preferred choice of editor to the post of publisher.[109] While formally staying within the terms of a guarantee of editorial independence, the appointment of other staff marginalised the editor's influence, which led to the editor's resignation.

The success of such a safeguard will also depend on who is appointed to enforce the guarantees of editorial autonomy and what powers they will have at their disposal in the event of a breach. Even where the independent board of directors has a broad jurisdiction, there are limits to the monitoring it can perform and it relies on a clear complaints procedure to bring any issues to its attention. While such a safeguard can provide a useful function, it will provide a check only on some instances of proprietorial interference; even then there will be limits as to what can be done.

The internal safeguards aim to ensure that the media's affairs cannot be determined by the will of one person or body and provide a check on the prerogatives of ownership.[110] An owner intent on influencing content can, however, do

---

[106] See House of Lords Communications Committee, above n. 32, at [214–20] for discussion.

[107] B. Page, *The Murdoch Archipelago* (London: Simon & Schuster, 2003) p. 320. Such a strategy was said to have been employed to pressure Harold Evans to resign as editor of *The Times*, despite the promises guaranteeing editorial independence made to the government when News International acquired that title.

[108] Similarly when allegations were made that Tiny Rowland had pressured employees into carrying stories favourable to the owner's business interests, the independent board of directors found that while the coverage had 'tarnished' the *Observer*'s reputation, there was no evidence of direct editorial interference, *The Times*, 28 June 1989. For an account see Greenslade, *Press Gang*, pp. 389–92 and Seaton and Curran, *Power without Responsibility*, pp. 81–3.

[109] M. Wolff, *The Man Who Owns the News* (London: Bodley Head, 2008) p. 6.

[110] This is not the only type of control on the owner's conduct; others include contractual terms guaranteeing journalistic independence. However, this will be subject to the owner's agreement

so by modifying their conduct in a way that falls outside the supervision of the board, or is not covered by the undertakings. These scenarios highlight the difficulty in attempting to preserve editorial independence while also recognising the owner's rights to protect and manage his own investment. Not every possible power can be overseen or handed to an independent board or trust. A clear line does not separate the commercial interests and the political output of the media; as a result the owner will have some degree of involvement that allows some influence over editorial staff. Despite the limits of this strategy, it can still play an important role as a constraint on the most direct interferences and as the embodiment of a commitment to editorial autonomy.

Subsidies

If controlling concentration and the conduct of owners only goes so far in serving democratic goals, an alternative strategy is to provide state support for some media entities. State support can be provided through grants to partially fund existing newspapers or broadcasters, or to fully fund the state-owned media. Funding for a subsidy does not have to come from general government revenues, but can be raised separately, for example through a levy on mass media advertising, or through a licence fee. The subsidy can also be provided through a benefit in kind where the state provides some asset to the media, such as the provision of broadcasting licences. These subsidies can assist the development of the polarised media sector, ensuring that financial support is provided to a diverse range of political perspectives and speakers. Alternatively, state funds can be provided to promote public service goals, for example where granted on the condition that the media entity provides balanced coverage or grants access to other speakers.[111] The imposition of public service goals, through a condition on a subsidy or through a legal duty, will be considered in later sections, the following section will examine the different methods for allocating funds.

Indirect subsidies

The decision to subsidise and the method of distributing the subsidy will partly depend on the relationship between the media and the state in the political system in question. At one extreme lies a view that emphasises the independence of the media from the state. Such a model is not hostile to all subsidies,[112] but will be less likely to attach conditions to the subsidies that allow the government to

to such terms, and even where it is agreed its provisions could be evaded in the same way as guarantees of editorial independence. See T. Gibbons, 'Freedom of the Press: Ownership and Editorial Values', at 290–1.

[111] The impact of such conditions on the expression rights of the private media owner will be considered below.

[112] For example, while the US system emphasises such a separation, the subsidised cost of mailing was an important factor in the development of the newspaper industry in the United States. See R. McChesney, *The Problem of the Media* (New York: Monthly Review Press, 2004) pp. 33–4.

influence the media content. However, even without such conditions, there will be concern that the media's dependence on state support could compromise its capacity to scrutinise the government for fear that its funding will otherwise be cut. Whether there is any evidence of state funds being used to undermine media independence is questionable,[113] but if the subsidy aims to support the polarised media sector, where political advocacy and criticism can be robustly pursued, a desire to minimise state interference is understandable.

The potential to compromise media independence can be avoided by decentralising the allocation of funds. This can be achieved by providing an indirect subsidy to all media entities regardless of content, or owner. In the UK, an example of this approach is the exemption of newspapers from Value Added Tax, which by helping to keep the cover price down encourages the public to purchase a newspaper.[114] Other types of indirect support include subsidising the cost of newspaper distribution and the cost of print paper.[115] In the United States, the current concerns about the financial stability of the newspaper industry have led to calls to increase indirect support to help existing papers, for example giving tax breaks to newspapers that are run on a non-profit basis,[116] or by providing a tax credit to encourage people to subscribe to a newspaper.[117] With such methods, the distribution of state funds is not fixed by a central agency, but instead depends on the buying habits of the public, or the activities undertaken by the media. Consequently, such methods will appeal in a system where there is a strong separation between the media and the state.

Indirect subsidies come with limits in fulfilling democratic goals. The first is that such support will tend to help existing media entities stay profitable, rather than bringing in excluded voices. A second limitation lies in one of its advantages; the support is not targeted. As a result, it may help those titles that are well resourced and need little help. Such indirect help could, therefore, be used to finance a mainstream title's price war, which in turn hurts smaller media entities. Furthermore, if the indirect support follows individuals' buying habits, or supports larger entities, the subsidy may amplify existing inequalities. For example, a tax credit for newspaper subscriptions may offer strongest support to those titles that already have many subscribers and are well financed. One way to avoid this problem would be to target this aid to smaller titles with a particular turnover or audience share, although such a qualification would make the scheme less simple to administer. There is much to be said for the indirect

---

[113] Hallin and Mancini, *Comparing Media Systems*, pp. 162–3.

[114] The possibility of removing this indirect subsidy has been raised on a number of occasions. For example, prior to the 1985 budget, proposals to extend VAT to newspapers and books were considered, but dropped following a campaign opposing the measure. More recently, the pressure to extend VAT has been thought to come from proposals to harmonise VAT in the European Union.

[115] Humphreys, *Mass Media and Media Policy in Western Europe*, p. 103.

[116] D. Swensen and M. Schmidt, 'News You Can Endow', *New York Times*, 27 January 2009.

[117] J. Nichols and R. McChesney, 'The Death and Life of Great American Newspapers', *The Nation*, 6 April 2009. Along similar lines, in January 2009, French President Nicholas Sarkozy announced a plan to give all 18-year-olds free subscription to a newspaper of their choice.

subsidies, especially at a time when the media sector as a whole is struggling financially, but it will provide limited results for pluralism and diversity.

Direct subsidies

An alternative is to provide direct subsidies to specific media entities, an approach that has been relied upon in mainland Europe. The success of such a scheme will depend on the criterion for distributing the funding and on the body that applies that criterion. For example, distributing a subsidy to those titles with the highest circulation may reflect public support for that media entity, but will tend to benefit the largest existing entities, rather than con-tribute to plural sources of information.[118] By contrast, subsidies could be allocated to those titles that contribute to the overall diversity of editorial con-tent.[119] This approach would seek to target funds in a way that supports a wide range of diverse voices and political perspectives in the media. The difficulty with this approach, as the regulation of media mergers highlighted, is in find-ing a standard to determine the ideal level of diversity to guide such an alloca-tion. One way to resolve this difficulty would be to take the range of political parties as a template for the ideal range of diverse views. In some countries subsidies are distributed among those newspapers that have a clear affiliation to a political party, where that party has a sufficient level of representation in Parliament.[120] This would not, however, be suitable in the UK where papers do not have a formal link with a political party and where the media's party allegiances shift over time. Furthermore, while funding in proportion to sup-port may be appropriate for political parties, it is less appropriate for the media that aims to contribute to the deliberative element by providing a more diverse range of voices.

A more promising strategy is to direct support to media entities that can-not find other sources of financial support, or which target funding in a way that supports a specific number of titles in a particular market. For example, in Norway support is 'directed towards papers with the weakest structural position in the market (smallest papers and papers with a minority position in the local market)'.[121] While in some systems such subsidies are granted on the condition that the editor agrees to abide by a professional code of practice, the allocation is not based on any viewpoint and attempts to target those titles that make some

---

[118] Humphreys, *Mass Media and Media Policy in Western Europe*, p. 104.

[119] *Ibid.*, p. 106.

[120] M. Osterlund-Karinkanta, 'Finland', in M. Kelly, G. Mazzoleni, D. McQuail (eds.), *The Media in Europe* (London: Sage, 2004) p. 60.

[121] H. Ostby, 'Norway', in Kelly *et al.*, *The Media in Europe*, pp. 163–4. On a similar subsidy directed toward 'secondary newspapers' in Sweden see L. Weibull, 'The Press Subsidy System in Sweden', in N. Couldry and J. Curran (eds.), *Contesting Media Power* (Oxford: Rowman and Littlefield, 2003); and Humphreys, *Mass Media and Media Policy in Western Europe*, p. 106. In January 2009, Dr Ashok Kumar MP suggested a similar model to support the British local press; see Hansard, HC, vol. 486, col. 188–9 (20 January 2009).

contribution to the plurality of the media. Such a strategy may be an important method of keeping a diverse range of sources going. However, in those countries that already provide this type of state support, the subsidy provides only a fraction of the total income for the media as a whole and has not prevented increasing concentration or commercialisation of the media.[122]

The financial crisis facing the media at the time of writing has put the state support of the media, including newspapers, back on the agenda. In the UK, the proposed response to the crisis has not been to follow the above strategies. Instead, in 2009 the government put forward a proposal for local news on the commercial broadcaster ITV and on multi-media outlets to be provided through local news consortia of broadcasters, newspapers and other organisations.[123] The consortia would receive some public funds, possibly taken from the BBC licence fee. The proposal would relieve the commercial broadcaster of the costs associated with local news production, but would maintain that service at the public expense. Under this proposal, the consortia gaining the contract would have to be impartial in its news coverage. This provides a separate method of allocating funds, on a contractual basis awarded on criteria including the fulfilment of certain professional standards. By requiring the contractor to be impartial, the difficult question of allocating money between the different viewpoints is avoided. Instead, the consortium would have to ensure their coverage of political issues is fair and to some degree inclusive. Aside from that proposal, other subsidy options include allowing media entities to use some of the BBC's resources, providing a subsidy in kind. For example, in July 2009 the BBC began sharing some of its current affairs video content with some national newspapers' websites. There have also been suggestions that further mergers of local newspapers could provide a way to keep the local press in business.[124] Permitting further mergers provides the cheapest way, from the taxpayer's perspective, to keep the local media running. However, it comes at the cost of the plurality of voices and enhances the potential influence of those controlling the more concentrated press.

State-owned media

Rather than funding the independent media entities, the final type of subsidy supporting a diverse media is through the state funding its own media outlet. The state-owned media avoids the question of who to allocate funds to, but raises broader questions in deciding who will determine the editorial standards for that media. One approach is for all editorial decisions to be made by the government itself. Here, the state-owned media would be an instrument

---

[122] See the account of the newspaper industries in Norway and Sweden in Kelly *et al.*, *The Media in Europe*, pp. 164 and 238–40.

[123] Department for Culture, Media and Sport and Department for Business, Innovation and Skills, *Digital Britain: Final Report*, Cm 7650 (2009) at [78].

[124] *Press Gazette*, 4 March 2009.

of government policy, promoting its goals, explaining policies and providing information. In the early years of broadcasting, the BBC and state broadcasters in other countries took a role in promoting government policies. Such a model has long since been rejected and the use of the state-owned media as an outlet for government propaganda does little to advance its democratic functions, or serve political equality. Instead the need is to separate the running and editorial decisions of the state-owned media from the government.

One method is to hand control of the state-owned media to an independent group. Under the polarised media model, the running of the state-owned media entities could be divided among political parties or certain groups. For example, in the 1970s and 1980s Italy's three main state-owned television channels were controlled by the Christian Democrats, Socialists and Communists; each effectively with its own channel.[125] An alternative to this polarised model is for a state-owned media to be governed by a single body, which consists of representatives from the relevant political groups. For example, state-owned German broadcasters are governed by independent bodies composed of representatives of the political parties (appointed through proportional representation) and 'socially relevant groups'.[126] This latter approach will normally arise in those political systems with a tradition of 'power sharing' among groups and parties, or of corporatism, where greater agreement about the level of representation is likely to be found.[127] With such a system comes the danger that it creates a sharp division between the included groups or parties and those without formal recognition in the system. Furthermore, it may also reward those political actors that are successful under the existing system and provide less representation of minorities, or unorganised interests. These approaches attempt to give the main political actors a central role in governing the state-owned media.

By contrast, the tradition in the UK has been to separate the state-owned media from political actors. This is illustrated by the BBC, which is governed by an independent trust, run according to professional standards and required by law to be impartial in its political coverage. Despite formal independence, there is scope for the government to interfere through its appointment of trustees, control over the BBC Charter, and the ability to determine BBC funding. Such scope for interference makes the relationship particularly sensitive. The BBC is generally willing to criticise the government of the day and is not a mouthpiece for those in office. However, the potential for the government to put pressure on the BBC through these channels was highlighted following the broadcaster's coverage of the war in Iraq and the subsequent negotiations over the licence fee and the renewal of the BBC Charter.[128]

---

[125] Humphreys, *Mass Media and Media Policy in Western Europe*, p. 154.
[126] Hallin and Mancini, *Comparing Media Systems*, p. 167.
[127] *Ibid.*, p. 31.
[128] See Freedman, *The Politics of Media Policy*, pp. 141–3 and 150.

State support raises a number of broader economic and legal issues, for example the EU laws on state aid.[129] Such concerns are beyond the scope of discussion here, and the point is to outline the numerous ways state support can be provided, both direct and indirect. However, these ways differ from the distribution of subsidies considered in other chapters, in particular the funding of political parties. There the goal was for party funding to support a responsive and competitive system of political parties; here greater weight is placed on the need for the media to carry diverse views and serve the deliberative goals. The funding is not proportionate to levels of support, but aims to enable the media to disseminate a range of different perspectives.

Rights of access

The media ownership rules seek to limit the number of media entities a person or company can own and the subsidies seek to make the control of some media entities less dependent on wealth. The measures in the remainder of this chapter are concerned with the content of the media. Such controls are not concerned with the structure of ownership, or the conduct of the owner, but with some of the editorial decisions.

The first such measure considered here is a right of access to the media, in which groups or speakers are allocated some time or space in the mass media to put across their own message. Access would give external groups some influence over the media coverage and provide a check on editors' or journalists' control of the agenda, or any influence secured by advertisers. It could lead to a fuller range of views being included in the media coverage and provide the audience with information of a different quality, such as the strength of feeling, or the type of person holding a particular view. Finally, access can also serve political equality by helping to make the media participatory and giving more people the resources to disseminate content.

While using the term a 'right' of access, it is not suggested that the provision of access is mandated under the Human Rights Act. Most media entities will not fall within the definition of a public authority,[130] and both the Strasbourg and UK courts have confirmed that freedom of expression does not require the state to provide a right of access even where the media is state-owned.[131] Only if the state decides to grant access to its own media will the courts step in to ensure that no viewpoint or speaker is unfairly discriminated against.[132] Consequently, the argument pursued here is not that the courts should judicially mandate a

---

[129] In relation to public service broadcasting, see J. Harrison and L. Woods, *European Broadcasting Law and Policy* (Cambridge University Press, 2007) ch. 13.

[130] The status of the BBC under the HRA remains unclear, and in *R (ProLife Alliance) v. BBC* [2004] AC 185 the point was conceded by the BBC but not argued before the court, see [106].

[131] *X and Association of Z v. United Kingdom* (1971) 38 CD 86; *R (ProLife Alliance) v. BBC* [2004] AC 185 at [8] and [57–61].

[132] *R (ProLife Alliance) v. BBC* [2004] AC 185.

right of access to the media, but that it could be created through legislative or administrative means.[133]

So far this appears to be similar to the right of access to land that was proposed in Chapter 6. However, the questions are more complex in relation to the media. With public land the competing demands for access can be more easily accommodated, even though access may raise some public order issues. Even in a well visited public space, access can often be granted to speakers without undermining the other uses of the property. By contrast, the general rule is that space in a newspaper, or on a television channel, is limited and will be used by its owners or editors for expressive purposes.[134] Granting access to one speaker will take space that could be used by another. Whether the right of access would make a positive contribution to political debate, therefore, depends on what it is replacing and how far it curtails editorial freedom. Before considering these competing rights, the following section will first look at paid access to the media.

Paid advertising

Access to the media can be allocated to those political speakers willing to pay, as is the case with commercial advertising. That way, space on the mass media is allocated according to a price mechanism. The main difficulty from the perspective of political equality is that the chance to communicate is determined by the distribution of economic resources. While political advertisements can be purchased in newspapers and on the Internet, paid political advertisements are prohibited in the broadcast media in the UK. The ban applies to advertisements by any organisation with a political objective, or seeking to advance a political message, such as a political party or single-issue group.[135] A number of critics have argued that the ban amounts to an unfair restriction on access to the media.[136] At the centre of the debate is the question of whether the ban violates freedom of expression under Article 10 of European Convention on Human Rights. This critics' stance is supported by the decisions of the European Court of Human Rights (ECtHR) in *VGT Verein*, in which the application of a similar ban in Switzerland that prevented an animal rights group advertising on television, was found to violate freedom of expression under Article 10.[137] The position was confirmed more recently in the case of *Rogaland*, in which a fine imposed on a Norwegian broadcaster for showing an advertisement for a minor political party also breached Article 10.[138] In contrast to the European decisions,

---

[133] Sunstein, *Democracy and the Problem of Free Speech*, p. 104.
[134] See Chapter 8 on the online media.
[135] Communications Act 2003, s.321.
[136] See Barendt, *Freedom of Speech*, p. 445 and pp. 484–6; A. Scott, 'A Monstrous and Unjustifiable Infringement? Political Expression and the Broadcasting Ban on Advocacy Advertising' (2003) 66 *Modern Law Review* 224.
[137] *VgT Verein gegen Tierfabriken v. Switzerland* (2001) 34 EHRR 159.
[138] *TV Vest As and Rogaland Pensjonistparti v. Norway* [2008] ECHR 21132/05.

the House of Lords have found the ban to be consistent with Article 10. In *Animal Defenders International*, an animal rights group challenged the UK ban after broadcasters refused to show a proposed advertisement highlighting cruelty to primates. In rejecting that challenge, the House of Lords concluded that the ban in the UK did not violate Article 10 and was a proportionate measure.

While the European Court of Human Rights and the House of Lords appear to come to different conclusions about bans on political advertising, both courts accepted that such bans serve a legitimate aim in protecting the integrity of the democratic process. The difference between the ECtHR and UK courts is on the question of whether a ban on political advertising is necessary to preserve the integrity of the democratic process, or whether it goes too far.

Critics of the ban argue that it is disproportionate for a number of reasons. The first reason is that the ban is discriminatory, as commercial advertising is permitted on television and radio, but political advertising is not. A commercial advertisement can, therefore, promote an airline, but an environmental group cannot advertise to advocate stricter controls on carbon emissions. While upholding the ban, this argument won some sympathy in the House of Lords; with Lord Scott suggesting that a future application of the ban that prevented an organisation responding to a commercial message might fall foul of Article 10.[139] The argument does highlight an important problem with the effect of a ban. The difficulty with the comparison to the freedom accorded to commercial advertisers is that different distributive values apply in the economic and political spheres. While substantive equality in the opportunities to participate is a central principle in the political process, the marketplace for commercial products does not require such conditions. In any event, if political advertising were allowed on television, the two types of advertising would still be subject to different regulations. For example, if commercial advertisers were permitted to engage in product placement advertising, there would be good reason not to extend such an opportunity to political speakers. Some level of discrimination between the two types of advertisement seems inevitable. Consequently, the critics' argument is not simply that the ban is discriminatory, but that the discrimination goes beyond that which is justified by the distinction between the commercial and political spheres.

A second argument against the ban is that it applies only to the broadcast media and such advertising is permitted in newspapers. Critics of the ban argue this has two consequences, the first being that speakers are being denied access to the most effective means of communication. However, the ban does not prohibit political expression, but prevents broadcasters making agreements to allocate space in return for payment. It does not prevent the broadcaster giving access to speakers on a basis other than payment and does not restrict the media's own choice of content. In so far as paid access is seen to be a matter of

---

[139] R (*Animal Defenders International*) v. *Secretary of State for Culture, Media and Sport* [2008] 1 AC 1312 at [41–2].

protecting the speech right of the advertiser, as already noted, there is no right for a speaker to access the most effective media. If there were strong reasons to grant the speaker access to the most effective means of communication, then it is not in the interests of democracy to limit that access to those with the resources to pay. That it is the most effective way of reaching a wide audience makes it all the more important to limit the role of wealth in deciding which speakers will get access. Critics also point to the second implication of applying the ban only to the broadcast media, as it provides a limited constraint on the use of wealth. Political advertisements can still be purchased in newspapers and the Internet. This line of criticism suggests the ban is ineffective in attaining its goal. However, while the differences between the types of media are beginning to blur, singling out the broadcast media is not arbitrary given the different histories of the two types of media and the higher costs associated with an effective broadcast advertising campaign. The ban thereby attempts to target the type of media that requires more economic resources for access.

A third argument against the ban is that concerns about inequalities of wealth could be addressed through alternative means, such as restricting the ban to party political advertisements, or limiting the amount any group can spend on advertising. Following the decision in *Rogaland*, it is not clear that the ECtHR would accept a ban limited to all party political advertisements, given the applicant in that case was a political party. Putting this point to one side, an attempt to limit the ban to electoral, or party political, advertisements may raise objections in principle and practice. As the chapter on party funding highlighted, this line between the electoral and the general political is difficult to draw and has generated much scope for evasion. Furthermore, concerns about political equality are not restricted to elections and can arise at the earlier stages of the process. While this does not mean that far-reaching measures like a cap on all political speech would be appropriate, the ban on paid political advertising curbs one of the most obvious ways that inequalities in wealth can impact on the opportunities to influence others prior to an election campaign.

Another alternative measure is to impose a limit on the amount that could be spent on political advertising. This would raise difficult managerial issues of its own. For example, if the limit is applied to each separate advertiser rather than to each viewpoint, overall coverage could be skewed in a particular direction if more advertisers seek to promote a similar stance. Then there is the level at which the expenditure cap should be fixed. Given the cost of making broadcast advertisements and the level of repetition required to have any effect on the audience, the limit would have to be set at a high level if it is to allow widespread communication. The new media landscape may change this, if technology lowers the cost of production and as some advertising space becomes less expensive. However, if the cap is fixed at a high level, like the election spending limits, considerable inequalities in the chance to access the media will remain.

If the ban is lifted, it raises the question of whether laws should be imposed to require broadcasters to allow all political speakers to buy advertisements at equal rates, or whether the private broadcaster should retain the discretion to exclude certain advertisers.[140] If a broadcaster has to carry a view, which he or she opposes, this would raise the difficult questions on editorial autonomy and freedom, which will be considered below.

Subsidised access

If direct access is necessary to fulfil the media's democratic function, access could be distributed regardless of the speaker's ability to pay. For example, access could be granted for free, or the state could provide a subsidy to cover all, or part, of the costs of access. This approach can be seen in the requirement that UK public service broadcasters provide free time to political parties during election campaigns, known as party election broadcasts.[141] This approach could be extended to provide access time for other political speakers. Taking such an approach, broadcasters in some European countries have provided access to speakers including religious groups and trade unions.[142]

The possible hazards of this approach can be seen in the difficulties experienced by the party election broadcasts. First, party election broadcasts are often criticised for being unpopular and for failing to engage the public.[143] Even though the length of the broadcasts have shortened considerably over the years, critics of the system argue that a broadcast lasting less than five minutes still fails to hold the audience's attention. Whether this would be true of a message from a pressure group, whose views have received less coverage in the mediated news, is uncertain, but the criticisms suggest caution in following the election broadcast model. A possible alternative is to grant access for very short slots, which by being repeatedly shown are likely to reach a wider range of people.[144]

The second problem is in deciding who should have access. While party election broadcasts have been a longstanding feature in the UK, deciding which parties are eligible for access and for how long has been far from simple. Under the current rules, 'major' political parties are entitled to a series of party election broadcasts and those contesting one-sixth of seats up for election are eligible for a broadcast. Much is left to the discretion of the broadcasters to decide how much time to allocate to each of the eligible parties. The formula attempts

---

[140] See *Columbia Broadcasting System* v. *DNC* 412 US 94 (1973), the US Supreme Court finding that a broadcaster's refusal to air a political advertisement did not violate the First Amendment; and *CBS* v. *FCC* 453 US 367 (1981), upholding a law requiring reasonable access for candidates for federal office during an election campaign. See also Judge Sajo's dissent in *Verein gegen Tierfabriken Schweiz (VgT)* v. *Switzerland (No 2)* [2009] ECHR 32772/02.

[141] Communications Act 2003, s.333. Outside the election campaigns, parties can be granted access under party political broadcasts.

[142] E. Barendt, *Broadcasting Law* (Oxford University Press, 1993) pp. 154–5.

[143] For discussion see B. Franklin, *Packaging Politics*, second edition (London: Arnold, 2004) pp. 125–8.

[144] See Electoral Commission, *Party Political Broadcasting: Report and Recommendations* (2003) pp. 31–3.

to distribute resources in a way that reflects both the level of support for the party and the need for diversity. However, complaints have been made that giving more time to the major parties operates unfairly on the smaller political parties.[145] Despite these difficulties, the election at least provides a formal institutional setting with defined participants among whom access can be distributed. If this model is extended beyond election coverage, this formal basis for distribution is lost and the questions of allocation become more difficult given the sheer number of potential speakers. It is one thing to manage access rights among a limited number of political parties; it is another to manage the competing access claims of an open-ended number of interest groups. The access right faces the same problem as that of subsidies discussed earlier.

A further difficulty is that demands for a right of access to the mass media may seem dated.[146] Given the ease with which people can access the Internet and disseminate content, newspapers and broadcasters no longer have a monopoly on the chances to reach a wide audience. However, while the Internet may have expanded those opportunities to communicate, it will be argued in the next chapter that a small number of media entities will continue to reach a mass audience. Some of those entities will still play a gatekeeping role, and access could ensure that diverse views actually reach a wider number of people. Yet access rights still face the problem of the ease with which people can now filter content and avoid any unwanted programmes. As a result, access may not guarantee attention.

Assuming the need for access to the main media outlets is still important, that goal can be pursued through the media's own policies to include diverse voices. Such an approach is reflected in the work of the public service broadcasters outside the context of election broadcasts. An early example being the BBC's Community Programme Unit in the 1970s airing *Open Door*, a programme which gave access and considerable editorial freedom to under-represented voices, such as social action groups.[147] Since then there have been various versions of access television with varying levels of broadcaster involvement in production, attempting to make the media more inclusive. While giving more people the chance to speak to a wide audience, some critics have questioned the extent to which such programmes help to inform.[148] Despite those reservations, such programmes had an important role in democratising the media. Aside from access programming, the broader obligations on the public service broadcasters may encourage access to be granted to those normally excluded from the mainstream media. For example, Channel 4 is under a duty to provide programming that, among other things, 'appeals to the tastes and interests of a

---

[145] See *R* v. *BBC, ex parte Referendum Party* [1997] EMLR 605.
[146] For discussion of this point from a leading advocate of access rights, see J. Barron, 'Access to the Media – A Contemporary Appraisal' (2007) 35 Hofstra L. Rev. 937.
[147] N. Lacey, *Media Audiences and Institutions* (Basingstoke: Palgrave, 2002) p. 142.
[148] Lord Annan (Chairman), *Report of the Committee on the Future of Broadcasting*, Cmnd. 6753 (1977) (Annan Committee) at [18.11].

culturally diverse society' and 'exhibits a distinctive character'.[149] The obligations do not give anyone a right to access the media, but the process of catering to those diverse tastes may in effect encourage the media to grant wider access. To some extent newspapers provide a limited form of access through their letters pages, although the newspaper policies for selection have been criticised for promoting established voices or those speaking on topics already deemed newsworthy. [150] Access is also developing in new ways, such as the use of user-generated content in the media. However, under these approaches access is not about a right held by a speaker, but arises through a more general responsibility held by the media to fulfil its democratic role. That role can be developed as a matter of self-regulation by the media, or in some cases through those public service obligations that require the media to be inclusive or to commission and assist in the production of content from some under-represented groups.

A more concrete type of access right can be framed as a right of reply, in which access is granted to a person or group that is subject to criticism or attack in the media.[151] Such a right could give the person criticised the chance to set the record straight and put across his own version of events. While there is no legal right of reply in the UK, such a right can arise in practice through the internal policies of the media, the broadcasting codes and the existing self-regulation of the press and in defamation laws.[152] A right of reply would provide a more precise definition of who can access the media, namely the person or group being discussed, and also provide a check on the potential abuses of media power. One difficulty is in deciding when the attack or criticism warrants a response, as not everyone discussed in the media can demand a reply. Furthermore, the goal of such measures is primarily to protect the person's reputation or dignity, rather than a more general redistribution of communicative opportunities. Finally, rights of reply can be seen to have a chilling effect. One reason why the US Supreme Court struck down a statute granting a right of reply to politicians subject to attack during an election campaign was the concern that newspapers may steer clear of controversial statements to avoid the access right.[153] As a result, critics of rights of reply argue that such rules potentially deprive the audience of valuable information. However, it is not clear that a right of reply would have such an effect, and in any event it is not clear that this concern justifies a large media entity's power to make statements about people without challenge. Instead, the problem with a right of reply for the purposes of discussion here is that it would arise in

---

[149] Communications Act 2003, s.265.
[150] M. Temple, *The British Press* (Maidenhead: Open University Press, 2008) p. 199.
[151] For discussion in relation to the broadcast media, see Barendt, *Broadcasting Law*, pp. 159–61.
[152] Whether a defendant attempted to contact the subject of the story and include that person's version of events in the publication are relevant factors in the qualified privilege defence in defamation cases, see *Reynolds* v. *Times Newspapers* [2001] 2 AC 127; *Jameel* v. *Wall Street Journal* [2007] AC 359. Clause 2 of the Press Complaints Commission Code of Practice provides 'A fair opportunity for reply to inaccuracies must be given when reasonably called for'. See also BBC Editorial Guidelines (2005) s.5 and Ofcom Broadcasting Code (2009) at [7.11].
[153] *Miami Herald Publishing* v. *Tornillo* 418 US 241(1974).

limited circumstances and play only a very small part of granting wider access to the media.

Impartiality

A final strategy is to regulate media content in a way that limits the use of the media to privilege any political viewpoint. Such an approach stops a media entity acting as an advocate, or campaigner. The requirement fits with a public service account of the media, which does not aim to favour any particular side in a political debate. One version of this approach is applied to all holders of a broadcasting licence in the UK, who are required to present the news, 'matters of political or industrial controversy' and 'matters relating to current public policy' with 'due impartiality'.[154] The rules also prohibit editorialising by a broadcaster. This does not stop partisan views and programmes being broadcast, or speakers advocating a stance or campaigning, but the broadcaster itself cannot endorse any political view or political party. These rules stop the broadcast media being used either by its owner, or by the owner's agents, as a vehicle for their own political views and aim to prevent the broadcast media being captured by any political actor.[155]

At the time of an election, broadcasters are subject to even stricter rules. 'Due weight' must be given to each of the major political parties and broadcasters must 'consider giving appropriate coverage to other parties and independent candidates with significant views and perspectives'.[156] Further rules require that individual candidates be treated fairly. For example, where a report on a particular constituency is broadcast during an election, an opportunity to take part must be offered 'to all candidates within the constituency or electoral area representing parties with previous significant electoral support or where there is evidence of significant current support'.[157] This approach reflects the change in priorities, as the voting stage gets closer, in which coverage becomes more even-handed and focused on the specific choices before the electorate.

These regulations are not the only way that public service goals can be pursued. Such an approach to politics may arise without legal regulation, for example where professional schools have influenced the style of journalism, or where the need to appeal to a broad audience means that no viewpoint is favoured. However, as the national newspaper market shows, impartiality will not arise as a natural consequence of professional or commercial constraints.[158] To guarantee such an approach, the impartiality requirements place a legal

---

[154] See Communications Act 2003, s.319(2)(c); Department of Culture Media and Sport, Broadcasting: *An agreement between Her Majesty's Secretary of State for Culture, Media and Sport and the British Broadcasting Corporation*, Cm 6872 (2006), cl.44; for further guidance see BBC Editorial Guidelines (2005) s.4, 'Impartiality and Diversity of Opinion', and Ofcom Broadcasting Code (2009) s.5. Communications Act 2003, s.320. Local radio services are subject to a requirement not to give 'undue prominence' to any particular view or body.

[155] House of Lords Communications Committee, above n. 32, at [344].

[156] Ofcom Broadcasting Code, s.6.   [157] Ofcom Broadcasting Code, s.6.10.

[158] Hallin and Mancini, *Comparing Media Systems*, p. 286.

obligation on broadcasters, which is monitored and enforced by the regulator Ofcom.

Impartiality as a concept is of limited help in guiding broadcasters and comes with a number of limits.[159] Broadcasters should not treat all arguments, whether good, bad, true or false, impartially. Some perspectives may be seen as off the table and no longer the subject of serious controversy. This may be obvious in some cases, as there is no need for an impartial media to cover arguments that the world is flat. However, in many instances it will not be clear whether a particular view is still seriously contested. For example, it is unclear whether the media has to give impartial coverage to those claiming that global warming is not caused by human activity, or whether such a view is now off the table.[160] Another limit to the standard is that broadcasters do not have to be impartial towards fundamental democratic principles and will oppose racism and intolerance.[161] In the context of media regulations, a requirement of impartiality does not provide a precise standard, but is a general aspiration to ensure that the media is inclusive of relevant viewpoints on contested and controversial issues, and takes into account the 'weight of opinion' holding those views.[162] The application of these standards is thought to be more difficult in a changing political landscape, where coverage can no longer be structured around the two major parties, but must include a range of other views and groups that go beyond the traditional divisions.[163]

Given these limits, the broadcaster retains considerable discretion in deciding what range of views are relevant and need to be included in its coverage. Impartiality rules may therefore provide a safeguard against the use of the media to blatantly promote the political agenda of its owner or advertisers, but is less likely to strike against good faith attempts to provide fair coverage. Consequently, impartiality obligations do not allow the regulators to micromanage the content decisions of the media, but provide a channel of accountability that allows the public to contest claims that the media have acted fairly.

One concern is that even with impartiality obligations, the media has much scope for its own political preferences to shape the selection of content. Such concerns are often seen in the claims that the broadcast media is politically biased despite the regulations. The argument being that while such biases are not overt in the sense of an editorial endorsement, it is present in the selection of speakers, issues and level of depth of coverage. Even where the impartial media does try to exclude its own political preferences, it will reflect some other

---

[159] See discussion of 'equality of ideas' in Chapter 2 pp. 49–51.

[160] See introduction in G. Starkey, *Balance and Bias in Journalism* (Basingstoke: Palgrave, 2006).

[161] Annan Committee, at [17.21]. See also T. Gibbons, *Regulating the Media*, second edition (London: Sweet and Maxwell, 1998) pp. 108–9.

[162] Annan Committee, at [17.10].

[163] Ofcom discussion document, *New News Future News* (July 2007) at [5.42], refers to concerns that under current impartiality rules views that 'do not fit easily within a conventional "both sides of the argument" approach can struggle to be heard'. See also BBC Trust, *From Seesaw to Wagon Wheel: Safeguarding Impartiality in the 21st Century* (2007).

political outlook. For example, biases may follow from the professional training of the journalists, which has its own assumptions about how issues should be framed. An attempt to be impartial may also lead the media to respond to the priorities of external actors, such as official government sources, pressure groups, or public relations officers, all of whom may have their own political agenda. The media may look to official sources and institutions to indicate what is newsworthy or relevant. Along these lines, the broadcast media has in the past been criticised for focusing on those working within the parliamentary system and excluding those who have not organised themselves within the formal political process.[164] The critics argued that focus leads to an unintentional bias towards the established views. Others may criticise the media for failing to question the basic assumptions underlying a market economy, so an impartial media may be too quick to assume that certain perspectives are no longer the subject of serious controversy. While impartiality may seek to limit the political actions of the media itself, the choices made in fulfilling this standard can still be rooted in some political outlook.

These criticisms need not call for the abandonment of impartiality as an ideal, but for changes in its practice. The critics may call for the underlying assumptions of the media to be more transparent, and that the standards should be open to debate and modified if their application is found to unfairly exclude any speaker. Calls have been made for a more radical account of impartiality that is inclusive of a wider and more controversial range of views.[165] However, impartiality still provides an important aspiration within the broadcast media. Even though the media cannot be strictly neutral, the experience in the UK shows that there is at least a qualitative difference between the broadcast media that seeks to be impartial and the print media, which pursues its biases more openly. While there are limits and difficulties with impartiality as a standard, the solution to the various criticisms is not simply to lift that constraint and allow the market pressures, or views of the owner, to shape the content.

Media sectors and freedom of expression

Earlier in this chapter media freedom was said to be different from the individual's freedom of expression and justified by its performance of certain democratic functions. The obligations relating to access and content discussed so far raise difficult questions about media freedom. However, the distinction drawn earlier between the polarised and public service sectors can provide a framework to address such questions. Under this view, attempts to regulate media content will be appropriate in relation to the public service media, which was characterised as a forum for people to hear diverse views. Access rights and

---

[164] A. Boyle, 'Political Broadcasting, Fairness and Administrative Law' [1986] PL 562, 574.
[165] BBC Trust, *From Seesaw to Wagon Wheel.*

impartiality rules arguably help the media perform these functions. In relation to the polarised media, the media should be free to determine their own content and not be subject to obligations to carry diverse content, whether through access regulation or impartiality rules. In the polarised sector, the equal distribution of the opportunities to communicate is served by ensuring a range of diversely owned media entities through ownership controls and subsidised media.

Even with this distinction, there are concerns that content controls could undermine the public service role in providing information and ideas. Such criticisms can be made in relation to the prohibition on broadcasters endorsing a political viewpoint. For example, the US Supreme Court struck down a requirement on non-commercial broadcasters not to editorialise, and emphasised the role of the editorial in 'informing and arousing the public'.[166] The Court distinguished such a requirement from rules that broadcasters provide balance in political coverage, as the balance requirement does not stop the broadcaster expressing its own view. By contrast, a ban on editorialising deprives the public from hearing the broadcaster's own opinion. Aside from a ban on editorialising, a further concern is that impartiality rules may also create a recipe for bland political coverage and force the media into the centre ground. The reporter may simply attempt to give both sides of the story, the official version and the opposing point of view, without attempting to engage in serious critical analysis.[167]

These concerns should not be overstated. The impartiality rules are based on content, but do not privilege any viewpoint.[168] Authored and partisan programmes are still permitted, and those controlling the media have other outlets to express their political views. The impartiality rules merely prevent the ownership or control of the media being used as a vehicle for these political views, which may be a desirable goal when thinking about the media as a public service.

The question is in deciding which media entities should be subject to public service regulations. The obvious target for such regulations is the state-owned media, as is currently the case with the BBC. UK laws go further and impose regulations on privately owned broadcasters. However, not all broadcasters are subject to the same level of regulation. The core 'Public Service Broadcasters' (PSBs) are subject to requirements to produce certain types of programme and meet quotas for original, independent and regional productions.[169] By contrast, the impartiality rules apply to all television channels with a broadcast licence, both publicly and privately owned, and including cable and satellite channels. So while impartiality has been described here as a public service

---

[166] *FCC* v. *League of Women Voters* 468 US 364 (1984) at 382.
[167] Hallin and Mancini, *Comparing Media Systems*, p. 226.
[168] See Justice Stevens' dissent in *FCC* v. *League of Women Voters1* 468 US 364 (1984).
[169] The PSBs are the BBC channels, Channels 3, 4 and 5.

obligation, within the regulatory framework the rule applies more broadly to all broadcasters.

By contrast, the print media is free from such restrictions on content. The distinction between the print and broadcast media emerged partly for historical reasons and its justification has been the subject of much debate.[170] Common reasons for distinguishing the broadcast media include the scarcity of broadcasting spectrum and concerns about the pervasiveness of television.[171] While such factors are important to certain regulatory issues, they need not be decisive for the current concern with the distribution in the opportunities to contribute to political debate.

In any event, the distinction between the broadcast and print media is coming under increasing pressure given changes to the current media landscape. Given the increasing number of broadcast channels and competition from the Internet, granting a broadcast licence is no longer seen as the generous subsidy it once was, with some arguing that these changes weaken the rationale for public service obligations. The impartiality rules have also come under pressure from broadcasters originating from outside the UK that are accessible through cable and satellite, such as Fox News. As a result of these developments, suggestions have been made that the impartiality requirements could be removed in relation to commercial broadcasters that are not categorised as a core PSB.[172] If there were a number of broadcasters that could all compete and produce diverse news coverage, there might be a case for some type of polarised broadcasting sphere. However, at present there is no such range. The only major UK television broadcaster producing regular news content outside of the core PSBs is Rupert Murdoch's BSkyB.[173] Given the continued dominance of a small number of news providers in the broadcast sector, the continued application of the impartiality rules provides a way of constraining the potential opportunities to influence held by those few media entities.

These changes, such as media convergence, do not remove the democratic rationale for a public service media. The concerns with political equality remain even as the technologies change. However, the current targets for regulation will need to be rethought in the future. For example, if the impartiality requirements were loosened in relation to some broadcasters, it would have to be decided which broadcasters should remain subject to those rules. Furthermore, if the distinction between the press and television is eroded and the two sectors are in more direct competition, then it may be argued that some parts of the press could be subject to similar obligations as broadcasters.

---

[170] Barendt, *Freedom of Speech*, pp. 445–6.
[171] In so far as the US First Amendment does permit the media to be regulated as forum, the reasoning of the US Supreme Court in *Red Lion Broadcasting Co.* v. *FCC* 395 US 367 (1969) is limited to the broadcast media in so far as it rests on the spectrum scarcity.
[172] Ofcom, *New News Future News*, at [5.42].
[173] House of Lords Communications Committee, above n. 32, at [351].

Obvious candidates for such public service obligations are the publicly funded media and monopolies. If newspapers do require some type of public subsidy to maintain their survival, then it could be subject to the fulfilment of some public service obligations, such as impartiality or a broader duty to include diverse or minority views. Aside from state funding, the level of 'dominance' of a media entity, or group of entities under the same ownership, in a particular market could help identify those subject to such obligations.[174] Under this approach, once the media entity has an audience or circulation in a particular market above a certain level, its democratic function changes. This does not cap the reach of any media entity, but imposes public service obligations as a condition of continuing that level of power. While much is being made of the decline in the established media's audience share and revenues, in the long term this may increase the importance of a handful of entities that continue to command mass audiences. However, the difficulty with a standard such as dominance is that it appears to punish the media entity for being popular. The problem therefore lies in determining whether the dominant position of the media entity is due to its advantage in resources or failures in the market, rather than the preferences of the audience. The arguments given earlier rejected a view of the media's political influence necessarily reflecting its audience's support. Consequently, a dominant position may give some basis for identifying those media entities that in practice act as a primary point of reference where people gain their political information.

This need not be an all-or-nothing approach. Some media entities have elements of the polarised and public service models. National newspapers in the UK are polarised in the sense that there is often a distinct editorial stance on political issues. The newspapers are not as committed to political parties as in previous years, but they are still politically committed, for example campaigning on single issues.[175] While a political stance may emerge from its overall coverage, newspapers carry a range of commentators with differing opinions, and provide some level of internal pluralism.[176] Not all newspaper coverage is politically committed, with the so-called 'quality' newspapers separating professional reporting from more overt partisan comment sections. The newspaper, therefore, performs a number of functions of which polarised commentary and advocacy are one, but also has a public service element in providing information and reporting. There are, therefore, arguments that some newspapers could be subject to limited public service

---

[174] Baker, *Media Concentration and Democracy*, p. 186. Similarly, Miller suggests that obligations could be imposed on newspapers with a certain level of readership, W. Miller, *Media and Voters* (Oxford: Clarendon, 1991) p. 218.

[175] Kuhn, *Politics and the Media in Britain*, pp. 221–4.

[176] *Ibid.*, p. 224.

obligations, although this may require some subsidy to offset any costs.[177] For example if a newspaper endorses a political party, it could be required to carry the print equivalent of a party election broadcast if it is to maintain its exemption from the party funding laws. The imposition of such an obligation seems unlikely and it would be a major departure from past practice in the UK. Furthermore, a time when newspapers are said to be in crisis and struggling for survival is not the time to introduce new burdens. There are also questions about the extent to which it really would balance the power of the media. However, such issues will need to be addressed in the long term once the business models of the media become more stable and as the current media sectors converge.

Conclusion

The media poses difficult issues if the influence of wealth in politics is to be checked. The arguments for political equality provide reasons to prevent the media simply being an instrument of its funders, or responding to commercial pressures. At the same time, some level of inequality in the chance to communicate is necessary if the media are to fulfil their ideal role in a democracy. In this chapter, a range of measures seeking to limit the threat of media power, while promoting the ideals of a free media, have been considered. All have some attraction, but come with potential drawbacks.

The approach taken here has not been to single out any one of these methods as the sole way to regulate media power. Instead it has been to sketch a pluralistic account to the media, in which different media sectors perform different functions and can be subject to different types of control. Two models were outlined, the polarised media and the public service media, both of which can complement one another. The controls on ownership and conduct may provide a way to promote a polarised media sector, whereas the public service sector may be more amenable to some regulations on content. It is also hoped that the media will have diverse sources of funding, with some privately run by trusts, corporations or interest groups, while others receive some state subsidy or are owned by the state. The pluralistic model may allow the limits of one sphere to offset the other, which will give people a more varied and complete picture of political coverage. As the different models sketched out are not clear-cut, overlap can occur. As suggested above, some media entities may fall between polarised and public service sectors and are thereby subject to more limited public service obligations.

As the media landscape is changing rapidly, some of the existing regulations and responsibilities are under attack. While these changes may call for reconsideration in the methods of regulation, the democratic arguments underlying

---

[177] See Miller, *Media and Voters*, p. 218; Barendt, *Freedom of Speech*, p. 450; Starkey, *Balance and Bias in Journalism*, pp. 66–7.

those goals remain. While the existing system is open to criticism and could be strengthened in some ways, the changes in the media do not call for deregulation in the belief that the market will serve all the citizens' needs. A system combining controls on ownership, conduct and promoting the public service element may help move away from the threat associated with media power, steering it closer to those democratic functions which justify its privileged place in political life.

8

Participation in the digital era: a new distribution?

The use of digital technologies may be thought to reduce the importance of wealth in politics.[1] The Internet and new media provide more opportunities and lower the cost for people to communicate, acquire information, pool resources and organise. Under this view, with a more equal distribution of the resources to participate, those with greater economic resources do not have the same power to control the agenda and to influence others. If this view is correct, then the concerns about wealth discussed throughout this book may be less of a problem, or even a thing of the past. However, as this chapter will argue, on closer examination, the impact on the distribution of political resources is more complex.

Idealised accounts of the Internet characterised its early days. For example, in 1995 Eugene Volokh wrote that digital technologies would promote 'cheap speech' and 'make it much easier for all ideas, whether backed by the rich or poor, to enter the marketplace'.[2] Yet, a more sceptical line of argument soon followed, looking at the possible harms that may arise. In a well-known argument, Cass Sunstein suggested that with Internet users having greater control over information received, people would tend to select those sources of information that support their existing outlook.[3] Choice over content could thereby emphasise divisions between different groups of people and lead to polarisation rather than democratic deliberation. Other critics focused on the 'digital divide', and the presence of 'systemic differences between those who have access and use digital technologies and those who do not'.[4] The concern was that such a division would reflect characteristics such as the users' socio-economic status, race, age and gender.[5] A further sceptical account suggested that a small number of corporations would continue to dominate the media market online. Under this view, through the process of commercialisation, the inequalities of wealth and ownership concentration associated with the traditional mass media would become a feature of the new media.[6]

---

[1] This chapter uses terms such as digital media, communications and technologies interchangeably, but will focus largely on the effects of the Internet.

[2] E. Volokh, 'Cheap Speech and What It Will Do' (1995) 104 Yale L.J. 1805 at 1847.

[3] C. Sunstein, *Republic.com* (Princeton University Press, 2001).

[4] See R. Klotz, *The Politics of Internet Communication* (Maryland: Rowman and Littlefield, 2004) p. 20.

[5] *Ibid.*, p. 21.

[6] See N. W. Netanel, 'Cyberspace Self-Governance: A Skeptical View from Liberal Democratic Theory' (2000) 88 Cal. L.R. 395.

Since these early accounts, the use of such technologies has become a feature of political life in the UK and elsewhere, and developed in some unforeseen ways. The evidence, however, remains mixed and the debate continues between the idealists and sceptics, though with a range of views in-between. The technologies and their uses continue to change rapidly and much of these debates involve some speculation about the future. Whether a more equal distribution of political resources will follow and the extent to which wealth will continue to play a major role in politics is unclear. The effects will depend on factors including people's habits in using the technology; the regulatory environment; the development of software and applications; the market; and the interaction between these factors.[7] The technology alone will not determine its democratic effects, and those effects will flow from choices that are the subject of political, legal and regulatory battles.

The use of digital technologies is taking place alongside traditional political activities, such as protests, face-to-face meetings, lobbying and publishing in the offline media. It is not clear whether this complementary role will continue, or whether some of the traditional activities will eventually be replaced or fall out of use. Some believe that the economic pressures that have put the newspaper industry in financial difficulty may result in the online media taking the place of local newspapers as a source of information.[8] Given that such outcomes have yet to emerge, it still seems appropriate to consider the effects of the digital communications separately, looking at the impact on the activities set out in previous chapters.

To assess the potential redistribution of political resources, this chapter will look at lobbying, political fundraising and the media. The argument will be that these developments have had dramatic effects and improved the opportunities for participation by individuals. However, the changes should not be exaggerated and some new sources of inequality may also emerge. Consequently, controls on the use of wealth to promote political equality will still be necessary.

Lobbying

A possible strategy to reconcile the lobbying of politicians and civil servants with political equality, mentioned in Chapter 4, is to open up the process for influencing officials to a wider range of people. The Internet and digital media potentially make such inclusion possible in a number of ways. The first way it is having an inclusive effect is in making more information about legislation and government policy accessible. Information including policy documents, reports and statistics are generally available from government websites, giving those interested greater chance to track policy changes and consider their

[7] L. Lessig, *Code Version 2.0* (New York: Basic Books, 2006) ch. 7.
[8] P. Starr, 'Goodbye to the Age of Newspapers (Hello to a New Era of Corruption)', *New Republic*, 4 March 2009.

effects. However, for the reasons outlined in Chapter 4, hiring a lobbyist will still be attractive for those with sufficient funds. Conventional lobbying techniques can acquire more sensitive, unpublished information and provide early off-the-record indications of policy changes. Meetings with officials also provide a different type of information from that found on the government websites, allowing the lobbyist to ask specific questions, seek clarification and find out what types of arguments are most likely to influence the official. The increase in the availability of information can help people participate, but does not level the playing field.

A second effect is to make lobbying potentially more accessible by providing easier access to politicians and other decision-makers. At the most basic level, email makes contacting officials and MPs much easier. A number of other channels also facilitate direct communication through the Internet. For example, some MPs have blogs that allow visitors to post comments[9] and Downing Street has set up an area on its website for people to sign e-petitions to be sent directly to the Prime Minister. However, whether such petitions, which require minimal effort from individuals, are the best way to get people involved in politics is questionable and how the government should respond to such pressure is unclear.[10] There are also a number of independent websites that perform similar functions, for example in providing information about MPs' voting records and statements in Parliament, and by making it easier to email those MPs.[11] Aside from such basic channels, government consultations and parliamentary calls for evidence are published online and responses can be submitted by email. Government departments are continuing to experiment with a range of different tools for consultation, such as blogs, wikis and forums, to provide a space for people to participate in a range of policy areas.[12] However, as Chapter 4 noted, some critics view such consultations sceptically, as public relations exercises.[13] Furthermore, these changes do not undermine the advantages to be gained from insider lobbying. Again, face-to-face meetings with an official are likely to remain an effective way to advance one's case, offering more opportunities to persuade than a written submission, email or petition. Those wanting to influence decisions through traditional lobbying techniques will also seek to shape policy at the earlier stages, before the information is published. Even though people may have more opportunities to communicate, the more capital-intensive lobbying activities are likely to persist.

A third effect of the digital media is to allow groups of people to organise collectively to lobby officials. Most obviously, collective action online allows

---

[9] For discussion see N. Jackson, 'Representation in the Blogosphere: MPs and Their New Constituents' (2008) 61 *Parliamentary Affairs* 642.

[10] J. Blumler and S. Coleman, *The Internet and Democratic Citizenship* (Cambridge University Press, 2009) p. 152.

[11] For example, TheyWorkForYou.co.uk.

[12] For an overview of some of these techniques see L. Miller and A. Williamson, *Digital Dialogues* (London: Hansard Society/Ministry of Justice, 2008).

[13] See discussion in Chapter 4, pp. 103–4.

Internet users to find like-minded people, coordinate their actions, and amplify their voices. For example, a template letter to be sent to an MP in relation to a particular issue can easily be distributed among activists throughout the country. Online organisation can also facilitate the pooling of resources and help people develop technical arguments and research to persuade decision-makers. For example, the digital media allows group members to collate different people's experiences of a particular government activity, building up research that can be put before an official. Collaborative projects allow the collective expertise of a group to be harnessed without expending vast amounts of money and put that knowledge to use in influencing government.

With these developments come some drawbacks. The first is that as more direct communications and representations are made, it may become much harder for voices to be heard, or to receive attention from the official. The advantages gained from hiring a professional lobbyist, in securing contacts and providing strategic advice, may be all the greater. Furthermore, with a wider range of voices potentially contributing to the process, the temptation for officials is to rely on sources that are known and trusted, or work in the area that the decision affects. The second drawback is that these developments may provide new ways to advantage those with greater economic resources. For example, such resources could be invested in an online 'astroturf' campaign, which has the appearance of popular participation, but which is sponsored by a paid lobbyist.[14] This could arise where the sponsor sets up a website or pays key individuals to form a social network campaign group. Such paid professionals may be crucial in getting the astroturf campaign noticed and to get a sufficient number of people to participate. These techniques of campaigning using the digital media may potentially make it harder to know or detect who is really behind or bankrolling the campaign.

The numerous ways that the new technologies can involve people more directly in decision-making are still being developed and tested through trial and error. The point is not to dismiss the democratic potential, but to note that while the digital media has provided new avenues for communication between citizens and officials, those with greater resources can still exploit such channels. The major lobbying campaigns are likely to hire professionals to advance their cause, continuing the capital-intensive channels of influence.

Party funding

A second area affected by the uses of the Internet is party funding and the cost of election campaigns. Chapter 5 considered the problems of super-rich donors to political parties, which have been a regular feature of UK politics. In the United States, some candidates have used online campaigning as part of a

---

[14] See P. Howard, *New Media Campaigns and the Managed Citizen* (Cambridge University Press, 2006) pp. 98–100.

strategy to secure funds from a wider range of donors. In particular, Howard Dean's presidential campaign in 2004 and Barack Obama's successful campaign in 2008 highlighted such a use of the Internet to solicit a larger number of small donations. The use of the technology to reach out to supporters, maintain their enthusiasm and provide an easy way to give money marked a shift away from the reliance on large donations. Reports about the Obama campaign highlighted how a greater proportion of financial support came from smaller donations of $200 or less.[15] Under this view, the trend towards small donations is a step closer to the ideal system in which a greater number of people have some say in party and election funding.

What at first appears to be a simple account of the Internet making election funding more egalitarian, gives way to a more complex account. There is some evidence that, in 2008, US presidential candidates relied more heavily on larger donations at the earlier stages of the campaign.[16] As candidates campaign not only for votes, but also for small donations, higher start-up costs may be required to attract the small donors. Furthermore, while much has been made of Obama's reliance on donations of less than $200, subsequent analysis has suggested that those sums were given by repeat donors, whose aggregate donations were at a higher level.[17] If this is correct, the greater reliance on the very small donor may have been exaggerated. The 2008 election clearly was a breakthrough in the use of the Internet, but further analysis is necessary to determine the extent to which it makes election funding more egalitarian.

Putting these issues to one side, the examples of Obama and Dean underline the role of money in politics. The broad base of donors was important because it gave candidates the resources to buy television advertising, hire consultants and pay for 'get out the vote' operations. Campaigns tend to use the Internet to engage with the existing committed supporters, but rely on the more traditional methods of campaigning to reach the non-committed voters.[18] Despite the changes in the use of the technology to raise funds, running an effective campaign in the United States is not getting cheaper.[19] The new media even has the potential to increase the cost of an election campaign, as campaigns will need to hire specialists in online activism and fundraising. Advertising and mobilisation strategies using the new media to target specific groups of voters may require extra expenditures to identify key groups, investigate what messages will appeal to those groups, and produce content with separate messages

[15] R. Hasen, 'Political Equality, the Internet, and Campaign Finance Regulation' (2008) 6 *The Forum*, art.7.

[16] M. Malbin, 'Small Donors, Large Donors and the Internet', CFI Working Paper (Washington DC: Campaign Finance Institute, 2009) pp. 13–14.

[17] *Ibid.*, pp. 14–19.

[18] C. Shirky, *Here Comes Everybody* (London: Allen Lane, 2008) p. 223; M. Hindman, *The Myth of Digital Democracy* (Princeton University Press, 2008) p. 28.

[19] The 2008 presidential election was the most expensive so far. According to FEC statistics, Obama spent over $700 million on his 2008 campaign. This figure does not include the expenditures

for each group.[20] For example, candidates may produce separate literature and videos tailored for different demographics, rather than having a blanket message across the whole media.

It is also important to note that reliance on small donations is just one approach that candidates and parties can take. It may become a more common path, given that such a strategy gives the candidate at least the appearance of popularity and greater freedom from special interests. However, candidates and parties can still rely on the larger donors. In a system without a cap on election spending (or a very high cap), the demand for funds provides an incentive for candidates to secure large donations, even where small donations are a substantial source of funds. If a candidate seeks to raise as much money as possible, she will be likely to pursue both large and small donor strategies. The role of wealthy supporters in election funding will continue, even if no longer essential for every campaign.

Politicians in the UK are keen to replicate the Internet strategy seen in the Obama campaign. This strategy could also help combat the public concern that wealthy individuals and institutions fund political parties. However, it is not clear whether this model is easy to transpose into the UK's political culture. Both Dean and Obama appealed to sections of the Democratic Party that were particularly unhappy with the incumbent administration at a time when US politics was highly polarised, providing a set of conditions in which more people were willing to make donations. Attracting small donors may also be easier where there is a particularly charismatic candidate, or one that a section of the public is strongly committed to. These factors could come about in the UK, especially in those elections where an individual is the focus of the campaign, whether the party leader, a constituency candidate, or an individual officeholder such as the Mayor of London. It may be that the political landscape or choices in a UK election have not been sufficient to motivate large numbers to donate, but this could change in the future.

A major difference from the United States is the regulatory environment. Unlike the United States, in the UK there is no limit on donations to political parties, but limits are imposed on election spending. Under that system of regulation, parties may find it easier to go to a small group of wealthy individuals for donations of tens of thousands of pounds, rather than to get thousands of individuals to donate hundreds of pounds. A low cap on donations could provide political parties with a steer towards a small donor strategy, by closing off the wealthy donors as the primary source of funds. Regulating donations could help to shape the way the Internet is used in elections.

---

of other candidates and independent organisations that also had the effect of promoting the Democrat presidential candidate.

[20] Although some data that facilitates market research may be more affordable as a result of the Internet, and there may be greater opportunity to test political messages without resorting to focus groups; see Howard, *New Media Campaigns*, ch. 3.

A final point on the election spending controls is that limits on third-party spending may need revision to take into account some online activities. The previous chapter noted that newspapers and broadcasters are exempt from the limits on third-party campaigns during elections.[21] This raises the question of whether the exemption should be extended to the online media. It is arguable that as some online speakers perform a similar function to newspapers and broadcasters in informing the public, an extension of the exemption is justified. The question cannot be answered by taking a uniform approach to all online speakers, as some larger scale entities do act as the equivalent of the mass media, whereas smaller scale speakers are just like leafleters, or campaigners in the offline world. One option may be to grant the exemption only to those online media entities willing to perform some public service functions associated with the offline media. The point to be made at this stage is that the blurring between the mass media and the individual speaker (and groups of those individuals) found on the Internet will require some revision of the exemption from third-party spending limits.

Political debate in the new media

The Internet and new media have revolutionised the way people organise and communicate. The Internet facilitates a wide range of communicative activities ranging from small audience websites, local discussion forums, and social networking sites. It changes the nature of such communications, with greater use of collaborative projects or conversations through blogs, rather than the traditional mass media top-down, one-to-many model. The interactive nature of the medium allows recipients of content to instantaneously post comments, use that content on their own site and receive real-time updates from various sources. Such communications include a wide variety of formats, such as the written word, audio and visual content. Given the range of activities and the fast pace of change, it is impossible to do justice to the topic in such a short space. However, activities that were once open only to a small number controlling the mass media are now possible for a much wider range of people.

The previous chapter justified the freedom of the mass media in terms of its performance of certain democratic functions, which partly aim to serve the needs of its audience as citizens. By contrast, in so far as the chance to communicate is distributed more evenly, online communications allow greater emphasis on the benefits offered to the speaker. Along these lines, activities such as setting up your own website, blog, or posting a comment may do little for the small audience that receives the content, but publicly articulating one's thoughts can develop the speaker's political skills. People can participate in online activities to exert political pressure, influence the agenda for discussion

---

[21] Representation of the People Act 1983, s.90A; Political Parties, Elections and Referendums Act 2000, s.87.

and persuade others. When groups of bloggers or websites all write about the same topic or advance a similar criticism, linking to one another and commenting on each other's posts, then it can create a buzz which leads to that issue getting more and more attention. The attention gained can be seen as representative of those people acting collectively. In such circumstances, the greater emphasis placed on the speaker's interest in communicating suggests that the audience-focused regulations applied to the mass media, considered in the previous chapter, would be inappropriate.

While this may be true of some forms of expression on the Internet, there are still opportunities for inequalities in wealth and ownership to confer an advantage to certain participants. There will be some online entities that are not just another speaker or participant, but play a more central role in shaping the agenda and deciding what will be heard. So far that role is still played by the established media whose websites are among the most popular in the UK.[22] Like the offline mass media, the value of its activities lies in serving the audience, rather than for the speaker's benefit. Online communications do not, therefore, require the abandonment of all regulatory strategies aiming to promote equality in the opportunities to participate in political debate. Instead, the task is to tailor any regulatory measures to target inequalities while preserving the freedom where opportunities to communicate are more equally distributed. To consider these issues, the next section will examine the role of online gatekeepers and intermediaries and then turn to the mass media.

Gatekeepers and intermediaries

With the Internet comes a new range of gatekeepers and intermediaries with the potential to promote certain voices and discriminate against others. For example, Internet service providers (ISPs), that supply individual users with access to a broadband connection, can exercise some control. By filtering or blocking content, ISPs can stop some content being accessed.[23] ISPs also have the power to charge content producers different amounts in order for their content to be more easily accessible, a prospect that has featured in debates on 'net neutrality'.[24]

---

[22] Ofcom, *New News Future News* (July 2007) at [3.105–3.125]. Statistics from Hitwise show that of the top ten news and media sites in Britain, for the week ending 27 June 2009, eight were the sites of newspapers and broadcasters. The other two were Yahoo News and Google News, both of which use content from external media sources. Two of the BBC's sites were also included in the top ten of all websites for the same week (www.hitwise.co.uk/datacenter/main/dashboard-7323, accessed 14 July 2009).

[23] Such powers of the ISP are sometimes used as a tool of government policy. The major ISPs in Britain will block access to URLs known to contain images of child abuse under the Internet Watch Foundation's self-regulatory system. In 2009, the government proposed to give regulators the power to require ISPs to block URLs and reduce users' bandwidth as possible strategies to combat copyright infringements; see Department for Culture, Media and Sport and Department for Business, Innovation and Skills, *Digital Britain: Final Report*, Cm 7650 (2009) p. 111.

[24] For discussion of net neutrality see T. Wu and C. Yoo, 'Keeping the Internet Neutral? Tim Wu and Christopher Yoo Debate' (2007) 59 Fed. Comm. L.J. 575.

That debate raises a number of complex questions about how to meet the costs of upgrading the broadband infrastructure. For example, one argument is that charging content providers for a privileged and more accessible position would give ISPs a source of revenue to invest in improving the infrastructure so that it can handle the increasing demands on Internet traffic. While the government currently does not see the need for any intervention to prevent differential pricing to fund such changes, the critics argue that such an approach could undermine the equal treatment of speakers on the Internet on the grounds of ability to pay.[25] However, the point here is not to look at that specific issue, but more generally to highlight the potential for intermediaries and gatekeepers to privilege certain voices. Under this view, the growth in the use of the Internet has not led to an egalitarian redistribution of political resources, but, in part at least, transferred the control once exercised by broadcasters to other actors.

Other gatekeepers include search engines, which enable speakers and webpages to be found by Internet users. The position of a webpage in a search engine ranking will often determine the extent to which that page gets seen.[26] There may be other ways to locate content, but the leading search engines are often the primary point of reference.[27] The way a search engine ranks pages is therefore a sensitive issue, and concerns have been expressed that the rankings are biased.[28] The first way such bias can arise is in the algorithm that determines the rankings, which may have effects that privilege certain speakers. Even though the rankings are produced through an automated process, the algorithm that produces those results will reflect the views of its designers as to what factors should determine the importance of a webpage.[29] The second channel for bias is the search-engine owner's deliberate intervention in the automated rankings. Search engines have the power to distort results by either excluding a site from its results or deliberately moving it to a lower ranking. So far, the leading search engines have shown little inclination to exercise this power to advance their own political agenda.[30] Instead, complaints about deliberate intervention have arisen where sites have been blacklisted under the search engine's policy to penalise those who attempt to manipulate their way into a higher ranking.[31] Another reason for deliberate intervention in ranking is where payment is received to promote a particular site.

[25] See Department for Business, Enterprise and Regulatory Reform, *Digital Britain: Interim Report*, Cm 7548 (2009) p. 22.
[26] See E. Laidlaw, 'Private Power, Public Interest: An Examination of Search Engine Accountability' (2009) 17 *International Journal of Law and Information Technology* 113 at 125; O. Bracha and F. Pasquale, 'Federal Search Commission? Access, Fairness, and Accountability in the Law of Search' (2008) 93 Cornell L. Rev. 1149 at 1164–5.
[27] Bracha and Pasquale, 'Federal Search Commission?', at 1179.
[28] See E. Goldman, 'Search Engine Bias and the Demise of Search Engine Utopianism' (2006) 9 Yale J. L. & Tech 188.
[29] *Ibid.*, at 192.
[30] R. Stross, *Planet Google* (London: Atlantic Books, 2008) pp. 75–6. However, for criticism of Google's policy on sponsored links by political speakers, see D. Nunziato, *Virtual Freedom* (Stanford University Press, 2009) pp. 14–17.
[31] See A. Halavais, *Search Engine Society* (Cambridge: Polity, 2009) pp. 133–4.

However, the leading search engines do separate paid and unpaid search results, a practice that avoids misleading users. To date, deliberate interventions are not a pressing problem for UK politics, but concern remains, as there is discretion to intervene, which could be applied in the future.

The extent to which search engines have power is difficult to determine because, unlike the ISPs mentioned above, they are not exercising physical control over Internet access. The search engine merely provides a service at a particular website which users find helpful. Power partly derives from its popularity and its expertise in discriminating among different webpages. If the user does not like the way results are ranked, then she can switch to other search engines.[32] Competition between the search engines may also impose a constraint on the potential for private censorship, as any bad publicity may encourage users to move to alternative sites.

There are, however, a number of limits to these constraints. First, the ability to switch to another search engine does little to empower the censored speaker. The person choosing the search engine is an audience member, who may not know or care what is being missed.[33] Second, if search engine rankings lack sufficient transparency, the user may have little idea about when interventions have been made or on what basis.[34] Without transparency, users may not have the knowledge to assess the performance of the search engine, and determine whether the results show any biases or miss any important sites.[35] Third, the users are more likely to stick with a particular search engine for convenience. They may already have links with that engine, such as an email account, use its blog software or instant messenger service, or have its toolbar in their web browser. The development of personalised search results, which rank results according to the user's previous preferences and habits, may strengthen such loyalty.[36] To receive the benefits of the personalised search, the user will have an incentive to stay with the engine that has the personal information. Finally, the high barriers of entry to the market limit the potential competition, in particular the costs of starting and maintaining a search engine.[37] The largest engines not only have the resources to invest in research and development to stay ahead of competitors, but can also buy up other competing search engines, or related applications that will help attract users. The search engine's power is not solely the product of its popularity or the users' approval of its biases.

Several strategies could be pursued to regulate search engine power.[38] The first is to require greater transparency about the way results are ranked. This need not compromise trade secrets, but requires that search engines do not

---

[32] J. Grimmelman, 'The Structure of Search Engine Law' (2007) 93 Iowa L. Rev. 1 at 50.

[33] Bracha and Pasquale, 'Federal Search Commission?', at 1185–6.

[34] Even where a notice is given to make clear that the search results have been truncated or altered, the user may still have minimal information to assess this. Halavais, *Search Engine Society*, p. 123.

[35] L. Introna and H. Nissenbaum, 'Shaping the Web: Why the Politics of Search Engines Matters' (2000) 16 *The Information Society* 169.

[36] Bracha and Pasquale, 'Federal Search Commission?', at 1182.

[37] Hindman, *The Myth of Digital Democracy*, p. 84.

[38] For discussion of these strategies see Jennifer A. Chandler, 'A Right to Reach an Audience: An Approach to Intermediary Bias on the Internet' (2007) 35 Hofstra L. Rev. 1095, at 1116–17.

exclude pages or manipulate the results except in accordance with clear publicly stated policies, and that they provide a reason to the affected speaker. A second type of control is to establish regulatory oversight to provide some channel of accountability.[39] Such an approach could require search engines to show some reasonable basis for any exclusion, or changes to the rankings and prevent the results being manipulated. Beyond such constraints, a regulator could go further still and attempt to impose a type of public service obligation. For example, separate from the general search rankings could be 'public service rankings' that, during an election, show candidates' websites when particular search terms are used. Alternatively, where a high-ranking article criticises a particular policy or candidate, the search engine could give a link to a competing point of view a prominent position on the site.[40] Finally, the state could attempt to develop its own search engine and use its power of ownership to develop a site that serves democratic values.[41] The difficulty with such an option is that it is unlikely to provide a service of the same quality as the current market leaders, or be as widely used. All of these options raise difficult questions and the point is not to advocate any of these particular reforms, but to sketch some potential options if it is found that search engines have biases that create problems for a fair democratic process.

As with other types of regulation, one objection is that some restrictions infringe the expression rights of the search engine.[42] Search engines do not merely carry other people's expression, but provide their own ranking of websites relating to a particular search term. Some US cases have gone as far as to suggest such lists are constitutionally protected statements of opinion.[43] The question is whether the search engine's expression should prevail over the need for other speakers to reach an audience. For the reasons given above, a small group of search engines tend to dominate the market and the potential to be included in its results is essential if there is a chance to be heard.[44] Like the mass media, the search engine's greater chance to influence political debate should be justified by its democratic function in informing citizens, which may point to the need for some process of accountability and possible check on arbitrary exclusions.

The potential power is not limited to search results, as some sites also aggregate news stories. One example is Google News, which provides news headlines and links to articles. Stories are selected through an automated process based on the algorithm, which aims to ensure some neutrality. Like the search discussed

---

[39] See Bracha and Pasquale, 'Federal Search Commission?'.

[40] For an argument for a more general right of reply, see F. Pasquale, 'Rankings, Reductionism and Responsibility' (2006) 54 Clev. St. L. Rev. 115.

[41] Halavais, *Search Engine Society*, p. 109.

[42] Chandler, 'A Right to Reach an Audience', at 1125–30.

[43] *Search King* v. *Google* [2003] US Dist. LEXIS 27193.

[44] According to statistics from www.hitwise.co.uk, in the four weeks ending 27 June 2009 Google had a 90 per cent share of the British search market (ranked by search volume).

above, this raises questions about possible biases in the automated process. Furthermore, Google first has to decide which news sources to include in the service, which does bring in questions of editorial judgement. Other search engines and news aggregators take a different approach and employ editors to select the top stories. Here, the most popular portals have considerable say in deciding what stories will gain attention. Yet this is not to criticise the presence of some editorial policy either in the choice of sources, or in deciding how to rank the news. Given the rapid pace of the news agenda, human choices may be necessary to ensure that no important stories are overlooked.[45] The concern here is with the way the decisions are made and any potential accountability in relation to those decisions.

Similar issues can also arise in relation to social networking sites, where owners have the discretion to remove and promote content as they wish. Rupert Murdoch's News Corporation, which owns the social networking site MySpace, has the freedom to remove content or block links.[46] However, it is still early days for such sites and they do generally provide an open space for the free exchange of user-generated content. In particular, the use of those sites by dissenters and campaigners in a number of countries has attracted much publicity, such as the protests following the elections in Iran in 2009. Furthermore, the terms and conditions of the service constrain the owner and set out some basis for interventions, although such terms can be open-ended and can be changed by the site.[47] Dangers of a backlash from users may provide some constraint on any heavy-handed interventions,[48] but like the search engine, in some cases there will be little the speaker can do if content is removed or access blocked. If the speaker wants to communicate with a particular audience, or participate in certain online activities, the leading social networking site may be particularly valuable given its

---

[45] Stross, *Planet Google*, pp. 78–80.

[46] So far the evidence of such controls is anecdotal. For example Common Cause reported that MySpace refused to accept an advertisement criticising media concentration; see 'MySpace Refused Our Ad', 10 January 2008, www.commonblog.com/story/2007/1/10/103219/774 (last accessed 1 June 2009).

[47] For example, Facebook sets out some conditions in its 'Rights and Responsibilities': 'You will not post content that is hateful, threatening, pornographic, or that contains nudity or graphic or gratuitous violence' (www.facebook.com/terms.php?ref=pf, last accessed 17 July 2009). Facebook also reserves the right to change the terms of use. While users can vote on some proposed changes, to be binding 30 per cent of all active users have to take part in the vote. The MySpace terms of use provide, 'MySpace reserves the right, in its sole discretion, to reject, refuse to post or remove any posting (including private messages) by you, or to deny, restrict, suspend, or terminate your access to all or any part of the MySpace Services at any time, for any or no reason, with or without prior notice or explanation, and without liability' (www.myspace.com/index.cfm?fuseaction=misc.terms, last accessed 17 July 2009).

[48] For example, criticism from users forced the social networking site Facebook to change the Beacon advertising program, see Stross, *Planet Google*, pp. 35–6. Similarly, in February 2009, Facebook had to reverse a change in its terms of service after negative publicity and protest from its users; see 'Facebook Backtracks after Online Privacy Protest', *Guardian*, 19 February 2009. However, in affecting all users of the network, both examples were more likely to trigger large-scale protest than a rule targeting a dissenting speaker or unpopular viewpoint.

number of users. Consequently, a person does not have the option of switching to another site if the target audience cannot be reached elsewhere. Given that these are early days, it is not clear whether any social network will develop such dominance for a substantial period of time, or whether users will keep moving to other sites. However, the leading social networks could play an increasingly important role as an intermediary in the future, especially as a way of targeting niche audiences and identifiable groups. While there is a need for social networks to develop their own rules and priorities, if those services do become more powerful in shaping political activity, calls may be made for content decisions to be open and accountable, with some rights to appeal, rather than at the discretion of the owner.

The mass media

The Internet and digital communications have had an impact on the mass media in a number of ways. The first is that by reducing the barriers for producing and distributing content, the mass media no longer has such strong control on what views and opinions will be heard by a wide audience. The second is in raising serious questions about the business model supporting the traditional mass media. Newspapers that have a cover price for their print copies now give content away for free online. At the same time, the advertising that supported the traditional mass media has migrated to other outlets online and, as yet, it is not clear whether the advertising on media websites will support existing levels of activity. The third change does not suggest such a radical challenge to the power of the mass media, but merely that the Internet and other online communications can make the mass media more accountable. The next section will consider these various changes and the impact on the influence of wealth, along with some possible regulatory options.

Equal chances to communicate

It may be thought that the Internet now creates a more equal chance for speakers to be heard. If anyone can create a website, post a video on YouTube or set up a blog, there is no reason why a speaker cannot reach a wide audience, as long as the content is appealing. At its most extreme, this type of argument makes a radical claim that people without vast economic resources can speak on an equal footing with the traditional mass media. While even the most idealistic accounts of the Internet tend to resist such a strong claim, it is important to outline the ways that some inequalities will persist.

Some people will continue to speak to a mass audience on a regular basis and therefore have greater ability to shape the political agenda. One reason lies in the nature of political reporting. Internet users generally do not know what story they are looking for in advance and go to the media to find out what has been happening. To lower the cost of locating material the need for an intermediary will remain, and the audience is likely to go to the same sources. Unsurprisingly, in the UK the most popular news sites are run by established media entities, possibly reflecting the previous habits in acquiring information.[49] Furthermore, the sources that cover a wide range of issues with sufficient frequency are likely to be a self-selecting elite compromising, in part, the established mass media. According to some, the variable quality of information online makes the traditional mass media even more important as a place that the audience can trust.[50] This may change and the audience share of some established media entities might decline, while some new media entities may become increasingly popular. The line-up may vary, but the argument is that a number of sites will continue to follow the mass media model.

Even if there is still a need for intermediaries for these reasons, once a citizen acquires this basic level of information about current affairs then he may turn to other online speakers to find out more about a particular issue. However, when an individual wishes to look beyond the usual sites, the methods of locating sources on the Internet may also contribute to a process in which a small number of sources gain greater attention from a wide audience. The vast range of sources available on the Internet means that audience members need to follow some cues in selecting content. One important way for users to find relevant sources is by following links from other websites and sources. However, if such links act as a signpost for Internet users, many point in the same direction. Some studies show that a small number of sites are more widely linked than others, and therefore attract a greater share of audience attention. As a result, according to Matthew Hindman, 'the number of highly visible sites is small by any measure' and 'comparative visibility drops off in a rapid and highly regular fashion once one moves outside the core group of successful sites'.[51]

The role of search engines in directing users to particular sites reinforces the importance of the link. With the example of Google, the search engine's algorithm ranks pages partly based on popularity. The number of links to a page measures its popularity, so the more links pointing to a particular page, the higher the Google ranking. Each link is not equally weighted, and a link from an already well-linked site will count for more in the rankings. A link from a popular website can therefore help a page move up the search results and possibly increase its audience. The formula has been important in Google's success, in helping users select content. However, the danger is that the automated algorithm may produce results that favour an elite group of sources, creating the bias referred to earlier.

When the user of the search engine enters a very specific search term, the distribution of links may have less impact, as the number of results will be low and the term used will determine the webpages listed. However, when a more general term is entered, pages that are already popular and well linked are likely

---

[49] Ofcom, *New News Future News*, at [3.105–3.125].

[50] However, for a contrasting view see W. Dutton, 'The Fifth Estate Emerging through the Network of Networks' (2009) 27 *Prometheus* 1.

[51] Hindman, *The Myth of Digital Democracy*, p. 54.

to be highly ranked and thereby become even more popular and receive more links. The concern is that the process may have a circular effect, in which the already popular are given the exposure that increases the chance of staying popular.[52] If this is correct, it can help to maintain the mass media paradigm in which a small group of speakers have greater influence over political debate. Furthermore, the established mass media, with its high existing level of exposure, is likely to be one of the main beneficiaries of this process.

A similar point can be made in relation to the blogosphere. Blogs tend to gain their audience through links from other blogs or publicity from other media sources. Consequently, once a blog has gained a substantial audience, more people are likely to hear about that site, visit it, and put links to it on their own blogs or websites. Journalists and public officials are more likely to read a well-known blogger and refer to that blog in the mainstream media. Under this process, the already popular speakers become even more popular and more widely linked. The process has led to the emergence of the 'star' blogger that attracts a mass audience on a regular basis. A small number of speakers thereby command a very high proportion of the audience, while the vast majority receive relatively few. A blog may be easy to set up, but only a few will be heard.[53]

Some of the elements of 'media power' discussed in the previous chapter may arise in relation to the small group of elite bloggers. For example, the star blogger can help determine the potential success of other bloggers, by deciding which sites to comment on and link to, thereby bringing that source to a wider audience. Star status may also enable the blogger to cultivate links with politicians, or other sources that assist with newsgathering. The trend should not be overstated; there are no guarantees that those at the top will stay there and new entrants can also gain an audience. Furthermore, whatever influence the star sites have, it is not a power to control the flow of information and exclude certain views.[54] Instead, there will be alternative channels for information to emerge. However, even with this caveat, the elite bloggers can be seen as a new form of mass media, and provide a reference point where people can find out what has been going on in national politics.[55]

That a small number of speakers command a much wider audience is not a surprise, nor is it a bad thing in itself. As the previous chapter outlined, the mass media provides a number of important functions in a democracy and a system in which everyone gains exactly the same level of attention is undesirable. It is important to have places that ensure people are well informed, hear a different range of views and where people focus on a common agenda. Gatekeepers and intermediaries that help to filter the information are an important part of that democratic function. The concern is how that status is achieved and maintained.

---

[52] Ibid., pp. 55–6; Halavais, *Search Engine Society*, p. 64.
[53] See C. Shirky, 'Power Laws, Weblogs, and Inequality' http://www.shirky.com/writings/powerlaw_weblog.html (first published 8 February 2003; last accessed 11 June 2009).
[54] Y. Benkler, *The Wealth of Networks* (New Haven: Yale University Press, 2006) p. 254.
[55] D. Drezner and H. Farrell, 'The Power and Politics of Blogs' (2008) 134 *Public Choice* 15, at 22.

One response to the concerns about inequality in the chances to reach people is that some online media speakers owe their status to a gradual process of audience building. Under this view, the process is consistent with democratic values as links and comments from other sites reflect a collective decision to draw attention to that speaker. Furthermore, the bloggers and the new media do not simply impose content in a top-down manner. Sometimes the blogosphere is referred to as an 'ecosystem' in which bloggers form communities around particular issues, topics or viewpoints, commenting on one another's articles and linking to each other's sites.[56] These conversations can collectively highlight the importance of that issue or topic. Within those communities, there will be speakers with a wider range of connections that act as an informal spokesman for that community, passing on some of its views and priorities to a broader audience.[57] Under this view, stories get into the best-known blogs through a gradual process of upward filtering through the network.[58] Consequently, those emphasising the 'ecosystem' of the blogosphere argue that it is a mistake to look at the star blogger as an isolated unit speaking to a mass audience, rather than the most visible point in a broader association.

This is an idealised account that should be treated with some scepticism, just like claims that a newspaper represents its readers. The network or community that helps to confer star-blogger status may be a fraction of the audience for that content. In any event, it is not clear that decisions to link really are endorsements by users or simply a result of the site being well known. While she may advance the concerns and views expressed by others within a particular network, the star blogger still retains considerable discretion over which issues to give prominence to, which slant to emphasise and which sites to link to. Furthermore, such a model of accountability will work most effectively in smaller online networks. Once the network becomes larger, the star blogger or website will not be as familiar with all the priorities and concerns of that community.[59]

Finally, the 'ecosystem' is not the only way that speakers can gain higher status in the online media. For example, the process may reward the early adopters who establish a web presence first and are in the best place to attract visitors as audiences grow. A speaker may also attract a wide number of links quickly because of their celebrity status, or ties with existing media entities or political parties. In the UK, *Comment is Free* is a blog set up by the *Guardian* newspaper and relies on posts by a number of established journalists as well as other well-known writers. Other examples include the *Huffington Post* and *Daily Beast*, which enlist a number of well-known individuals to contribute to the blog. Celebrity is just one resource. Rather than working through the

---

[56] See Benkler, *The Wealth of Networks*, pp. 172–5 and pp. 253–5; Drezner and Farrell, 'The Power and Politics of Blogs', at 22.

[57] See Shirky, *Here Comes Everybody*, pp. 211–25.

[58] For criticism of such an account see Hindman, *The Myth of Digital Democracy*.

[59] Shirky, *Here Comes Everybody*, pp. 89–93.

'ecosystem', speakers may achieve star status through money, namely in paying for the content, staff and publicity necessary to run a wide audience site. While sites such as the *Huffington Post* are low cost by the standards of the traditional media, it still has to pay a staff of 50–60. As attempts to buy into the system may result in a hostile reception, most sites will seek to play this down and take on an appearance associated with the ecosystem. While there are some online speakers who have emerged from and remain accountable to a grassroots system, there will be others that have not and more closely resemble the mass media.

Aside from the ecosystem argument, another counter-argument to the analogy with the mass media is that it exaggerates the inequalities and over-emphasises the 'mass' online speaker. That counter-argument contends that while a small number of speakers may enjoy much greater levels of attention, the activities of the sites with a smaller audience are still significant.[60] The smaller communities can provide a greater level of easily accessible niche content, which may previously have gone unheard.[61] As Professor Yochai Benkler explains: 'There is a big difference between a situation where no one is looking at any of the sites on the low end of distribution, because everyone is looking only at the superstars, and a situation where dozens or hundreds of sites at the low end are looking at each other as well as the superstars.'[62]

The extent to which niche content and smaller sites really are gaining more attention is still being debated.[63] The matter certainly requires further study in relation to UK politics, with some previous studies suggesting that the vast majority of political blogs were 'virtually ignored'.[64] However, if there is significant activity among the smaller scale sites, it at least provides a chance to influence, and gets individuals actively involved in politics. Benkler also argues that many of the smaller sites are not so remote from the broader audience and can be accessed fairly easily through a number of links.[65] The conclusion Benkler draws from this is that whatever the shortcomings compared to a democratic ideal, from the perspective of a democratic system it is an improvement on the traditional mass media.

However, even if these developments do make content more easily accessible, they do not alleviate the concern with inequality expressed here. While there may be greater chances for individuals to communicate, the elites at the very top of the online media may become more powerful than some of the traditional mass media in the offline world. Larger media entities such as the BBC, Fox or the *New York Times* can now reach a wider audience and are not subject to the limits imposed by the old methods of distribution. The changes may benefit those at the very top and bottom of audience share, but squeeze those media entities that had

[60] Drezner and Farrell, 'The Power and Politics of Blogs'.
[61] See C. Anderson, *The Long Tail* (London: Random House, 2006).
[62] Benkler, *The Wealth of Networks*, p. 251.
[63] Compare Hindman, *The Myth of Digital Democracy*, p. 45.
[64] S. Coleman and S. Ward (eds.), *Spinning the Web* (London: Hansard Society, 2005) p. 7.
[65] Benkler, *The Wealth of Networks*, p. 252.

occupied the middle ground.[66] This much is speculative, but further consideration is required to assess the various democratic effects of the new media.

The central point in this section is that some speakers and entities will command a regular mass audience. While that status can be achieved in a number of ways, the next section will argue that economic resources are a significant factor. While Benkler argues that money is not 'necessary or sufficient' to command attention online,[67] money alone has never guaranteed the success of a media entity. A newspaper cannot command attention without providing content with some appeal. However, money will still provide considerable advantages in political communications, and whatever the democratic benefits, the concerns expressed in the earlier chapters remain present.

Financing the online media

One reason why economic resources will remain a significant factor is the need to gain enough attention to attract the initial audience. This may require large expenditures on publicity and advertising to ensure the site is known. Even when the site has gained a sufficient level of publicity, there are the costs of producing content that can attract and maintain a wide audience. If a site covering news and politics is to be influential, it will need well-presented and up-to-date coverage. Following the model of the traditional mass media, the online media can produce the content itself by employing staff, or purchase it from another source. While the distribution and some production costs may be lower, other costs such as staff and running an office will remain beyond the reach of most. Furthermore, while the technology makes it easier to put together a webpage, or edit a video, to stand out the speaker requires greater investment in presentation and visuals.[68] Also the expectations of the audience may rise, requiring that news coverage be updated as it happens, increasing the costs associated with hiring reporters and other production staff.

With the traditional mass media, it was easier to point to the instances where ownership of the channels of distribution or means of production gave the speaker an advantage. The difficulty found now is that the way economic resources generate potential influence is fused with the appeal of the content and harder to identify. However, the concern is that to become a regular and comprehensive news outlet, the sort that will be most people's primary reference point rather than a lone commentator, may be more expensive than ever. This explains why many of the well-known blogs and websites provide opinion and comment on news reported in the mass media, rather than original reports or investigations. It also reflects the criticism that bloggers are 'parasites' dependent upon the mass media. Under this view, although there may

---

[66] See Hindman, *The Myth of Digital Democracy*, p. 100.
[67] Benkler, *The Wealth of Networks*, p. 254.
[68] E. Noam, 'Will the Internet Be Bad for Democracy?', November 2001, Camden, Maine (www.citi.columbia.edu/elinoam/articles/int_bad_dem.htm, last accessed 3 June 2009); N. Netanel, 'Cyberspace Self-Governance', at 463.

be many new voices, those voices tend to comment on and discuss the content provided by the traditional mass media. This may be true of many speakers on the Internet, but the criticism is unfair in so far as some sites do provide original stories. In some cases, the stories may come from the speaker's personal experience, or area of expertise. However, such sites will often focus on a specific area. If a site wishes to carry regular reports covering as many areas of political life as possible, it will require considerable resources, whether in terms of money or volunteers.

While the costs associated with a mass audience point to the continued dominance of the mass media model, they also pose a challenge to existing media entities. At the time of writing, the sources of funding available to support the mass media appear to be limited. The media also gives most of its content away for free online, with only some newspaper sites still charging a subscription fee. Whether this will continue remains to be seen, with some speculation that a subscription model may return to online newspapers.[69] However, this option may be unattractive, especially in the UK where media entities will be competing with the state-funded BBC, which will continue to make content accessible online for free. If subscriptions are not a major source of funding, the media may rely more heavily on advertising. The difficulty here is that the revenues attracted by the online media are reported to be a fraction of the costs of running a media entity. This may change in the future, especially as the Internet takes on a more central role as a place where people get their news and political coverage. However, for the moment it poses a considerable challenge to the media industry.

If the traditional sources of funding are not sufficient, then one alternative is for a wealthy patron or company to subsidise the online media. This could arise where the owner is willing to pay for some losses, and wants to keep the online media entity going for reasons of prestige, or to promote other interests. However, reliance on a set of 'new media barons' is hardly appealing from the perspective of political equality.

The prognosis need not be so pessimistic. The financial crisis that broke out in 2008 could provide an opportunity to address the various concerns with traditional sources of media finance and move to a different model of media funding. At the most basic level, people could make voluntary donations to support the media entity. A variation is for members of the audience to pledge sums of money in advance for the media to research or investigate a particular story.[70] This source of funding would then allow people to use purchasing power to set the media's agenda. One difficulty of a voluntary donation approach is that it is not clear whether individuals will make such payments, or whether they would be more likely to act as free-riders if the final product were to be given away.

[69] Rupert Murdoch has been reported to suggest that charging for newspaper content will be a more common business model, *The Times*, 7 May 2009.
[70] C. Beckett, *SuperMedia* (Oxford: Blackwell, 2008) p. 76; D. Gillmor, *We the Media* (Sebastopol: O'Reilly, 2004) pp. 156–7.

The extent to which such a model is truly egalitarian would depend on the level of payment necessary to support the entity. Like donations to political parties, if bankrolled by large donations from wealthy individuals, then there is the danger that those individuals will influence its content.

An alternative is to adopt a 'micro-payments' model, in which the individual reader does not pay a subscription, but a very small sum to access an article. This approach faces the difficulty in getting a critical mass of media entities to sign up for such a scheme. If enough media entities adopt that system, users would come to expect such charges and use the same payment system across a number of sites. Like the donations model, it is not clear whether micro-payments could provide the media with a stable source of income for the production of quality journalism on a regular basis.

An alternative model is for the state to provide subsidies to support a diverse media. For example, content produced by the BBC, which is funded by the licence fee and governed by impartiality obligations, is disseminated over the Internet. However, subsidies could also extend beyond the BBC. This could be in the form of a new entity to provide support to independent speakers and commission diverse content, especially from those traditionally excluded from the mainstream media. Along these lines, Blumler and Coleman call for a publicly funded agency to establish a 'civic commons' to mediate between different speakers and coordinate various online initiatives, ensuring that different views reach an audience and connect citizen activities with government.[71] Establishing such an agency seems unlikely after Ofcom abandoned plans for a new 'public service publisher'. Other plans include a proposal for a state-funded consortia of newspapers and broadcasters to provide local news on television and through the Internet, subject to impartiality requirements.[72]

The subsidies need not come from general tax revenues. One approach would be to impose a levy on broadband providers, so that subscribers to their services contribute to a fund to support a sufficiently diverse range of online newspapers.[73] The subsidy need not come in the form of cash, but could be in the provision of access to facilities to make quality media content. For example, in 2009 the BBC began sharing some content with national newspapers, possibly opening up opportunities for other resource-sharing arrangements.[74] There is considerable appeal in these proposals, which could help foster a well-resourced online media with a range of differing funding bases along the lines discussed in the previous chapter.

---

[71] See Blumler and Coleman, *The Internet and Democratic Citizenship*, ch. 7.

[72] Department for Culture, Media and Sport and Department for Business, Innovation and Skills, *Digital Britain: Final Report*, Cm 7650 (2009) at [78].

[73] Although Ofcom found that the case for such an approach was not being made; see Ofcom Second Review of Public Service Broadcasting Review, *Putting Viewers First* (2009), at [5.52–5.58].

[74] Although the arrangement drew criticism from those providers that sell content to newspapers, *The Times*, 29 July 2009.

A voluntary alternative

A separate approach is to reduce the role of money in the production of media content and move to a voluntary model, which relies on people providing content and their expertise for free. Volunteers collaborating on a joint website could produce high-quality content on a regular basis from around the world. If there is a wide enough pool of volunteers, then it can potentially tap into resources that would stretch a traditional media entity. This follows the model of collaboration found in Wikipedia, in which collective expertise provides a new method of production.[75]

Such an approach could support investigative journalism, traditionally seen as requiring a high level of investment. A simple example is where MPs' expenses or donations to a political party are published online. A group of volunteers could divide up the data and its analysis among themselves, with each citizen agreeing to monitor the expenses of a particular MP, or donations to a particular branch of the party, and then pooling any findings. In other situations, volunteers can collaborate in the analysis of information. For example, where a Freedom of Information Act request provides an internal policy document, a group could post that document online with space for each member to offer comments, with each group member then checking and verifying the conclusions of others. A level of collective expertise can emerge through this process. This turns traditional journalism around, as the investigation and its refinement take place openly in public view.[76] It also suggests that even for a news site there are alternatives to the high-cost model of investigation.

It is not yet clear how far voluntary production can work as an alternative to the traditional mass media. It depends on whether there are enough volunteers to provide reports on a regular basis. It may also raise questions about inequalities in time, where those who can afford to put the time aside have greater chance to participate. To make journalism an unpaid profession would hardly be to make it egalitarian and could favour those who do not require an alternative source of funds. This could also raise concerns that the activities of some 'volunteers' are really being subsidised by an outside interest.

The voluntary model may be more suitable for certain types of content. It may be appropriate for Wikipedia, where the project is not usually time-sensitive and tasks can be more easily divided up among different users.[77] Such collaboration is also most likely to be successful where primary materials are available online, where the issues are relatively defined and where individuals have already taken a position, or have a stake that motivates them. By contrast, the traditional media may be better placed to research other stories, having an advantage when newsgathering through an established range of contacts and sources. There are also broader issues about the voluntary media, as it may lack training in professional ethics and skills in questioning sources.[78] To deal with

---

[75] Benkler, *The Wealth of Networks*, pp. 261–6.   [76] *Ibid.*, pp. 225–33.
[77] *Ibid.*, p. 101.   [78] Gillmor, *We the Media*, ch. 9.

some of these issues, Wikipedia, for example, has an extensive set of rules for contributors, which requires internal policing and has an arbitration committee to resolve disputes. There is also the question of how the voluntary media should deal with legal issues including defamation and privacy. Given these reservations, it seems that even if collaborative volunteer media does become more successful, it will complement rather than replace the traditional mass media.

An accountable media

A mid-way approach between the extremes of citizen media and the traditional mass media is for the latter to draw from the former. In other words, by utilising the contributions of volunteers in their reporting, the professional mass media can help facilitate citizen journalism. A connection between the voluntary and small-scale online speaker and the traditional mass media points to a possible channel of media accountability. The blogs and smaller websites provide stories that can feed into those media entities with a mass audience. Journalists are frequent readers of blogs and online media, using them as sources for stories. Many of the celebrated instances where blogs and other digital media have made a difference in politics arose once the professional mass media took up the story.[79] Furthermore, by commenting on and criticising stories that appear in the mass media, the smaller sites can help hold the media to account and help to check any abuses of media power. Journalists can encourage this by running their own blogs to test ideas and receive comments before publishing in the mass media. Such practices do not suggest an idealised ecosystem, but at least provide a channel of communication between the media and its audience.

There are other uses of the technology that can make the mass media more accountable. One example is for newspapers to allow users to have some say in selecting the stories to be given a prominent place on the site. People would not contribute content, but could vote for articles, as is found with Slashdot and aggregators such as Digg. Even if media websites do not want to relinquish control, newspapers could create an alternative homepage reflecting users' choices.[80] This is not to advocate this specific measure, but to highlight the various ways that the media can attempt to engage with the audience. Such experiments could run risks. An open format of audience-selected content could be subject to manipulation from interested parties.[81] Like the ecosystem of blogs, such a channel of accountability is likely to work in the case of niche sites with a relatively small community of users. Furthermore, as the previous chapter outlined, responsiveness is only one element of a democratic media, so practices such as voting may have less value. While there may be limits as to what can be gained from such practices, there are at least opportunities to experiment in ways that could lead to greater accountability.

---

[79] For discussion of this point in relation to the US blogs, see J. Rowbottom, 'Media Freedom and Political Debate in the Digital Era' (2006) 69 *Modern Law Review* 489 at 506–7. In Britain, the treatment of Ian Tomlinson by the police at the scene of a protest in London in May 2009 was filmed by a bystander, but was brought to public attention after it appeared on the *Guardian*'s website.

[80] D. Tapscott and A. Williams, *Wikinomics* (London: Atlantic, 2008) pp. 145–7.

[81] L. Strahilevit 'Wealth Without Markets?' (2007) 116 Yale L.J. 1472, at 1496.

Advertising and public relations online

The potential for inequalities in wealth to shape political debate online also arises when people pay to be seen on a well-visited site. So far, the costs of UK political campaigns have been kept down by the ban on political advertising in the broadcast media. However, if the Internet becomes a more important way to reach audiences, then the costs of political campaigning which, so far, have been avoided could arise through spending on Internet advertising. While generally cheaper than its broadcast equivalent, as the section on party funding noted, online advertising can bring new costs. For example when targeting audiences, there is potential for a wealthy advertiser to buy up spaces for all the various niche audiences and reach a mass audience in total, in a way that would not be open to those with less money. While the spending limits discussed in Chapter 5 will control the expenditures in an election, political advertising on the mass online media may call for some further controls.

The use of wealth to gain access to the media goes beyond traditional advertising. For example, those with sufficient resources may hire a public relations firm, or adopt in-house strategies, to get their content promoted in others' websites. This may include astroturfing techniques, or approaching certain websites with press releases or other content to include on their blog or webpage. Given that there will be pressures on the blogger or site to keep introducing new content and update posts, there is a danger that the online speaker will be open to manipulation by public relations campaigns. Such vulnerability may be greater where the website operator does not have the professional training or experience of a journalist, or lacks the resources to make checks and scrutinise such releases. Alternatively, the public relations firm may pay the website or blogger not for an advertisement, but to publish sympathetic content in the site author's own name. This method is high risk, as if found out the blogger may lose credibility and the trust of the audience. However, this tactic is not unheard of and blurs editorial and advertising content, the separation of which has generally been a feature of journalistic ethics.[82]

There are piecemeal rules that help to prevent such misleading advertising strategies. For example, it is an offence to make a payment to an elector for the exhibition of 'any address, bill or notice' promoting a candidate in an election, unless that payment is made to an advertising agent in the course of business.[83] The purpose of this provision is to stop individuals being paid to put election posters up in gardens and windows, but it could be interpreted to include payments to websites to display election messages that are not overt advertisements. This offence is limited only to election communications and will not affect other political campaigns. Non-electoral advertising is governed by a self-regulatory body, the

---

[82] While normally associated with commercial product placement, some political bloggers in the United States have been accused of accepting payments from political campaigns without disclosing the payments to the readers. For discussion, see D. Perlmutter, *Blog Wars* (Oxford University Press, 2008) pp. 151–2.

[83] Representation of the People Act 1983, s.109.

Advertising Standards Authority (ASA), whose code of conduct requires a separation between advertising and editorials, or at least for paid editorial content to be clearly labelled.[84] There are limits to the self-regulation, as it only applies to members of the ASA, who have agreed to be subject to the code.[85] In addition to the self-regulatory code, there are a number of legal provisions that limit astroturfing in commercial advertising. For example, communications in which a trader falsely represents himself to be a consumer are a prohibited 'unfair commercial practice', which potentially stops a business giving itself favourable reviews on a consumer website while posing as a happy customer.[86] The prohibition applies to commercial communications relating to a product, and will not normally cover political communications (unless it has a commercial dimension such as selling merchandise). However, the piecemeal laws and regulations show that it is possible to devise strategies to address astroturfing in some contexts, and that such communications are not to be accepted as an inevitable feature of the Internet.

Beyond advertising, there is little transparency about the major sources of funding of some high-profile websites and blogs in the UK. It may be unknown when a wealthy patron is sponsoring the online speaker, either to meet the costs of running the site, or to allow the speaker to spend more time producing content. One possible area for transparency is in electoral material. At present, printed election material that promotes a candidate or party must include the name and address of its printer, promoter or person on whose behalf the material is being published.[87] One area of debate is whether this requirement should be extended to online election material, such as websites.[88] The extension of this rule has yet to be enacted[89] and raises difficult questions about what type of online message it could apply to. Such details may be appropriate for some websites, but would be harder to impose on more informal or shorter communications such as Twitter messages. There are also other transparency requirements that affect political communications; for example direct marketing by a political party via email should include the identity and an address of the sender.[90] However, online speakers are under no general obligation to

---

[84] Advertising Standards Authority, *British Code of Advertising, Sales Promotion and Direct Marketing*, cl.23. The Code does not cover advertisements aiming to influence voters in an election.

[85] Furthermore, in some cases it will be difficult to identify when content constitutes an advertisement subject to the code or where it is editorial. See *R* v. *Advertising Standards Authority Limited, ex parte Charles. Robertson (Developments)* [2000] EMLR 463. In deciding what constitutes an advertisement, the ASA will consider whether the advertiser or editor had control over the final content.

[86] Consumer Protection from Unfair Trading Regulations 2008, Schedule 1.

[87] Representation of the People Act 1983, s.110; Political Parties Elections and Referendums Act 2000 (PPERA) s.143.

[88] Electoral Commission, *Vote for Change* (2003), recommending the imprint requirements 'be applied to online communications, web, email, SMS, digital TV'.

[89] PPERA s.143(6) provides a power to extend the rules.

[90] Privacy and Electronic Communications (EC Directive) Regulations 2003, reg. 23. Communications by political parties made by phone and email have been found to be 'direct

disclose their identity, permitting some level of anonymity that is viewed by some as a key feature of the Internet.[91] The difficulty with a stricter regulatory regime, such as a general blanket requirement of disclosure, is in making online expression more burdensome for individuals and discouraging participation. An alternative may be a self-regulatory system in which online media speakers or campaigns can register and disclose major sources of funding. While such an approach would not be comprehensive, it might at least give the audience a point of reference when assessing an online campaign. After viewing a political communication, the viewers of the message would be able to find out further information about who is behind the message or have a greater sense of whether the source can be trusted.

Possible solutions

The previous sections argued that, while the Internet may bring about many improvements for political equality, the inequalities associated with the mass media are likely to remain. It is likely that some media entities will continue to command a mass audience and thereby have greater chances to influence political debate. While there may be alternatives to the commercial model and there are ways to make the mass media more accountable, it remains to be seen if these developments will provide a counterweight to the voices of the well-funded. As a result of the various trends discussed so far it remains likely that economic inequalities will impact on who gets heard and influence the content disseminated in the online media. The difficult question is whether anything can be done to address these inequalities. One solution is for the laws that apply offline to curb political spending to be applied online. For example, at present, where a third party incurs expenditures on a website for a party, or candidate in an election, it falls under the election spending limits. As discussed, whether online communications should be subject to those restrictions or exempted, like other media entities, is open to debate.

Outside the context of elections there are a number of other measures that could address the inequalities, such as the subsidies and transparency requirements discussed in earlier chapters. In addition to such measures, those online media outlets that perform public service functions can continue to be subject to rules in relation to political reporting, such as the impartiality rules, access

marketing' under the regulations, see *Scottish National Party* v. *Information Commissioner* (2006), Information Tribunal, Appeal Number: EA/2005/0021.

[91] For a criticism of online anonymity see Gillmor, *We the Media*, p. 180. Online speakers do not enjoy complete anonymity; court orders have been used to discover the identity of the speaker when defamatory or unlawful content has been anonymously published on the Internet. See *Totalise* v. *Motley Fool* [2001] All ER (D) 213 (Feb); *Sheffield Wednesday Football Club* v. *Hargreaves* [2007] EWHC 2375. The Queen's Bench Division rejected a claim for misuse of private information brought by a blogger seeking to restrain a newspaper from publishing his identity. The court found that there was no reasonable expectation of privacy in relation to a blogger's identity, see *The Author of a Blog* v. *Times Newspapers Ltd* [2009] EWHC 1358.

rights or duties to carry diverse content that were discussed in Chapter 7. However, public service goals are arguably served without the need for any intervention. On the Internet a more diverse range of sources and new channels for original reporting can be found. People can access a range of political sources at little cost, and have greater opportunity to explore the different perspectives. Furthermore, sites with differing political stances often link to one another and encourage visitors to go to the different sites. Under this view the network as a whole could be thought of as providing a form of public service, and the diversity of sources may be seen to undermine the rationale for the existing model of public service regulation.

The problem with the view of the Internet as a whole providing a public service is that it does not serve all the democratic functions of the media.[92] One difficulty is that the increase in choice allows people to rely on sources that reflect existing views and avoid opposing opinions.[93] The fact that people can choose partisan content is unproblematic and, as Chapter 7 highlighted, there is a need for people to have access to a polarised media sector. Concern arises when such sources account for most of an individual's media experience. One study has suggested that there is some evidence for this fear, showing a tendency for political sites in the United States to link more heavily to sources with a similar perspective.[94] While this does not exclude opposing viewpoints, the network promotes those sites with a similar political stance. However, such selectiveness is not the main concern here and further study of the networks will be required to see if similar patterns emerge in the UK before any conclusions can be drawn.

A second concern is that the network of political sites may provide new sources for 'news junkies' who are willing to explore the various sites, but does less for those who choose to avoid politics altogether.[95] These are the people who have traditionally received political information from public service broadcast media and who may be harder to reach given some audience fragmentation. Again, this is not the primary concern here, but it suggests that some form of public service obligations would help communicate with those audiences. Third, even if the network did function in the ideal way, with sites linking to opposing views, the audience arguably still needs a mediator to help navigate the sources and provide some basis for evaluation.[96] The central argument

[92] See Chapter 7.
[93] C. Sunstein, *Republic.com 2.0* (Princeton University Press, 2007). A study of the role of the Internet in the 2008 Presidential Election found that as people visited a wider range of sources, greater reliance was placed on partisan sites which reflect the visitors' existing view; see A. Smith, *The Internet's Role in Campaign 2008* (Washington: Pew Internet and American Life Project, 2009) p. 66.
[94] L. Adamic and N. Glance, *The Political Blogosphere and the 2004 U.S. Election*, Proceedings of the 3rd International Workshop on Link Discovery (2005) (www.blogpulse.com/papers/2005/AdamicGlanceBlogWWW.pdf, last accessed 16 June 2009); Sunstein, *Republic.com 2.0*, p. 149.
[95] M. Prior, *Post-Broadcast Democracy* (Cambridge University Press, 2007).
[96] Blumler and Coleman, *The Internet and Democratic Citizenship*, pp. 179–81.

made earlier was that such sites are likely to emerge in any event and command greater audience attention. These sites will perform the functions traditionally carried out by newspapers and broadcasters, acting as a primary point of reference, rather than just one source in the overall network. The danger is that such sites will have the power, but lack the responsibilities associated with the public service media. It is in relation to these sites that the public service obligations will be most relevant.

The question is how public service requirements in relation to news and political reporting can be promoted online, and who should be subject to its obligations. One approach is for those currently subject to public service obligations offline, such as the BBC and other broadcasters, to be subject to the same regulations online. This provides a short-term answer. As there is greater convergence in the media, some organisations playing a similar role to the broadcast media will exist online only. If the Internet becomes the dominant mode and the equivalents of broadcasters exist in the online world only, the current regulations will not apply. An alternative method is to target certain formats, such as audiovisual content. This approach has been taken in the European Union through the extension of some limited broadcast regulations to scheduled and on-demand commercial audiovisual services.[97] While this approach may be appropriate for some regulations, such as the protection of minors, it does not identify the public service media. If the concern is that media power reflects inequalities in wealth and is based on ownership of the resource, there is little reason to isolate audiovisual content.

The obvious alternative is to regulate only the state-funded or subsidised media. However, this will not redress the inequalities reflected in the privately owned media, where some media entities may perform the functions equivalent to the traditional broadcasters. There are, however, difficulties in identifying such online media entities. While the dominance and market share of the entity can provide some indication, it is important not to punish sites merely for being successful. Given the rapidly changing nature of the Internet, the point here is not to prescribe any particular solutions. The changes in the digital media make identifying the targets for regulation harder, but to respond by abandoning all the regulations that govern the UK's political coverage would undo the conditions that have helped to define the political culture. None of this is clear-cut and the lines drawn may be arbitrary, but the hurdles are not insurmountable and an absence of media regulation is not inevitable.

An argument advanced against the regulation of online content, is that even if all the above were desirable, enforcement would be difficult, particularly as online media is global and consequently some content comes from other jurisdictions. Consequently, self-regulatory models that promote public service may be more fitting with the tradition of the Internet. Furthermore, the capacity to impose such controls might also be subject to some EU law restrictions, such as

---

[97] Audiovisual Media Services Directive 2007.

state aid rules that can restrict subsidies to the media. However, given that the mass media entities targeting a UK audience will tend to have offices, staff and assets in the UK, enforcement against those bodies is more realistic. While the global nature of the Internet poses regulatory challenges, this has not stopped other regulations, such as those relating to commercial activity, copyright law, public order or pornography, being imposed on Internet content.

Conclusion

This chapter has sketched an argument suggesting that the uses of wealth to influence democratic politics are likely to remain. The changes in online communications do not point towards deregulation of controls on money in politics. Instead, controls on the use of wealth may encourage more egalitarian uses of the Internet and digital media, for example with a limit on donations to political parties providing greater incentive for online fundraising. It is also important to look for new threats to political equality, such as the power of online intermediaries. Even if the control of such an intermediary has been unproblematic so far, it is a power that could be used in future.

The most important change considered in this chapter is the way people can now communicate. Chances to communicate and be heard are spread more widely, not as a result of legislation or direct state subsidies, but through changes that make the channels of communication more accessible. Yet on closer examination, the extent of the changes in the distribution of political resources and the major beneficiaries of these developments are unclear. A central point in this chapter is that the chance to communicate and be heard is still characterised by inequalities and that economic resources still have an impact in determining who will be heard and who will shape the political agenda.

Consequently, expression on the Internet cannot be viewed as a single category. The types of speaker in the online world are as varied as those found offline. In most cases the websites are participants in the democratic process whose expression should be protected and where possible facilitated. However, those sites gaining the very highest levels of attention and deciding which views will be heard are more like the mass media and, in some cases, act as a forum for other speakers as well as providing a point of reference. The argument in this chapter is that such potential to influence should not arise purely from the ownership of, or the economic resources needed to run, such an entity.

There are difficulties with this approach. Limiting the inequalities through state regulation is at odds with the non-state forms of governance associated with the Internet. While a number of legal provisions have substantially eroded that freedom, one hope may be for the concern outlined above to be self-correcting. This view suggests that the freedom to organise online will provide a natural counterweight to any power attained through economic resources. Such an argument appeals to the pluralist democratic theory discussed in Chapter 1, in which no one political resource was thought to give any group control over the political process. Chapter 1 outlined the reasons for rejecting such a view, and the danger of relying on those pluralist arguments in legitimising the advantages gained through wealth. There is much to be said for caution in any state intervention, but for the state to keep out completely may allow the inequalities discussed above to become stronger, entrenched and harder to remedy once apparent.

Finally, there is no clear-cut way of identifying the most powerful sites and redressing any inequalities, and some types of regulation may deter the participation of other speakers. This presents one of the biggest challenges to promoting equality online. With low voter turnout and declining membership of political parties, new forms of political activism need to be encouraged rather than burdened. However, a continued commitment to public service goals in the online mass media and the protection of grassroots activity are not in tension. Requiring some responsibility and accountability from those at the very top of the hierarchy and constraining the power of its owners or advertisers may help those at the grassroots level to be heard.

9

Conclusion

Political equality is a central principle in a democracy. It is a principle that runs through the different stages of the political process. Yet it is compromised when opportunities to influence political decisions are secured through a person's wealth. The unequal distribution of wealth in the economic sphere stands in contrast to the democratic ideal that people have the same opportunities to participate and influence decisions. As the previous chapters have shown, the potential for inequalities in wealth to enter the political sphere arises at various points. These points include the funding of political parties, the channels for influencing MPs and ministers, and in the opportunities to communicate with the public.

The impact of the inequalities in wealth in politics has not gone unchecked and is subject to a number of legal restraints. Controls on election spending have been in place since 1883, and laws of corruption and the various codes of conduct have prevented influence being bought. Furthermore, large sums of money are not essential for many forms of participation. Yet the tension between political equality and inequalities in wealth remains. That tension is also heightened, not as a result of any conspiracy or deliberate design, but as a result of the separate trends discussed in earlier chapters. Chapter 4 discussed the growth of professional lobbying techniques, which offer more capital-intensive methods to influence MPs, ministers and civil servants, and potentially increase the costs associated with certain political activities. The effort to prevent inequalities in wealth entering electoral politics was considered in Chapter 5. While much has been done in recent years to update the party funding laws, that chapter noted the continuing inequalities in political donations and the very large contributions made by some wealthy individuals.

Public spaces are generally seen to offer a place for people to engage in political activities without involving substantial economic resources. Allowing access to such spaces provides a political resource that is more equally distributed. Yet this is coming under pressure not only from the various legal restrictions on the right to assemble, but also from the private management and ownership of those places. The other major forum that has been discussed here, the mass media, has long posed a challenge to political equality. However, some of the controls that have helped keep the media in check and promoted its democratic functions are also coming into question. For example, recent years have witnessed a liberalisation of the media ownership laws, and the future of the public service media in the digital era is the subject of debate. Even with the Internet, long seen to promote the equal opportunities to participate in politics, the picture is mixed. Alongside the new voices disseminating their views, some intermediaries and media organisations continue to play a powerful political role.

In looking at each of these areas, various strategies to separate economic inequalities from the political sphere have been discussed. As Chapter 1 noted, these strategies are primarily focused on direct attempts to participate in formal politics. This discussion did not try to deal with the privileged position of business in government, or the problem of broader background inequalities, such as the different opportunities in education. Yet even this narrower type of inequality is difficult to address. One recurring problem is that of loopholes, in which those with sufficient resources look for other ways to spend their money, or use their property to evade any restrictions. In other cases, the strategies may not be easily evaded, but still leave plenty of scope for the use of wealth in politics. For example, while some controls have been imposed on media ownership, its owners still have considerable opportunities to influence political decisions. Similarly, caps on political donations or spending mitigate inequalities, but those with greater economic resources can still spend and contribute more within the limits set.

Identifying the way that inequalities affect opportunities to influence is easier in some contexts, but a greater challenge in others. Where a person gives money to a political party, it is easy to see how money transfers into the political sphere. In other contexts, the line is not so clear-cut. Much of the mass media are commercial enterprises, but their products, information and news are directly related to politics. Various measures can attempt to constrain some of the effects of economic pressures on media content and supplement the commercial media with other sources of funding. However, there is no bright line dividing the media's economic and political activities. The difficulty in separating the two spheres also arose when looking at lobbying. There the difficulty lay in drawing a line between a politician's legitimate associations with outside groups and the potential to give privileged access to some external organisations. While an organisation sponsoring certain parliamentary activities is open to the criticism that access is being bought, it can also be defended as a way of sharing expertise with legislators. This does not mean the strategy of insulation should be abandoned, but rather acknowledges that difficult lines need to be drawn and that the division will never be watertight.

Given the difficulties in separating the two spheres, it is tempting to focus on the most blatant and obvious affronts to political equality that can be most easily remedied. The wealthy person who makes very large donations to a political party and the company that owns several national newspapers are often characterised as the villains that threaten the integrity of the democratic process. Such examples do pose serious problems for political equality and there is good reason to seek to control those uses of wealth. However, simply addressing the most high-profile cases will not secure more opportunities for people to participate or address the less visible impact of inequalities in wealth. For example, even if political donations are capped at £50,000, as argued in Chapter 5, the political parties may become responsive to the very rich who have thousands to spare, rather than the super-rich who have millions. Similarly, the media may still be responsive to the needs of advertisers even where the power of its owner is constrained. When looking at the forums for expression, such as the media and public spaces, where that property is not being used as an instrument for the owner's political views, structural constraints may still lead to the exclusion of some participants. It is still important to address the most obvious instances of political influence being secured through economic power. However, those measures curtail only the most visible part of a broader trend, and it is important to address the more subtle ways inequalities in wealth have an impact in the political sphere.

While the focus of the present discussion has been on political equality, that value has a close relationship with the political freedoms. If political equality means an equal opportunity to influence, in practice this will rely on freedom of expression and association. The protection of those freedoms can play a central role in promoting equality. When the right to assemble in public places is restricted, it impacts on the opportunity to engage in a low-cost form of communication. In protecting such rights, the courts have a role in securing political equality and will sometimes impose a positive obligation on the state to support political freedoms. Yet the argument pursued here has not been that steps to promote equality should be mandated under the ECHR, except in extreme circumstances. Of greater concern is the potential for the Convention rights to be used to challenge those laws that attempt to promote political equality. However, as argued in Chapter 2, Convention rights should be read in a way that gives considerable freedom for states to take measures to protect the fairness of the democratic process, and that such measures can go some way to furthering the values underlying freedom of expression.

Some of the methods for promoting political equality would require new measures to be introduced in the UK, such as the controls on lobbying or access to the public spaces. In other parts, the argument defended certain existing arrangements from the perspective of political equality, such as the public service media. These are just a selection of steps that can be taken, and there are other measures to promote equality in a range of contexts. While open to criticism and subject to limits, the existing policies and regulations have had important effects and helped to define and shape the way politics is conducted. For example, the media regulations have helped to keep down the cost of election campaigns, as political parties and other organisations cannot purchase advertisements on television. While the various measures such as party funding laws, corruption controls and media regulations were introduced at different times and for different reasons, the discussion has shown how these measures and policies in separate areas are connected, and shape the political environment. Consequently, all these measures have a role to play in creating a fair democratic process.

The measures discussed may not fully establish political equality, but can take an important step in that direction. The impact may also go beyond a more egalitarian distribution of some political resources, and have a symbolic role which can shape people's expectations of the political system. As noted in Chapter 5, the reforms brought about in the nineteenth century not only helped to change the methods and costs associated with election campaigns, but also contributed to a broader change in ethical standards and attitudes. Attempts to prevent inequalities in wealth entering politics can play an important role in acknowledging the value of political equality. Taking steps that address the issue can show a commitment to respect people's equal status as participants. For these reasons, while the approaches discussed in the previous chapters raise many difficult issues, the outlook should not be pessimistic and the various strategies can have important effects in creating an egalitarian democratic system.

If the approaches discussed in the earlier chapters are rejected, the tensions between economic inequalities and political equality will remain. The question is then whether such a tension should be accepted and left as it is, or whether alternative steps should be taken. At one end of the spectrum is a laissez-faire approach in which equality is protected only formally, providing more opportunities for inequalities in wealth to secure a political advantage. At the other end of the spectrum, a more equal distribution of economic resources could provide a way to reduce the tension between inequalities in wealth and political equality. Eradicating differences in wealth that give rise to inequalities in the opportunities to participate and influence political decisions would, however, require radical measures of redistribution. In the current political climate such redistributive policies are not a realistic prospect. The approach taken here, for all its difficulties, does not demand such an outcome. What is attempted is a mid-way approach of insulating the political sphere from inequalities in wealth. The measures proposed do not seek to level economic resources, but attempt to impose various barriers and other mechanisms to stop those inequalities entering the political sphere. The aim is to ensure that the opportunities for political influence are as open to the many as to those with the money, and that way protect the principle of political equality that lies at the heart of a democracy.

Index

For EU product safety concerns, contact us at Calle de José Abascal, 56–1°,
28003 Madrid, Spain or eugpsr@cambridge.org.

www.ingramcontent.com/pod-product-compliance
Ingram Content Group UK Ltd.
Pitfield, Milton Keynes, MK11 3LW, UK
UKHW030900150625
459647UK00021B/2708